# Sustainability Acc
# Accountability



## Fourth Edition

Matias Laine and Helen Tregidga

Routledge
Taylor & Francis Group
LONDON AND NEW YORK

Designed cover image: redstallion / Getty Images®

Fourth edition published 2026
by Routledge
4 Park Square, Milton Park, Abingdon, Oxon, OX14 4RN

and by Routledge
605 Third Avenue, New York, NY 10158

*Routledge is an imprint of the Taylor & Francis Group, an informa business*



First edition published by Routledge 2007
Third edition published by Routledge 2022

*British Library Cataloguing-in-Publication Data*
A catalogue record for this book is available from the British Library

ISBN: 978-1-032-87542-2 (hbk)
ISBN: 978-1-032-87540-8 (pbk)
ISBN: 978-1-003-53320-7 (ebk)

DOI: 10.4324/9781003533207

Typeset in Bembo
by codeMantra

Access the Support Material: www.routledge.com/9781032875408

Dear Jeffrey,

You gave us the opportunity to work with you on the last version of this book. You were with us in the early stages and guided us when it mattered. Your limited time gave us motivation to write, and write fast. You never did get to see much of what the book contained, but we wanted your name next to ours to recognise your contribution – to us and to the topic.

We know you would now want us to "go alone". It was the plan from the start. But we do so with your advice in our heads and your smile and laughter in our hearts.

Thank you,
Matias and Helen

# Contents

# Detailed contents

# Figures

# bles

# Preface

This fourth edition of *Sustainability Accounting and Accountability* is an update to the previous edition published in 2022. Such a revision was required due to the fast-paced developments that occurred in the intervening years, most notably in the areas of the regulatory environment relating to sustainability reporting as well as developments in the financial markets and their growing interest and influence on sustainability accounting and accountability. This revised version of this book reflects those changes. While all chapters have been updated, some more extensively than others – most notably, and in line with the above, Chapters 5, 6 and 7 have seen the most significant changes.

In preparing this edition, we are mindful that the field continues to develop and evolve – and in some areas, this development is at a faster pace than others. As such, we have tried to write with a focus that is at the level of the principles, assumptions and ways of thinking, rather than concentrating on too many specifics. However, where specifics are required or useful, these are relevant at the time of writing. While we have tried to write this in a way that ensures the text does not date too quickly, we will also be pleased if it does as the overriding message of this book remains: developments are needed – and the faster, the better.

# Acknowledgements

We wish to acknowledge the large number of students who have passed through our sustainability accounting and accountability courses over the years. We have been involved with courses on this subject at a number of different universities and value the conversations and engagements with students from diverse backgrounds and views. These have undoubtedly shaped the way we approach the topic and influenced the content and tone of this text. We also wish to thank those who have provided comment on the previous version of this book. We have benefitted from conversations with those who have read and used this book in various country contexts, and the feedback received has been valuable as we have revised this version. We welcome further feedback from students, educators and practitioners.

We also wish to acknowledge the continued support of the CSEAR community and everyone involved in the network, as the discussions, presentations and debates we have engaged with there over the years have aided us to better understand the complexity of sustainability accounting and accountability. In particular, we are grateful to Jan Bebbington, Brendan O'Dwyer and Jeffrey Unerman for giving us the opportunity to write the last version of the text. We would also like to thank Lies Bouten, Robert Charnock, Colin Dey, John Ferguson, Giovanna Michelon, Gunnar Rimmel, Shona Russell and Eija Vinnari for their comments on specific chapters of the third edition and Jeremy Osborn and two anonymous reviewers who provided useful feedback which has assisted in this revision.

On a more personal note, we would also like to thank the ongoing support of our families Eeva, Nuutti, Minttu and Todd.

We are very grateful to the editorial team at Routledge for their help and encouragements in the writing and compilation of this book. In particular, we would like to thank Michelle Gallagher and Chloe Herbert.

Matias & Helen

# About the authors

**Matias Laine** is Professor of Accounting at Tampere University, Finland. In his research, Matias seeks to understand the interface of business, societies and the natural environment, and to use his privileged position to critically explore the roles sustainability accounting, accountability and reporting can play in the pursuit of a less unsustainable world. Matias is co-editor of the *European Accounting Review*, and has for a number of years served both the European Accounting Association (EAA) and the Centre for Social and Environmental Accounting Research (CSEAR) in various roles.

**Helen Tregidga** is Professor of Accounting at Royal Holloway, University of London, UK. Helen's research focuses on social and environmental accounting, accountability and reporting with a particular interest in corporate discourses on sustainability and how they can be resisted and changed to enable the transition to a more sustainable environment and society. Helen is co-editor of the *Critical Perspectives on Accounting* journal and an active member of the CSEAR.

CHAPTER

1

# Introduction to sustainability accounting and accountability

Before starting to explore the topic of this book, it is perhaps useful to take a moment to reflect on some key questions. What kind of world do we want to live in? What is the state of the natural environment in that world? How are the societies organised? How do the economies function, and in whose interests? And, importantly, how does that vision compare to our present reality?

If our vision is one that includes a healthy environment able to sustain life on Earth, social justice for all and fair economies which promote the fair distribution of wealth and opportunity, then we must acknowledge that there is a (growing) gap between our vision and our shared current reality. Scientific consensus regarding climate change as a result of human activity is well established, and the effects of climate change (now commonly referred to as climate emergency, climate breakdown or climate crisis) are all around us from extreme weather events, changing landscapes and climate refugees, the result of displacement due to rising sea levels, extended droughts or the natural environment otherwise becoming increasingly difficult for human communities. High levels of biodiversity loss are causing alarm, given the many crucial roles of a healthy biosphere for all life. For example, healthy biodiverse soil can sustain the growing of more nutritious foods in greater long-term quantities needed by humanity and other animals than severely degraded soils. The devastating effects of biodiversity loss are resulting in individuals, organisations and countries across the globe working on ways to restore threatened or already lost habitats, protect species of flora and fauna and curb growing levels of extinction, especially in ecosystem hotspots. And climate and biodiversity are just two examples which illustrate the current state of the natural environment and the effects of environmental destruction. There is also attention being placed on growing levels of economic inequality in many parts of the world, especially in the West, and people living in poverty across the globe, in particular the Global South[1] and increasingly as a result of war and conflict. It is now commonplace to hear about social injustices occurring across the globe and crises within the financial and economic systems. The socio-ecological crisis is also closely related to heightened social tensions concerning migration, as it is an important factor driving growing numbers of people seeking better life conditions and opportunities.

DOI: 10.4324/9781003533207-1

Overall, the negative consequences and impacts of our current way of life are increasingly being understood. Importantly, the role of human activity is also (finally) being acknowledged and placed at the fore. How this way of life compromises our ability for ecological integrity, social justice and economic stability is also being recognised, leading to critical reflection and awareness that we must act – and act now. Dominant ways of organising our economies so as to maximise short-term economic growth which operated nearly unquestioned for decades are under scrutiny. Economies and systems of organising that work for the few, rather than for the many in current and future generations, are widely considered to be part of the systemic reasons behind the current critical situation – the unsustainability of our planet and livelihoods.

Issues of sustainability (and relatedly unsustainability) are the focus of this book. While expanded upon in Part I, sustainability in this book relates to the medium- and long-term viability of the natural environment, society and the economy or how we might ensure social, environmental and economic sustainability beyond the short term. Or, put another way, how we might move from the current unsustainable system to a sustainable one. Organisations, including business organisations as key economic actors, not only impact the environment and society but also are dependent on the environment and society. As such, organisations and systems of organising are central to any movement towards sustainability.

Accounting and accountability, and their relevance to sustainability, are the particular focus of the chapters that follow. While all the above might be familiar to you, you might be thinking, what has all this got to do with accounting? Accounting is a powerful tool within societies. It is a key function in organising economic activity and plays a central role in decision-making. Accounting is traditionally conceptualised as financial and management accounting and related to financial decision-making by those both internal and external to the entity. Take a moment to think about what you know about accounting. It is possible that you may be thinking about financial accounting and accounting as focusing on numbers and finance, a process of collecting, analysing and communicating financial information on the financial performance of an entity for financial decision-making. A range of financial accounting techniques have been developed to communicate to owners of an entity how the entity's management has used economic resources, demonstrating accountability for the financial resources for which it is responsible and the financial impacts of its operations.

But, as is now commonly understood, organisations no longer have responsibility and accountability only for financial resources. As the array of environmental, social and economic impacts and dependencies of organisations have become evident (in particular the environmental and social impact of large corporations), organisations have increasingly been required to be accountable for these impacts and for their use of environmental and social resources. This has seen the need for accounting to evolve and adapt. In practice, attempts to account for, and be accountable for, environmental and social impacts have grown to be relatively commonplace. However, many would argue, and as you will see in the chapters that follow, that accounting and accountability practices still have a long way to go if they are to be "fit for purpose" in a sustainable world.

At the same time, the tangible (financial) consequences sustainability has for organisations would have become clear to anyone paying attention, as, for instance, changing weather patterns and extreme weather events cause material damage and we consider the stages of the reporting process and key influences, debates and discussions that occur at each stage.

Chapter 7, "ESG and Financial Markets", presents and discusses the role of sustainability and ESG in the financial markets. In the ESG context, there is growing awareness of the increasing risks which escalating global sustainability challenges are causing – not only to organisations but also to social and economic systems more broadly. Indeed, the development and influence of financial markets have been a defining feature in the development of sustainability accounting and accountability in recent years. In this chapter, we discuss how sustainability accounting information and accountability relationships are interconnected with financial markets and increasing ESG activity. This includes an understanding of how sustainability can affect the financial performance and long-term success of an organisation and also reflects on how the financial markets can influence the social and environmental activities of organisations. While understanding the sustainability impacts of organisations is important, this chapter also highlights how accounting for dependencies can be significant in the context of financial markets, risk management and investments.

The last chapter in Part II, Chapter 8, "Counter Accounting", discusses the practice of counter accounting. This form of accounting essentially refers to accounts prepared by those external to an entity and often associated with the accountability relationship. We discuss the various practices which can collectively be referred to as counter accounting as they are relevant to sustainability accounting and accountability. In addition to introducing this area of sustainability accounting and accountability, this chapter is also useful in thinking through the complexities of the topic – both in relation to encouraging critical thinking, and for engaging in discussion on how the practice of accounting could be different in order to move towards sustainability. This latter aspect is also useful as background for discussions in Part III.

Part III, Issues in Accounting for Sustainability, consists of five chapters which each address a separate sustainability issue. Specifically, we discuss climate (Chapter 9), water (Chapter 10), biodiversity (Chapter 11), human rights (Chapter 12) and economic inequality (Chapter 13), respectively. While each chapter's structure is influenced by the nature of the topic, they generally follow a similar structure. In each chapter, we outline the issue that is the focus of the chapter and consider why it is an issue for organisations and accounting more specifically. We overview the key global, national and organisational level institutions, frameworks and governance structures which influence each issue, paying particular attention to those which relate to accounting and accountability. Each of these issues has, to varying degrees, been addressed in accounting and accountability practice. We discuss current practice in each of these areas and consider the role of sustainability accounting and accountability, now and into the future, in relation to these five sustainability issues.

It is important to recognise here that the five areas selected are not the only sustainability-related issues relevant for accounting and accountability. Indeed, there are a myriad of other issues that could have been included here. We have chosen issues that are either established or receiving increasing attention in the sustainability accounting and accountability field – both in organisational practice and academic research. In doing so, we are conscious of the topics that have been excluded. For example, accounting for other forms of inequality beyond economic are an obvious exclusion. Gender, racial (in)equality, disability and LGBTQI+ issues are just some of the topics that are essential considerations for sustainability accounting. In addition to these and other social issues, environmental issues such as waste, energy, soil and animal welfare/rights would appear to be some obvious omissions. In presenting each issue separately, we also risk presenting them as disconnected. We wish to highlight that these issues are all interconnected, so while it is useful to consider each issue in turn, we should also be thinking about the dependencies and interconnections between them. For example, as you will see in Chapter 11, "Accounting for Biodiversity", one key factor in biodiversity loss is climate change, the focus of Chapter 9. Likewise, climate change also has relevance for other issues discussed such as water, human rights and economic inequality. These interconnections will be noted in each of the chapters but are worth reflecting on throughout the book.

While we are unable to cover all possible topics in this text, we would encourage you to consider the relevance of sustainability accounting and accountability to the range of sustainability-related issues as you engage with all chapters of the book, Part III in particular. For practitioners and researchers in the area, we would stress that there is as much of a need for further knowledge and attention on the issues that do not appear in this book as there is on issues that do. Common across all these topics – those that are usually the most relevant and so are covered in this book, and those that are (knowingly and unknowingly) absent – is that they all require further consideration from an accounting and accountability perspective if we are to make the urgent transition towards a more sustainable society.

These reflections are carried through to Part IV, Conclusion, where we make, in Chapter 14, some closing remarks. In this final chapter, we reflect on some of the discussions presented. In particular, we highlight how the book has identified the challenges posed by sustainability to organisations and accounting. While accounting can, and we would argue needs to, play a number of important roles in the transition towards a more sustainable society, we reflect on how, to be effective, this would require a fundamental change to a number of accounting and accountability practices, going beyond the current state of practice and knowledge presented in this book.

## 1.2 A note for instructors

This is the fourth edition of this title. The third edition, published in 2022, was a completely rewritten edition of the second edition, undertaken due to the demand for a textbook suitable for use in the now large number of courses on the topic of sustainability accounting and accountability. As we discussed in the preface, this fourth edition is an update of that text to reflect the fast-evolving nature of this field, in particular in relation to reporting and financial markets. While the book is written to appeal to a broad audience, the book covers the range of topics you might expect to find in an entry-level course on the topic or as essential foundational knowledge for more advanced or specialist courses.

We have designed this book to be used at both undergraduate and postgraduate levels. This includes courses dedicated to the topic or where sustainability accounting and accountability features as a topic within a broader course. Many chapters include examples from the practitioner literature or practice which help contextualise and ensure the text has practical relevance. These examples can be used and followed up in preparing class materials and exercises alongside the resources that accompany this text, or the myriad of resources now available online. Where this book is being used for a postgraduate course the instructor might like to consider supplementing the chapters with academic readings. To assist with this, each chapter includes an inset highlighting a research paper related to the topic as well as an additional reading list along with the usual reference list.

This text has been structured in a way that an instructor can work through the book in its entirety, for a long course, or focus on particular chapters to accommodate a shorter course. For example, each chapter is suitable for an individual session (one or two hours) on each topic. Chapters 5 and 6, both of which discuss sustainability reporting, can either form the basis of two sessions or be combined into one. While we would suggest Chapters 2 and 3 are useful for all courses on the topic, some instructors might like to focus on topics in Part II, while others on the range of issues presented in Part III. Any comments that readers and instructors may have on the structure and content of this book are most welcome.

## 1.3 Conclusion

In this chapter, we have introduced the focus and approach taken in this book. We hope that readers find the material presented both useful and informative. It has been written to not only introduce the topic of study but also encourage readers to consider more broadly the potential and limits of accounting and accountability in the transition to a more sustainable society. We hope you enjoy the material that follows.

## Note

1 We should note here the challenges related to the use of simplistic dichotomies, such as first world and third world, industrial West and Global South, high-income and middle- and low-income countries, as well as developed and developing countries. None of these are perfect, as they for instance signal the primacy of particular areas (first world), emphasise path-dependency and the superiority of a specific growth model (developed and developing countries), or just otherwise group very different countries, regions and cultures together (Global South). We nonetheless use such categories occasionally in this book when we think it is relevant to point out significant global differences or otherwise highlight some specific features that should be considered.

PART

I

# Setting the context

CHAPTER

# 2

# Background and global context

Sustainability simply means to maintain, to endure into the long term. It is also understood as a state where things can keep going and can sustain themselves. The focus of this book is on the sustainability of life on Earth (humans and others) and the role of accounting and accountability in transitioning to a more sustainable environment, society and economy. In this chapter, we discuss the background and global context within which the discussion in this book is situated. We begin by discussing the key concepts of sustainability and sustainable development. We briefly trace the development of the concepts by outlining their emergence onto the global political and business agendas and consider more recent articulations and efforts to promote the urgent need to address global sustainability issues. We then turn our attention to considering how sustainability is relevant to economies, organisations and accounting. We also outline how different types of organisational forms are relevant and how we discuss them in this book. The aim of this chapter is to provide the essential context to the topic of sustainability accounting and accountability and locate our discussions that follow in the forthcoming chapters of the book.

By the end of this chapter, you should:

- Understand the key concepts of sustainability and sustainable development.
- Be aware of the various and interconnected global sustainability issues.
- Have a critical awareness of how sustainability relates to, and requires a rethinking of, economic systems.
- Have a critical awareness of how sustainability relates to, and requires a rethinking of, business models.
- Be aware of sustainability accounting and accountability, in particular what it means and why it is important.
- Be able to identify various organisational forms and consider their relevance to sustainability accounting and accountability.

DOI: 10.4324/9781003533207-3

## 2.1 Sustainability and sustainable development

### 2.1.1 Defining the terms

As noted above, sustainability is about living within the limits of the Earth. It is considered to be a desired state that we not only wish to achieve but must achieve if the life that the Earth currently supports is to continue into the future. It can be useful to think of sustainability in relation to unsustainability. That is a state of living beyond the means of the Earth.

In 1972, in their well-known book *Limits to Growth*, Meadows et al. (1972) predicted that economic growth, consumption and population growth would lead to humans exceeding the carrying capacity of the Earth (the maximum number of individuals the Earth can support indefinitely). This, they noted, would lead to a condition of overshoot, a condition in which human demands exceed the regenerative capacities of the biosphere, the planet. Overshoot, that is unsustainability, is the state we are now living in as evidenced by the problems currently facing life on the planet, problems such as climate change, mass extinction, water scarcity and poverty.

In addition to the term "sustainability", sustainable development is also a key term. While sustainability can be considered to be a desired state, sustainable development can be understood as the process to get there. So, while the two terms can be seen to be different, they are often used interchangeably.

**PAUSE AND REFLECT...**

Earth Overshoot Day is marked each year to represent the day in which humanity's demand for the Earth's resources and services in a given year exceeds what the Earth can regenerate in that year. In 2025, Earth Overshoot Day fell on 24th July (www.overshootday.org/). Earth Overshoot Day tends to get earlier each year meaning we are not only living unsustainably, but we are becoming more unsustainable with time.

### 2.1.2 The United Nations Sustainable Development Goals

A prominent contemporary attempt to define or conceptualise sustainable development and what is needed to achieve it is provided by the United Nations (UN) through their Sustainable Development Goals (hereafter the SDGs). Released in 2015, the SDGs consist of 17 goals which relate to various social, ecological and economic issues. They are commonly referred to as the Global Goals as they outline 17 goals which the globe needs to address in its transition towards sustainability. As you will see from the visual representation of the goals in Figure 2.1, in addition to some social, environmental and economic issues such as poverty, education, climate and inequalities, the SDGs highlight important concepts such as peace, justice, the role of institutions and the importance of partnerships to achieve the goals. The goals are intended to be ambitious, and the aim is to achieve them by 2030.

The SDGs are useful in highlighting global challenges and sustainability issues. Each goal presents a key global challenge that requires a range of individuals, groups

**FIGURE 2.1** The UN SDGs

and institutions to achieve it. Each goal also includes a set of targets (there are 169 targets in total) that help understand what might be required to achieve this 2030 agenda for sustainability.

One important and useful aspect of the SDGs is the recognition that the goals, and thus sustainability issues, are interconnected. The problems facing life on Earth, problems such as those mentioned above, climate change, mass extinction, water scarcity and poverty, are intrinsically linked systems problems. And systems are complex. Activities to address one aspect can also affect, positively or negatively, another. And these effects often cannot be predicted or they are not well understood. So, while we may argue as to whether environmental destruction causes poverty or whether poverty causes environmental destruction, for example, it is clear that the two issues are interconnected. We cannot address one problem without considering the other.

While not without their critics and limitations, the SDGs have been very successful in promoting key sustainability issues and have been widely adopted by governments, organisations and other civil society groups. They also provide a good platform for our understanding of key sustainability issues in this book and a consideration of the roles of accounting and accountability in addressing these key sustainability issues. We refer to the SDGs throughout this text, and you will see a consideration of some of the specific goals in Part III. We should also point out here that while we at times refer to some specific targets included in the SDG's overall set of 169 targets, we mostly stay on a more generic level and with the 17 goals. As you make your way through the chapters, we nonetheless recommend you to have a closer look at the SDGs and consider the key targets and indicators listed for some key goals you are interested in. As you do so, it might also be useful to reflect on the lack of progress in achieving these goals. A UN 2024 report, for example, finds that "only 17 per cent of the SDG targets are on track, nearly half are showing minimal or moderate progress, and progress on over one third has stalled or even regressed" (United Nations, 2024). There is, therefore, a long way to go and some concerning trends.

### 2.1.3 A brief history

It is useful, we suggest, to recognise the history of the concepts of sustainability and sustainable development. This enables us to further understand them, as well as consider how they have developed over time.

Being grounded in the disciplines of, for example, conservation and ecology, the concept of sustainability (and relatedly sustainable development) has a long and complex history. However, what we think of as sustainability as a field of study today, and what we are focusing upon here in this book, has its beginnings in the environmental movement of the 1960s and 1970s. Several key publications mark the beginning of the movement, such as Rachel Carson's *Silent Spring* (1962), Paul Ehrlich's *The Population Bomb* (1968), E. F. Schumacher's *Small Is Beautiful: A Study of Economics as If People Mattered* (1973), as well as *Limits to Growth* mentioned above. Some key events also mark the beginning of the focus on sustainability at a global level, including the first image of Earth from space (showing visually and powerfully the Earth as a bounded system) and the chemical and nuclear disasters of Union Carbide in Bhopal, India, in 1984 and Chernobyl, Soviet Union, in 1986.

However, it is perhaps the World Commission for Environment and Development (WCED) in 1987 that provided a definition of sustainable development which launched the concept onto the global political and business agenda. They defined sustainable development as "development that meets the needs of the present without compromising the ability of future generations to meet their own needs" (WCED, 1987, p. 43). However, while it is often only this first part of the definition we see quoted, it is important to note that they followed this definition with the following statement:

> It contains within it two key concepts: The concept of needs, in particular the essential needs of the world's poor, to which overriding priority should be given; and The idea of limitations imposed by the state of technology and social organisations on the environment's ability to meet present and future needs.
>
> (WCED, 1987, p. 43)

While it could be argued that the content of this latter part of the definition was neglected for some time, a look at the SDGs above, as well as a closer look at the targets underlying them, will demonstrate that the concept of essential needs of the world's poor in particular has again been highlighted and takes prominence in many current discussions. Advances in technology and artificial intelligence (AI) also bring this latter part of the definition to the fore.

In Figure 2.2, we provide a timeline noting some of the significant events in sustainability thinking. Given the focus of this book, we include the events most relevant to the global and organisational context.

### 2.1.4 Contested concepts

While we have provided definitions of sustainability and sustainable development, as well as identified the SDGs as a useful way to understand the concepts and what is needed to achieve these, it is important to recognise that transitioning towards sustainability is complex and not agreed by all. For example, while many (even all) of us would agree that sustainability is the goal, there is not necessarily agreement on what is required to get there, and how fast change should or needs to take place.

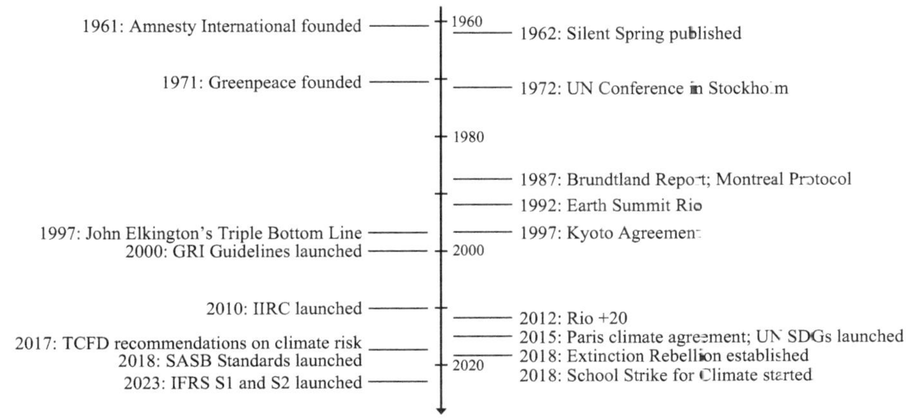


**FIGURE 2.2** Timeline of Key Sustainability Events

While the SDGs represent sustainable development via 17 goals, previously, sustainability and sustainable development were generally and commonly understood to consist of three dimensions – ecological, social and economic. These three dimensions were oftentimes referred to as the triple bottom line (TBL), a term coined by John Elkington. You may still see this term being used by some organisations and authors, although it is less common these days. These three dimensions can also be found labelled as the three pillars, the three Es (environment, economy and equity) and, especially within the business context, as the three Ps (people, planet and profit). This three-dimensional conceptualisation of the term has been very powerful. However, the TBL also has its limitations, as Elkington himself acknowledged 25 years after introducing the concept (Elkington, 2018).

The limitations of the TBL approach to sustainable development relate to different understandings of how the three dimensions relate to one another. Different understandings lead to different views on how sustainability can be achieved. Let's reflect on these different understandings, which can be referred to as weak and strong sustainability and illustrated in Figure 2.3. While you probably won't see these terms being used much now, they are useful for introducing and understanding the core concepts in use today. They help us consider the different views that exist and are also likely to be useful as you start to form your own perspective as to how we might transition towards sustainability and what is needed to get there. The weak and strong sustainability models are also helpful in understanding our discussions of economic systems and sustainability below, as well as in providing a basis for which we can reflect on various sustainability accounting and accountability tools and practices throughout the book.

The key difference between these two different understandings of sustainability relates to trade-offs, that is the extent to which one or more of the dimensions of sustainability can be traded-off against each other. For example, a perspective informed by a weak conceptualisation of sustainability, the interlinking diagram on the left, allows for trade-offs. When operating under a weak conceptualisation of sustainability a focus is placed on achieving "win-wins". A win-win is an action or opportunity that benefits two dimensions. However, this often occurs without a consideration of the third dimension (requiring a win-win-win). An example could be seeing an increase in production in a coal mine leading to jobs as good (a win) for

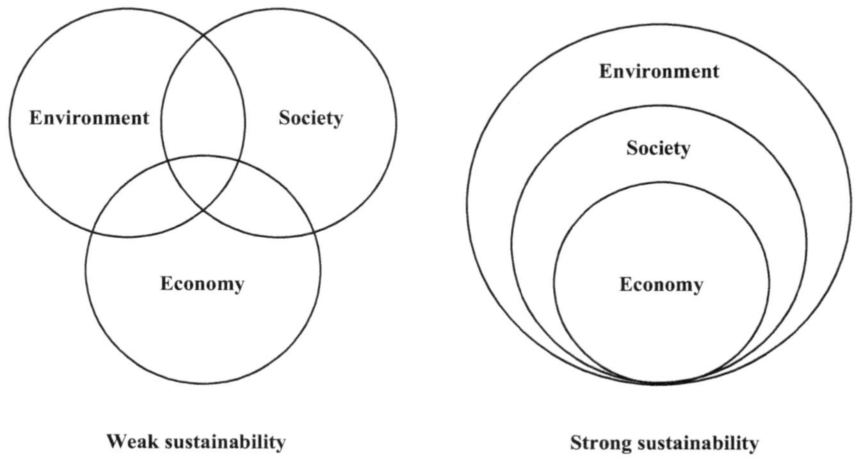


**FIGURE 2.3** Weak and Strong Sustainability

society and good (a win) for the economy. However, the environmental dimension, and subsequent negative impacts on the environment, is not considered here.

A perspective informed by strong sustainability, the nested diagram on the right, sees the relationship between the dimensions differently – and operating under such a conceptualisation has very different outcomes. Here, you can see that the strong view sees the economy to be reliant on the society and the society to be reliant on the environment. It holds that a healthy and stable economy relies upon a well-functioning society, and such a society relies on a healthy and functioning environment. Here the dimensions are seen as interdependent and there is no room for trade-offs. Furthermore, the environment is seen as the overarching system within which all other dimensions rely. So, while the strong sustainability model still involves the three dimensions, they are conceptualised very differently.

In summary, a weak sustainability perspective, still common in many organisations, sees each of the dimensions in silo, rather than as interdependent, as part of a system. This is a key limitation of the TBL. This systems perspective and the strong model of sustainability is also relevant when looking at how a consideration of sustainability affects the economic system.

**PAUSE AND REFLECT...**

The language we use is important. In this book, we use the terms "sustainability" and "sustainable development" as we are interested in exploring accounting's role in the transition towards sustainability as conceptualised in the discussion above. But it is perhaps useful to pause and reflect on other terms, in addition to the TBL introduced above, that you may come across.

*Corporate Social Responsibility* (CSR) and *Responsible Business*: the use of these terms usually involves a focus on the business/corporation and the activities that they engage in. Unlike sustainability which looks more at systems, these are organisation-centric topics.

*Corporate citizenship*, or simply corporate citizen, is a term often used to highlight the role corporations play in society. That is, just like (human) citizens, corporations take part in the daily life of societies. The term *corporate citizenship* highlights the social and ethical responsibilities towards the community that corporations have. Again, there are different views with regard to what the role of a corporation in a society is, as well as what it should be.

*Business ethics* concerns organisational decision-making, or perhaps more correctly the decision-making by individuals within organisations. In essence, business ethics focuses on questions of right and wrong. Business ethics decisions range from those which are highly controversial, such as engaging in bribery to get access to a deal, to the mundane, such as everyday policies concerning customer relationships. As is the case with philosophy and ethics in general, there are very few absolute answers here, since our view of right and wrong depends on such things as the philosophical perspective we approach decisions with.

*ESG* is a prevalent abbreviation used especially in connection with the financial markets. Standing as a shorthand for environmental, social and governance, ESG is used widely to refer to sustainability matters. While various ESG frameworks exist with differing emphasis, in general terms the letters refer to three main topic areas firms provide disclosures on. A core feature in ESG thinking is the identifying and assessing of different kinds of risks and opportunities that relate to the company's activities. Further, within ESG, the focus is usually on the outside-in perspective, meaning the impacts sustainability matters can have on the company, its financial performance and future outlook.

While some organisations and authors might use the above terms interchangeably with sustainability, we would argue that it is wise not to do so as there are important differences. Consider the following: *can an organisation be responsible without being sustainable?*

This is an interesting question and one which is likely to create discussion and even disagreement. Take time to reflect on this question and discuss it with others. It is likely to be useful in understanding the differences between the terms: responsible business, CSR, business ethics, ESG and sustainability.

### 2.1.5 Planetary boundaries

The Planetary Boundaries is a highly popular framework, which is used to illustrate the impact human activities have on key processes of the Earth system (see Figure 2.4). The first public iteration of the framework was introduced in 2009, originating in the work of an international group of scientists led by Swedish scholar Johan Rockström, who at the time was working at the Stockholm Resilience Centre (Rockström et al., 2009). At the core of the planetary boundaries framework lies the identification and assessment of nine Earth system processes, which are considered to be critical for maintaining a stable and resilient planet. Amongst these processes are familiar ones such as climate change and freshwater change, but also some which are discussed more seldom such as biogeochemical flows, novel entities and ocean acidification. While the illustration depicts these processes as separate, it is important to recognise their interdependence. As we have noted already, Earth systems are complex, and it is evident that these critical processes have various feedback loops affecting one another.

Since their introduction in 2009, Rockström and colleagues have continued their work to assess the critical processes and develop the framework. In 2023, the group

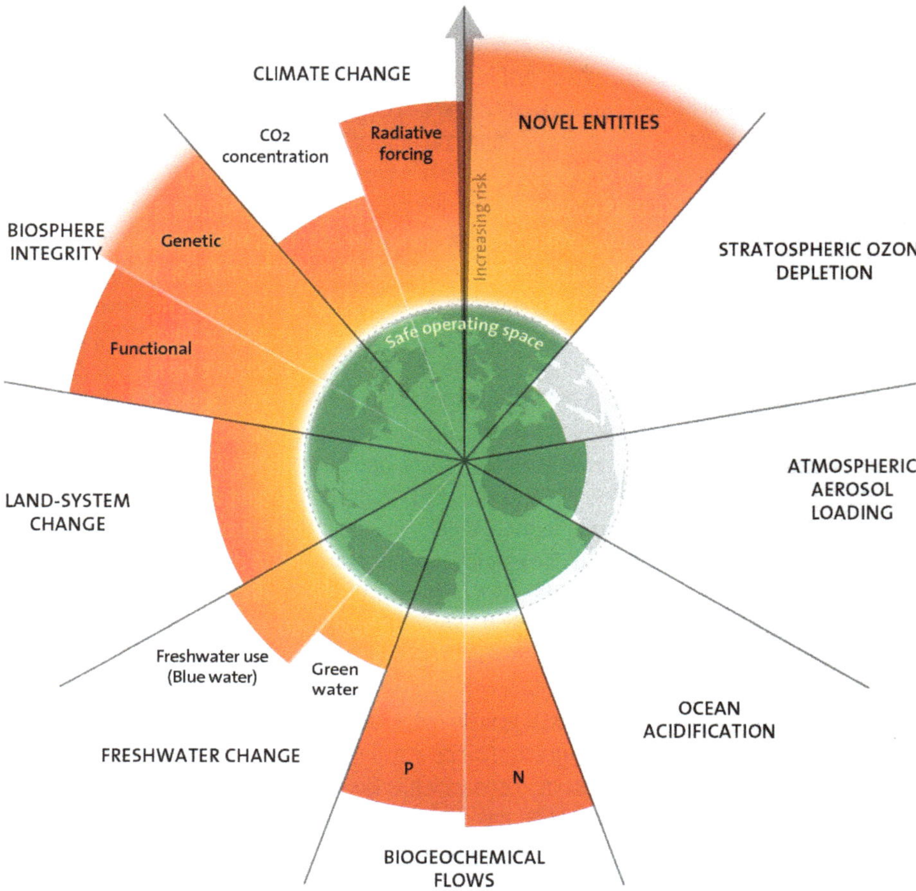


**FIGURE 2.4** Planetary Boundaries

published their work to provide a quantitative assessment of all nine boundaries, highlighting that human activities would now have transgressed six of them (Richardson et al., 2023). Understanding the timescale of events is increasingly relevant here: Earth system changes can occur slowly and hence it is quite unlikely that we would notice anything dramatic occurring today or even this year. However, the compromising of these planetary boundaries can lead to exceeding potential tipping points in global ecosystems. That is, as we transgress these boundaries, it is increasingly likely that some large-scale and irreversible changes in the global environmental processes occur. In other words, staying beyond the boundaries brings growing risks for compromising the stable and resilient Earth that has withheld human life as well as the ecosystems we live together with and are dependent on.

### 2.1.6 Doughnut economics

Doughnut economics is a visual framework developed by economist Kate Raworth. The visual (see Figure 2.5) depicts a framework for sustainable development and how societies aspiring to reach an inclusive and sustainable

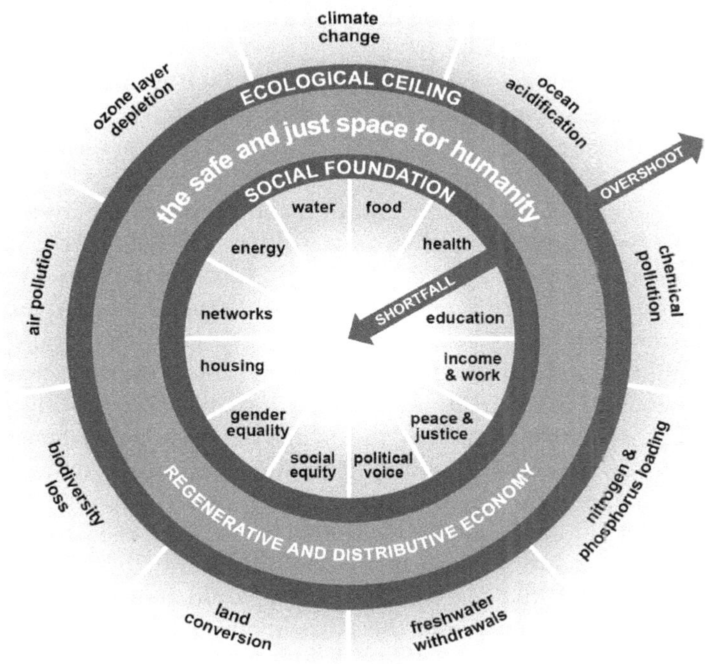


**FIGURE 2.5** Raworth's Doughnut Economics

economy need to be structured. The framework is based on social thresholds and ecological boundaries and as such sees the economic system as interlinked with the social and environmental systems as discussed above. The framework gets its name from the shape, a ring doughnut, where the aim is to live within the doughnut ring, that is, not to fall into the middle or outside the outer crust. The first iteration of the doughnut was presented in an Oxfam discussion paper in 2012 and since then it has had substantial traction as a framework through which we can see the interconnections of social, environmental and economic issues (e.g. Raworth, 2017).

Let's explore Raworth's framework further by examining more closely the above doughnut economics diagram. If we start from the middle we see the visual's inner boundary, the social foundation. This inner boundary highlights the key foundations for a safe and just humanity, issues like sanitation, food, health care, equality and so forth. These need to be achieved in all communities or societies in order for everyone living there to have the key capabilities to flourish. If these factors do not exist in a society then the system falls short of the inner ring and there is an inadequate foundation to support the fair and safe economy needed for humanity to live within and thrive. The outer boundary, the ecological ceiling, describes the planetary boundaries above which humanity cannot go without risking its global ecosystem's carrying capacity. The planetary boundaries draw on the influential work of Rockström et al. (2009) discussed above and highlight key ecological processes and ecosystem services (services we receive from the ecosystem such as regulation and stabilisation of climate, see Chapter 9). If this ecological ceiling is exceeded, again meaning the system moves outside the ring of the doughnut, then we have overshoot, a concept we introduced earlier.

Raworth's doughnut is a powerful visual, which usefully shows us that when seeking to achieve sustainability it is essential to understand that economic, social and ecological issues are intertwined. Take major ecological challenges: some suggest that the only way humanity can avoid an ecological collapse would be an instant and radical change in consumption and production patterns, including, for instance, the banning of things like air travel, fast fashion and the use of oil. While such actions, if somehow agreed upon on a global scale, would definitely reduce the ecological strain, they would also have substantial impacts on the social and economic dimensions, as entire sectors of the economy could disappear and people would abruptly lose their livelihoods. Such impacts would also not be spread out evenly, since many societies, regions and communities have over time specialised in particular industries and hence become highly dependent on them, as is the case in Bangladesh with the clothing industry, or as the COVID-19 pandemic showed with tourism in Spain, Italy and Greece. As such, while some radical actions could help, and are indeed needed, with the ecological boundaries, they might simultaneously push many communities below the social foundation, which together with the sense of inequality could result in substantial unrest in societies. The doughnut model therefore requires us to think more holistically about our ecological, social and economic systems and the connections between them. Given these connections, before we proceed to discuss accounting and accountability, we need to look more closely at the broader social systems in which organisations operate.

### INSIGHTS FROM RESEARCH: ACCOUNTING AND THE PLANETARY BOUNDARIES

Are you thinking "what have the planetary boundaries got to do with accounting?" After reading Sobkowiak et al.'s (2023) paper you may be left thinking "a lot". Even how accounting is needed when it comes to articulating and achieving the planetary boundaries.

In recognising the prominence of the planetary boundaries as a framework for "comprehending and, ideally, remaining within the Earth's ecological limits", Sobkowiak and colleagues reflect on the future of accounting research and practice in relation to the planetary boundaries framework.

Sobkowiak et al.'s discussion starts with the recognition that, despite the prominence of the planetary boundaries, they have been the subject to critiques. Such critiques include the prioritisation of the environment over the social, cultural and political (you might find it useful to consider the other models mentioned in this chapter including the SDGs, strong sustainability and doughnut economics) and the lack of engagement with others. It is those critiques which provide the basis for their exploration of the role of accounting. They argue that a more "interdisciplinary, inclusive, and not one-sided technoscientific approach that incorporates social, cultural and political perspectives into the understanding and management of planetary boundaries" is needed. This is where accounting enters the story.

Several roles for accounting are identified, including, but not limited to, accountings, role in collecting information about ecological limits and also raising awareness of planetary boundaries. However, key to their discussion is the nature of accounting they discuss. This includes accounting that is participatory, narrative, literary and arts-based, amongst other things. As such, in prompting us to consider the critiques of the planetary boundaries and the role of accountings in addressing them, they also challenge us to consider what accounting is and the form that it takes – especially when it comes to human-nature interactions. After reading this paper, you will be left with the challenge of thinking about how accounting might help in "articulating planetary boundaries and sensing the ecological limits of our shared existence" (p. 259).

And we would argue this is highly relevant. While many accounting research papers begin by mentioning planetary boundaries and emphasising their relevance, it is much less common to see scholars engaging in a more in-depth conversation about the interface of accounting, accountants and planetary boundaries. Such discussion is arguably more advanced in the field of management and organisation studies (see Williams et al., 2025), but there are also parallel conversations in accounting scholarship to draw on, such as those exploring the interface of accounting and sustainability (Gray, 2010) and accounts of nature (Russell et al., 2017).

**Sobkowiak, M., Senn, J. and Vollmer, H. (2023). Rethinking Planetary Boundaries: Accounting for Ecological Limits. *Social and Environmental Accountability Journal, 43(3),* 259–272.**

## 2.2 Sustainability and the economy

In order to consider accounting and organisations, it is useful to understand the broader socio-economic and political landscape within which they operate. In thinking about what a particular organisation could, should or even can do, we need to remember that organisations do not exist separately from their context. While it is outside the scope of this book to cover all possible aspects of this context, several key ones warrant acknowledging.

The socio-economic and political context an organisation operates in not only sets boundaries, for instance in the form of regulation, but also sets general expectations with regard to how an organisation is expected to operate. This relates to the norms operating within any given society. For instance, and in very simplified terms, publicly listed companies are usually expected to increase the shareholder value for investors, state-owned organisations are expected to have some broader ambitions, while non-governmental organisations tend to be considered advocates for the benefits of some particular group or at times for some broader good.

While we note that each of these perceptions can be problematic, and indeed in need of critical consideration, in each case, it is worthwhile recognising them. While an organisation's management can go to great lengths in deciding how the organisation goes about its business and activities, they are nonetheless dependent on preconditions, structures and institutionalised norms of the operating context and the networks they sit within. Thus, to understand organisations, and to be able to discuss the role and relevance of sustainability accounting and accountability within organisations in pursuing sustainability, we must begin from the macro level.

### 2.2.1 Capitalism

The economic system within which organisations operate, which in many contexts is capitalism, plays an important role and affects the ways in which organisations, in particular profit-seeking corporations, operate. Capitalism is an economic system in which the means of production of goods and services are privately owned and operated for a profit. It is a system that has as its basis three things – wage labour, private ownership of the means of production and production for exchange and profit. Capitalism is distinct from the market. Capital is not a thing but a process in which money (capital) is perpetually sent in search of more money. This drive for increasing capital has a range of effects, many of them negative in relation to the natural environment.

There are varying views as to whether or not capitalism can be reformed to address sustainability. Some believe capitalism can be re-invented, reformed to include such things as equality, solidarity, responsibility and caring to deliver a sustainable future. Some even maintain that capitalism is the only system through which sustainability challenges can be solved. Such a perspective leads to, for example, the creation of market mechanisms in response to sustainability issues (e.g. carbon markets to support emissions trading schemes). It also can lead to a faith in, and incentivisation of, innovation in technology and disruptive competition as they are considered the best mechanisms to produce the swift and widespread changes required to move away from unsustainability. There are varieties in this way of thinking of course, but in general terms, ideas such as green capitalism and conscious capitalism fall under this umbrella. These ideas underscore that within a capitalist system business can both seek profits and work for the broader social good.

Others argue that capitalism is fundamentally irreparable. They believe that the very nature of the system, including power imbalances and relying on continuous growth, will continue to destroy nature and perpetuate social inequalities. While we don't have the scope to engage in such important (and complex) discussions here, the economic system within which organisations and society operates is important to recognise. It has a direct impact on the way in which organisations, accounting and society, more broadly, operate.

### 2.2.2 Globalisation

Organisations, in particular large corporations, often operate across multiple contexts. Likewise, supply chains have become increasingly global with many organisations engaging in the outsourcing of production. As such, globalisation increasingly affects the way in which organisations and societies operate and is again relevant to any discussion of sustainability accounting and accountability.

The global nature of operations and their effects on the environment and local communities have been scrutinised for some time. In many communities, concerns for job security and the challenges globalisation and web-based commerce have brought for independent businesses have generated moves to a greater consideration of the local – supporting local business and local community initiatives. In the 2020s, also governments and large multinational corporations became increasingly concerned about the evident downsides of economic globalisation: first the supply chain problems and subsequent inflation hikes in many economies caused by the COVID-19 pandemic exposed how dependent businesses and societies more broadly had become on global trade. Simultaneously, the heightened geopolitical tensions, related primarily to Russia's invasion of Ukraine in 2022 and the longer-term developments in the relationships between China and the United States, made the risks related to the outsourcing of production to distant countries more tangible. As a result, we have seen substantial interest of both nation states and corporations in reconsidering their supply chains. However, despite the increased awareness and increasing trend towards a consideration of the local for various reasons, it is important to recognise that much of our economic system is still organised globally.

Together with heightened global sustainability concerns, discussed above, globalisation is setting challenges for accounting and accountability. In the global markets, capital is moving increasingly fast and relatively freely in its search for better returns. Supply chains in the production of goods, for example, have become increasingly complex and fluid. Global supply chains mean that social and environmental impacts can take place across the globe at a very distant location from a company's headquarters. Companies can have their subcontractors regularly compete against one another in seeking to receive best offers. So how does this relate to accounting and accountability? Take fast fashion for example. Products sold on the high street or to internet customers in Europe are often produced in Bangladesh, Vietnam or India, where workers can experience low pay and harsh health and safety conditions. How do we account for the associated questions of human rights and inequality? And who should be held accountable across such a supply chain consisting of several subcontractors and multiple organisations? Such matters are at the heart of sustainability accounting and accountability, and we will return to discuss these questions further.

## 2.3 Sustainability and organisations

In a book about sustainability accounting and accountability, it is important to consider the role of humans and their organisations within this broader context of sustainability. For example, what is the role of humans and human activity which has led to SDG 13 on Climate Action, the need to act on climate change and its effects? What is the role of humans and their organisations in biodiversity loss and what is their role in addressing SDGs 14 Life below Water and 15 Life on Land?

We are still learning about the role of humans and human activity in relation to various aspects of sustainability and ways in which humanity transforms the planet and planetary processes. However, scientific knowledge has gone a long way in understanding some of the relationships between, for example, human activity and climate change and biodiversity loss. The effect of humans and human activity on the Earth is recognised by reference to the fact that we are living in what has become known as the Anthropocene.[1] The Anthropocene refers to the idea that we have entered a new geological epoch in which human activity has become the major driver behind planetary change. Essentially, the Anthropocene recognises that humans have become a geological force on a planetary scale. One way in which humans affect the planet is through their organisations and the economic system within which they are a part and, important for our purposes here, the role of accounting within those organisations.

### 2.3.1 Organisations and their context

Looking at the operational level, organisations, no matter what their form or size, are reliant on resources – both natural and social resources. Some of this resource use can be subject to public scrutiny, and we are seeing an increase in public attention and concern in relation to some aspects of this. For example, scrutiny of organisations in relation to climate and such things as plastic continues to grow. It is perhaps important to recognise however that these issues are not new. Many have known about and shown concern for issues such as these for a long time. We must also be aware that there are other effects, some of them long-term and equally important in relation to sustainability, that we do not know or hear so much about, or at least do not hear much about in relation to organisations. For example, you may not have previously heard much about important issues such as the nitrogen cycle or soil retrogression and degradation, which we introduced above when discussing planetary boundaries. Growing awareness, concern and scrutiny within civil society is important. It has effects on how organisations operate and creates a sense of urgency in relation to these critical contemporary issues. The role of the media in highlighting such issues, and the role of social media in providing additional channels within which information can be spread, are also central considerations in this context.

### 2.3.2 Organisational impacts and dependencies

Organisations, which take many forms as we discuss below, are an important institution within any society. Organisations, in particular large corporations, have power within those societies and are connected with the society and environment in numerous ways. Organisations have a range of social, environmental and economic impacts. For example, it is hard, impossible even, to think of an organisation which does not involve people or use resources in ways that emit carbon. The impacts that organisations have can be both positive and negative.

In addition to impacting society, the environment and the economy, organisations are also dependent on them. This dependence is being increasingly recognised. Not only do organisations require employees to work for them and customers to buy from them, but they are dependent on, for example, the economic equality of the society/ies within which they operate (see Chapter 13 for further discussion). Organisations also have a range of dependencies when it comes to the environment. For example, organisations are reliant on a range of ecosystem services (such as climate regulation). These are discussed further in a latter chapter of the book (Chapter 11).

The impacts and dependencies of each organisation are different, and some organisations clearly have more impacts and higher dependencies than others. For example, the roles of corporations in relation to sustainability (in particular corporations in the industrial West, or providing goods for the industrial West) are key given they disproportionately drive environmental damage and have immense social impacts.

### 2.3.3 Linear and circular economy

Given this context, we have outlined it is perhaps not surprising that we are seeing increased attention in the way in which organisations operate and a consideration of business models.

Many organisations have operated, and indeed still operate, on a "take-make-use-waste/dispose" model. This is referred to as the linear economy model. Here organisations, as well as consumers, take resources from the natural environment, use those resources in the production of goods and services, and dispose the by-product of that process as waste. This business model is unsustainable. This unsustainability is not only due to the fact that many of the resources used are non-renewable, but also the large amount of waste produced that the natural environment is not able to assimilate, or not able to assimilate fast enough. While the adverse results of this type of production are very visible, take vast landfills and the Great Pacific garbage patch for example, the challenge is that many profit-seeking organisations are dependent on consumers engaging in swift throw-away consumption, such as changing their smartphone each time a new model is released or getting a new outfit for each party they attend.

Attempts are nonetheless being made to change these business models. The notion of the circular economy, for example, is an important move to try and alter the ways in which organisations operate. In a circular economy innovative ways of reuse, repair, redesign and remanufacture of products are sought and emphasised, as this reduces the need for new raw materials and the creation of waste. Moreover, the circular economy not only attempts to reduce waste in the process but also considers how any waste that cannot be avoided could be reused. This reuse can be by the organisation itself or by another organisation or group (see the below "Focus on practice" for an example). A circular economy highlights the need to work co-operatively and collaboratively in transitioning to a sustainable state. These concepts will be returned to throughout the course of this book.

At the same time, it is important to recognise that circular economy or circulation of materials for production does not automatically mean that such activity would be beneficial for our collective pursuit of sustainability. Production of goods, no matter whether the raw materials are virgin or recycled, requires energy and other materials, and is also going to result in the production of waste and emissions to varying degrees. Here, the role of accounting can be important, as sometimes following circular principles can in effect require more resources and inputs than doing so with a linear production model, in addition to which it can also lock-in, even encourage, waste generation as waste needs to be available to enable production. This does not mean that we should simply keep following the linear approach. But we should not assume that circularity is a good thing by definition – even if firm marketing materials and social media discussions might make it seem that way. Likewise, sometimes the key principles of collaboration and co-operation are left aside, and instead organisations end up focusing on elements of circularity within the boundaries of a single business only, which can lead to sub-optimisation or simply into the development of more and more products.

Transitioning away from a linear economy model to a circular one requires a fundamental shift in business approaches. A shift that requires new forms of accounting and accounting practices and, given the need for partnerships and collaboration, new, or at least increased, attention to existing accountability relationships. Let's consider just one example here. Within a linear model waste is

**Focus on practice: Circular economy thinking**

Food waste is an oft talked about environmental issue. Within the UK, it is widely reported that more than a third of all food enters the waste stream. And bread is one foodstuff widely discarded. As a relatively low-cost food item with a short shelf-life, it is reported by the Ellen MacArthur Foundation that a staggering 44% of bread produced in the UK is thrown away!

However, in a return to a previous practice, some brewers are turning waste bread into beer. Incorporating waste bread collected from, for example, bakeries and supermarkets, into the brewing process can replace approximately a third of the malted barley usually required. A simple action, but a good example of how waste can be rethought of in the circular economy.

From an accounting and accountability perspective, there are clearly implications. Ensuring cost accounting practices not only support but also promote the use of waste products over virgin raw materials in the production process is one such consideration. As is managing accountability relationships that arise from working in partnership with others to ensure such arrangements in a circular economy are supported.

Brewing beer from surplus bread is just one example of circular economy thinking in action. Possibilities are everywhere. Some of which are obvious, while others will require more creativity and innovation – and the development and refining of related accounting and accountability practices and processes.

Sources: Ellen MacArthur Foundation (2021), Smithers (2018).

considered a costly or non-valuable item. However, within a circular model, waste needs to be designed out of the system, translating it into a source of value. What accounting practices are needed, or existing practices in need of change, to facilitate this? You are probably starting to see that sustainability accounting and accountability is complex and pose many fascinating challenges.

### 2.3.4 The role of organisations and other institutions in shaping the context

While much of the above discussion considers the way in which context affects organisations, we must also recognise the role that organisations and other institutions play in shaping context. Not only do organisations and institutions innovate and set examples, and we will highlight examples of this throughout the following chapters, but they also shape the context through other activities.

While not exactly an organisation, we cannot bypass the role of financial markets here. Related to capitalism and globalisation, the financial markets are, in many societies globally, a significant institutional force, which have substantial implications on the organising of economies and societies. As such, they need to be recognised as a crucial factor in the pursuit of sustainability. Market dynamics are highly complex, and there are libraries worth of books written about them, but at risk of over-simplification, it here suffices to briefly illustrate their significance through three avenues. First, markets have demonstrable effects on politics and political choices, as nation states are prone to consider "what the markets would think" when making political decisions. Second, the markets have an impact on organisations and organisational behaviour, as managers take into account the preferences of various market actors and institutions when making decisions. Third, with their visible role in societies, the financial markets and market discourses can be argued to influence how individuals, organisations and societies come to understand what is preferable and prestigious in the world. We will obviously return to discuss financial markets and the various aspects of them and their influence in the context of the transition towards sustainability in more detail throughout this book.

A different kind of example here can be seen through a consideration of lobbying and advertising. While there are times where organisations lobby for environmental, social and economic development in ways that promote sustainability (for increased regulation for example), unfortunately, much lobbying, especially by industry groups and large powerful corporations, often works against sustainability interests. This may seem counter-intuitive at first, and one might ask why anyone would want to oppose a healthy environment and flourishing communities. There are a number of reasons here, including the different views on sustainability we highlighted earlier. For example, short-termism and financial interests, as well as pure ignorance of scientific facts, or perhaps personal interests and beliefs. Again, we can see here why organisations are so important from a sustainability perspective and why they require transforming if we are to transition to a more sustainable society. However, we can also start to see why doing so is a challenge.

There is another significant reason why organisations and individuals seem at times to work against sustainability. This is a more systemic one and concerns the way societies have over time come to perceive economic success and assess organisational activities in relation to that perception, which also ties into the points we made with regard to financial markets above. This reason relates to how we account for the resources that are used, the environmental and social systems that an organisation is dependent on, and the social and environmental impacts that the activity causes. Or, perhaps if we consider this further, it is often not just how we account for them presently, but rather whether we account for them at all. Many are considered to be external to the economic indicators conventionally used to judge the performance of organisations. We therefore do not take many of these "externality" impacts and dependencies into account at all in assessing, for example, which types of activities are laudable, which modes of production are better and which organisations are the most successful. This is where sustainability accounting and accountability comes into play.

## 2.4 Sustainability accounting and accountability

As we identified in the previous chapter, sustainability accounting refers to a range of techniques, tools and practices that are used in the measurement, planning, control and accountability of organisations with regard to environmental, social and economic issues. Accounting is a powerful mechanism used to assess, measure, control and communicate organisational activities. Accounting as we traditionally view it, perhaps the type of accounting that you have spent time studying, does not work when it comes to sustainability. While that accounting may be effective at measuring, planning and controlling in relation to the financial aspects of an organisation, it is not fit for purpose when it comes to accounting and accountability for a sustainable world.

### 2.4.1 Problems with conventional accounting

So, what are the problems with conventional accounting? Well, for one, conventional accounting tends to focus on the information needs of stakeholders (internal and external to the entity) with a financial interest. In that sense, it is limited in its aims and scope. Accounting for sustainability and its concern with broader accountabilities has inherent within it a focus on a broader range of stakeholders. Indeed, accountability and stakeholders are key concepts within sustainability accounting and accountability and are therefore discussed in depth in the following chapter.

Conventional accounting also holds within it commonly accepted principles and practices that make it unsuitable for accounting within a sustainable society. For example, the entity assumption, encouragement of substitution and externalisation, the recognition criteria of measurability and profitability all require rethinking when accounting for sustainability. Conventional accounting also excludes from expenses the impacts on resources not controlled by the entity, or costs of their practices borne by others. We could go on, but you should be starting to see the limitations of our accounting practices for a sustainability context.

At this point, we should also consider the increasing interest for non-financials or sustainability-related financial matters, which focus on assessing and communicating the potential (financial) impacts sustainability might have on the firm and its financial outlook. This is the outside-in perspective we noted in Chapter 1. It is still unclear how useful such information is for accounting for sustainability, as well as to what kind of implications the proliferation of this perspective will have for sustainability over time. Given the underlying assumptions and their limited focus on the interests of financial stakeholders, such accounting may arguably suffer from similar limitations that conventional accounting does. The global sustainability challenges are enormous however, and we hence need to do as much as possible to mitigate the impacts and adapt to the rising implications. As such, and despite its potential shortcomings which we discuss further in the chapters that follow, an outside-in perspective focusing primarily on the financial risks and opportunities of sustainability for organisations can potentially be helpful for enticing some groups and institutions, such as the financial markets, to work on sustainability.

### 2.4.2 The role of accounting in transitioning towards sustainability

As we have highlighted, organisations and various other institutions will be essential in any transition towards sustainability. Accounting supports change and therefore can play a role in identifying and stopping unsustainable actions and processes. Accounting is also central to decision-making processes and the information provided is important to ensure decisions take into account extended understandings of financial implications (i.e. include financial implications of sustainability issues such as climate and biodiversity), as well as provide appropriate information on the consequences of the decisions made. Accounting is also central to allowing organisations to construct and understand the relationship between internal and external stakeholders.

So, it is quite clear that we need new types of accounting and accountability in order to address sustainability challenges. This type of accounting and accountability is developed and discussed throughout this book. It is perhaps important to acknowledge that this form of accounting while having a reasonably long history and being quite well-established, is fast evolving and developing. The changing nature of the sustainability challenge is a central consideration. As the global sustainability-related challenges emerge and evolve, and become increasingly urgent, so too must accounting practices.

### 2.4.3 Sustainability accounting and accountability practices

The emergence of sustainability accounting is usually identified as occurring in the 1970s. It is generally associated with the emergence of corporate reporting on the environment and society. As you will see in Chapters 5 and 6, this practice is an important one in the sustainability accounting and accountability domain, and a lot of attention has been given to reporting practices. While initially developing as separate disciplines, that is environmental accounting and social accounting and their related reporting, and waxing and waning in popularity for a number of years, since the 1990s the practice of sustainability reporting has become commonplace and institutionalised – at least within large corporate organisations. Various frameworks and standard-setters for sustainability reporting, for example the Global Reporting Initiative (GRI), Sustainability Accounting Standards Board (SASB), EU's Corporate Social Responsibility Directive (CSRD) and International Sustainability Standards Board (ISSB), have emerged in this space over the years and been of significant influence in the sustainability accounting field. We discuss these further in latter chapters.

Another example of where sustainability accounting practices are most common or visible is in relation to the issue of climate change. A range of accounting and accountability tools and practices have emerged in relation to climate and carbon emissions. Carbon footprinting, a tool to assist an entity to understand, measure and record their carbon emissions, is one such example. Have you ever thought of the accounting implications of carbon emissions trading schemes? You will find these schemes have many implications for accounting. This is just one of many areas which highlight the nature of "new" and "evolving" accountings.

As you will see throughout this book the examples are numerous. While we attempt to cover some of the main ones, we are well-aware that it is not possible to consider them all. We encourage you, as you read this book and engage with the text, to consider other areas where accounting for sustainability is evident. Perhaps more importantly, we would also encourage you to consider areas where such accounting is needed.

### 2.4.4 The accounting profession

The influence of the global sustainability context on accounting can also be seen when considering the changing nature of the accounting profession and the range of professional accounting bodies that support it. Many accountancy practices, including the global Big4 firms, are active in developing and providing "innovative sustainability and ESG accounting solutions" to their clients. This is partly in response to recognition of the importance of sustainability to a growing number of their clients, with demands for tools to embed understandings of social and environmental impacts and dependencies into clients' strategic and operational decision-making. Emerging regulation in the sustainability reporting landscape is also a big driver here, including in the area of sustainability reporting assurance. An additional important influence here which we mentioned briefly above is also the investment community as those in the financial markets (e.g. analysts and investors) are increasingly interested in this information and companies' performance and preparedness in relation to, for example, reputational and sustainability-related risks (e.g. financial risks associated with climate change). We discuss this in more detail in Chapter 7. And we should not forget that there can also be a pro-active driver in providing these services, with firms recognising an ethical need to support a transition to a more sustainable society as well as the ability to attract top talent to sustainability and ESG-related roles.

## 2.5 Accounting for sustainability in different organisational settings

When we think of sustainability accounting and accountability we often think of large corporations. This makes sense. We noted above how large corporations are highly visible in society. They use a lot of resources and have significant impacts. However, sustainability accounting and accountability is not just relevant for large corporations, or even just business organisations. All types of organisations, not-for-profits, non-governmental organisations (NGOs), small- and medium-sized enterprises (SMEs) and public sector organisations, for example, are relevant.

Here, in this book, we are concerned with sustainability accounting and accountability in all types of organisations. While much of our discussion in the following chapters relates to large corporations, given their disproportionate impacts and influence, and also the recognition that a large amount of practice has developed in this type of organisation, we also consider a wider variety of organisational forms. In this section, we unpack some common organisational forms. As you will see, this highlights how sustainability accounting and accountability is relevant for all organisations, and also how sustainability accounting and accountability is needed for all organisational forms if we are to transition towards sustainability. For ease, we divide our discussion into three parts: the private sector, the public sector and the third sector. These categories are somewhat fluid, however, as not every organisation or organisational type fits nicely into a single category. Moreover, regulatory differences and geographically or culturally specific features and characteristics can exist affecting both how they are structured and how they are perceived in different societies.

### 2.5.1 Private sector organisations

#### 2.5.1.1 Corporations

Corporations are a dominant form of business entity in the modern economy. Corporations, in particular large multinational corporations, have significant impacts and influence. A corporation is an organisational form that is largely defined by its legal status and also in relation to ownership of assets. A corporation is defined by the law as a separate entity and is often referred to as an "artificial person", given that this legal status gives them certain rights and responsibilities, just as individual citizens have. This legal status and structure of privately owned corporations has implications for corporate responsibility and accountability. Interesting discussions of this can be found in Crane et al. (2019) and Bakan (2005).[2]

#### 2.5.1.2 Small- and medium-sized enterprises

While defined differently in different contexts, the main form of for-profit business organisation and driver of many economies is the SME sector. While it would be easy to think that SMEs have relatively small or minor sustainability impacts, taken together the impact of SMEs is significant. With the increasing expectation (regulatory and otherwise) set upon large companies to be aware of and accountable for the sustainability impacts in their supply chains, many SMEs are facing requirements to provide social and environmental information to their customers. These can place strain on their often limited resources, which at times can be exacerbated by limited knowledge and capacity many SMEs have concerning sustainability and sustainability accounting. While SMEs are perhaps underrepresented in the sustainability accounting and accountability research literature (although well-covered in the management research literature) they are an important organisational form and as such we would encourage you to think about how the range of tools and techniques that feature in the book could be applied and adapted to the SME context. Limited resources within SMEs can mean they look for innovative ways in which to adopt sustainable practices which can also make them an interesting context to consider.

#### 2.5.1.3 Partnerships and co-operatives

Other forms of for-profit organisations include partnerships and co-operatives. Partnerships and co-operatives come in various forms. For example, co-operatives include consumer co-operatives, such as those operating in retail, banking and housing, worker co-operatives, found across different industries, and producer co-operatives, often found in agriculture. And while the legal form for co-operatives can differ, the common characteristic of most is that they are owned jointly by the members and governed democratically, meaning each member has one vote. Co-operatives also often strive to serve their membership, implying that the pursuit of economic profit is not given priority as the driving force of operations. This does not mean that all co-operatives would by definition enhance sustainability. Like any economic activity, co-operatives also have social, environmental and economic impacts, and their activities have dependencies just like any other forms of organisations.

#### 2.5.1.4 Other emerging for-profit organisational forms

There are a myriad of other for-profit organisational forms that have developed, many in direct response to the sustainability challenge. These organisational forms have a range of names, for example, hybrid organisations, social enterprises or benefit corporations. While the exact legal form and thereby some characteristics differ across contexts, a common feature across these types of organisations is their pursuit of a dual mission. That is, they pursue financial success but at the same time explicitly seek to create positive social and/or environmental impact. The relative importance of these two purposes may vary over time, across contexts and between organisations, as does how the achievement of such goals is assessed. While many social enterprises remain small organisations and operate locally, there are also several larger and prominent examples. Patagonia, a US-based clothing and outdoor gear company, for example, is a certified B-corporation paying substantial attention to its environmental footprint and pledging to donate 1% of its annual sales to the preservation and restoration of the natural environment. In the context of such hybrid organisations, learning how to assess, measure and communicate the pursued environmental or social outcomes is highly critical, since without this, it would be hard to distinguish actual positive results from mere narratives or feel-good stories. This again underscores the relevance of sustainability accounting and accountability.

### 2.5.2 Public sector organisations

The public sector has been usefully defined by Broadbent and Guthrie (1992, p. 3) as

> that part of a nation's economic activity which is traditionally owned and controlled by government...the public sector is composed of those public organisations which provide utilities and services to the community and which have traditionally been seen as essential to the fabric of our society.

As such, the public sector consists of a very wide range of organisations. There are, for instance, cities, local councils and regional authorities. These often consist of a number of smaller subsections and units. For example, a city often owns and runs publicly owned companies, which perform specific tasks or are given responsibility for particular operations. In many societies, universities are public and hence part of this group.

Given the scale and operational impact of the public sector on the economy, environment and community, it is important for sustainability, and thus sustainability accounting and accountability. National governments too are an important focus for sustainability and thus sustainability accounting and accountability. Countries have for a long time produced environmental reports (sometimes referred to as "State of the environment" reports) outlining each country's performance, progress and strategy in relation to a range of sustainability-related issues like biodiversity. In similar terms, many elements of the social, such as level of education, health and human rights are often assessed and discussed on the national level. The SDGs introduced above, while being considered by business organisations, are essentially written for national governments. It is therefore not surprising that there is some reporting at country level against SDG performance.

The rising sustainability challenges require action from all sectors of the economy. Public sector organisations in general, and nation states in particular, have long engaged in international agreements regarding various social and environmental questions. Such agreements, whether dealing with human rights, water or biodiversity, require mechanisms through which the situation and potential progress can be assessed, measured and reported. Again, we are potentially within the realm of sustainability accounting and accountability. While accounting for human rights or carbon accounting can look at the same elements in any organisational form, one particular question in the realm of public sector relates to allocation and the idea of an entity: does a city include in its carbon emissions all the emissions that occur within its regional boundaries – i.e. also those of any private organisations or citizens residing there, even if the city has no direct control over those? In other words, how should the accounting and accountability systems be structured so that not only all necessary impacts and dependencies are included but also the associated accountability relationships are identified.

## 2.5.3 The third sector

The third sector is a common term to describe the variety of organisations which fall outside both private and public sectors. While lumping everything together under this broad label risks missing the diversity and results in oversimplification, this generic categorisation is perhaps required due to the range of possible organisational forms.

The third sector label covers a diversity of organisations from charities and churches to sports clubs and civil society groups. It is sometimes called the non-profit or voluntary sector. Again, all organisational forms within this sector are relevant and important to sustainability accounting and accountability. Indeed, if we take a moment to reflect on the impacts and accountability relationships these organisations collectively have, we can see it is vitally important. We cannot feasibly include a discussion of all of these here, although you will see us refer to some throughout the book. We will, however, raise attention to two forms: NGOs and social movements.

### 2.5.3.1 Non-government organisations

NGOs are diverse. It is for this reason that they are quite hard to define. NGOs can, for example, take the form of voluntary associations, unions, religious organisations and consumer groups. Table 2.1 provides a useful classification. Some of the more well-known NGOs operating in the sustainability arena that you may know are Amnesty International, Friends of the Earth, Greenpeace, the World Wildlife Fund (WWF) and Oxfam International.

A large number of NGOs exist within societies. There are perhaps a number of reasons for this. For example, the perceived failure of the state in many regions to support civil society and therefore the need for other organisations to fill the void, or the increased awareness and concern for both local and global sustainability issues such as environmental degradation and human rights abuses which saw a growth in

**TABLE 2.1** Attributes of NGOs

| | |
|---|---|
| NGO orientation – type of activities they engage in | Advocacy |
| | Development |
| | Development education |
| | Development-orientated |
| | Research |
| | Welfare |
| NGO level of operation | International |
| | National |
| | Community |

Source: Adapted from Boomsma and O'Dwyer (2014), Vakil (1997).

these kinds of NGOs in the past. Concerns with democratic processes and the need for NGOs to represent different civil society and environmental voices are another potential reason. With this rise has come an increasing influence of NGOs. Unfortunately, growth and the associated level of funding received by NGOs has also been accompanied by a number of scandals emerging from the sector, and overall a greater concern with NGO accountability.

NGOs are an important organisational form for sustainability accounting, not only because they have sustainability impacts, but they can also act as an organisational form which promotes sustainability ideals. NGOs demand accountability of others, but there is also the need for NGOs to be accountable. NGO accountability has been a significant area of sustainability accounting and accountability research and practice. We do not focus extensively on NGOs here in this book. While we do consider how accounting and accountability mechanisms are important to NGOs, including how NGOs demand accountability and how they can use accounting in their practices (e.g. see Chapter 8), we would encourage you to consider how the topics, tools and practices outlined in this book are relevant to the NGO context more broadly.

#### 2.5.3.2 Social movement organisations

Social movement organisations (SMOs) are another organisational form. SMOs can be considered to be a group, or organised sector, of a social movement. Examples you may be familiar of are those organisations that have emerged out of the climate movement. SMOs can be local or global, and also vary significantly in form and level of formal structure. Given their diversity, they are not easy to characterise. However, they are the subject of increased attention, likely due to their growing presence in society, especially in relation to social and environmental justice issues, and research. We refer to several SMOs throughout the chapters, although do not consider their own unique accounting and accountability needs. You might find it interesting to reflect on these further however.

### 2.5.4 Summary of different organisational settings

Organisations, be they multinational corporations, public sector entities, NGOs or others, sit within societies and engage in a network of relations to other organisations as well as individual citizens. The activities of organisations always have implications on other members of the society and the society at large. At the core of the relationships are both implicit and explicit expectations with regard to how an organisation should behave in a given society or any other context. While it may be easy to assume that certain types of organisations, such as major multinational corporations, have larger sustainability impacts and hence should be the focus of sustainability accounting and accountability, sustainability accounting and accountability has relevance across the organisational forms discussed above.

Bearing this diversity in mind, it is relevant to understand that one will not be able to find a single model of sustainability accounting and accountability which could be applied in all contexts and for all sustainability issues. Instead, sustainability accounting and accountability includes a diverse and evolving field of practices, which are based on recognising the interconnections of social, economic and ecological dimensions. While some tools in the field might appear relatively straightforward, other approaches can seem highly complex and open-ended.

## 2.6 Conclusion

Sustainability will depend on having informed, ecologically literate citizens working towards healthy ecosystems, genuine social inclusion and equitable distribution of resources. We will need strong and just institutions to support this. Organisations and their systems of accounting and accountability are institutions that will be central to sustainability and the transition towards sustainability.

In this chapter, we have discussed the background and context to the topic of sustainability accounting and accountability. We began by discussing the concept of sustainability itself. While we have identified the SDGs as a useful framework for understanding sustainability, we have also discussed how we need to consider sustainability as a systems-level concept and introduced the planetary boundaries as well as the doughnut economics model as useful visual representations to consider this. We have also noted how a transition towards a more sustainable environment, society and economy will require a reconsideration of business models. Here we have introduced the concept of the circular economy to begin to reflect on how a consideration of sustainability requires a transformation of current dominant models. Lastly, we have spent some time defining and examining sustainability accounting and accountability. That is, the role of accounting and accountability practices in this transition towards sustainability and achievement of the SDGs. We included a discussion of various organisational forms to indicate how sustainability accounting and accountability is relevant in many different contexts.

This chapter has provided the background and context to the chapters that follow. However, before delving into a more specific discussion of the various practices and issues, we will in the following chapter explore some of the key concepts that provide further clarity as to the topic of sustainability accounting and accountability.

## Notes

1 The Anthropocene was proposed as a new epoch to follow from the current Holocene. While the Holocene is "a period of warm and extraordinary stable climate conditions between ice ages that was ideal for the development of human civilization" (Robertson, 2017, p. 23), the Anthropocene was proposed as an epoch which highlights changes, and the role of humans in bringing about those changes (anthropo – human, cene – "new", "recent"). While the proposal to have the Anthropocene officially recognised was rejected in 2024, it is a useful term to consider the effects of humans as a geological force. The Anthropocene and its relevance for organisations and accounting have also been discussed (see Wright et al., 2018; Bebbington et al., 2020).

2 Reference here is to Bakan's book (2005) *The Corporation*. It is also available as a documentary. A follow-up book and documentary were published in 2020.

## References


Bakan, J. (2005). *The Corporation: The Pathological Pursuit of Profit and Power.* Free Press.

Bebbington, J., Österblom, H., Crona, B., Jouffray, J.-B., Larrinaga, C., Russell, S. and Scholtens, B. (2020). Accounting and Accountability in the Anthropocene. *Accounting, Auditing and Accountability Journal, 33(1)*, 152–177.

Boomsma, R. and O'Dwyer, B. (2014). The Nature of NGO Accountability: Conceptions, Motives, Forms and Mechanisms. In Bebbington, J., Unerman, J. and O'Dwyer, B. (eds), *Sustainability Accounting and Accountability* (2nd edn), pp. 157–175. Routledge.

Broadbent, J. and Guthrie, J. (1992). Changes in the Public Sector: A Review of Recent "Alternative" Accounting Research. *Accounting, Auditing and Accountability Journal, 5(2)*, 3–31.

Carson, R. (1962). *Silent Spring.* Houghton Mifflin.

Crane, A., Matten, D., Glozer, S. and Spence, L. (2019). *Business Ethics: Managing Corporate Citizenship and Sustainability in the Age of Globalization* (5th edn). Oxford University Press.

Ehrlich, P. (1968). *The Population Bomb.* Sierra Club/Ballantine Books.

Elkington, J. (2018). 25 Years Ago I Coined the Phrase "Triple Bottom Line:" Here's Why It's Time to Rethink It. *Harvard Business Review*, 25 June 2018.

Ellen MacArthur Foundation (2021). Brewing Beer from Surplus Bread: Toast Ale. www.ellenmacarthurfoundation.org/case-studies/brewing-beer-from-surplus-bread (accessed 16 January 2025).

Gray, R. (2010). Is Accounting for Sustainability Actually Accounting for Sustainability...and How Would We Know? An Exploration of Narratives of Organisations and the Planet. *Accounting, Organizations and Society, 35(1)*, 47–62.

Meadows, D., Meadows, D., Randers, J. and Behrens, W. (1972). *Limits to Growth: A Report for the Club of Rome's Project on the Predicament of Mankind.* Earth Island.

Raworth, K. (2017). *Doughnut Economics: Seven Ways to Think Like a 21st-Century Economist.* Random House.

Richardson, J., Steffen, W., Lucht, W., Bendtsen, J., Cornell, S. E., et al. (2023). Earth Beyond Six of Nine Planetary Boundaries. *Science Advances, 9*, 37.

Robertson, M. (2017). *Sustainability: Principles and Practice.* Routledge.

Rockström, J., Steffen, W., Noone, K., Persson, Å., Chapin III, F. S., Lambin, E., Lenton, T. M., Scheffer, M., Folke, C., Schellnhuber, H., Nykvist, B., De Wit, C. A., Hughes, T., van der Leeuw, S., Rodhe, H., Sörlin, S., Snyder, P. K., Costanza, R., Svedin, U., Falkenmark, M., Karlberg, L., Corell, R. W., Fabry, V. J., Hansen, J., Walker, B., Liverman, D., Richardson, K., Crutzen, P. and Foley, J. (2009). Planetary Boundaries: Exploring the Safe Operating Space for Humanity. *Ecology and Society, 14(2)*, 32.

Russell, S., Milne, M. J. and Dey, C. (2017). Accounts of Nature and the Nature of Accounts: Critical Reflections on Environmental Accounting and Propositions for Ecologically Informed Accounting. *Accounting, Auditing & Accountability Journal, 30*(7), 1426–1458.

Schumacher, E. F. (1973). *Small Is Beautiful: A Study of Economics as if People Mattered.* Blond and Briggs.

Smithers, R. (2018). Raise a Toast! New Beers Made from Leftover Bread Help to Cut Food Waste. *The Guardian.* www.theguardian.com/lifeandstyle/2018/apr/28/new-beers-made-from-leftover-bread-marks-and-spencer-adnams (accessed 30 June 2020).

United Nations. (2024). *The Sustainable Development Goals Report 2024.* Available at https://unstats.un.org/sdgs/report/2024/ (accessed 6 May 2025).

Vakil, A. C. (1997). Confronting the Classification Problem: A Taxonomy of NGOs. *World Development, 25(12)*, 2057–2070.

WCED (The World Commission on Environment and Development) (1987). *Our Common Future.* Oxford University Press.

Williams, A., Perogo, P. and Whiteman, G. (2025). Boundary Conditions for Organizations in the Anthropocene: A Review of the Planetary Boundaries Framework 10 Years On. *Journal of Management Studies, 62(4)*, 1811–1846.

Wright, C., Nyberg, D., Rickards, L. and Freund, J. (2018). Organizing in the Anthropocene. *Organization, 25(4)*, 455–471.

## Additional reading and resources

Arjaliès, D.-L., Rodrigue, M. and Romi, A. (2023). "Come Play with Us!" A Grassroots Research Agenda for Accounting and the Circular Economy. *Accounting Forum, 47*(4), 497–524.

Bakan, J. (2020). *The New Corporation: How "Good" Corporations Are Bad for Democracy*. Vintage Books.

Bakan, J. (2020). *The New Corporation: The Unfortunately Necessary Sequel*. Available at https://thenewcorporation.movie/.

Bebbington, J. and Larrinaga, C. (2014). Accounting and Sustainable Development: An Exploration. *Accounting, Organizations and Society, 39(6)*, 395–413.

Bebbington, J. and Unerman, J. (2018). Achieving the United Nations Sustainable Development Goals: An Enabling Role for Accounting Research. *Accounting, Auditing and Accountability Journal, 31(1)*, 2–24

Ellen MacArthur Foundation. www.ellenmacarthurfoundation.org/ (Circular Economy).

Gray, R. (1990). *The Greening of Accountancy: The Profession after Pearce*. Chartered Association of Certified Accountants.

Larrinaga, C., and Garcia-Torea, N. (2022). An Ecological Critique of Accounting: The Circular Economy and COVID-19. *Critical Perspectives on Accounting, 82*, 102320.

Vollmer, H. (2024). *Handbook of Accounting in Society*. Edward Elgar Publishing Ltd.

CHAPTER

3

# Accountability, stakeholders, materiality and externalities

## Examining key concepts

In this chapter, we introduce and discuss some of the key concepts that are essential for understanding the role and position of sustainability accounting and accountability in societies and organisations. These key concepts are important in understanding much of the discussion that follows in the next two parts of this book as they help us make sense of the assumptions and perspectives that provide the foundations for the topic. With this in mind, in this chapter, we introduce and examine four related concepts: accountability, stakeholders, materiality and externalities. We begin by discussing the notion of accountability. Accountability is probably the broadest and most complex of the four concepts. We begin our discussion here however because accountability is arguably the overarching concept which informs the practice of sustainability accounting, or at least how the practice is understood in this book. We then discuss the concepts of stakeholders, materiality and externalities in turn relating these to the concept of accountability and the practice of sustainability accounting.

By the end of this chapter, you should:

- Understand the concept of accountability and why it is relevant to sustainability accounting.
- Be able to define accountability and identify various accountability relationships between organisations and others.
- Be able to define and identify relevant organisational stakeholders and understand the various ways and reasons why organisations engage with them.
- Understand the concept of materiality and why materiality is an important concept for sustainability accounting and accountability.
- Understand the concept of externalities and their relevance to sustainability accounting and accountability.

DOI: 10.4324/9781003533207-4

## 3.1 Accountability

In most contemporary societies, there are laws and other regulations that outline the basic rules for how both individuals and organisations are allowed to operate. Such laws and regulations cover both how individuals and organisations should operate in general, and in relation to one another. A variety of governance systems stipulate how organisations can operate, how they can make use of various resources and what kind of requirements they need to fulfil in order to do so. However, these explicit and official governance regulations are only part of the complex social structures forming the rules and guidelines of society. There are a plethora of other, sometimes informal and implicit, expectations which affect individuals, organisations and organisational activities.

In other words, individuals and organisations cannot base actions and operations only on the idea of following the legal rules and formal regulations in place in a given society. Some areas and aspects of social and economic life are not governed by any formal regulation. There obviously cannot be a rule for every single aspect. Moreover, sometimes rules only set some minimum thresholds, which are then not, for one reason or another, considered sufficient by the public at large. This means that individual citizens and organisations need to get by without them. To do so, norms are established which guide behaviour and set informal and implicit expectations.

As we noted in the previous chapter, corporate responsibility is a common term used when discussing the need for organisations to be responsible in their activities in societies. While the concept is vague and subject to various interpretations, at the heart of it is the idea that organisations have a responsibility towards others in society. These responsibilities are various. For example, an organisation is responsible to its financiers to use the capital it has been provided with in an efficient way to produce financial returns to owners and creditors. There is a responsibility to employees with regard to, for instance, suitable work conditions and financial compensation. Towards customers, there is a responsibility to deliver safe and reliable products and services, including ensuring they match what the organisation has promised in relation to them. There is also a responsibility towards society. All organisations receive various types of resources and services, such as an educated workforce and infrastructure, and there is hence a responsibility in relation to how the use of those resources serves the broader good. Likewise, an organisation uses environmental resources and causes environmental impacts. This leads to a responsibility towards the environment and others with regard to how those resources are being used.

While there can be regulations in place regarding some of these responsibilities, for the most part, there is no legal governance. Where regulations are put in place, often they are developed with a considerable time lag behind changes in social values that have motivated new or amended regulations. Therefore, responsibility is oftentimes based on the implicit social and institutional norms mentioned above, rather than being codified in current regulations. It is this consideration of responsibility and the potentially complex responsibilities that organisations have that leads us to the concept of accountability.

### 3.1.1 What is accountability?

So, how do we know what an organisation's responsibilities are (i.e. the extent of their responsibilities), and whether an organisation is fulfilling those responsibilities? This is clearly a complex question. In addressing this question, information is often considered key. An essential element of the expectations surrounding an organisation's responsibility relates to the provision of information on organisational activities. Simply put, the act of giving an account. As organisations populate the shared social space, make use of environmental, social and economic resources, and have implications on human and non-human beings as well as on other organisations, it is reasonable to expect them to provide accounts of, and for, their actions. This goes directly to the idea of accountability, which for the purposes of this book, we will define as the duty to provide an account of the actions over which one is considered to have responsibility (see Gray et al., 1996).

To explore this concept further, it is perhaps useful to think of accountability in relation to financial accounting and accountability which may be more familiar to you. When we think about financial accounting and the act of providing financial accounts, we often think of this in relation to decision-usefulness. That is, we consider that the act of giving a financial account enables the users of this information to make financial decisions. Oftentimes in the case of financial accounting these users would be current and potential investors, and in the case of management accounting, they would often be internal users such as managers. From this perspective, accounting is concerned with providing financial information that is useful for the user for financial decision-making.

However, financial accounting can also be seen through an accountability lens. That is, we can consider the act of providing financial accounts as an act of discharging accountability, being accountable for the financial resources that the entity is responsible for.

Both decision-usefulness and accountability are relevant for sustainability-related accounting. For example, sustainability-related information can assist in making a variety of decisions such as who we buy from, who we work for, and, as will be discussed in Chapter 7, who we might invest in. Indeed, with the consequences of climate change and sustainability crisis more broadly becoming more tangible, the term decision-usefulness has become increasingly used in association with sustainability accounting. The establishment and swift rise of the International Sustainability Standards Board (ISSB) is at the crux of this development, with their standards seeking to enable the production of decision-useful sustainability-related information to investors. This perspective is however limited to a specific kind of an accountability to a specific group of stakeholders, and as such it underscores how the accountability lens taken in this book is a key consideration in sustainability accounting. Indeed, much of sustainability accounting is concerned with organisational responsibility relating to environmental, social and economic resource use and impacts, and the associated act of giving an account to provide the accountability expected and needed in these relationships beyond investors, analysts and other stakeholders with a financial interest. Contrasting the approach of ISSB, signs of a broader accountability approach can be seen in other prominent sustainability reporting frameworks, such as the Global Reporting Initiative (GRI) and the EU's European Sustainability Reporting Standards (ESRS). Given we approach sustainability accounting with a focus on accountability in this book, let us explore the concept further.

### 3.1.2 Legal and moral duty

It is relevant to distinguish between the legal duties to provide information (to give an account) and a moral duty to do so. In this book, both are covered. We are interested in both aspects but note that the latter is often at the crux of discussions regarding what kind of roles and responsibilities organisations have in societies. A consideration of the moral as well as legal duty to discharge accountability also situates organisations within their environmental and social context and clearly positions accountability as relational. That is, accountability is not simply about organisations, but about organisations and those to whom they are responsible and therefore accountable. We can refer to stakeholders here. A term we explore further below.

Being subject to accountability implies that organisations need to provide information about what they have been doing and what kind of implications these actions may have had. For members of society, having access to such information is essential, as otherwise it could be highly difficult to make sense of organisational activities and evaluate whether these have positive implications for oneself or for the environment and society more broadly. Again, we can see why the act of giving an account is important.

As we noted above, an organisation has a range of responsibilities towards both various social groups and the society as a whole. These responsibilities also bring with them accountability relationships, which as we have noted, are similarly diverse and varied. In addition, these relationships are arguably expanding over time. While in the past it mostly sufficed if an organisation produced financial disclosures and thereby fulfilled its accountability towards owners, investors and creditors, there is now an increasing number of issues that organisations are considered to be accountable to and hence are being held to account for. One reason for this is our increased collective understanding of sustainability and the higher awareness of the importance of how we use and impact the Earth's social and ecological resources. Hence, organisations are seen to have a wider range of sustainability-related responsibilities. Consider the SDGs discussed in the previous chapter. Organisational responsibilities and accountabilities relate to many, if not all, of these 17 goals (GRI and UN Global Compact, 2022).

### 3.1.3 Social licence to operate and legitimacy

As established above, the responsibilities an organisation (or perhaps more correctly individuals within an organisation) can be considered to have are often broader than those set by formal regulation. In a similar vein, we can draw a distinction between a legal or regulatory licence to operate and what we call a social licence to operate (see Gray et al., 1996).

A legal or regulatory licence to operate is relatively straightforward and likely to be familiar to you. That is, an organisation operates within the regulations that exist within a context. For example, an organisation may follow the required regulation or have been granted specific permission to operate.

A social licence to operate however is perhaps less straightforward, but equally as important. A social licence to operate is essentially the approval granted by the various social groups or the society in general. This licence to operate is not set out in the legal regulatory context, but rather the normative and moral context. Clearly, there is no social licence or a social contract in any tangible form, instead it is intangible, relating to the relationship an organisation has with those that surround it. If an organisation for some reason is not perceived to fulfil its responsibilities in society, it risks losing its social licence to operate. This is obviously a crude simplification, as the situation is by no means clear in all cases.

In practice, losing the social licence to operate can materialise through negative publicity, diminished customer interest, active consumer boycotts, negative reactions by suppliers or corporate customers, visible social protests outside organisation's facilities or on social media and so forth. Think of Uniper, a German energy company, which in 2020 opened a major new coal-fired power plant called Datteln 4. This was clearly legal, and the company did not break any legal rules as it started operating the plant. Indeed, the power plant ranks amongst the most modern and environmentally efficient coal-fired power plants in the world. However, at the time of its opening the social context and societies' attitudes towards coal and coal use were not positive and the decision was not viewed favourably. The organisation faced constant protests on-site and online, as social groups cited urgent climate concerns and demanded an end to coal. Likewise, Fortum, a Finnish energy company, which was Uniper's parent company at the time, became a target of environmental NGOs and shareholder activist campaigns, which labelled the organisation's claims of being a leader in clean energy as being hypocritical. As such, while Uniper could be seen to have had a legal or regulatory licence to operate, its social licence to operate was less clear. Indeed, while the social licence to operate was not lost entirely, it was clearly at risk. Subsequently, and illustrating the changing nature of accountabilities, the Russian invasion of Ukraine in 2022 and the associated geopolitical tensions and economic sanctions against Russia caused major disruptions to Uniper's businesses, resulting eventually in a German government bailout, which the European Commission approved with a set of conditions, including a requirement to sell the Datteln power plants. This example demonstrates the need for both legal and social factors to be considered in the organisational context.

In relation to the social licence, we can also speak of organisational legitimacy. This is a useful term for discussing how an organisation is positioned in society. As is the case with social contract and social licence to operate, legitimacy is likewise an intangible aspect. That is, we can consider the above examples in relation to whether the organisation's operations are considered to be legitimate within the social context. Like the social license to operate, if an organisation loses legitimacy it can have tangible consequences.

When considering the social licence to operate, it is perhaps useful to reflect on the changing nature of society. Our above example of Uniper mentions social media, protests, NGOs and shareholder activists. These things influence both visibility and information sharing of organisational activities and accountabilities. Protest and activism related to climate change, for example, are likely to be known. Extinction Rebellion (XR), School Strikes and Parents for the Future (PFF), for example, are just some of the groups seeking to raise awareness of various organisational and government accountabilities relating to climate change. They also demonstrate the diverse nature of those involved in such actions. We discuss related aspects further in Chapter 8.

### 3.1.4 Accountability and the social licence to operate

All these ideas (social contract, social licence to operate and organisational legitimacy) relate closely to responsibility and accountability. They imply that an organisation needs to fulfil some basic requirements and responsibilities to maintain its social licence to operate within a particular society. To show this, organisations discharge their accountability by providing accounts of their actions. Or that is at least what is expected of them, since in many cases, these accounts go beyond areas where there is a legal duty to produce the information. These accounts are also important in how others perceive an organisation and its actions.

A key challenge however is determining what kind of accounts and information an organisation can and should give. What type of account is needed to discharge accountability? As the social contract and legitimacy relate more to how other social groups perceive the organisation than to how it actually operates, it has often been suggested that organisations can seek to enhance their reputation and maintain their legitimacy in society through publishing positive information, such as sustainability reports highlighting their achievements and good intentions. While an increasing number of reporting frameworks and some regulatory requirements have emerged across societies, the question still remains. Furthermore, social groups seldom have any direct access to an organisation's activities, which means that they are for the most part dependent on the information the organisation is providing them. Hence, characteristics such as balance, comparability and trustworthiness are pertinent questions in sustainability accounting and accountability, and we will return to this theme throughout this book.

**Focus on practice: Dieselgate and the social licence to operate**

The 2015 emissions scandal at Volkswagen (VW) provides a useful illustration of the social licence to operate. In what has become known as Dieselgate, VW was found to have intentionally programmed some of their diesel engines so that full emission control was only engaged during testing. This was referred to as a "defeat device". This meant that when the vehicles were being tested their emissions were within the legal requirements and were within limits which enabled the company to promote them as "Clean Diesels" – leading to several environmental awards, tax breaks and increasing sales amongst environmentally concerned car users. However, when in daily operation on the road, emissions were, in fact, much higher.

When exposed, this scandal had immediate impacts. Those impacts went well beyond the legal and regulatory aspects and the formal legal charges raised against the company. For example, consumers – including many previously loyal to the brand – indicated a loss of trust with some demanding to return their vehicle. The impact was also evident amongst shareholders with shares in the company falling immediately after the announcement.

While a relatively dated example now, it is nonetheless a useful one to consider the concepts introduced above. For example, we can see that in addition to the company breaching the legal or regulatory licence to operate in relation to the specific vehicles included in the scandal, the company can also be seen to have lost legitimacy and breached the social licence to operate. This loss of legitimacy and the effects of the breach to the social licence were broader than the particular vehicles and applied to the company more broadly. Despite the company's efforts to change course and rebuild its brand through an active sustainability strategy and public engagement in climate discussions, Volkswagen's name continues to be associated with Dieselgate a decade later, with the public still receiving reminders of the events through ongoing court cases and students studying the case as an illustrative example of corporate culture and ethical questions. Dieselgate continues to have ongoing effects so the company needs to be prepared for backlash and increased scrutiny anytime it promotes something in environmental terms.

### 3.1.5 The broadening of accountability

It is important to recognise that accountability is a contested concept. This means different individuals and groups hold different views on the responsibilities that organisations have, as we have already noted above. For a long time, private organisations were mainly expected to provide information about their financial activities. Environmental issues were not considered to be relevant, and social matters were seen as more the responsibility of the public sector than that of private corporations. However, this has clearly changed. Different groups may have varying expectations for organisational accountability, but in general terms, these expectations have increased and, importantly, continue to increase.

However, as we established in the previous chapter, there is growing awareness not only of the various sustainability issues but also how those issues are interconnected. This means that in seeking to account for the various social, economic and ecological responsibilities and accountabilities that an organisation has, the organisation faces increased complexity. This complexity relates not only to the number and interconnectivity of the issues but also to the accounting used to produce the accounts. That is, the typical accountability questions relating to *accountable for what* and *accountable to whom* are expanding (Dillard and Vinnari, 2019). This is leading not only to more complexity for organisations but also to greater complexity for accounting which is central to these relations. But this perhaps makes accountability appear much simpler than it is.

### 3.1.6 Who is an organisation accountable to?

Thus far, we have noted that an organisation might be accountable to various social groups, or perhaps to the society as a whole. While the social contract and the idea of legitimacy in society have provided interesting insights for our understanding of the relationship between organisations and society, it needs to be acknowledged that speaking of a unitary society with common views and values is too simplistic. Societies consist of different kinds of individuals, groups and organisations, each with their own values, prioritisations and assumptions. As such, a more fine-grained analysis of society and social actors is needed. In order to better understand the significance of accountability and how those accountability relationships are formed, we need to take a closer look at the concept of stakeholders.

## 3.2 Stakeholders

As is highlighted through the notion of the social licence to operate, no organisation can operate without having relationships with other institutions, individuals or groups in society. Some of the most obvious ones include financial services, employees, subcontractors, customers and owners. From an organisation's perspective, these individuals and groups are collectively known as stakeholders.

There are numerous definitions as to who and what counts as a stakeholder, but according to the classic definition of Freeman (1984), stakeholders include any groups or individuals who can affect or are affected by the achievement of the organisation's objectives. While some stakeholders, like the employees or the community around a production site, are fairly obvious, easy to identify, and also uncontested, there are other perhaps less obvious and more contentious ones. For example, nature and future generations. Despite having more subtle relationships to the organisation, both nature and future generations are clearly affected by an organisation's activities. Stakeholder identification is thus also politically contentious: the results are different based on who gets to make the decisions.

### 3.2.1 Stakeholder mapping: Who are an organisation's stakeholders?

While there are some evident stakeholders each organisation tends to have, stakeholders are always context-specific and hence unique to each organisation. As such, it is important for an organisation to execute stakeholder mapping to identify its stakeholders. This can be done with regard to the organisation in general, or alternatively on a more detailed level concerning a new production site, a specific project or product.

In addition to identifying the various stakeholders an organisation has, stakeholder mapping should also include looking into the characteristics of those stakeholders and the relationship they have with the organisation. This helps an organisation to understand the overall setting: who are the key stakeholders, which groups can have most influence on the organisation, which groups would be most impacted by the organisation's activities, which groups might speak out and which ones might not and so forth. Having such an understanding is essential when considering the accountability relationships an organisation has. For example, it is important to acknowledge to whom an organisation is responsible and should be accountable to. As each organisation is different, with a different history and currently operating with different types of activities and policies, the stakeholder relationships and associated accountabilities are also different.

### 3.2.2 Stakeholder salience: Power, legitimacy and urgency

Organisations are dependent on stakeholders when they seek to achieve their organisational goals. Investors provide the organisation with financial capital. Employees are needed to carry out work and duties. Customers are relied upon to purchase products and services offered. And so forth. At the same time, there are other groups which might be less relevant from the organisation's point of view in the short term. Consider civil society groups, who challenge the organisation's environmental policy. Or the aforementioned future generations, who have no voice in the present to state their views. Accordingly, various classifications have been presented to categorise an organisation's stakeholders, such as external and internal, primary and secondary, or proximate and distal stakeholders.

It is evident that stakeholder groups are not equal – especially in the eyes of the organisation which is likely to consider some stakeholders as more important. Mitchell et al. (1997) refer to this as stakeholder salience, identifying that, from an organisation's perspective, some stakeholders have more salience than others. They suggest organisations, or more correctly the managers within organisations, use the three concepts of power, legitimacy and urgency to determine which stakeholder groups are the most important. Different stakeholders vary in terms of the power they hold over an organisation, and this balance also differs from organisation to organisation. The position of some groups, say creditors providing the organisation with short-term capital, can be such that the organisation has no option but to answer the demands. Some other groups might present vocal criticism and post demands, but without having any leverage or power over the organisation. Hence, they might get overlooked by the organisation. Or alternatively, the requests might be considered to be less urgent, and hence the organisation might opt to leave answering to a later point. In the Mitchell et al. model, the stakeholders considered to possess all three attributes, power, legitimacy and urgency, are called definitive stakeholders.

This stakeholder salience view on stakeholders is critiqued by some as being overly organisation-centric, that is, considering stakeholders from the perspective of the organisation. They suggest that this leads to a narrow definition of stakeholders as we discuss further below. In response, there are attempts to rethink and challenge who gets to define stakeholders and a consideration of the limits, in particular, who and what is overlooked, when the organisation undertakes stakeholder identification and prioritisation. We discuss this further below.

Another thing that must be kept in mind, however, is that a stakeholder's relationship with an organisation can change. Such positionings are not static or stable. This is particularly so in today's society where civil society movements are becoming more widespread and social media, for example, can have a big effect on who gets heard and what information becomes available. Another example is how investors and analysts have become more interested in an organisations' sustainability activities over time and demanded more information in relation to such activities. Moreover, the attributes defining a stakeholder's status, power, legitimacy and urgency, are not anything that can be objectively measured. So within stakeholder identification by organisations, the question is how the managers of an organisation perceive the various stakeholders and their respective relationships with the organisation, and thereby assess how important each group is from the organisation's viewpoint.

Within management studies, stakeholder thinking and stakeholder theory are well-known schools of thought (Johnson-Cramer et al., 2022). The main interest here is the relationships organisations have with their stakeholders. Using stakeholder theory, scholars have pointed out how organisations emphasise the needs and expectations of the more powerful stakeholders in shaping their activities over sustainability issues. In working with the various stakeholders, the organisation's management seeks to take into account the different demands set by them. This not only includes adjusting organisational activities to better fit the expectations, but may also include providing the stakeholders with information they are expecting. That is, who an organisation recognises as their stakeholders (whether through choice or due to stakeholder demand) affects their accounting and the discharging of accountabilities.

There is also an inherent challenge here. Both organisational managers and the stakeholder salience framework presented above focus on looking at the stakeholder relationships from the organisation's viewpoint. If we took a different perspective, setting ourselves in the position of a particular stakeholder group or approaching the setting from a broader sustainability point of view, the relationships are likely to look very different. While a local social group calling for the protection of a particular ecological habitat next to the organisation's production site might not be considered very important by the organisation, the relationship might be crucial for sustainability more broadly. Likewise, different groups could have very different views in different settings. Consider, for example, where the livelihoods of particular indigenous people are dependent on a major multinational company abandoning its plans to expand pulp and paper production in the Amazon basin. As such, it is important to recognise that stakeholder identification and subsequent relationships are not given. Instead, they are based on subjective assessments and judgements, which can also involve political choices regarding who and what counts in a particular situation. Considering the perspective from which stakeholder decisions are made is also important. We should not, for example, take for granted the stakeholders identified and selected by any one organisation as some important ones may be absent.

This concern with the prioritisation of some stakeholders while others are overlooked or marginalised, has led some to suggest that rather than focus on who are the stakeholders of a particular organisation, another way to consider stakeholders is to consider who has a stake in an issue or sustainability more broadly, for example, thinking of stakeholders in relation to the climate crisis or biodiversity (Tanima et al., 2024; Tregidga and Milne, 2022). Considering these different perspectives on stakeholders and their implications is useful and again highlights the contested nature of stakeholders and their identification.

**PAUSE AND REFLECT...**

Let's take a moment to consider organisational stakeholders and their accountability demands a little further. We can do this through a series of steps.

1. Choose a specific organisation familiar to you and then write down as many stakeholders as you can think of. You may start by listing some of the more obvious ones but also try to think of those that are not so obvious. Avoid looking up the organisation or looking online for this information. You can do that later.
2. Consider the stakeholder claims or demands on the organisation for some of the stakeholders you have identified. What are the responsibilities/accountabilities that exist between the organisation and the stakeholder?
3. Consider any conflicts between the stakeholder groups. Do any of the claims or accountability demands compete against each other? Consider what challenges this would bring in relation to stakeholder engagement.
4. You may now wish to go online and consider how your selected organisation has discussed stakeholders. Who have they recognised and not recognised? In what way? It might be useful to reflect on the stakeholder salience model discussed above here.

While each of the stages above might appear quite straightforward, you should be seeing how they lead to quite complex outcomes. And this is before we even start to consider how these things may change over time. It is also likely that you have considered these things from the position of the organisation. Perhaps challenge yourself to consider how such an approach leads to omissions of stakeholders and stakeholder groups that might have an interest in, or be affected by, indirectly by, or at a distance from, the organisation. These relationships and accountabilities go to the heart of much of the discussions in the following chapters.

### 3.2.3 Stakeholder engagement and stakeholder management

From an organisational perspective, and in seeking to understand accountability obligations, once stakeholders have been identified, we need to consider how organisational managers then know what the various stakeholders think about and expect of the organisation or some of its specific activities. For this purpose, stakeholder engagement can be made use of. In broad terms, stakeholder engagement refers to a process in which an organisation engages with its stakeholders to learn about their expectations, assumptions and viewpoints (see Kujala et al., 2022). There is no specific form that a stakeholder engagement process needs to take. Some organisations try to do these online, some organise individual events and see who attends, while others prefer running regular meetings with the specific stakeholders to maintain good communication and enhance the relationship. Some also use data analytics in seeking to identify key stakeholder interests from Big Data sources such as trends in social media postings.

It is important to acknowledge that simply having a one-off event with the organisation's managers giving PowerPoint presentations on stage does not take an organisation very far here. Instead, interaction and communication should be at the core of any stakeholder engagement process. Still, it is not entirely surprising that organising stakeholder engagement processes can be challenging. Already in the 1960s, Arnstein (1969) illustrated this through what is known as Arnstein's ladder of participation (see Figure 3.1). By discussing citizens' participation in public planning processes in the United States, Arnstein distinguishes between eight different degrees or types of participation. At the lower end of the ladder, there are degrees which Arnstein calls non-participation. These non-participation positions on the ladder are, in practice, about trying to win public support for something. In the middle, there are degrees such as informing, consultation and placation. Arnstein labels these as tokenism as they appear to offer the public an opportunity to provide views and influence, but in practice offer the participants no real power. At the top of the ladder, mechanisms such as partnership and delegation refer to settings in which the participating public actually possesses some power to affect the outcomes. Arnstein's highest positions on the ladder therefore represent citizen power.

Similar ideas can be seen to take place in many stakeholder engagement processes. Too often, stakeholder engagement processes remain at the lower end of participation. This implies that stakeholders are left in a passive role. In many ways, they are simply informed of the organisation's activities. From an organisation's point of view, the goal of such engagement can also be considered stakeholder management. Stakeholder

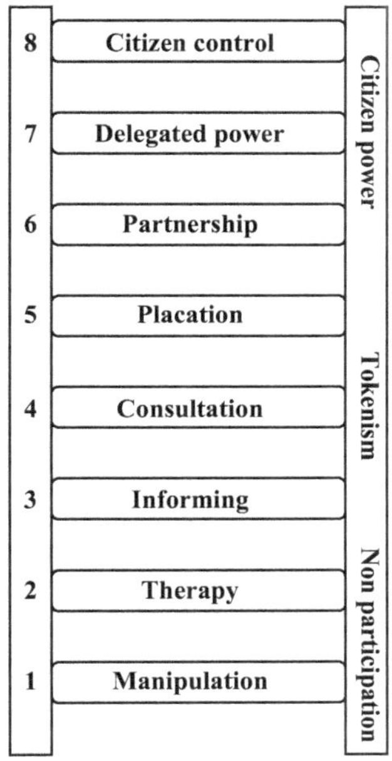


**FIGURE 3.1** Arnstein's Ladder: Degrees of Citizen Participation

management refers to an organisation seeking to influence its stakeholders and to affect their views so that they would be more favourable towards the organisation. Sometimes, however, stakeholder engagement processes turn out to include higher levels of participation, resulting for instance in actual stakeholder dialogue taking place. In such situations, the process can consist of a longer-term interaction, in which the organisation and its stakeholders are able to learn about the goals, doubts and expectations each of them have, and perhaps carve out some mutual solutions bringing positive outcomes to all those involved.

The key point here is that while stakeholder engagement processes, as opposed to stakeholder management, can seem burdensome for an organisation, there is much to be gained through them. Such processes help the organisation learn of and about their stakeholders, provide opportunities to enhance the stakeholder relationships, aid in identifying organisation's responsibilities in society, and eventually help out in discharging an organisation's accountability towards its stakeholders.

### 3.2.4 Stakeholder and accountability in different types of organisations

As is often the case in accounting, discussion of stakeholders and accountability tends to focus on the activities of major corporations, which, as we have pointed out, are visible and powerful players in societies. This does not mean, as discussed in the previous chapter, that the questions of accountability and stakeholder relationships do not apply to other types of organisations.

When it comes to other organisational forms, such as public sector organisations or NGOs, stakeholders and the related accountability relationships are also varied. Think about one typical public sector organisation, a public university. It is relatively simple to list some key stakeholder groups, such as employees, students, other universities, the local community, local authorities and the state. There are also plenty of responsibilities a university can be said to have. However, when we discuss accountability, the setting can get more complicated. Who is the university accountable to? Students? Employees? Ministry of Education? Ministry of Commerce? Society more generally? Moreover, are some of these stakeholders more important in the sense that the university would have a higher responsibility with respect to its actions towards them? Would this imply that there would be a stronger accountability demand towards particular groups than towards some others? Consider Japan, where in 2015 the government ordered national universities to scale back their involvement in social sciences and humanities, and to focus on areas which the government considered would better serve the society's needs. Or think about the United States, where student activism and political involvement have long been standard fixture on university campuses. More recently, alongside increased polarisation in the society in general, universities have become a field of heightened political struggle and culture war. Expectations are set on universities to take certain actions (or not) and to provide accounts and justifications (or not) for a range of political controversial issues, including foreign politics, as well as choices over curricula content and pedagogical methods. Overall, there are complexities that are inherent when we begin to explore organisations' stakeholder relationships and associated accountabilities.

Similar questions are also present in the third sector. Consider a major NGO such as Amnesty International. The stakeholder networks are again diverse and context-specific, and you can find many of the usual stakeholders to be relevant also in this setting. Most NGOs, such as Amnesty International, are generally considered to be working for the common good. There are however some specific elements that are worth considering here. For instance, there is substantial complexity that arises in relation to both upward (to funders) and downward (to beneficiaries) accountabilities these organisations have (see the "Insights from research" below). Likewise, in many societies, NGOs and civil society groups have faced higher scrutiny after operational problems or outright misconduct have come to public view. Such scrutiny often manifests through accountability demands concerning how the groups are using the funds they have received through donations, e.g. how much is spent to support administration compared to "proper work", and whether the donated funds are used effectively to achieve the impacts they proclaim. Such demands may be coming from those supporting the organisation, but also from other stakeholders, who could for instance be adversary to the cause or otherwise claim that such NGOs and citizen groups are avoiding accountability by hiding behind their reputation and purported claims to work for the common good.

### INSIGHTS FROM RESEARCH: NGO ACCOUNTABILITY

International development NGOs have for several decades been influential in shaping the relationship between the first world and less developed countries, also known as the developing countries or the third world. Governments as well as individual citizens in various countries have funded NGOs' work to enhance the living conditions and livelihoods of the people living in poverty. While in general terms NGOs have been considered to work on important issues, much emphasis has not always been put on evaluating their work or its impacts.

This paper by Roel Boomsma and Brendan O'Dwyer focuses on a large Dutch NGO and examines how accountability was shaped over time in the relationship between this NGO and its main funder, the state. The study discusses how the accountability of the NGO developed in an interplay between government programmes focusing on assessing and improving the quality of the work, and the NGO's counter-conduct which stemmed from an interest to be governed differently. Boomsma and O'Dwyer illustrate how this process affected the move towards emphasising cost consciousness, increased professionalisation and enhanced NGO cooperation. As an interesting observation, they also note how competition for funding among NGOs came to have a central role in their accountability.

On a more general level, this paper illustrates how the role of major NGOs started to be seen differently, and how a government funder can aim at using the idea of accountability to influence how an NGO operates. Accounting and accountability were significant in a process where some elements of NGO activities were made visible and thinkable, and thereby also subject to intervention. As such, the paper also highlights how powerful stakeholders can seek to influence NGOs, while also showing how an NGO can actively try to affect how it will be governed.

**Boomsma, R. and O'Dwyer, B. (2019). Constituting the Governable NGO: The Correlation between Conduct and Counter-Conduct in the Evolution of Funder-NGO Accountability Relations. *Accounting, Organizations and Society, 72,* 1–20.**

### 3.2.5 Accountability to stakeholders: But for which issues?

Sustainability accounting underscores that organisations should engage with stakeholders when developing their sustainability accounting and reporting systems. The interaction provides the organisation with opportunities not only to learn about the stakeholders and their needs but also to enhance their ability to respond to those needs and to collaborate in attempts at creating more relevant practices. It is evident that not all stakeholders are interested in similar issues. Likewise, as we have noted, the needs and wants of stakeholders are also context-specific, implying that organisations cannot necessarily rely solely on some boilerplate standards and guidance in seeking to understand their stakeholders. This applies not only to developing an organisation's activities but also, in the context of sustainability accounting, to the provision of information.

It is relevant to bear in mind that providing information to stakeholders is not the only element of accountability. Organisations also need to understand their own activities, be able to assess their impacts and dependencies, and thereby consider how they fulfil their responsibilities in society. To be able to do so, managers need to have access to suitable and relevant information, which allows them to evaluate the organisation's activities and make decisions. As sustainability has become increasingly prominent in societies, there is more and more need for accounting and reporting, which gives relevant information for such considerations. So, how is the relevance of information determined – both in relation to an organisation's external stakeholders as discussed above and to information used for decision-making by managers? Here, the concept of materiality is highly relevant, and we move on to discuss it next.

## 3.3 Materiality

Materiality is a core accounting concept. It is a regular feature in financial accounting and reporting standards and practices. In essence, materiality refers to the need to identify whether particular topics, issues or incidents are significant for the organisation or the organisation's stakeholders. While this may sound rather straightforward in the first instance, identifying the most significant sustainability issues from the perspective of both the organisation and its stakeholders is a challenging task, especially if a broad stakeholder view, as discussed above, is taken.

From the outset, we note that the materiality considerations related to sustainability accounting and reporting can differ from how the concept is used in financial accounting and reporting. In financial accounting and reporting, information and items are considered material if they could potentially influence the economic decisions of those using the information. This is the approach ISSB has taken in their approach to sustainability disclosures, known within the sustainability accounting space as financial materiality. Now, it is highly important to recognise that in sustainability accounting and reporting, materiality is much more diverse than this: there is no single way of performing a materiality assessment and the definitions of materiality differ across frameworks, contexts and standards. This is illustrated by prominent terms such as financial materiality, impact materiality, double materiality and dynamic materiality (see Table 3.1). Moreover, the perspective taken with regard to sustainability is a core consideration here: are we interested in an outside-in perspective, i.e. how sustainability can affect the organisation and its future outlook, or an inside-out approach, i.e. the sustainability impacts caused by the organisation and its activities. We will return to these questions in more detail below, but it will be helpful to acknowledge these differences together with the significant consequences they bring in relation to the underlying assumptions and expected outcomes of sustainability accounting. The difference in the meaning of materiality and who decides material issues is, as we will discuss in Chapter 5, also a defining difference across different approaches to sustainability reporting standard setting.

**TABLE 3.1** Different Types of Materiality

| | |
|---|---|
| Financial materiality | Considers the impact of sustainability issues on an organisation's financial performance. Sometimes referred to as single materiality. |
| Impact materiality | Considers the impact (actual and potential) of an organisation's operations on the society, environment and economy. |
| Double materiality | The consideration of both financial and impact materiality. |
| Dynamic materiality | Recognises that materiality changes over time and what is not considered important today may be in the future (and vice versa). Encourages proactivity in identifying and acknowledging emerging issues/topics. |

Source: Cooper and Michelon (2022).

As discussed in Chapter 2, sustainability accounting deals with a very broad range of issues. Moreover, we have discussed how the significance of those issues varies greatly across regions and industries and across different stakeholder groups. For instance, while water availability and consumption would be highly relevant for an organisation producing agricultural products and soft drinks in water scarce and highly populated regions of, for example, Australia, Egypt or Pakistan, it is not likely to be relevant for a company offering IT services in Norway. Or, take a mining company dealing with substantial human rights and environmental issues in places like Congo or South Africa, and compare it to an organisation offering day care in Japan. While we must be careful not to take such things for granted (e.g. see the discussion of modern slavery in Chapter 12), clearly the most important and pertinent sustainability issues are very different in different places and contexts. As such, materiality assessments are an essential element of the sustainability accounting processes no matter whether the organisation is seeking to use the information mainly for internal decision-making purposes, for reporting to external stakeholders in general, or for disclosing specific details to the investor community in particular. Moreover, materiality is not only about which sustainability issues are the most relevant for a given organisation. The importance of different elements varies over time, as for instance social interest can move the public interest quickly from one aspect to another.

### 3.3.1 Material impacts and dependencies

It is worth highlighting that even if some aspect of sustainability is particularly urgent or severe on a global scale, it does not necessarily mean that the same aspect would be material for a particular organisation. This again relates to the fact that materiality assessments are highly context-dependent, organisation-specific and influenced by the perspective of materiality that one takes (again, see Table 3.1). Moreover, another layer of materiality comes into play when we note the difference between accounting for impacts and accounting for dependencies. While the former focuses on what kind of consequences the organisation's actions may have on society, different stakeholders and/or the natural environment, the latter puts emphasis on identifying and assessing those aspects of sustainability that the organisation is the most dependent on. A change in these aspects might lead to substantial consequences for the organisation's operations over some time period. For instance, if the organisation needs a large amount of clean water in its production, issues of water pollution and water security in a particular region should be considered highly material. Organisational dependencies and their sustainability impacts might not always be related to the same sustainability issues, or might become substantial over a very different timeframe. Hence, acknowledging the difference between accounting for impacts and accounting for dependencies is an important part of understanding organisational sustainability accounting and accountability.

### 3.3.2 Materiality is subjective

Another key factor is that not everybody sees materiality of the different issues in the same way. Individuals might, for instance, perceive the value and relevance of some elements of sustainability differently: for some, elements of biodiversity might be much more important than questions of social inequality, whereas someone else might perceive social issues as the fundamental priority in any setting. Likewise, major differences can also result from individuals approaching materiality from different time perspectives. While someone could argue that impacts on ecosystem services are paramount and need to be taken into account, since ignoring them can result in major consequences in the medium-term, say 15 years, someone else could counter by highlighting the immediate implications on livelihoods, and thus maintain that those would be the most material aspects.

Materiality also depends on whose perspective we are taking. From an organisational point of view, it is important to remember how those aspects that are considered to be material for the organisation's decision-making might not always be the same as the ones that stakeholders regard as crucial. Or that just some of the stakeholders consider crucial, for that matter, since the range of stakeholders are likely to have different views regarding which issues are more material for them. Understanding and dealing with such diverse viewpoints is relevant for organisations, and it relates closely to the stakeholder engagement processes discussed above.

### 3.3.3 Materiality and sustainability reporting

Sustainability reporting is perhaps the area in which the differences in materiality definitions become most evident, or are at least the most evident in discussions. As we have noted above, organisations and their stakeholders usually have different views about the organisation's responsibilities. The same applies then when an organisation seeks to discharge its accountability by reporting on sustainability. As it is not reasonable to expect to have any organisation report everything on all aspects of sustainability, such reporting requires choices to be made. One guiding principle here is that reporting should focus on material issues. However, an obvious question follows: how is this decided on? Given its importance and prominence, we cover materiality in the context of sustainability reporting in detail in Chapters 5 and 6. For now, it perhaps suffices to say that the different parties involved in setting standards and developing frameworks for sustainability reporting come from different perspectives. This has a range of implications on sustainability reporting.

**PAUSE AND REFLECT...**

Take a company that you are familiar with. Consider what might be material from each of the materiality perspectives noted above (financial, impact, double and dynamic). Now reflect on the question:

To what extent does taking a different perspective of materiality affect the outcome of topics/issues identified?

## 3.4 Externalities

In addition to changing social interests, the materiality of different issues can change due to new or enhanced knowledge. This is particularly pertinent in the realm of sustainability. As our collective knowledge of interconnected sustainability impacts as well as their relationship to economic activity has developed, it has become increasingly evident that we should ensure all necessary impacts are taken into account. This brings us to our fourth and final key concept discussed in this chapter, externalities.

In simple terms, externalities are the impacts of activities which affect some others, but which are not taken into account when assessing the activity (Unerman et al., 2018). In economics, externalities are often described as being costs or benefits affecting a third party, while not being reflected in the market prices. Air pollution would be a common example here.

Let's look at some further examples to consider the concept of externalities and its importance to sustainability accounting and accountability. Think about an individual who wants to get rid of an old couch. Instead of taking it to a landfill, the person decides to leave it on the roadside parking lot, since this is an easy option and does not cost anything. Eventually, the municipality decides to clean the area and take the couch to the landfill. This means that the individual's decision to leave the couch in the parking lot involved an externality, in this case a financial cost for the municipality. Or how about a manufacturing company which wants to cut costs by making the employees work in poor working conditions. Being exposed to noise and dust over an extended period is likely to have consequences not only for the employees, as having health problems lowers their quality of life, but also for the society through increased costs for the provision of health care for those people in countries where this exists, or to their families and communities through caring for sick relatives where they do not. Again, there was no direct cost for the organisation, but we can start to see how the decisions resulted in externalities borne by other parties.

From the perspective of an organisation, we can consider externalities as the costs and benefits which are not borne by the organisation. Externalities exist on different levels and scales, and the impact of their (non-)consideration varies significantly. Conventional accounting practices do not recognise these externalities.

### 3.4.1 Externalities and their relevance to sustainability accounting and accountability

Again, it is perhaps useful to consider another example to illustrate why externalities are particularly important for sustainability accounting and accountability. While hard to imagine now, for a long time, organisations did not need to care about the $CO_2$ and other greenhouse gas emissions from their manufacturing processes. Emissions did not feature as part of the organisations' accounting practices. Broad sectors of society were not aware of the possible long-term implications of the increasing greenhouse gas emissions and $CO_2$ concentration in the Earth's atmosphere, and as such organisations did not need to consider them either.[1] But, the thing with externalities is that the benefits and costs, while not borne by the entity, are borne by others (most commonly, in a sustainability sense, by societies and nature). As the costs of greenhouse gas emissions have become known, and as the science behind climate change has become well-established and awareness of the climate emergency has increased within societies, the situation has become substantially different. Organisations of all forms now must consider their climate impacts. Governments and communities are looking for ways to reduce $CO_2$ levels, including responses such as developing carbon calculators, carbon trading schemes and carbon taxes.

From the perspective of accounting, this relates to the possibility of internalising an externality. As long as $CO_2$ was not considered relevant by an organisation, it was not considered in any accounting calculations. As such, this could show that it was beneficial for an organisation to proceed with high $CO_2$ emissions, as tackling them would only have caused additional costs. In this setting, $CO_2$ is an externality borne by the broader society. However, if $CO_2$ emissions are given a price, through for instance a carbon market, carbon tax or an intra-organisational pricing mechanism, the situation changes significantly. The option of continuing with high $CO_2$ emissions becomes more costly, as the previously invisible $CO_2$ emissions are suddenly given a price and subsequently included in the accounting calculation. And, consider this further in relation to our discussion of accountability above. Things get more complicated when we move beyond consideration of the financial cost and market mechanisms to consider responsibilities and accountabilities. In this example, there are reputational risks, also likely to have financial implications, of continuing with high $CO_2$ emissions. We will discuss this more in Chapter 9.

### 3.4.2 Accounting for externalities

There are several reasons why externalities are fundamental to sustainability accounting and accountability (see "Insights from research" below). A key consideration is due to the effects of externalities on societies and the environment. However, another reason is that our societies are run based on financial considerations. Consumers, businesses and public sector entities all consider the price of alternative choices before deciding on buying a piece of clothing, investing in a particular energy source, or deciding whether to construct new railroads or wider highways. Including externalities, and therefore the "true" cost of environmental and social resources, in the pricing decisions would change the landscape substantially. Taking externalities into account (or omitting them) has a significant impact on one of the key criteria used for evaluating success in contemporary societies: the bottom line (i.e. profit). As put by high-level business leaders in a report titled *Better Business Better World*, "Sustainable competition depends on all the competitors facing prices that reflect the true costs of the way they do business – internalising the externalities, to use the jargon" (Business and Sustainable Development Commission, 2017, p. 16).

While the role of prices has been noted several times in the above, it needs to be emphasised that taking externalities into account does not necessarily mean that everything would be monetised. Other types of assessments are also possible. Some sustainability information might be in qualitative form and others could be presented in quantitative terms. This is also a typical feature of sustainability accounting and accountability. In much conventional financial and management accounting, information is mostly presented in a single and comparable unit, money. However, in sustainability accounting and accountability, one needs to be prepared to deal with settings where information concerning different elements of sustainability is presented in a variety of ways, types and units, and hence cannot be readily compared or aggregated.

We will return to the questions of quantification and monetisation again in the following chapter when we discuss the role of information in organisational decision-making. Externalities will also be covered in more detail in Part C of the book, as they relate closely to a number of key sustainability topics covered such as biodiversity and human rights.

## INSIGHTS FROM RESEARCH: ACCOUNTING FOR EXTERNALITIES

"Externalities comprise social, environmental, and broader economic impacts arising from the activities of an entity that are borne by others and do not feedback directly into the short-term financial consequences for the entity" (Unerman et al., 2018, p. 498). However, as Unerman and colleagues discuss, the potential financial impacts of externalities are "not usually systematically communicated in either sustainability or financial reports".

While there have been significant developments in this area, in particular with the increased attention to the financial implications of sustainability in recent reporting practices and in the investor mindset, improving information on externalities remains an important area for both financial and sustainability accounting. And it is an area where Unerman et al. (2018) note that there is a need to break down the silos of financial and sustainability reporting – that is, seeing the connections between financial and non-financial impacts. In this paper, the authors draw on a review and synthesis of academic literature and practices of accounting and reporting on externalities in their discussion. In addition to providing us with a greater understanding of externalities and their importance, this paper also looks at why we need to consider them for effective corporate reporting, and introduces us to key aspects in the accounting for externalities such as identification, quantification and commensuration.

Their discussion of commensuration and the credibility of the quantification of externalities is particularly interesting and worth considering further given its central place in sustainability accounting. Commensuration is the process of transforming different qualities into quantities, reducing information into something (usually numbers) that can easily be compared. Commensuration in accounting usually takes the form of money, and as such, things are monetised (recorded as a monetary value or cost). The monetisation of externalities is one way to ensure they are included in financial accounting as well as non-financial information, but as Unerman et al. (2018) illustrate, this is not entirely straightforward or unproblematic. There are problems with quantification and monetisation as these authors explain. And these aspects have consequences for what externalities are identified and information provided on. There can, for example, be perceived issues of reliability and there are limits to monetisation.

On these issues, the authors provide useful insights and points of reflection. Their discussion of intersubjectivity is, for example, useful in reminding us that there can be consensus on some values (e.g. carbon) and as such these measures can be considered intersubjective (as opposed to entirely subjective). They also draw on the role and importance of narrative when quantification is less useful. A key takeaway from their discussion is however to remind us of the risk of only considering externalities that are easily quantifiable/monetised, and excluding those that are more difficult to measure.

**Unerman, J., Bebbington, J. and O'Dwyer, B. (2018). Corporate Reporting and Accounting for Externalities. *Accounting and Business Research, 48(5),* 497–522.**

### 3.4.3 Materiality and externalities

As our discussion above highlights, the accounting and reporting information that is used as the basis of decision-making in organisations and societies does not include everything it should. This is also highly relevant from the perspective of materiality. Let's consider this through another example, an example in which the financial and sustainability issues intertwine: the risk caused by climate change.

Scientific reports highlight how climate change not only involves rising temperatures but also means that extreme weather effects, such as flooding, droughts and storms, become stronger and more frequent. From an organisational viewpoint, this can clearly have substantial implications. Flooding can disrupt logistics, droughts can compromise raw material supplies in agriculture and all water-dependent industries, and storms can cause substantial damage to production facilities. As a combination, while this causes higher risks for everyone, it also indicates that some organisations are more vulnerable than others when it comes to sustainability risks. However, if we look at the financial statements, it is evident that such risks are currently not sufficiently accounted for, even if their potential financial consequences would be major, making them potentially material also from a financial perspective. There are initiatives that have developed to change this, however, whether or not they are likely to be successful in doing so is debated. Again, this is a matter we return to several times in later sections of this book.

## 3.5 Conclusion

In this chapter, we have introduced and discussed some key concepts for sustainability accounting and accountability. In addition to accountability, stakeholders, materiality and externalities, we have also touched upon other significant terms such as responsibility and legitimacy.

In the following chapters, we will discuss how sustainability accounting and accountability can help individuals, organisations and societies contribute to the much-needed global sustainability transition. This is not, however, only a matter of replacing conventional accounting with a new set of sustainability accounting tools, techniques and systems. As you will have come to note, we have constantly highlighted how the issues we have raised often involve subjective judgements. In this chapter, we have emphasised that accountability, stakeholders, materiality and externalities, which are key concepts for sustainability accounting, all involve subjectivity and potentially political choices. While these aspects are not absolute and cannot be defined objectively, we are not suggesting that anything would be acceptable. Instead, and as we will emphasise throughout this book, learning sustainability accounting and accountability requires one to reflect on the assumptions, choices and rationales underlying such practices. Such critical awareness is essential, since global sustainability transition is likely to require rethinking many practices (including new practices emerging), institutions and conventions we currently take for granted in societies – including accounting and accountability.

## Note

1 In more technical terms, within climate science and politics, various types of greenhouse gas emissions, such as $CO_2$, methane and nitrous oxides are converted into a common unit, known as $CO_2$ equivalent or $CO_2e$, to facilitate calculations, approximations and creation of models. We will return to this in Chapter 9.

## References


Arnstein, S. (1969). A Ladder of Citizen Participation. *Journal of the American Planning Association, 35*(*4*), 216–224.

Boomsma, R. and O'Dwyer, B. (2019). Constituting the Governable NGO: The Correlation between Conduct and Counter-Conduct in the Evolution of Funder-NGO Accountability Relations. *Accounting, Organizations and Society, 72*, 1–20.

Business and Sustainable Development Commission (2017). Better Business Better World. https://sustainabledevelopment.un.org/index.php?page=view&type=400&nr=2399&menu=1515 (accessed 5 November 2020).

Cooper, S. and Michelon, G. (2022). Conceptions of Materiality in Sustainability Reporting Frameworks: Commonalities, Differences and Possibilities. In Adams, C. (ed.), *Handbook of Accounting and Sustainability*. pp. 44–66. Edward Elgar.

Dillard, J. and Vinnari, E. (2019). Critical Dialogical Accountability: From Accounting-Based Accountability to Accountability-Based Accounting. *Critical Perspectives on Accounting, 62*, 16–38.

Freeman, R. E. (1984). *Strategic Management: A Stakeholder Approach*. Pitman.

Johnson-Cramer, M., Phillips, R. A., Fadlallah, H., Berman, S. L. and Elms, H. (2022). What We Talk about When We Talk about Stakeholders. *Business & Society, 61*(*5*), 1083–1135.

Gray, R., Owen, D. and Adams, C. (1996). *Accounting and Accountability*. Prentice Hall.

GRI and UN Global Compact (2022). *Business Reporting on the SDGs: An Analysis of the Goals and Targets. Updated Edition 2022.* www.unglobalcompact.org/library/5361 (accessed 25 Feb ruary 2025).

Kujala, J., Sachs, S., Leinonen, H., Heikkinen, A. and Laude, D. (2022). Stakeholder Engagement: Past, Present, and Future. *Business & Society, 61*(*5*), 1136–1196.

Mitchell, R., Agle, B. and Wood, D. (1997). Toward a Theory of Stakeholder Identification and Salience: Defining the Principle of Who and What Really Counts. *Academy of Management Review, 22*(*4*), 853–886.

Tanima, F., Brown, J. and Hopper, T. (2024). Doing Critical Dialogic Accounting and Accountability Research: An Analytical Framework and Case Illustration. *Accounting, Auditing and Accountability Journal, 37*(*1*), 1–30.

Tregidga, H. and Milne, M. (2022). Not at Our Table: Stakeholder Exclusion and Ant/agonistic Engagements. *Critical Perspectives on Accounting, 85*, 102265.

Unerman, J., Bebbington, J. and O'Dwyer, B. (2018). Corporate Reporting and Accounting for Externalities. *Accounting and Business Research, 48*(*5*), 497–522.


## Additional reading and resources

Bebbington, J., Larrinaga, C., O'Dwyer, B. and Thomson, I. (eds). (2021). *Handbook on Environmental Accounting*. Routledge.

Gray, R. (1992). Accounting and Environmentalism: An Exploration of the Challenge of Gently Accounting for Accountability, Transparency and Sustainability. *Accounting, Organisations and Society, 17(5)*, 399–425.

Hines, R. D. (1988). Financial Accounting: In Communicating Reality, We Construct Reality. *Accounting, Organisations and Society, 13(3)*, 251–261.

Quattrone, P. (2022). Seeking Transparency Makes One Blind: How to Rethink Disclosure, Account for Nature and Make Corporations Sustainable. *Accounting, Auditing & Accountability Journal, 35(2)*, 547–566.

Wang, D., Cooper, S., Chapman, C. and Calace, D. (2025). Sustainability (Environmental, Social and Governance) Reporting: Tracing Materiality's Visionary and Relational Role over 25 Years through Boundary Objects and Boundary Work. *The Accounting Review*, 1–25. https://doi.org/10.2308/TAR-2023-0675.

PART

# II

# Accounting for sustainability

CHAPTER

4

# Sustainability management accounting and control

If managers and other organisational decision-makers are to steer organisations in line with a transition towards sustainability, then we need to ensure that those decision-makers have appropriate information at their disposal. Information is needed to reduce the organisation's environmental impacts, understand dependencies, enhance the social good organisational activities create and to bring about fair and equitable economic impacts. Management accounting and control plays a major role in creating this information and therefore needs to be considered as societies seek to transition towards sustainability. Management accounting and control is also important from an organisational performance point of view. In order to prosper, those who manage organisations need to make sustainability management accounting and control a core element of the organisation's management systems and integrate multidimensional sustainability factors into strategic and operational decision-making at all levels. All this means the creation of new management accounting and control tools and practices which integrate sustainability issues. It also requires a critical look at how we apply and use the tools and practices of conventional management accounting which tend to focus on the provision of financial information.

By the end of this chapter, you should:

- Understand the role of (conventional) management accounting and control in organisational decision-making in relation to sustainability.
- Be able to define sustainability management accounting and control and have an awareness of the relevance of externalities and resource allocation in relation to sustainability management accounting and control.
- Be aware of the variety of sustainability management accounting and control tools and practices.
- Have a critical awareness of sustainability management accounting and control, including some key considerations of tools and practices, and the implications for the transition towards sustainability.

DOI: 10.4324/9781003533207-6

## 4.1 Introduction to management accounting and control

Management accounting and control generally refers to accounting tools, practices and methodologies used inside an organisation to assist managers and other individuals in strategic and operational decision-making. Most often, management accounting refers to practices focused on financial information and includes a wide range of institutionalised practices such as cost accounting, budgeting and investment appraisals. Management controls are then considered to be a broader set of things, including all systems, tools and practices designed for and used in an organisation to affect the activities, behaviour and decisions of the employees so that they are in line with the organisation's overall goals. While many conventional management accounting and control tools and practices have been used for decades (e.g. activity-based costing and the balanced scorecard which were introduced in the 1980s and 1990s), they continue to develop and take new forms. This is essential to keep up with developing organisational forms and the evolving needs of organisational decision-makers, including the increasing sustainability concerns and related accountabilities.

As we have established in previous chapters, organisations have to look beyond financial information in their decision-making. Sustainability is changing the operating context of organisations. Corporate executives, for example, have to understand the potential sustainability impacts and dependencies of an organisation not only because these issues can have direct implications on financial success but also because a good command of sustainability is needed for success in the marketplace. Sustainability management accounting and control has become highly important as it allows embedding complex multifaceted sustainability factors into organisations' strategic and operational decision-making. In essence, high-quality sustainability information enhances managers' capabilities to make far-reaching decisions regarding the future.

## 4.2 Management accounting and control and sustainability

An important element of how societies could become more sustainable relates to how, and on what basis, decisions are made in organisations. The information, tools, practices and approaches used internally in organisational decision-making are therefore highly relevant. Accordingly, in this chapter, we focus on the role of sustainability management accounting and control in the context of sustainability accounting and accountability.

In the discussion that follows we do not restrict our focus only to tools and practices falling under the categories which can be labelled environmental or sustainability management accounting and control, or in other words to management accounting and control tools and practices that have been developed with the express purpose of providing internal information on environmental and/or social aspects. While these tools and practices are important, as you will see from the following discussion, the so-called conventional management accounting and control tools, practices and institutional arrangements are relevant for sustainability as they can both support and hinder organisational transitions towards more sustainable practices. Furthermore, as is the case with many of the topics discussed in this book, new approaches are still needed to address the sustainability challenge and as such a reflection on a range of tools and practices is useful when reflecting on what is needed.

### 4.2.1 Defining sustainability management accounting and control

So, what exactly do we mean by *sustainability* management accounting and control? In essence, we are referring to a very diverse set of tools and practices which help corporate executives bring sustainability considerations into the organisational decision-making processes on both strategic and operational levels. This can be done in a range of ways. It is, for instance, possible to develop conventional management accounting practices so that they better incorporate sustainability considerations (e.g. the balanced scorecard becomes the sustainability balanced scorecard, see Figge et al., 2002). Another option is to use measures focusing solely on specific sustainability-related aspects, such as energy use, water consumption, emissions or amounts of waste. There are also a range of dedicated tools and practices seeking to provide more sophisticated information on some areas of sustainability, such as material flow cost accounting (MFCA) or social return on investment (SROI) introduced below.

Sustainability management accounting and control therefore refers to a broad range of activities aimed specifically at measuring, assessing and communicating an organisation's sustainability activities internally. As with more conventional management accounting, it is useful to make the distinction between sustainability management accounting and sustainability management controls. As above, the former can be considered to be a narrower realm, focusing primarily on tools and practices used to develop information regarding sustainability issues. The latter can then be conceived of as a broader area, which Crutzen et al. (2017, p. 1293) describe as follows: "sustainability management controls can be said to include all devices and systems that managers develop and use to formally and informally ensure that the behaviors and decisions of their employees are consistent with the organization's sustainability objectives and strategies".

These definitions are obviously broad. The key point, however, is that we are dealing with a wide range of tools, practices and systems, which are used to aid managers in seeking to integrate complex and multifaceted sustainability factors into organisational decision-making. Such considerations include, for instance, assessing, following and evaluating how organisational activities are related to sustainability, analysing how certain decisions might affect the organisation's sustainability performance, and ensuring that the actions taken by employees, groups and divisions are in line with the organisation's broader sustainability strategy and approach. We introduce a number of these tools and practices in the next section; however, first we outline some basic characteristics of sustainability management accounting and control to help contextualise this discussion.

### 4.2.2 Diversity of sustainability management accounting and control practices

Diversity is a defining feature of sustainability management accounting and control. As we outlined in Chapter 3, organisational managers may have very different needs since sustainability considerations can vary considerably across industries and contexts. The information and practices used for internal decision-making can vary substantially, not only in regard to the form of organisation (e.g. profit or non-profit) but also in terms of the significance of the setting, organisational history and culture and the preferences and individual views of the managers, to name but a few. This means organisations are likely to have and need different approaches to sustainability management accounting and control. Likewise, given that we are dealing with a swiftly developing area, some organisations already have implemented sophisticated systems and dedicated tools, whereas others are at an earlier stage of the learning curve. We should also bear in mind here that most regulation concerning accounting information relates to accounting directed at external stakeholders (e.g. reporting which will be discussed in the following two chapters) rather than internal stakeholders. Furthermore, the regulatory requirements concerning sustainability reporting can also have implications on the internal practices. For example, organisations may prefer to get by with the information they have to collect for external reporting purposes. The key question here is obviously whether data collected for external reporting purposes is also useful for internal decision-making. Overall it is useful to recognise that, the most part, there are no clear rules or ready-made templates for sustainability management and control that can be applied to all organisations.

### 4.2.3 Inherent flexibility in sustainability management accounting and control practices

In addition to the diversity of sustainability management accounting practices, we should also consider the flexibility which is inherent to internal accounting processes. That is, further to having different types of tools and practices at their disposal, managers can also apply them in different ways, as there are again no rules or overarching principles stipulating their use and interpretation. Moreover, as with other types of accounting information, assumptions underlying such information and the starting points used for these calculations, as well as the subjectivity involved in their interpretation, all need to be considered key factors affecting the information.

Like other forms of accounting, sustainability management accounting and control is sometimes seen as a neutral and technical activity which is used to provide objective information and assessments of particular situations or settings. At the same time, accountants acknowledge that management accounting and control is full of choices and judgement calls. Simply put, which aspects are included, and which are excluded, from various calculations, for example, have implications on the outcome. Likewise, questions such as how is the entity, or the object of analysis, defined; how are the boundaries and the timeframe of an investment appraisal set; and, in more general terms, what kind of assumptions are the calculations based on, are all subjective and include room to manoeuvre. It is also highly relevant to consider the various types of information that can be prepared (financial and non-financial), as in decision-making processes managers rely on assessments and calculations to compare various alternatives. How these questions are framed and answered all have consequences for the outcome of the assessment and for the subsequent decisions as we explore further below.

### 4.2.4 Defining sustainability management accounting and control summary

Sustainability management accounting and control is an extensive and diverse field. Alongside new tools and practices focusing explicitly on some aspects of sustainability, we also need to consider the conventional management accounting tools, practices and methodologies used inside an organisation. These practices guide managers and other individuals in their decision-making, and they are intertwined with sustainability whether this is explicitly recognised or not. Our aim in the rest of this chapter is to introduce you to the field and also to encourage you to reflect on the current state of practice as well as on where developments are still required to address the sustainability challenges we outlined in Chapter 1. We next outline some specific tools and practices before discussing some key considerations in their application.

## 4.3 Some sustainability management accounting tools and practices

There is no need for an organisation to start its journey with sustainability management accounting and control from scratch. Even though there are no uniform tools, a wide range of tools and practices exist which an organisation can adopt and adapt. These come with varying degrees of complexity. While some organisations manage their processes by using broad-based integrated enterprise resource planning (ERP) systems which may have particular elements focusing on sustainability included, many rely on separate applications, which may either be off-the-shelf tools or have been developed in-house. In general terms, we must again be mindful that the appropriateness and relevance of management accounting is highly context-specific: any single tool, practice or approach does not necessarily fit every organisation.

To illustrate the diversity, we next discuss some of the more common and well-known sustainability management accounting and control tools and practices. Like many aspects discussed in this book, it is not possible for us to cover them all, or even provide a comprehensive examination of those we do include. Each could fill the contents of a book itself. Our purpose, therefore, is to introduce some of the various types that exist which we reflect on further in the following sections of this chapter. Furthermore, we will return to some of these in Part III, where we delve deeper into several key areas of sustainability, such as biodiversity, water and human rights, to discuss how these tools, practices and considerations are relevant in those specific topics.

### 4.3.1 Material flow cost accounting

Material flow cost accounting (MFCA) is one of the more commonly used forms of environmental management accounting. Mainly used in process-based manufacturing industries, MFCA is intended to help organisations reduce their environmental impacts and improve environmental efficiency. It does so by focusing on the tracing and quantifying of the material flows and stocks within processes. These material flows and stocks are different for each organisation, but generally speaking include raw materials, energy and water, as well as various forms of residuals and waste. A systematic look at these material flows and stocks allows managers to identify potential inefficiencies as well as substantial sources of waste. In addition to the quantified volumes of material streams, MFCA also includes the associated costs, such as those incurred from the sourcing, production and logistics of materials eventually disposed as waste. Focusing not only on the physical volumes but also on the costs can be important, since in complicated processes, substantial costs can remain hidden in the aggregate numbers. Producing more detailed cost information will provide managers further details on the processes, and can prove helpful, for instance when seeking to understand which material flows or parts of the process could potentially be improved cost-efficiently.

MFCA can be a useful tool for organisational decision-makers looking to reduce the negative environmental effects of processes while simultaneously gaining potential financial benefits through improved efficiency. One starting point for organisations would be ISO standard 14051, which outlines the terminology, principles, key elements and implementation of a material flow cost accounting framework, as well as ISO 14052, which extends the discussion into how MFCA can be applied in supply chains. As MFCA also helps understand the material flows into, through and out of the organisation it also has the potential to help support an organisation transitioning to a more circular business model (see Chapter 2).

### 4.3.2 Life-cycle assessment

Life-cycle assessment (LCA) is a tool similar to MFCA as it seeks to assess the impacts of a product, process or service. A key difference to MFCA is that it does not necessarily focus on costs, although reducing costs can be an outcome of an LCA.

While there are various methodologies, in general terms, LCA attempts to record and assess the environmental inputs and outputs of a product, process or service as well as to understand the impacts associated with the life-cycle. To do so, the life-cycle (sometimes referred to as cradle to grave) of a particular product, process or service first needs to be identified. That is, a product, process or service is broken down into its various stages from raw material extraction, to manufacture, distribution, use and disposal. This life-cycle enables a decision-maker to understand the inputs and impacts at each stage of the life-cycle with the aim of providing information required to make informed decisions. Think about a standard cotton T-shirt for example. A comprehensive LCA will help us understand the environmental impacts associated with the different stages of its life-cycle, such as the growing of cotton, production of yarn and fabrics, sewing the shirt at a factory, transportation of raw materials and finished products, selling on the high street or over the internet, the washing of the shirt by the user, as well as the eventual disposal of the T-shirt. In addition to helping with comparisons of alternatives, such as whether it would be environmentally more beneficial to use pristine cotton, modern wood-based fabrics or synthetic polyester as the main material, an LCA can aid in identifying sustainability hot spots, that is the most significant or risky stages in the life-cycle. Such information could be used to direct attention to those stages where there are more potential sustainability benefits to be achieved, as well as to such stages of the life-cycle in which the sustainability impacts are identified to be the most sensitive to some specific underlying conditions or assumptions.

The LCA has proven a relatively popular approach with organisations, in particular large corporations. As was the case with MFCA above, there are also ISO standards in place for LCA, with ISO 14040 covering the principles and frameworks, and ISO 14044 taking a more practical perspective on the requirements and guidelines. As you look into some organisational practices and examples relating to sustainability accounting and accountability, you are likely to see examples of LCA. One company that uses LCA to understand their products and their impacts on the environment is Unilever.

**Focus on practice: Unilever and LCA**

Unilever, a multinational consumer goods company, uses LCA in several ways including new product design, assessments of existing products and product lines, and developing science and methodologies (see Unilever, 2025).

In terms of product design, Unilever highlights how LCA has helped them analyse the environmental profiles of existing and potential products. Such insights are then fed into the product development processes. This is significant as a substantial portion of the environmental impacts of any product are essentially set during the innovation, planning and design stages, which dictate many of the characteristics of subsequent production and use. An example here would be Unilever's project to redesign plastic bottles to allow the use of recycled plastic, expected to reduce greenhouse gas emissions and the need for virgin raw materials.

In addition to using LCA information to assess and reduce the environmental impacts of their products and production across their supply chain, Unilever acknowledges how LCA analyses needs to be continuously developed and refined. The company hence engages with other organisations, scientists and policymakers in initiatives aimed at improving the knowledge underlying LCA assessments. The Life-Cycle Initiative, hosted by the United Nations Environment Programme (UNEP), is one such example. The Life-Cycle Initiative targets both public and private decision-makers and seeks to provide a science-based forum for enhancing credible knowledge and use of LCA tools and methodologies.

Again, like MFCA, an LCA is likely to be useful in supporting a circular economy model. However, preparing a comprehensive LCA of a product is not always a straightforward exercise, particularly where the product involves several tiers of suppliers, retailers and users. As such, a carefully developed LCA requires considerable expertise not only of the approach in itself but also of organisation-specific aspects such as the business model and the particularities of the supply chain. It has therefore been unlikely an organisation has had the resources to prepare LCAs across its whole product range. It is worth pointing out however that there are in the marketplace various software applications and service providers who offer organisations fast and easy access to LCA calculations. These have been feasible as LCA is largely based on standardised methodologies and calculations can be executed by drawing extensively on secondary data consisting of benchmarks and industry averages. The development of AI tools is amplifying this trend further. While such numbers can be helpful, a caveat is in order for both the producers and users of the information: the quality and usefulness of an LCA is highly dependent on the quality of the data. Given for instance the significance of choices concerning system boundaries and underlying assumptions, it is possible that LCAs looking ostensibly at the same question end up providing different answers. Therefore, the results of LCAs always should be interpreted through a consideration of how the LCA was conducted.

Nonetheless, as an LCA considers inputs and impacts across the life-cycle and thus usually involves multiple entities as well as requires understanding the inputs and impacts outside of the entities' own control, such preparation will not only bring an organisation insights on the environmental profile of products but also aid in considering the various accountabilities involved in such complex value chains.

### 4.3.3 Social return on investment

SROI is an accounting method used for assessing the range of impacts an investment has. Different from other methods of calculating return, SROI is interested in calculating the societal value of an investment beyond the financial return. In simple terms, SROI tries to identify different types of social, environmental and economic outcomes an activity has, provide a monetary value for them, and then show the results as a ratio between the generated outcomes and the original investment. An SROI approach has become increasingly popular in today's society which seeks to measure and evaluate performance beyond financial indicators.

SROI has been used in a number of fields. Many NGOs and non-profits, for example, have applied SROI in seeking to figure out how effective their activities have been in creating value for society. Take for instance UEFA, the main body administering European football, which has commissioned studies on the social value of football activities in several countries and regions (for an example of Scotland see SSFA/UEFA, 2018). Again, the main point of such a study is to highlight the value of a particular activity, extending beyond mere financial outcomes. SROI has also been applied in evaluating public policy alternatives and thereby in providing policymakers with more information for making policy choices. Likewise, within the investment community, investors and companies exploring the potential of impact investing have sought to make use of SROI, and it has also been applied by social enterprises aiming at achieving both financial and social results. Here, SROI might be used to evaluate the benefits of some investment choices or modes of operating, which would perhaps not be justifiable if decided upon the basis of financial criteria only.

Despite its popularity, SROI has also received a fair share of criticism. The method relies on the idea of monetising different types of outcomes, which is known to pose challenges and risks leading to potentially artificial figures, as we will discuss below. Moreover, before being converted into monetary units, these outcomes need first to be identified, which can also be an area of debate. As an end result, SROI produces figures which at face value appear to be highly accurate and detailed (see the below "Pause and reflect" for a relevant discussion). The question, however, is whether the underlying assumptions and methodological choices are communicated along with the results.

**PAUSE AND REFLECT...**

Terms such as social impact and impact investing are common phrases when discussing the achievements and results of organisations and various organisational initiatives and projects. But what does impact mean? And why is it relevant to discussions about sustainability management accounting and control?

First, to understand impact, it is beneficial to acknowledge the differences between inputs, outputs, outcomes and impacts. All these provide different knowledge regarding an activity or a product.

- *Inputs* refer to resources used to do something, such as money, labour or physical resources.
- *Outputs* describe the direct consequences of the use of inputs, such as the number of training sessions or how many people attended them.

- *Outcomes* go one step further and seek to capture the changes that took place due to the outputs. In the case of training sessions, this could for instance refer to how many participants changed the way they work or do something.
- *Impact*, the most complicated, refers to changes on a broader level, such as the improvement of individuals' quality of life or, on a smaller scale, well-being at work.

The key point here is that we should pay attention to what is being measured and offered to describe the desired results of an activity or a project. For instance, while input-based numbers are sometimes used to describe the volume of an activity, for instance through presenting the amount of money used for environmental investments in a given year, such resource-based metrics tell us little about whether or not anything was achieved.

At the other end of the spectrum, assessing the actual impact of something is highly challenging. In principle, measuring impact would require one to be able to show that some changes have happened exactly because of a specific activity and not due to some other reason. Still, the challenges inherent in the assessments of outcomes or impacts should not be seen as a reason to avoid looking at them. Staying at the level of inputs or outputs might be easier in the short run, but would likely result in decision-making being based on lower-quality and less relevant information, which can subsequently lead to adverse consequences for both the organisation and its stakeholders.

Again, a key reflection here is the need to critically evaluate the information being produced and communicated through management accounting and control systems and reflecting on its usefulness and limits.

Having highlighted the differences between these concepts, however, a word of caution is perhaps in order. You will come to note that these terms are not always used with exactly these meanings, with for instance the term "impact" being commonly used in a more general sense to refer to the various kinds of effects an organisation has on its stakeholders and the environment. This is the case also in this textbook when we refer to the distinction between impacts and dependencies.

### 4.3.4 Sustainable investment appraisal

Including sustainability considerations in management accounting decisions does not necessarily require the use of any specific tool, however. What matters is how the information concerning a particular decision is collected, which dimensions are being considered and how they are evaluated in relation to one another. One such example relates to embedding sustainability considerations into capital investment appraisals (see A4S CFO Leadership Network, 2019 for a useful guide).

For many organisations, investment appraisals are amongst the most long-standing and consequential decisions, as they will affect organisational activities for years, if not decades. Consider, for instance, such far-reaching investments as a new coal-fired power plant, or the establishment of a new major oil refinery. While for a long time such investment decisions were driven almost entirely by financial factors, sustainability considerations can substantially alter the logic, and therefore outcomes, of such decisions. It might not be possible to include all elements in a model of discounted cash flow, but in making appraisals other types of information can be considered, potentially also reaching across the organisational boundaries.

It is relevant to keep in mind that embedding sustainability into capital expenditure appraisals requires more than just adding new figures into the mix. Sustainability considerations force organisational decision-makers to re-evaluate how different dimensions of sustainability are identified, assessed and considered, and subsequently how the decision-making criteria are set in a situation, in which all the relevant information might not be presented in a similar form. Multi-criteria analysis, minimum thresholds and specific hurdle rates for various aspects may have to be implemented, as it is likely that simple aggregation of all information is not feasible. Eventually, organisations also need to acknowledge how conducting such investment appraisals with embedded sustainability might require constant learning as well as individuals with different types of expertise and knowledge. It may therefore be worth reconsidering the governance practices of such projects, and also considering the inclusion of cross-functional teams in their development, evaluation and management.

### 4.3.5 Key performance indicators

For information to have an influence in organisational decision-making, it needs to be embedded into the processes through which performance is evaluated and goals for actions are set. One mechanism for this is integrating sustainability into key performance indicators (KPIs). As KPIs can have a major influence on organisational culture, they are an important management control consideration.

KPIs refer to some measurable values which tell us how an organisation is performing against particular objectives, or indicators, set in advance. KPIs are used across organisational hierarchies, ranging from daily metrics concerning operational performance of small units, such as the amounts of recycled and mixed waste at a particular facility, to strategic KPIs geared towards evaluating the entire organisation's performance against long-term goals, such as the total greenhouse gas emissions of a multinational company. In other words, KPIs are a common way in organisations to assess how targets are being reached on multiple levels.

There is no one right way for an organisation to set their KPIs. As is the case with traditional KPIs focusing on financial performance, the same metrics cannot be directly applied for all individuals, units or organisations. At the same time, it is well-established that metrics such as KPIs affect the behaviour of individuals and groups. We can for instance try harder in order to achieve higher performance on a given KPI, and particularly so when incentives are set for such achievements. KPIs can be effective in steering an organisation in a particular direction and therefore provide opportunities to integrate sustainability considerations into decision-making across multiple organisational levels. However, focusing on performance alone does not necessarily suffice, and hence other types of controls, such as planning controls concerning budgets, objectives and resources, as well as administrative controls consisting of organisational structures and policies, also need to be considered.

**INSIGHTS FROM RESEARCH: MANAGEMENT CONTROL FOR SUSTAINABILITY**

Questions concerning organisational strategy have long been of interest to both management and accounting scholars. How strategies are set, and why are they set in a specific way? Further, once a strategy has been decided upon, how does it get implemented into business activities? From an accounting perspective, we should also ask what role does accounting information and management control systems play in strategy implementation? And furthermore, from a perspective very pertinent to this book, how is sustainability included in a firm's strategy, implemented in the business activities and integrated into the organisation's accounting and management control systems?

Peter Beusch, Jane Elisabeth Frisk, Magnus Rosén and William Dilla seek to provide some insights on such questions in their study based on a longitudinal examination of a Swedish multinational organisation. More specifically, they discuss how this major industrial case organisation sought to align its management control system and sustainability control system, and whether this integration supported the attempts to develop and implement an integrated sustainability strategy in the organisation.

Presenting insights from a 15-year period, Beusch and colleagues note that developing and conducting substantial changes in the sustainability-related organisational and control practices of a major firm takes time. Further, they also highlight how different control systems play a role in shaping how the sustainability practices of a firm evolve. One of the interesting features of the study is how, instead of relying primarily on specialists, the case organisation's top management emphasised that all employees should be responsible for sustainability. Beusch and colleagues argue that such an approach can be important for creating interactive dialogues, which may be helpful for avoiding sustainability initiatives becoming marginalised even in situations where sustainability metrics are not as well developed as the more established financial performance measures.

At the same time, it is evident that in this particular case of organisation, the level of ambition for sustainability transformation over the period examined was not particularly high. Beusch and colleagues for instance note how the firm and its CEO have in public presentations and materials stated that "There is no longer any contradiction between environmental and commercial targets. They are one and the same". While the study is informative in discussing how management control systems are intertwined with sustainability practices, and in presenting how sustainability improvements can be achieved through small steps in organisations, it does at the same time challenge scholars to explore how strategic changes aimed at major sustainability transformations which are not compatible with the current business models can be implemented, and what kind of a role sustainability management accounting and control systems play in doing so. A word of caution is hence in order for those who are highly optimistic of the ability of sustainability management accounting tools to bring about major organisational changes since both the underlying institutional structures (including market mechanisms and customer expectations) as well as the institutionalised assumptions (such as the taken-for-granted assumption that an organisation needs to prioritise profit) and beliefs can remain strong and resistant to changes challenging the way things have usually been done.

**Beusch, P., Frisk, J. E., Rosén, M. and Dilla, W. (2022). Management Control for Sustainability: Towards Integrated Systems. *Management Accounting Research,* 54, 100777.**

Sustainability is complex with various interconnections between social, economic and environmental aspects, making setting appropriate KPIs for an organisation, unit or individual difficult. It should be underscored that even if some sustainability information is readily available or easy to collect, it is not necessarily useful for decision-making. Consider raising environmental awareness in an organisation for instance. If a KPI is set to measure the number of people attending a training event, the unit responsible for the training has an incentive to organise multiple training events. Such a KPI however tells us little about whether the training had resulted in a higher environmental awareness.

### 4.3.6 Cost accounting

Our final example, cost accounting and allocation, takes us to the very heart of conventional management accounting practices. Cost allocation relates to the way in which the various costs caused by organisational activities are distributed within the organisation. These can be allocated to, for instance, projects, processes or products. From the perspective of sustainability accounting and accountability, cost allocation provides us with an illustrative example of how management accounting and sustainability considerations are interlinked.

Let's take a simple example of waste costs in a manufacturing facility to help illustrate. How waste is allocated has implications, and as we have identified there is flexibility here. Are all waste costs bundled into generic cost pools from which they are allocated to all processes and/or products? Or are systems in place which allow for the identification and recording of which processes and/or products are actually causing specific waste and therefore waste costs? While the former is usually more straightforward and easier, it is unlikely to lead to information which allows for the best sustainability-related decision-making. For example, a management accounting system bundling all waste costs into generic cost pools could lead to cleaner processes and products ending up looking more expensive as the waste costs allocated to them are derived from broader operations. In addition, processes and products causing more waste and waste-related costs are likely to end up looking cheaper and hence more beneficial to the organisation (see Schaltegger and Burritt, 2000). A more detailed tracking of social, environmental and economic costs can allow the organisation to diminish both the financial costs and the sustainability impacts of its activities, but it is obviously more complex. In this task, specific tools such as the MFCA and LCA discussed above can prove helpful.

As you can see, cost allocation can have major implications for how organisational decision-makers assess different situations, how various projects, processes and products look when compared against one another, and what types of decisions are supported and incentivised by the management accounting information. This highlights the range of information and accounting practices that are relevant to keep in mind as managers and corporate executives seek to integrate sustainability considerations in their decision-making.

### 4.3.7 Summary of tools and practices

We have presented a short introduction to a number of tools and applications that organisational managers can use in bringing elements of sustainability into their decision-making. The list could easily be expanded with a range of other tools and practices such as ecological footprints, sustainability balanced scorecards and water management accounting.

Some of the approaches may appear fairly distant from what you usually consider to be "accounting". For example, you might consider that instead of accountancy an LCA would fall into the expertise of an environmental scientist. If you are feeling this way, it is worth remembering that instead of being something stable, accounting has always been an evolving craft, art and profession. As Peter Miller (1998) aptly pointed out, practices currently perceived to be at the core of accounting have usually at some point in the past been considered to be peripheral, and practices currently seen to be on the periphery and of limited relevance to accounting will include those that form the core of accounting in the future. Many elements of sustainability, such as carbon accounting which began on the edges of accounting and is now a core part of accounting practices for many organisations, clearly illustrate the relevance of Miller's observation.

## 4.4 Sustainability management accounting and control: Key considerations

Sustainability management accounting and control practices should enhance the ability of the organisational managers to understand and make informed choices regarding the sustainability impacts of their decisions as well as to understand how the organisation and its activities are dependent on various aspects of sustainability. While such considerations can complicate sustainability management accounting and control systems compared with more conventional forms concerned primarily with financial costs, they should not be seen as a burden. Providing better information to decision-makers, considering what is important to the organisation's various stakeholders, and ultimately directing the organisation towards more sustainable practices, should be seen in light of the overall performance of the organisation. Considered another way, not including sustainability considerations in organisational decision-making is likely to put at risk the organisation's short-term performance and long-term survival. Moreover, placed within the accountability perspective taken within this book, management accounting and control tools and practices such as the ones introduced above should also enable the organisational decision-makers to both understand and discharge their accountabilities to various stakeholders.

Here we identify and discuss some of the key choices which need attention no matter whether one is trying to develop and apply sustainability management accounting and control in an organisation, or alternatively aiming to interpret information already produced.

### 4.4.1 The level of analysis: What is the entity being measured?

One of the first questions that needs to be asked in relation to sustainability management accounting and control relates to the entity and the level to which it is appropriate to consider the entity and its operations. Is the object of analysis an organisation, a business unit, a process, or a product? Take our examples above. Many of the tools discussed (e.g. MFCA, LCA and KPIs) can be applied to various levels, from single products to entire organisations, so it is important to consider what the most appropriate and useful level of analysis is (see Table 4.1).

**TABLE 4.1** Levels of Measurement

| Level | Example | Relevance |
|---|---|---|
| Organisation (i.e. consider organisation as a whole) | System tracking energy use of the organisation | Enables organisation wide decision-making when appropriate |
| Production site | System looking at water use and discharge at individual production sites | Can be used to compare the performance of different facilities, and subsequently use this information to find internal benchmarks and to improve performance on the poorer performing sites |
| Process | Measuring waste generated from different production processes | Can be used to consider alternative production methods or in seeking to understand which processes are more dependent on the availability of particular natural resources or ecosystem services |
| Product | Carbon or environmental footprint of a particular product | May be needed to meet regulatory or legislative requirements, for gaining environmental certification, or if the organisation wishes to add credibility to their marketing of the product as "environmentally friendly" |

While some single sustainability management accounting systems or tools can be used to achieve information across these various levels, this is not always the case. There are also other factors that require consideration. As such, when designing, implementing and assessing sustainability management accounting and control practices, a consideration of the level of analysis is essential.

### 4.4.2 The scope of analysis: What are the boundaries?

With the scope of the assessment, we are here referring to how broadly one attempts to capture the sustainability impacts related to the level they are assessing. Are we looking within the boundaries of our own organisation only, or at what is taking place at a particular facility? Or, are we trying to assess and understand the situation across a broader life-cycle of a product or a process, perhaps crossing organisational boundaries and out of a single organisation's direct control? The latter, as illustrated above with the LCA tool, is clearly more difficult, but arguably needed if operating within a circular economy model (see Chapter 2) or attempting to ensure that the broader multidimensional sustainability impacts and dependencies are properly considered.

The choice of scope is relevant for the assessment and the implications and outcomes of the assessment. Take the example of a chocolate bar. Do we consider the environmental impacts taking place in the supply chain, such as potential deforestation and biodiversity loss occurring due to intensive cocoa farming? Do we assess the risks related to child labour and human rights? In most cases, the firm producing the chocolate bars does not operate the cocoa farm, or the sugar mill, hence, we are crossing organisational boundaries here. At the same time, if the assessment does not include these, an LCA or a carbon footprint of such a product would be left essentially meaningless, since it would have left out most of the sustainability impacts and dependencies. In addition to the results themselves, the way boundaries are set and considered has implications for organisational accountability. If something is represented to be outside an assessment, it can also appear that the organisation has no accountability over those issues, nor the ability to control or influence them. But if you take the chocolate bar example, many in society would argue that the producer does have responsibility and the related accountabilities for the environmental impacts of the supply chain. We invite you to take a moment to consider such supply chain controversies in the following "Pause and reflect".

**PAUSE AND REFLECT...**

It is perhaps worth pausing at this stage to consider further LCA controversies.

The choices made regarding the scope of an assessment can not only have substantial implications for the results but also lead to situations in which comparisons between apples and oranges are made. That is, if the assessments of two products or processes have been prepared with a different scope or by using different assumptions, any comparison between them can be outright meaningless.

Still, such situations feature regularly in the media. Sometimes they might be due to pure misunderstanding, as would be the case when someone simply puts two assessments side-by-side without knowing the underlying assumptions or understanding their relevance. On other occasions, these comparisons are used to achieve desired outcomes, such as making a particular product or process look more sustainable than its alternative.

An example here would be the debate regarding the relative sustainability of electric cars versus gasoline cars. Here, outcomes of an assessment can be substantially different based on how the batteries of an electric car are considered, and how far into the upstream and downstream one goes. In addition to scope, outcomes will vary according to any assumptions made concerning the durability of the cars or their parts, including the batteries.

The main message would be that any comparisons should include information regarding the underlying choices and assumptions used in the assessment, and furthermore that anyone using such comparisons should look into these before rushing into any hasty conclusions. We should also remain open to results which may appear counterintuitive at first. For example, while cotton tote bags have long been considered a superior alternative to plastic bags, the matter can get complicated. Many studies have pointed out the high environmental impacts cotton production has, and we must also take into account how many times the cotton alternative is used.

Take a moment to reflect on where you have seen such comparisons made between organisations, products or services. Have you ever stopped to think about how the assessments, and therefore comparisons, have been made? As these examples show, it is important that we take time to critically evaluate such claims if we are going to make informed decisions.

### 4.4.3 Materiality: What issues should be assessed and focused on?

Sustainability includes a very wide range of issues, and hence it is difficult, if not impossible, for any one assessment to include everything. Organisational decision-makers and organisational stakeholders must decide which issues are important – which issues are material. Materiality, as discussed in Chapter 3, refers to considerations regarding how relevant a particular sustainability issue is for an organisation and its stakeholders. Here, it is significant to recall the differences between different perspectives on materiality, such as financial, impact and double materiality, and acknowledge that the perspective taken has also implications on how an organisation approaches sustainability in its internal decision-making. At the same time, we should emphasise that differences between financial and impact materialities are not clear-cut black and white, but instead can and often do intertwine, especially when looked at on different time horizons.

Like in other areas of sustainability accounting and accountability, materiality considerations are important in the area of sustainability management accounting and control. It is important to focus efforts on identifying the most material issues, those which would be likely to have most relevance for the organisation and organisational stakeholders and the decisions being made. Given the internal focus of the information being produced, internal stakeholder views are often prioritised in materiality discussions relating to management accounting information. However, external stakeholder views should not be ignored. External stakeholders' views can be extremely useful in identifying relevant aspects to focus on, enabling organisations to understand the external context including any changes in societal views. An example here is the increasing societal concern relating to plastic waste in recent years. If an organisation produced plastic waste, being mindful of material issues of external stakeholders could help inform and direct management accounting information to relevant matters.

When considering materiality for internal decision-making, it is again important to look into both impacts and dependencies. This can lead to vastly different material issues. For example, an organisation might be strongly dependent on the availability of water resources, while its impacts might mostly be in the area of social justice and human rights. Thereby, the first could be highly relevant from a financial materiality perspective, while the latter could be more in the focus when thinking of impact materiality while having less (immediate) significance from the financial perspective. Finally, when considering materiality, it is important that we keep in mind another key concept introduced and discussed in Chapter 3, externalities.

### 4.4.4 The role of externalities

Externalities are the costs and benefits deriving from the impacts of activities which are not borne by the organisation. Externalities exist on different levels and scales, and the impact of their (non-)consideration varies significantly.

So, how do externalities relate to management accounting and sustainability management accounting more specifically? Let's take the example introduced in Chapter 3, $CO_2$ emissions, and consider it specifically from a management accounting perspective. While hard to imagine now, organisations for a long time did not need to consider the amount of $CO_2$ emissions their manufacturing processes caused. But as the science behind climate change has become well established, and the associated costs have become better understood, the situation is now substantially different. Governments and communities are looking for ways to reduce $CO_2$ levels, and mechanisms such as carbon trading and carbon tax have been established. From the perspective of management accounting, this relates to the possibility of internalising an externality and the effect that this has on decision-making. When $CO_2$ was not seen as relevant to an organisation's operations (or could be externalised), it was not considered in any management accounting calculations. Management accounting information could have shown that it was beneficial for an organisation to proceed with high $CO_2$ emissions, as tackling them would only have caused additional costs. However, when the climate is taken into account, and when $CO_2$ emissions are internalised (for example, given a price) through for instance a carbon market, carbon tax or an intra-organisational mechanism such as internal carbon pricing (see Chapter 9), the situation changes significantly. The option of continuing with high $CO_2$ emissions becomes costly (the degree to which is dependent on the pricing mechanism), as the previously invisible $CO_2$ emissions are suddenly given a price and subsequently included in the management accounting calculation.

Such examples where externalities are given a price or a monetary value, and there are many, also begin to demonstrate why some believe that the best way to transition organisations towards sustainability is to internalise externalities through such pricing and costing mechanisms. And it is perhaps an effective way in which to enter sustainability considerations into decision-making. However, such pricing and costing mechanisms, essentially the monetisation or financialisation of sustainability impacts, are far from straightforward and uncontested, as research on *full cost accounting* has demonstrated (see Antheume and Bebbington, 2021). This is also why other ways of internalising externalities, such as through narratives, have been considered. We will return to some of these aspects of externalities further in Part III.

## 4.4.5 Valuation: Which metrics are being used, how and why?

In conventional accounting, we have become used to having a single unit, money, dominate our calculations. This keeps things simple. Although sometimes such simplicity may cover up the underlying complexities. When preparing sustainability management accounting and control information, there are a range of alternatives to be considered and while money can be one of these, it is often not the only one, or even the most useful.

### 4.4.5.1 Qualitative and quantitative information

In making decisions, managers may need to rely on both qualitative and quantitative information. It is therefore useful to consider their differences and some of the assumptions surrounding the use of both forms of information within management accounting and control. Much of this discussion also applies to sustainability accounting and accountability more broadly.

Qualitative information, that is information not involving numbers, is useful. Indeed, qualitative information is often unavoidable in communicating different types of information within internal settings. Narrative disclosures are a common example of qualitative information. However, for many, quantitative information, that is information involving numbers, is considered necessary for a meaningful management accounting and control system. Some even consider quantitative information to be by definition "better" than qualitative information.

One of the reasons for this is that quantitative information can be aggregated, compared and presented in a simple and easily digestible form, for example. However, while physical metrics, such as $CO_2$ emissions or extracted water amounts can be measured with fairly high confidence, it is substantially more complicated when dealing with some other areas, such as human rights or employee wellbeing. While it is definitely possible to come up with a number, it is reasonable to ask whether it is the right number, or whether there can be a right number at all. For some elements, it is possible to create proxies or ratios which then allow presenting things in a quantitative form. However, such proxies or ratios often cannot capture all aspects of what is being measured so again leave us with problematic or incomplete information. An additional challenge in considering the nature of information is that numbers appear exact, and hence can result in the decision-makers having superior confidence in them.

When it comes to qualitative and quantitative information for the purposes of management accounting and control, and sustainability accounting and accountability more generally, it is likely that a combination of qualitative and quantitative information is beneficial. The key, however, is to consider what is the most appropriate and the effects of using the various information forms.

#### 4.4.5.2 Relative vs. absolute numbers

In a similar way, there are also important considerations to be had with regard to the use of relative and absolute numbers within management accounting and control information. Relative numbers, such as how much energy is being used to produce one ton of steel, can be insightful as they can show how the performance has become relatively better (or worse). At the same time, relative improvement can hide the fact that the absolute numbers (e.g. total energy being used to produce steel) might still be going up if the company is producing more steel.

To take another example, even if the water efficiency of a production facility in an arid region shows improvement in relative terms and hence demonstrates that the company is being more water efficient (sometimes referred to as eco-efficiency), the facility might still be using more water in absolute terms as its production volume has increased. As such, while the relative numbers might look good, the organisation would overall be having more of an impact on the environment due to total water use increasing. As these examples demonstrate, relying only on relative numbers might mean that management loses sight of the overall situation. This could not only have negative impacts on the environment but also expose the organisation (and the community) to risks, such as water shortages in the future in our example above. In other words, being more efficient in its water use does not necessarily help the organisation in the long run if its absolute water use keeps increasing, and as a result, the water basin it depends on dries up. Likewise, such efficiency can cause harm to the organisational stakeholders, surrounding communities and the ecosystem, as they would also be affected by limited water availability.

#### 4.4.5.3 Monetary vs. physical information

As we noted above in the context of externalities, the use of monetary valuation, i.e. monetisation, is an increasingly popular approach when seeking to embed sustainability information into organisational decision-making. There are clear reasons for this. For instance, while corporate executives, managers and other decision-makers are likely to have a hard time estimating whether a particular quantity of carbon or sulphur dioxide emission is a lot or just a negligible amount, turning sustainability impacts and dependences into financial language can help understand and consider them. Our discussion of carbon emissions in Chapter 9 provides further details on this. Likewise, monetisation can aid in making different dimensions of sustainability more readily comparable. Going a step further, it can also be argued that unless sustainability issues are converted into financial numbers (i.e. money), they will remain peripheral in any organisational decision-making process. The rationale here is that most organisational decision-makers are so used to monetary information that it is prioritised over other types of information expressed in physical units or in qualitative terms.

At the same time, there are substantial caveats when it comes to monetising sustainability impacts and dependencies, some of which we have already mentioned in passing above. From the perspective of corporate management, it is worth underscoring that monetisation is not simple and that for many sustainability issues, no common and generally accepted or appropriate methodologies exist. Engaging in monetisation can be a highly resource-intensive and expensive process. Moreover, there are limits to monetisation, although there might not be a shared view on where these limits are. Consider trying to put a monetary value on a key employee burning out due to extensive work stress. An organisation needs to find and train a replacement, for which a monetary price could perhaps be estimated, but there would still be other intangible effects through for instance how the morale of other employees in the team would be affected. Moreover, from the individual's perspective, what is the value of losing one's capability to be an active citizen for, say, six months?

Monetising and associated valuation have benefits, but they also include considerable pitfalls (see Antheume and Bebbington, 2021). For example, monetisation can create an assumption that all social, environmental and financial aspects are interchangeable, which would mean that any major social and environmental impacts can be remedied, and dependencies understood with financials. Monetisation can also mean that decision-makers lose sight of no-go zones, which we know to exist frequently in both social and environmental realms (see the discussion of weak and strong sustainability and the doughnut economics model in Chapter 2 for an illustration related to environmental overshoot and social shortfalls). What is the monetary value of someone losing one's life in a work-related accident, an ancient cultural heritage site of Aboriginals located at a potential mining site, or the last remaining healthy ecosystem of an endangered species? An often-cited example of such controversial calculation is the case of designing the Ford Pinto in the 1970s. A faulty design of the fuel tank was noted to substantially increase the risks of fire in car accidents, but Ford decided against modifying the design, as a cost-benefit analysis including monetary values for injuries and loss of lives showed that it would be cheaper to keep the design and pay compensations to victims (van der Kolk, 2019).

Assigning monetary values to sustainability aspects can be highly informative, but they need to be approached with caveats and not used without paying attention to the underlying information. Clearly, this is not as simple as many would like, but what can we do, the ecosystem is complex and messy. You will find more discussion of monetisation as you move through the chapters that follow, for example, accounting for climate (Chapter 9) and accounting for biodiversity (Chapter 11).

### 4.4.6 Timeframe: What is a useful timeframe?

The relevance of considering different timeframes in sustainability management accounting and control needs to be underscored. As with financial accounting, many sustainability indicators tend to produce lagging information. The focus is on what has already happened. For decision-making purposes, however, it is valuable to be able to develop forward-looking indicators, which can provide decision-makers with information concerning potential scenarios and developments. Clearly, forward-looking indicators do not entail that they would be expected to predict the future and produce exact forecasts, but they may enhance management's ability to assess how decisions made now will impact on the various elements of sustainability in the coming period.

Another element of time includes consideration regarding whether the information collected and presented focuses more on short-term or long-term information. These are different and require managers to interpret and make decisions differently. In an organisation, there are likely to be differences as to what kind of information managers operating at different organisational levels need in order to be able to integrate sustainability into their decision-making. While at the operational level, the day-to-day decisions can often be based on short-term and more immediate information, at the strategic level, corporate executives usually need to have more complex information at their disposal. Given that sustainability concerns develop swiftly, organisational decision-makers can benefit from keeping a close eye on the macrotrends of sustainability and incorporating those considerations in scenario analysis concerning future developments. In these cases, long-term forward-looking information is essential. Here, we should keep in mind however that some inherent features of sustainability include complex feedback loops and tipping points. Ecosystems for instance can for long appear to be seemingly resilient, only to eventually falter after a specific tipping point gets reached through accumulated strain over time. This means that impacts of organisational activities may only become visible slowly, which poses challenges for managers as they seek to make decisions and take action at an earlier point when the consequences of activities are yet to clearly manifest.

### 4.4.7 Summary of key considerations

As should be clear, the quality of decisions made with the aid of sustainability management accounting and control systems is dependent on the underlying information. In addition to the above, there are also other aspects that are useful to mention here. For example, how accurate the measurements are, is the information complete, does it include both positive and negative elements and so on.

No organisation should rely on a single metric without considering the context and underlying principles. Likewise, an organisation should not assume that it can find the most suitable tools and practices by merely imitating other organisations, since a practice designed for one context might not provide relevant information in another. Therefore, when considering the design and use of sustainability management accounting, every organisation should pay attention to a range of questions, including those we have discussed. Careful consideration of these questions helps as managers will have access to information that is fit for purpose.

## 4.5 Challenges and future developments

Sustainability management accounting and control practices have developed substantially. They have also become increasingly commonplace, and many large organisations are showing how sustainability can be integrated as a core element in management information. While all this is important and shows progress, there are still major challenges that need to be looked at to ensure that sustainability management accounting information contributes positively to the transition towards a more sustainable society. We next outline some of these challenges.

### 4.5.1 Ensuring sustainability management accounting is core not peripheral

A long-term challenge that remains relates to ensuring that complex and multifaceted sustainability factors are integrated into organisational decision-making. While knowledge has grown substantially, it is still often the case that traditional financial-based management accounting information dominates when it comes to what information managers rely on and prioritise in making decisions. The structuring of the organisation's accounting systems is relevant. Is sustainability management accounting information included within the core of the organisation's information systems, such as being included in the same system with the financial information and on an equal footing? Or is it a supplementary system? Sustainability information being supplementary tends to position this type of knowledge as peripheral and secondary to the financial information. This has been one of the reasons why there has been increased focus by some on the financial considerations of sustainability issues (i.e. the financial related risks of climate or biodiversity loss). However, this must be considered in relation to our discussion above regarding the monetisation or financialisation of sustainability-related impacts and dependencies.

Moreover, the tone set at the top of the organisation is also likely to be important. If an organisation publicly emphasises the importance of sustainability, the top executives show knowledge of sustainability and use sustainability management information in making strategic decisions, it is likely to have an impact on how managers further down in the organisational hierarchy approach such topics. Conversely, should the employees note that the top executives use sustainability primarily for public relations, it is increasingly likely that any sustainability management accounting information remains more peripheral across the organisation.

### 4.5.2 Ensuring the relevance of indicators used

A highly significant question regarding the efficiency of any sustainability management accounting tools and practices relates to the relevance of indicators used and the level of ambition taken.

Bebbington and Thomson (2013) noted their disappointment that most sustainability management accounting practices focus on relative measures, such as improving eco-efficiency as discussed above. Such an approach seldom challenges the organisation's business model in a fundamental way as it is possible to improve the relative sustainability performance of virtually any activity. The problem from a broader sustainability perspective, as has been discussed, is that such an improvement may still lead to a higher adverse impact on sustainability in absolute terms.

In addition, Bebbington and Thomson (2013) noted that there continue to be significant barriers for organisations to engage in initiatives which do not appear to be profitable, again indicating the continued prioritisation of financial performance. Likewise, Schaltegger (2018) points out how most environmental management accounting tends to focus only on a few selected environmental aspects, and usually on those closest to business operations, rather than on aspects which would be the most important from a sustainability perspective. This means that instead of focusing on the most material issues stemming from the perspective of global ecological limits and planetary boundaries, the focus remains limited to issues that are material for the organisation's financial performance.

This is not to say that such focused information could not offer clear signals for managers and other decision-makers to improve an organisation's sustainability performance. However, from a sustainability perspective, it is evident that more ambitious approaches are needed. The global sustainability crisis is so urgent that tinkering with mere eco-efficiency does not suffice. Burning coal in a more eco-efficient manner does not help us, since if we are really to address sustainability and the climate emergency we should not be burning coal at all. The trick is that indicators looking at eco-efficiency can show the former option as a good thing, whereas a science-based approach derived from global planetary boundaries would call for the latter. Here, it can be useful to consider our earlier discussion concerning inputs, outputs, outcomes and impacts, as the distinctions between these levels can help in evaluating available information.

### 4.5.3 Understanding why organisations do (not) implement sustainability management accounting and control

In many organisations, particularly large corporations, various sustainability management accounting and control tools and practices can be seen as everyday practices. Nonetheless, their use can be sporadic or even outright non-existent once we move to the context of smaller companies, NGOs or other types of organisations. Integrating sustainability into decision-making does not have to be dependent on size, however. Still, increasing the number of organisations which have integrated sustainability into their management information is among the key challenges (see Johnson and Schaltegger, 2016; Journeault et al., 2021). To understand why some organisations are slow in adopting these practices, it is useful to consider the motivations organisations have for engaging with them. We can consider both internal and external drivers.

A key external driver, that is a motivation from outside of the organisation, can be a regulatory requirement. An organisation in a particular industry or at a particular site could be required to record and monitor an element of its environmental performance in a systematic way. In addition to reporting requirements, such regulatory demands can relate for instance to environmental permitting, requiring the organisation to deliver a regular report to the authority on particular emissions, discharges or the use of substances. The organisation may then include such compulsory record-keeping as an element of its information system and use the metrics as indicators of operational efficiency. External drivers may also relate to responsibilities and accountabilities to stakeholders. An organisation may publicly commit to strive for excellence in some aspect of sustainability, and as such decide to use particular metrics like noise levels or safety incidents to monitor their progress over time and enable them to demonstrate that they are achieving their stated commitments. Expectations of major customers have also proven to be strong external drivers. The sustainability efforts of IKEA, a leading Swedish furniture company, for instance, are highly dependent on how all its suppliers perform with energy use, water consumption and sustainable raw material procurement, and hence its emphasis on sustainability has created a strong external driver for companies in its supply chain to integrate sustainability into their management information.

Internal drivers can also provide an impetus for organisations to engage in sustainability management accounting and control. Behind the use of sustainability management accounting and control tools and practices, there is the assumption that an organisation can improve its sustainability performance. After all, through regular measurement, control and benchmarking one can follow how particular dimensions of the operations are developing over time. However, again we recognise the need to consider which tools and practices are being used and whether they assist in achieving the organisational aims. Given the broad range of sustainability matters that can be assessed, the organisation should also consider which elements are the most significant, or material, for it and its activities, and thereafter ensure that the tools and metrics are capturing those elements instead of some less relevant ones.

Engaging in sustainability management accounting can bring a range of other benefits for an organisation and for society, the environment and/or the economy if they bring about improved sustainability performance. Considering the escalating global sustainability challenges, it is very likely that regulatory demands on organisations will get more stringent in many operating contexts. Tackling such changes in the future will be easier if an organisation has already been measuring and managing its sustainability performance. This could entail a better understanding of the future risks related to the organisation's dependencies on some natural resources, such as water. Or, from a more positive perspective, having strong internal sustainability data of its activities gives an organisation a good footing to prosper in the future.

It should be acknowledged that there are times when engaging with sustainability management accounting will not bring financial benefit to an organisation, but instead will result in increased costs. Potential sustainability benefits might also be incremental, given many organisations begin by focusing on a small part of their business or a single aspect of sustainability. It might however be that one of the key barriers relates to awareness and knowledge. Sustainability has not traditionally been considered to be inside the domain of accountancy, and hence many accountants do not have the necessary skills to tackle these questions in organisations. This is where the accounting profession and professional bodies could have a substantial role to play.

### 4.5.4 The role of the accounting profession

It is perhaps useful to end our discussion of the challenges and future developments with a note about the accounting profession. The accounting profession is a core link in the area of sustainability management accounting and control. Through professional accounting groups such as AICPA and CIMA (the America Institute of CPAs and the Chartered Institute of Management Accounting), as well as large accounting practices, the profession plays a role in developing new indicators, tools and approaches and also in their promotion.

As we have noted, we must also pay attention to the role of conventional management accounting in the transition towards sustainability. Conventional management accounting tools have a major impact on sustainability through for instance the assumptions made regarding the relevance of some aspects, the inclusion or exclusion of externalities, as well as the valuation given to sustainability issues. As this information is used for decision-making and for setting goals for projects, units and organisations, the way sustainability is taken into account (or not) has substantial implications. Many accounting institutions and professional bodies have high significance here. In a number of countries, such as Australia and the United States, accountancy is a regulated profession and hence academic institutions offering accounting education need to consider the requirements set by the professional bodies when shaping the curricula. Even though such a system is not in place in all societies, accountancy tends to be a global profession. Universities and training institutions across the world use the same core textbooks and follow by and large similar approaches in delivering their education. In this sense, the tone set by professional bodies and major accountancy institutions is important in facilitating new practices and challenging old ones. It is thus important that examples of how the profession is seeking to engage with sustainability are emerging. This is highlighted for instance in how ACCA in its report "Accounting for a better world: priorities for a Transforming profession" included sustainability as one of the core priorities for accountancy in the future (ACCA, 2022). International Federation of Accountants also discusses how the expected professional competencies on sustainability are expanding the scope of professional accountancy (IFAC, 2024).

### Focus on practice: Accounting for Sustainability (A4S)

"To help ensure that we are not battling to meet 21st century challenges with, at best, 20th century decision-making and reporting systems", a quotation attributed to the then HRH The Prince of Wales, is the founding logic behind Accounting for Sustainability Project (A4S), established in 2004 (Accounting for Sustainability, 2025). A4S is an influential network working with the global accounting community, investors and capital markets and business schools, as well as regulators and policymakers across the world.

In simple terms, A4S aims at transforming sustainable decision-making into an everyday thing in corporations and other organisations. The reasoning for this is captured in the quotation above: A4S perceives that the dominant financial and accounting systems are not fit for purpose when it comes to responding to the sustainability challenges faced by contemporary societies. Hence, the A4S aims to raise awareness within the profession, enhancing the skillsets of accounting and finance professionals, and developing new types of tools and approaches that would help embed sustainability considerations into decision-making.

An example of their work is the series of A4S Essential Guides, which have been produced by the A4S CFO Leadership Network. The guides focus on a range of accounting and finance topics, such as debt finance, managing future uncertainty, and strategic planning, budgeting and forecasting, and provide case studies, practical tools and guidance for those seeking to learn how to develop their organisation's decision-making systems and approaches.

## 4.6 Conclusion

In this chapter, we have discussed the broad area of sustainability management accounting and control. We have sought to provide a definition and understanding of the topic and to introduce and critically reflect on a number of tools and practices. Again, we note that there are a vast number of tools and practices that have not been included, but you should now have an understanding of the role management accounting information has in the transition towards sustainability, from the perspective of both the conventional and the emerging sustainability-related practices.

Integrating environmental, social and broader economic considerations into management information and decision-making processes can help provide insights to decision-makers. Given the increased need to consider and address sustainability challenges which relate beyond the boundaries of a single entity, well-designed and properly implemented sustainability management accounting and control tools and practices have become essential for corporate executives and organisations seeking long-term success. While we would argue that all this is needed for the future sake of the planet, we recognise that such tools and practices also play a role in ensuring the financial performance of many organisations going forward. At the same time, improved sustainability management accounting practices will help managers gather information, which is needed when organisations seek to understand and fulfil their diverse accountability relationships. We will delve deeper into this in the following two chapters, which focus on organisations' sustainability reporting.

In concluding this discussion, we reiterate not only the need to develop new tools and practices which help us address the sustainability challenges we face, but also the need to reflect on and challenge the limits of existing, or conventional, tools and practices. We provide opportunities to do this in Part III where various sustainability accounting and accountability issues are discussed.

## References

A4S CFO Leadership Network (2019). *Essential Guide to Capex: A Practical Guide to Embedding Sustainability into Capital Investment Appraisal.* www.accountingforsustainability.org/content/dam/a4s/corporate/home/KnowledgeHub/Guide-pdf/Capex%20(2019).pdf.downloadasset.pdf (accessed 11 February 2025).

ACCA (2022). *Accounting for a Better World: Priorities for a Transforming Profession.* https://www.accaglobal.com/gb/en/professional-insights/pro-accountants-the-future/accounting-for-a-better-world.html (accessed 11 February 2025).

Accounting for Sustainability (2025). A4S's Aims. www.accountingforsustainability.org/en/about-us/overview.html (accessed 11 February 2025).

Antheume, N. and Bebbington, J. (2021). Externalities and Decision Making. In Bebbington, J., Larrinaga, C., O'Dwyer, B. and Thomson, I. (eds), *Handbook on Environmental Accounting.* pp. 224–235. Routledge.

Bebbington, J. and Thomson, I. (2013). Sustainable Development, Management and Accounting: Boundary Crossing. *Management Accounting Research, 24*(4), 277–283.

Beusch, P., Frisk, J. E., Rosén, M. and Dilla, W. (2022). Management Control for Sustainability: Towards Integrated Systems. *Management Accounting Research, 54*, 100777.

Crutzen, N., Zvezdov, D. and Schaltegger, S. (2017). Sustainability and Management Control: Exploring and Theorizing Control Patterns in Large European Firms. *Journal of Cleaner Production, 143*, 1291–1301.

Figge, F., Hahn, T., Schaltegger, S. and Wagner, M. (2002). The Sustainability Balanced Scorecard – Linking Sustainability Management to Business Strategy. *Business Strategy and the Environment*, *11*(*5*), 269–284.

IFAC (2024). *Educating Accountants for a Sustainable Future*. https://www.ifac.org/knowledge-gateway/education/publications/educating-accountants-sustainable-future (accessed 11 February 2025).

Johnson, M. P. and Schaltegger, S. (2016). Two Decades of Sustainability Management Tools for SMEs: How Far Have We Come? *Journal of Small Business Management*, *54*(*2*), 481–505.

Journeault, M., Perron, A. and Vallières, L. (2021). The Collaborative Roles of Stakeholders in Supporting the Adoption of Sustainability in SMEs. *Journal of Environmental Management*, *287*(*1*), 112349.

Miller, P. (1998). The Margins of Accounting. *European Accounting Review*, 7(*4*), 605–621.

Schaltegger, S. (2018). Linking Environmental Management Accounting: A Reflection on (Missing) Links to Sustainability and Planetary Boundaries. *Social and Environmental Accountability Journal*, *38*(*1*), 19–29.

Schaltegger, S. and Burritt, R. (2000). *Contemporary Environmental Accounting*. Greenleaf.

SSFA/UEFA (2018). Measuring the Value of Football Participation in Scotland. https://www.scottishfa.co.uk/media/4961/sfa-uefa-grow-pp-screens-mar19-web.pdf (accessed 11 February 2025).

Unilever (2025). Plastics. https://www.unilever.com/sustainability/plastics/ (accessed 11 February 2025).

van der Kolk, B. (2019). Ethics Matters: The Integration of Ethical Considerations in Management Accounting Textbooks. *Accounting Education*, *28*(*4*), 426–443.

## Additional reading and resources

A4S CFO Leadership Network (2020). *Essential Guide to Management Information: Supporting Decision Makers with Information That Is Fit for the Future*. www.accountingforsustainability.org/en/knowledge-hub/guides/management-information.html (accessed 25 February 2025).

Baker, M., Gray, R. and Schaltegger, S. (2023). Debating Accounting and Sustainability: From Incompatibility to Rapprochement in the Pursuit of Corporate Sustainability. *Accounting, Auditing & Accountability Journal*, *36*(*2*), 591–619.

Bebbington, J., Larrinaga, C., O'Dwyer, B. and Thomson, I. (2021). *Handbook on Environmental Accounting* (Section C – Management Accounting). Routledge.

Garcia, S. and Thomson, I. (2018). The Case of Assabi: Expanding the Learning on Sustainability through an Experiential Qualitative Multi-Criteria Decision Making Activity. *Social and Environmental Accountability Journal*, *38*(*3*), 197–217.

Kuokkanen, N. (2024). A Problematizing Review of the Financialization of Living Beings. *Critical Perspectives on Accounting*, *99*, 102739.

Kurki, M. and Järvenpää, M. (2024). Engaging Management Accountants in Corporate Sustainability. *Accounting, Auditing & Accountability Journal*, *37*(9), 100–127.

Ligonie, M. (2021). Sharing Sustainability Through Sustainability Control Activities. A Practice-based Analysis. *Management Accounting Research*, *50*, 100726.

Milne, M. J. (1996). On Sustainability, the Environment and Management Accounting. *Management Accounting Research*, 7(*1*), 135–161.

Yang, C., O'Leary, S. and Tregidga, H. (2021). Social Impact in Accounting: Is It at Risk of Becoming a Hembig Concept and Does This Matter. *Qualitative Research in Accounting & Management*, *18*(*3*), 313–331.

CHAPTER

5

# Sustainability reporting

## History, frameworks and regulation

Sustainability reporting is a term commonly used to describe a range of practices where organisations provide information on sustainability matters. Sustainability reporting can relate to the reporting to stakeholders of an organisation's strategies, priorities, policies and practices concerning sustainability issues, the sustainability performance of an organisation and the sustainability impacts the operations have. Sustainability reporting can also, among other things, discuss how an organisation is dependent upon the environment, society and economy, the risks and opportunities associated with these dependencies, as well as an organisation's sustainability-related responsibilities and accountabilities.

Sustainability reporting is not only prominent and visible but also a complicated phenomenon. For this reason, we split our discussion of the practice into two chapters. In this chapter, we focus on providing an overview of the practice. We discuss sustainability reporting's historical development, some of the main frameworks and standards that exist for this form of reporting, and discuss ongoing debates surrounding regulation. In Chapter 6, we delve deeper into the process of reporting including questions such as who reports are produced for, what is being reported and how this is done. We also discuss the assurance of such reports. That is, while in this chapter we look at the practice of sustainability reporting more generally, in the following chapter, we consider more closely the reporting process and key influences, debates and discussions that relate to reporting.

By the end of this chapter, you should:

- Understand what sustainability reporting is and the practices defined by this term.
- Be aware of the historical roots and development of sustainability reporting from early voluntary disclosures to current institutionalised and increasingly regulated practice.

DOI: 10.4324/9781003533207-7

- Be aware of the various standards and frameworks that exist within the field of sustainability reporting and gain an awareness of their similarities and differences.
- Have a critical awareness and understanding of the ongoing debates surrounding the regulation of sustainability reporting.

## 5.1 Introduction to the practice of sustainability reporting

As introduced, "sustainability reporting" is a term commonly used to describe a range of practices where organisations provide information on sustainability matters. Sustainability reporting has become a widespread feature across societies and it is now a standard practice in many large organisations, particularly in the business world. It is relevant to acknowledge right from the start that sustainability reporting practices are diverse. There are several reasons for this. One such reason is that, while regulation is evolving, sustainability reporting emerged as, and in many cases remains to be, largely a voluntary practice. This implies that in many contexts, organisations choose whether they publish a sustainability report, how they prepare it, what information they include, as well as the form and medium they publish the information.

Furthermore, while sustainability reporting practices are increasingly regulated, especially for large corporations, there exists various regulatory bodies and non-state organisations with differing viewpoints on, aspirations of, and expectations for, such reporting. There are thus a number of reporting initiatives, frameworks and standards, which place various expectations on organisations and the reports they publish. While seeking both to help organisations prepare their reports and to create a more standardised practice the diversity of approaches means differing practices still exist. We will discuss these aspects, including some of the debates surrounding regulation and standardisation, in more detail below.

### 5.1.1 Different names and forms of sustainability reporting

Sustainability reporting is not the only name used for this type of reporting. Earlier, it was common for organisations to publish environmental, social or EHS reports (environment, health and safety). There are also plenty of corporate citizenship reports, corporate responsibility reports, accountability reports and corporate social responsibility reports out there. The term "non-financial reporting" is prominent (although often broader in scope than sustainability issues), perhaps because it provides a contrast to conventional financial reporting (e.g. the annual report), and the label ESG (Environment, Society and Governance) reporting is increasingly being used. For ease, and in line with the overall focus on sustainability taken in this book, we will here mostly refer to this practice as sustainability reporting.

Sustainability reports also come in various forms. While a standalone sustainability report, published on an annual basis in addition to the financial report, continues to remain a common form in many organisations, many have turned to producing integrated reports, in which various types of social, environmental and broader economic information is presented alongside the financial information in a single report. It is also common to see a series of supplementary reports being produced alongside an integrated report, covering, for example, disclosures on climate or modern slavery. We discuss some of these in the chapters that follow.

As would be expected in today's online society, in addition to the reports published with a regular cycle, many organisations are reporting sustainability information through their websites or on social media. Such reporting offers an organisation the possibility to reach different stakeholder groups than it would with a regular report, as well as potentially facilitate interaction and dialogue with the stakeholders. This will be discussed in more detail in the following chapter (see also Tregidga and Laine, 2021).

## 5.1.2 The purpose of sustainability reporting

Sustainability reporting plays a role in accountability relationships as it is a means by which organisations communicate with a range of stakeholders. While an organisation can produce reports on sustainability-related performance for internal purposes (such as those for internal decision-making purposes discussed in the previous chapter), here, in this chapter and the next, we focus on those that seek to communicate to a broader range of stakeholders. While stakeholders to an organisation's sustainability reporting are usually external to the organisation (e.g. investors, customers, suppliers and civil society), they can also be stakeholders internal to the organisation (e.g. employees).

At this point, however, it needs to be noted that while sustainability reporting has developed into a common practice and is increasingly regulated, the credibility of sustainability reports is not always considered to be very high. As sustainability reporting is still developing, and to varying extents voluntary practice, and often without a formal audit or assurance mechanism, stakeholders regularly express concerns that sustainability reports could be used for green-, blue- or white-washing. At the same time, in the investment community, there is an increasing awareness of how relevant an organisation's sustainability impacts and dependencies can be for risk levels and medium to long-term success. This serves as a driver compelling organisations to focus on the quality of the information they provide.

We would also emphasise that the role sustainability reporting plays in the aspired transition to a sustainable society remains unclear. For some, corporate sustainability disclosures are a medium which has the potential to enhance democracy by providing further transparency and increased accountability in organisations' operations (Gray et al., 2014). This would happen as citizens and various interested social groups gain more information about the organisation, and hence these disclosures are considered to have the potential to facilitate informed public dialogue and debate through civil institutions. Likewise, together with the growing involvement of the investment world, sustainability reporting is argued to create mechanisms driving major changes in organisations, as they provide investors with the necessary information to incorporate sustainability into their decision-making models, and thereby harness the power of the markets to nudge organisations towards less unsustainable practices.

For others, however, such development is merely idealistic, and waiting for it to materialise is inherently harmful for societies. Those with a highly critical perspective maintain that sustainability reporting creates an illusion of positive development and places false hope on organisations' ability to fundamentally transform their operating model to the extent needed for sustainability transition. Holders of such critiques are often not persuaded by efforts to regulate sustainability reporting practices as many see such initiatives as primarily prioritising and enhancing private and financial interests and not aligned with aspirations regarding enhanced accountability. As such, focusing on sustainability reporting is seen as harmful, as it can distract societies from taking steps urgently needed in the global sustainability crisis.

Keeping these different viewpoints in mind as we work through the content of this and the next chapter is helpful when trying to make sense of corporate sustainability disclosure practices and considering the role of such reporting in the transition towards a more sustainable society and environment.

### 5.1.3 The focus of this chapter

Before proceeding further, a few words about our focus in this chapter are in order. While acknowledging that sustainability reports are produced by all types of organisations, the focus of the majority of this chapter is on private corporations. There are several reasons for this decision. While not discounting or meaning to diminish the importance for all organisations to report on sustainability, the sustainability reporting practices of corporations (in particular large corporations) arguably have more prominence and visibility in societies than those of other organisations (e.g. public sector, not-for-profit). This is not only because of their size, but also their impacts. It is also predominantly large corporations that are affected by the range of emerging reporting regulations discussed in this chapter. Moreover, and largely for these reasons, scholarly research has in the main focused on corporate reporting practices, and hence our knowledge of them is substantial (see Andrew and Baker, 2020 for a review).

Furthermore, just as this and the next chapter do not discuss reports prepared for internal purposes, (these, to the extent they relate to management accounting and internal decision-making, were discussed in Chapter 4), they also do not discuss what have become known as counter accounts, that is reports of an organisation prepared by someone outside the organisation. These will be the focus of Chapter 8. This is not to suggest that these practices are not interrelated – quite the opposite in fact, as there can be substantial interplay between organisational disclosures, internal reports and counter accounts of an organisation – but rather, for the sake of clarity, we delineate our discussion to the practice of sustainability reporting prepared by business organisations.

**PAUSE AND REFLECT...**

Are you familiar with the practice of sustainability reporting?

We suggest before you proceed further with this chapter that you take a few minutes to look at an example of the practice (if you are not able to now, make a note of it and do so when you can). As we have identified, most large corporations now produce such reports, so many examples can be found via a quick online search. You can search for one of your favourite companies, or perhaps a company that produces the clothes you are wearing or the smartphone you are using, or perhaps the company that provides your accommodation with utilities or who you rely on to move around (transportation firm or petrol provider).

There is no need to look in detail at this stage but take a look at a sustainability report taking in the structure of the report, what topics they talk about and any initial impressions.

Do also consider if the organisation is following a framework or standard in its reporting. You might find it useful to compare two reports to see any differences, perhaps from two different geographic contexts. We suggest you look at this same report after you have read this and the next chapter – it will be useful to provide context and help understand much of the content that now follows.

## 5.2 A history of sustainability reporting

Corporate sustainability reporting is today a widespread practice. The forms and practices of sustainability reporting have developed swiftly over the past decades, and current forms of reporting are very different from the reports published in the early stages of their emergence. We will next provide a brief overview of how the practices have evolved over time, as awareness of the history helps position the contemporary practices, standards and debates into a broader context and acknowledge how current initiatives have not been set on a whim, but are instead a result of long-term developments and conversations.

### 5.2.1 Early pioneering examples

While the more rapid uptake of organisational social and environmental reporting began in the 1990s, some organisations have provided information beyond the usual financial disclosures for much longer. Historical work has shown that some companies published social information in the early 20th century, focusing mainly on employee issues, housing projects, as well as other social initiatives (Guthrie and Parker, 1989). Subsequently, during the 1970s, there was a more substantial increase in the number of companies reporting on social issues. In the United States, for instance, corporate annual reports at this time included disclosures on topics such as human resources, community involvement and fair business practices (Buhr et al., 2014; Ernst and Ernst, 1976). Similar themes were visible also in Europe. In the UK, companies were publishing value-added statements, which highlighted the additional value that organisational activities contributed to the society, making clear that corporations were not only producing value to investors but also to and by various other groups in society (see Burchell et al., 1985). The interest in social disclosures fell in the late 1970s and early 1980s, perhaps due to the broader political trends prevailing in Anglo-American societies at the time.

### 5.2.2 Environmental reporting and reporting initiatives

Environmental issues began to gain more prominence in societies and international discussions towards the end of the 1980s through a series of international events, such as the disasters of the nuclear explosion at Chernobyl (1986) and the Exxon Valdez oil spill in Alaska (1989) as well as international agreements like the Montreal Protocol (1987) and the Brundtland Report (1987) (see Chapter 2). Alongside these broader developments, pioneering companies began to publish environmental information in the annual reports or as separate standalone publications. The early reporters tended to be companies from the more environmentally sensitive and impactful industries, such as oil and gas, mining, pulp and paper and chemicals, or alternatively companies like Body Shop, which wanted to showcase the environmental and social values their operations were built on.

These early reports were published on a voluntary basis, as there was no regulation nor any standards in place at the time. Still, there were various initiatives through which environmental reporting was being promoted, including the Reporting Awards Schemes run by the Association of Chartered Certified Accountants (ACCA), which started in the UK in 1991. Likewise, the Environmental Management and Audit Scheme (EMAS) developed in 1993 with its requirement regarding environmental statements was an influential driver for environmental disclosures, particularly in German-speaking countries in Europe (Larrinaga and Bebbington, 2021). Towards the end of the 1990s, around one-third of the largest 250 companies in the world were publishing voluntary disclosures (KPMG, 2020).

### 5.2.3 The Global Reporting Initiative and the broadening of reporting

An important milestone for sustainability reporting took place in 2000 when the first edition of the Global Reporting Initiative (GRI) guidelines was released. The GRI has since become established as arguably the most influential set of sustainability reporting guidelines. Corporate disclosures were already at the time expanding from environmental reports to broader reports including social, environmental and economic issues, and the publication of the GRI guidelines incorporating these three dimensions further strengthened this development. The first version of the GRI published in 2000 was a rather fledgling attempt to establish a framework for corporate disclosures, and there continued to be a broad variety in the reports with regard to which issues were being reported on and how they were covered. As is still often the case, the reports were published under a variety of names, such as triple bottom line reports, corporate citizenship reports, CSR reports and sustainability reports, with a common denominator being the expansion of the breadth of topics discussed. Since its inception, the GRI has developed through several iterations and, despite many more frameworks and standards setters entering the area, continues to be influential and widely used across the world (KPMG, 2024). It is for this reason that we return to discuss the GRI further below.

### 5.2.4 Reporting becomes mainstream

In the 2000s, sustainability reporting swiftly became an everyday practice for most large corporations. Reporting had expanded to all sectors, as a vast majority of the biggest companies in many industrial countries disclosed sustainability information in reports. In the 2010s, reporting also became standard practice in Asia as well as in some major economies in Latin America and Africa. On a national basis, the bulk of major companies in many countries produced sustainability reports (see KPMG, 2020). It is evident, however, that for business organisations, there was a size threshold for the disclosures, since reporting was not as common outside of the large corporations. Despite the scholarly interest and public eye often being set on the major multinationals, as we have noted, there was a wide range of other types of organisations, such as universities, utilities and other public sector organisations, NGOs, as well as cities and regions, publishing sustainability reports on an annual or biennial basis.

### 5.2.5 The maturing of reporting

Over time, the amount of content and breadth of topics covered by sustainability reports varied. Starting in the 1990s and continuing until around the mid-2000s, there was a fairly constant trend during which the reports of most organisations expanded. More aspects were being covered, different perspectives were taken into account, and additional details were included. As a result, the standalone reports of major corporations were rather lengthy, easily surpassing 200 pages on many occasions. This began to change around the year 2010, as organisations together with their stakeholders started to be more critical with regard to reporting practices. Questions were being asked as to whether the key issues were being covered, even buried underneath an overwhelming amount of data, whether anyone was interested in all those details, and also whether the extensive reports were worth the resources and costs needed to put them together. Subsequently, materiality emerged as a key principle of sustainability reporting, replacing the earlier emphasis on transparency, a change reflected in the GRI Guidelines (i.e. GRI 3.1 to GRI 4) and other reporting frameworks.

During the 2010s, the landscape evolved also through the emergence of other reporting initiatives alongside the already well-established GRI. These would include the International Integrated Reporting Council (IIRC), which was founded in 2010 and subsequently launched the <IR> framework on integrated reporting in 2013, as well as the Sustainable Accounting Standards Board (SASB), which was established in 2011. While it took until 2018 for the SASB reporting standards to be published, the emergence of both IIRC and SASB indicated how capital market actors began at this point to acknowledge and have more interest in the potential relevance of non-financial information.

### 5.2.6 The continued development of reporting

More recent times have seen a new era of activity in the field of sustainability reporting. Two key features are particularly notable here. First, there is an increase in regulation and disclosure requirements. The EU's regulatory package, including the Corporate Sustainability Reporting Directive (CSRD), Sustainable Finance Disclosure Regulation (SFDR) and EU taxonomy is probably the most notable of these, but sustainability reporting or elements thereof is being increasingly mandated in other countries and regions. The emergence of the International Sustainability Standards Board (ISSB) and the IFRS Sustainability Disclosure Standards it is developing is perhaps the main example here. Second, in this most recent period, we have seen a considerable increase in the interest of investors, capital providers and other financial market actors in sustainability information. This is a development which has had a substantial influence on how reporting is being discussed in different forums. This has also led to the distinction between "inside-out" and "outside-in" perspectives on reporting, with the first referring to focusing on the impacts and implications organisational activities have on various sustainability aspects, while the latter being concerned with the potential impacts the various sustainability aspects have on the organisation and its future outlook. This distinction is significant, and you will note in the discussion below that there are in this question important differences between the various reporting frameworks.

Overall, the field of sustainability reporting is undergoing substantial changes, with the general interest being at a high level and an increasing number of parties expressing views on, and taking an active role in, the development of the field. In the early 2020s, the landscape has commonly been referred to with terms such as "alphabet soup", "tectonic shift" and "regulatory tsunami", describing the swift, substantial and sometimes confusing nature of changes in the field. This is perhaps most evident in the emergence, and in some cases demise (see O'Dwyer et al., 2024), of sustainability reporting guidance, frameworks, emerging standards and regulations. While many of these initiatives (discussed further below) were motivated by a stated desire to, amongst other things, improve comparability, this has not yet necessarily had a substantial impact on the practice and is hence still to become evident for the users of these reports. Differences in approaches, emphasis and perspectives, also on the fundamental level as it comes to the role of reporting in society in general, means that variability still exists. Flexibility within the frameworks and standards also means diversity is likely to continue even amongst organisations following the same reporting guidelines and frameworks. This most recent period in the history of sustainability reporting is no doubt an important one where we see fast moving developments and influences on the practice.

## 5.3 Characteristics of sustainability reporting

We have already noted that sustainability reporting practices are not uniform as organisations have flexibility in terms of how they want to engage with the practice, including how they report in line with various standards and frameworks. There are also major differences when it comes to reporting practices in different regional contexts, stemming for instance from historical developments, the features of different societies, as well as regulations and other guidance in place. For example, in Australia, where water is scarce in many regions, reporting and performance indicators concerning water use and policies are required and have been in place for some time.

It should be highlighted that despite calls for uniformity, such variance in reporting practices is not necessarily a negative thing. We should bear in mind that among the various roles sustainability reporting has, it also serves as an accountability mechanism from the organisation to its stakeholders. Given that organisations (including their contexts) and stakeholder groups are different and have different priorities, expectations, needs and aspirations, the reports are bound to be different. As such, striving for uniformity might not be beneficial. At the same time, there are certain characteristics that are generally accepted that an organisation should follow in producing a sustainability report, no matter where and in what form this takes place.

Three concepts are particularly useful when considering reporting: accountability, materiality and reporting boundary. While all of these have been touched upon in the earlier chapters, a brief recap in relation to sustainability reporting is in order here. In addition to being useful to consider important aspects of the practice, there are also areas where the standards take different approaches and therefore are relevant when we consider the various approaches of regulators and standard setters.

While Table 5.1 represents these concepts separately, choices made relating to accountability, materiality and boundary are closely related. For example, how far an

**TABLE 5.1** Key Concepts and Their Relevance to Sustainability Reporting

| Concept | Description | Relevance for Sustainability Reporting |
|---|---|---|
| Accountability | Accountability relates to the duty to provide an account of the actions over which one is considered to have responsibility. | Sustainability reporting is a mechanism through which an organisation can discharge accountability duties to its stakeholders. Key considerations here to whom and for what the reporting organisation is accountable. |
| Materiality | Materiality relates to those issues or elements considered important. Materiality defines what is included and what is excluded from a report. | An organisation and its various stakeholders can have different views on materiality and as such, from whose perspective materiality is considered when it comes to reporting can influence what is reported and how it is reported. |
| Boundaries | Reporting boundaries relates to the scope of the report. Boundaries help define the scope of the report – and therefore also which issues are included. | While financial reporting boundaries are set based on ownership and control, in the context of sustainability the reporting boundary is much more fluid. Just like in life-cycle assessment (Chapter 4), in the context of sustainability reporting an organisation needs to consider how far upstream and downstream in its supply and value chain it will include in the report. |

organisation's responsibility is considered to reach (reporting boundaries), and which aspects are perceived to be material for the organisation and its stakeholders are not unrelated choices. We will discuss these choices in more detail from an organisational point of view in the next chapter. From a broader perspective, however, these concepts help us identify some key characteristics, which can be seen as building blocks of good sustainability reporting. While there is likely to be variance in the reporting practices, as each organisation is different when it comes to its activities, its operating context and key stakeholders, as well as the potential reporting guidance, frameworks and regulations it chooses or needs to follow, the characteristics in Table 5.2 can be seen to apply in general across all organisations.

It is evident that some of the characteristics presented above are not only ideal types but also likely to be contested in practice. Individuals and institutions who seek to influence practice have different views as to, for instance, what is required for information to be reliable and accurate, whether something is expressed clearly enough and what balanced reporting actually means. This does not mean, however, that organisations could not strive to reach these characteristics in their reporting, or that those using the reports could not expect organisations' disclosures to follow them, and hence use the characteristics as a basis against which the reports are evaluated.

## 5.4 Sustainability reporting standards and frameworks

We have already mentioned reporting frameworks and standards which are playing a key role in defining sustainability reporting and influencing practices. We therefore discuss these in more detail here. One thing we do need to keep in mind, however, is that these are fast-developing and in a state of flux. This state of flux includes who the key institutions will be, and what their standards and frameworks will eventually

**TABLE 5.2** Characteristics of Sustainability Reporting

| Concept | Description | Points to Consider |
|---|---|---|
| Accuracy | Information in a report should be sufficiently accurate and detailed to allow readers to assess an organisation's performance. | Organisations are at times vague when presenting negative information. Are graphs and tables structured properly, or have they been skewed or distorted? |
| Balance | A report should include both positive and negative aspects so that users can assess the overall performance of the organisation. | Organisations often emphasise positive information. Frameworks and assurance practices hope to help in getting more balanced reports. |
| Clarity | Information in a report should be presented in a clear, understandable and accessible form. | User groups vary in their knowledge and ability to understand information. What is complex to some can be self-evident and simplistic to others. |
| Comparability | Information should be selected, compiled and reported consistently. It should allow analysis of changes both over time and in relation to other organisations where possible. | Reporting frameworks can help by providing standard practices. Does the organisation provide information from previous years to allow reader to see trends and developments easily? |
| Reliability | Reported information should be derived from reliable processes, which could also be subject to independent evaluation. | Implies that in addition to the reported information, it is also relevant to discuss how the information has been collected and compiled. |
| Stakeholder inclusiveness | An organisation should identify and engage stakeholders, and discuss how it has responded to their expectations and interests. | Stakeholder groups can have very different expectations. Different forms of reporting have different audiences, who can have varying expectations. |
| Timeliness | Reports should be published on a regular schedule and in a timely manner so that it allows the report users to make informed decisions. | Web-based reporting can often be more timely, but an annual and regular reporting cycle can have other advantages. Timeliness is not just about speed, but also regularity. |

Source: Adapted from Tregidga and Laine (2021).

look like. Likewise, while mandatory reporting requirements have emerged in various countries and regions, we still have only limited experience on how these are being and will be, applied in practice, and hence their eventual impact remains to be seen. Other factors such as expectations set by industrial bodies and stock exchanges will also ultimately play a role. Overall, while there have been early signals from practice of the general direction we are heading, the specificities of reporting and regulatory landscape remain uncertain.

There is no doubt that one of the big drivers to the development of sustainability reporting and key to its institutionalisation has been the myriad of guidance standards and frameworks for this form of reporting. The influence of these has become increasingly evident in the early 2020s. As the significance of sustainability information has risen, and reporting has become a standard practice for many corporations, there has also been growing interest in standardising the practice. Standards and frameworks are often advertised as an opportunity to get more reliability, consistency and comparability into the voluntary disclosures, but also with the claim to enhance the materiality of the disclosures. This implies that the standards and frameworks help organisations focus on the more important and relevant matters while leaving the less important issues with limited or no attention. Obviously, those that produce these standards and frameworks, including large corporations which have influenced them, all have their own interests, and hence the standards and the choices made therein always imply some political choices regarding how reporting has developed. This influence ultimately affects organisational accountability achieved through such reporting, including which stakeholders are considered most important (or even important at all), as well as how broadly an organisation's duty to provide an account ranges across diverse issues.

Guidance standards and frameworks are emerging globally and they focus on various levels. For example, while we concentrate our discussion on what could arguably be considered three key ones next (i.e. GRI, ISSB and CSRD), we also discuss some of the smaller scale and/or regional efforts. In the remainder of this section, we outline these guidance standards and frameworks. As it is not possible to cover all possible standards and frameworks, we have chosen to discuss those that represent the most well-known global guidelines at the time of writing that will enable us to consider a variety of practices.

### 5.4.1 The Global Reporting Initiative

The GRI has been the household name for sustainability reporting guidelines for many years. You will probably have noted that we have already mentioned it in places throughout this text. According to the widely cited KPMG surveys which usefully have traced the development of sustainability/CSR reporting since 1993, most of the world's largest companies make use of GRI in their sustainability reporting. Notably, the influence of the GRI is international, with the same survey noting that around 70% of the top 100 companies of the surveyed countries and around three-quarters of the world's largest 250 companies use the GRI guidelines (KPMG, 2024).

Founded in 1997, the GRI published their first reporting framework in 2000. The GRI was initially established, and the framework produced, with the expressed purpose of increasing the prevalence of reporting. Over time, the GRI reporting framework has developed into its current form and continues to evolve. Their aim and focus have also broadened in line with the reporting context. While the GRI started out as a broad multi-stakeholder initiative and continues to emphasise multi-stakeholder process in its work, it has nonetheless been at times criticised for having moved increasingly towards a corporate-led and investor-focused initiative. More recently, the advent of ISSB and other initiatives geared primarily towards the financial markets (see below) has however again strengthened GRI's position as the reporting standard perceived to be more inclusive and having a broader stakeholder orientation. GRI describes itself as focusing on the reporting of impacts of organisational activities, taking in other words an inside-out perspective on sustainability reporting.

**TABLE 5.3** The GRI, ISSB and CSRD Sustainability Reporting Frameworks

| | Global Reporting Initiative (GRI) | International Sustainability Standards Board (ISSB) | The Corporate Sustainability Reporting Directive (CSRD) |
|---|---|---|---|
| Standards | GRI Standards | International Financial Reporting Standards (IFRS) Sustainability Disclosure Standards | European Sustainability Reporting Standards (ESRS) |
| Date released | 2000 | 2023 | 2023 |
| Structure of standards | Universal standards (apply all); sector standards (use those for your sector); and topic standards (report on those that are material) | General requirements (IFRS S1); climate related disclosures (IFRS S2) | General requirements (ESRS1); general disclosures (ESRS2); environmental (ESRS E1–E5); social (S1–S4); governance (G1) |
| Main users for the report | Stakeholders at large | Financial markets, investors | Stakeholders at large, financial markets |
| Approach to materiality | Impact materiality (double materiality) | Financial materiality | Double materiality (financial and impact) |

The GRI reporting framework is essentially the publication of a set of social, environmental and economic indicators for which organisations can report. For each indicator, there are supporting guidelines regarding their assessment and measurement, as well as how they should be reported upon. The underlying idea of the GRI approach has been to enhance the quality of sustainability disclosures by standardising the way different organisations report, thereby making the information more consistent and comparable both over time as well as across organisations.

The provision of guidelines for sustainability reporting is regarded as helping organisations engage with reporting, and also aiding them to focus on the more relevant questions. A key role here is played by materiality analysis, which has been a core feature of the GRI guidelines since the G4 version published in 2013. With materiality considerations at the centre of the GRI reporting process, organisations need to evaluate and focus on the most essential sustainability matters. Within the GRI, these are evaluated not only from the perspective of the organisation's activities but also from the viewpoint of stakeholders. This approach is envisioned to help organisations and their stakeholders focus on the most significant issues, and thereby also spur further action towards them. As materiality and materiality determination processes are key aspects of the process of reporting, we build on this discussion in the following chapter.

## 5.4.2 International Sustainability Standards Board

The sustainability reporting landscape entered arguably a new era when the IFRS Foundation announced the establishment of the ISSB in late 2021 at the UN COP26 climate negotiations in Glasgow. Given that the IFRS Foundation is the dominant standard-setter for financial reporting with the IFRS Accounting Standards developed by the International Accounting Standards Board (IASB), it was quite evident from the get-go that this decision by the IFRS Foundation to formally enter the sustainability reporting field was going to have substantial ramifications on the landscape internationally. The announcement was preceded by a period of consultation and active lobbying, during which it became clear that there was a need and growing interest amongst investors and the financial markets more broadly for the IFRS to engage with sustainability reporting. Likewise, the ISSB was founded on work conducted over the preceding years by other initiatives, such as the Task Force on Climate-Related Financial Disclosures (TCFD), Climate Disclosure Standards Board (CDSB), Sustainability Accounting Standards Board (SASB) and International Integrated Reporting Council (IIRC). Some of these continue to function or otherwise remain relevant, and we will discuss them in more detail below.

The IFRS Sustainability Disclosure Standards are explicitly geared towards the needs of investors and the financial markets. The rationale here is that as different aspects of sustainability have become increasingly relevant factors for contemporary investors and investment decisions, they believe there is a growing need to develop reporting standards, which would help companies to produce high-quality, consistent and comparable information on sustainability-related risks and opportunities. In other words, it was perceived that the information already available at the time would not respond to the needs and fulfil the expectations of market participants. As a result, the ISSB has set out to develop standards, which would result in a "high-quality, comprehensive global baseline of sustainability disclosures focused on the needs of investors and the financial markets" (IFRS, 2024a). Essentially, while the GRI above takes an inside-out perspective, the orientation of the ISSB is based on the outside-in perspective and has at its core the potential financial implications sustainability and sustainability-related risks and opportunities might have for the organisation.

In organisational terms, the ISSB is "an independent standard-setting body within the IFRS Foundation" (IFRS, 2024b), sitting alongside and in co-operation with the IASB. Close collaboration is considered important, since the growing relevance of sustainability implies that the traditional accounting information and sustainability information are perceived to complement each other in meeting investor requirements for comprehensive information. Therefore, in developing the sustainability disclosure standards, the ISSB seeks to ensure that they are consistent with the IFRS Accounting Standards as it comes to for instance definitions and various expectations. This shows in the ISSB's approach to materiality, as the firms are expected to "disclose material information about the sustainability-related risks and opportunities that could reasonably be expected to affect its prospects", where "material information" is defined similarly to the IFRS Accounting Standards: "information is material if omitting, obscuring or misstating it could be reasonably expected to influence investor decisions" (IFRS, 2024c).

The ISSB published its first sustainability disclosure standards, the IFRS S1 and S2, in June 2023. Of these, IFRS S1 focuses on sustainability-related risks and opportunities that firms are expected to face over different time horizons. The standard requires "an entity to disclose information about all sustainability-related risks and opportunities that could reasonably be expected to affect the entity's cash flows, its access to finance or cost of capital over the short, medium or long term" (IFRS, 2024d). As you will note, this is remarkably different from the aims of the GRI standards, and places a specific stakeholder group, the investors, at the heart of the reporting. The IFRS S2 then is dedicated to climate. IFRS S2 sets out specific climate-related disclosure requirements. The goal and approach of S2 are similar to that of S1, with the focus being on climate-related risks and opportunities. Going forward, the ISSB seeks to publish further dedicated disclosure standards to supplement the IFRS S1 and S2, with the first research projects in 2025 focusing on Human Capital and Biodiversity, Ecosystems and Ecosystem Services, implying that these were identified as potential future areas for disclosure requirements.

Given their recent emergence, it remains unclear how the IFRS Sustainability Disclosure Standards are going to be applied and how the reporting practices will evolve. There has been substantial interest however, and towards the end of 2024, the ISSB reported that 30 jurisdictions had already decided to use or were proceeding to introduce the IFRS Sustainability Disclosure Standards in their regulatory frameworks. It is therefore likely that the IFRS Sustainability Disclosure Standards are going to have an impact on sustainability reporting practices globally.

From a critical perspective, it is essential to acknowledge that ISSB's approach to reporting and the use of materiality is much narrower than that of GRI and clearly strategic in focus. As such it does not necessarily take into account those issues which may have the most significant social and/or environmental impacts for a diverse range of stakeholders or for the broader society. At the same time, it needs to be said that this is not what the framework seeks to achieve.

As we already mentioned above, in addition to the IFRS S1 and S2 standards, there are other reporting frameworks and initiatives under the auspices of the ISSB which remain relevant as they either have been influential or continue to be applied in practice for specific purposes. We will introduce three of these below – SASB, TCFD and Integrated Reporting. It is worth pointing out again however that as was the case with the reporting landscape more broadly, also the development and status of these specific frameworks continue to evolve, and hence it is worth keeping an eye on the most recent developments.

#### 5.4.2.1 Sustainability Accounting Standards Board

SASB was established as an independent US-based organisation in 2011. SASB started out with the aim to create sustainability reporting standards that would help organisations produce material information to investors in a cost-effective way. After publishing the first version of the SASB Standards in late 2018, SASB was involved in the consolidation processes in the sustainability reporting landscape. First, SASB merged with the IIRC in 2021 to form the Value Reporting Foundation. This was soon thereafter consolidated into the IFRS Foundation. Since 2022, SASB has operated as part of the IFRS foundation, with the ISSB having assumed responsibility for the maintenance and development of the SASB Standards.

After SASB became a part of the ISSB, there was an initial period of uncertainty about the future of the SASB Standards. However, the SASB Standards have become one element in the IFRS Foundation's sustainability reporting infrastructure and hence continue to exist and remain in use. The more specific guidelines included in the SASB Standards provide firms a reference point that assists them in applying the more general level IFRS S1 disclosure standard. Moreover, the IFRS Foundation also notes that the industry-specific materiality assessments of the SASB Standards can be made use of as firms seek to identify material information about sustainability-related risks and opportunities and subsequently develop their disclosures on this basis, should there be no specific IFRS Sustainability Reporting Standard available.

As noted, the SASB Standards were originally published in late 2018 after a prolonged draft and consultation stage. At the time SASB was still an independent organisation, and in the public view, there were no strong signals on the potential interest of IFRS. The response to the publication of the SASB Standards showed that there was clearly demand for such an investor-focused approach, as the standards gained notable traction immediately upon publication, especially in the US market. The popularity has continued to increase thereafter, as KPMG (2024) reports that over 70% of the top 100 companies surveyed in countries such as Brazil, Canada, the United States and Taiwan as well as over half of the world's largest 250 companies follow the SASB standards. Alongside the figures provided on GRI above, this illustrates that firms often consider multiple frameworks in their sustainability reporting.

Despite firms potentially applying the two frameworks to an extent side-by-side, it is worth underscoring that SASB has some key differences to GRI. For example, SASB has a focus on accountability to investors, rather than the GRI's broader multi-stakeholder accountability orientation. A further distinction is that whereas the GRI emphasises how each organisation should consider which issues are material for the organisation and its stakeholders, the SASB guidelines aim at simplifying the process, and define material aspects on the level of the industry, with the focus being on the financially material sustainability information. Thereby, the goal is explicit in serving the corporations so that they can easily and cost-effectively identify and manage a well-defined set of key sustainability performance indicators. Investors are also considered by providing them with comparable and concise information to aid decision-making.

#### 5.4.2.2 Task Force on Climate-Related Financial Disclosures

You may have noticed the acronym TCFD shows up quite frequently for instance in corporate reports and reporting guidance. TCFD refers to the Task Force on Climate-Related Financial Disclosures, which was an initiative launched in 2015. While the TCFD has since been disbanded in 2023 after it was considered to have fulfilled its remit, it is worthwhile to know some key details about the initiative, not only because the disclosure recommendations put forth by TCFD remain relevant and form the basis on which the IFRS Sustainability Disclosure Standards further build on, but also due to the significant role the TCFD arguably played as a catalyst in initiating the tectonic shifts that have been occurring in the sustainability reporting landscape (O'Dwyer and Unerman, 2020).

The TCFD was established and governed by the Financial Stability Board (FSB), with considerable influence deriving originally from the G20 Finance Ministers and Central Bank Governors. In essence, the initiative was established to develop recommendations for more effective climate-related disclosures that could "promote more informed investment, credit, and insurance underwriting decisions", and subsequently "would enable stakeholders to understand better the concentrations of carbon-related assets in the financial sector and the financial system's exposures to climate-related risks" (TCFD, 2021). The underlying logic related to the quality of data and power of the markets: once there is better data in an accessible format, the markets and market actors will be more equipped to assess, price and manage climate-related issues, opportunities and risks appropriately. This then, the logic followed, would create incentives for organisations and individuals to innovate and develop their activities, since carbon risks and exposure would get properly included in the financial information, decision-making and investment appraisals. TCFD sought to achieve its aims by producing guidelines on how organisations could produce climate-related financial disclosures. Moreover, TCFD also emphasised the application of scenario analysis, which would help organisations to identify, assess and disclose potential risks and opportunities related to climate change. The guidelines put forth by the TCFD have now been incorporated into the IFRS S2 Climate-related Disclosures standard.

The quick emergence and rapidly growing significance of TCFD in the late 2010s signalled how there was a substantial need for climate-related information in the financial markets and highlighted that the information that had been previously available had not been sufficient or of sufficient quality for investors. This provided strong impetus for IFRS Foundation as it was considering its own role in the sustainability reporting landscape. It is however also worth acknowledging that the investor focus TCFD strongly advocated for has meant particular viewpoints being emphasised in its recommendations, implying that the concerns of financial markets and investors have received substantially more attention than those presented by vulnerable communities or critical NGOs. Depending on the perspective one has, this can be seen as a positive or negative thing. In any case, it is clear that the TCFD initiative had a major effect on organisational understandings as to climate and risk exposure due to climate, which has potential implications on the type of information organisations produce and make use of in their decision-making (see also O'Dwyer and Unerman, 2020). It has also played a role in providing information that might steer the markets towards sustainability. The success of the TCFD has also encouraged subsequent initiatives building on its footsteps, including the Taskforce on Nature-related Financial Disclosures (TNFD), established in 2021, and Taskforce on Inequality and Social-related Financial Disclosures (TISFD), established in 2024. We will return to these in Chapters 11 and 12.

#### 5.4.2.3 Integrated Reporting and Integrated Thinking

As our discussion indicates, as sustainability became increasingly commonplace, and as perspectives on the best way to advance such reporting varied, initiatives were developed and sought to gain traction. One of these was Integrated Reporting as defined and promoted by the IIRC. The IIRC was formed in 2010 and received substantial attention as it was readily backed by a range of major corporations and accountancy organisations. While the IIRC has now been disbanded after what has been described as an "institutional demise" following a notable presence in the reporting landscape (O'Dwyer et al., 2024), the Integrated Reporting Framework and Integrated Thinking Principles continue to be maintained jointly by the IASB and ISSB under the auspices of the IFRS Foundation.

Like SASB and TCFD above, the IIRC also had an explicit focus on the investor. However, the key idea the IIRC developed related to having organisations produce a single integrated report, which would speak of the organisation's ability to create value in the short, medium and long term (IIRC, 2021). For this purpose, the report would have provided both managers and investors information on how the organisation's value creation process operates within a particular external environment and interacts with six forms of capital to create value. These forms of capital were financial, manufactured, intellectual, human, social and relationship, and natural. While integrated reporting has not been presented to be about any of those capitals in particular it has, together with the promotion of integrated thinking, nonetheless been coveted as a mechanism through which organisations can better address and manage various social, environmental and governance challenges in contemporary societies. Despite often being considered vague and unclear, the ideas of Integrated Reporting and Integrated Thinking received considerable attention and influenced reporting practices in organisations. Moreover, it is interesting to note that producing an integrated report became mandatory in South Africa, and the Integrated Reporting Framework hosted by the ISSB is endorsed as an example of good practice for developing such a report.

### 5.4.3 Corporate Sustainability Reporting Directive

The EU has arguably emerged as the trailblazer of sustainability reporting regulation. While its first widely discussed regulatory initiative, the Non-Financial Reporting Directive, adopted by the EU in 2014 and subsequently introduced in the member states' national legislations, can in hindsight be described as a relatively modest attempt to regulate the practice, the more recent regulation introduced as part of the EU Green Deal is substantially more ambitious and potentially far-reaching. A core element of this regulation is the Corporate Sustainability Reporting Directive (CSRD), with the Sustainable Finance Disclosure Regulation (SFDR) and the EU Taxonomy discussed in Chapter 7 serving as other key elements of the regulatory package in the EU. The CSRD has the potential to have broad and visible impacts on the reporting practices not only in Europe but also in other contexts.

After the directive was being transposed into national regulation across the EU, the first companies were set to report according to the requirements in 2025, with additional organisations falling under the scope during the following several years. The directive is set to be broad-based and hence the requirements will affect a range of companies from large multinationals to relatively small and medium-sized non-listed entities, many of which have not had any prior experience with sustainability reporting. Firms operating EU subsidiaries meeting specific criteria are also expected to comply with the regulatory demands, hence its anticipated ramification beyond the EU. Overall, it was originally estimated that some 50,000 firms would have had to comply with CSRD once all the requirements were in place. The eventual number might be significantly smaller however after the so-called omnibus proposal European Commission adopted in February 2025. Seeking to simplify EU rules in the name of competitiveness and more favourable business environment, the Commission for instance proposed raising the employee and turnover thresholds of the CSRD, which would reduce the number of firms within the scope of the directive by some 80%. Despite the proposed changes, the mandatory requirements would nonetheless continue to affect many organisations.

A core feature of the CSRD is the double materiality principle, which implies that reporting organisations should consider both inside-out and outside-in perspectives in their reporting. In other words, similar to GRI, firms should consider the impacts their activities have on various sustainability aspects, while also, akin to ISSB, provide disclosures on how the different sustainability matters might have an effect on their financial performance and business. The disclosure requirements are then set out in the European Sustainability Reporting Standards (ESRS, yet another acronym), which provide detailed and comprehensive guidelines on how the reporting should be conducted. There are 12 ESRS Standards in total, spanning environmental, social and governance topics, and including a substantial number of data points that the organisations are expected to provide information on, subject to the double materiality assessment mentioned above. In addition, in seeking to combat greenwashing and improve the reliability of the reported information, there is a mandatory assurance requirement in the CSRD for all the sustainability information organisations are reporting. Overall, the requirements included in the CSRD are extensive and have the potential to implicate major shifts in how sustainability reporting is going to be executed within the EU and beyond. However, similar to the IFRS Sustainability Disclosure Standards, it still remains to be seen how the eventual implementation and practical feasibility of the regulatory package unfolds.

### 5.4.4 Other notable frameworks

Another few sustainability reporting guidelines warrant consideration here. In particular those that have found prominence in particular geographical areas, relate to a single sustainability issue, or are emerging as significant developments.

#### 5.4.4.1 The CDP

CDP is an investor-led initiative, originally founded under the name Carbon Disclosure Project, seeking to gather comparable information about corporate actions related to climate change. The CDP runs a large dataset, which has been collected through annual surveys of large corporations and other large organisations. The first Carbon Disclosure Project's survey was launched in the year 2000 and focused on collecting climate-related information from corporations at a time when organisations seldom included such information in their sustainability reports. Since then, CDP has expanded its scope, and it now hosts a large database of corporate information around climate, water, forests and supply chains, hence the name change.

#### 5.4.4.2 SDGs and sustainability reporting

The influence of the SDGs introduced in Chapter 2 is also being felt in the corporate reporting space, with many organisations referring to the goals in their sustainability reporting to discuss action plans, aims and achievements (see KPMG, 2024). While the SDGs are clearly not a reporting framework per se, nor were they explicitly designed to be implemented at the organisational level, their overall structure with the defined goals and targets appears to have been attractive to many organisations as a way to organise and report on. Perhaps partly due to the substantial traction, the

SDGs gained swiftly after they were launched in 2018, the GRI and UN Global Compact led an initiative to produce a series of guidance documents for organisations concerning how the SDGs could be integrated into organisational reporting. Given the prominence of the SDGs together with their visual appeal, we would expect their influence on corporate reporting to continue for some time. It is a different question, however, what kind of implications reporting on SDGs, or through SDGs, might have on organisational stakeholders, accountability relations, or societies more broadly. The KPMG (2024) survey would seem to suggest there is much scope for improvement, pointing out how organisations are seldom taking a balanced approach to reporting both negative and positive impacts when it comes to the SDGs, and even going on to note how "this suggest that many companies are using SDG-based targets primarily for marketing purposes rather to guide corporate strategy" (p. 62). In all, while the SDGs are likely to remain quite visible and persist as reference points for many private and public-sector organisations, they have not become a default mode for sustainability reporting, nor should they be seen as one of the main players in this field.

### 5.4.5 National and regional mandatory reporting requirements

As we have noted, sustainability reporting emerged as a voluntary practice, which evolved over time as organisations experimented with ideas, benchmarked and imitated others, responded to stakeholder needs and followed guidance and frameworks presented by different institutions. Alongside this development, mandatory legislation began to emerge in different forms. We have discussed the EU context as well as mentioned how Australia, due to the national context, has some reporting requirements surrounding water, for example. France is another notable example as it has had some mandatory disclosure requirements for some corporations relating to employees (known as "le bilan social") for some time. These are not the only examples and many countries have national and/or regional requirements and drivers influencing reporting behaviour. As sustainability reporting practices have become increasingly commonplace, there have been an increasing number of regulatory initiatives and instruments set mainly by governments. The nature of change is illustrated by the title of KPMG's influential survey in 2024: "The move to mandatory reporting" (KPMG, 2024).

An interesting example is the development of sustainability reporting in the United States. The development of reporting regulations in the US has been different to many other regions in the world, in particularly when compared to Europe. While there were some early examples, sustainability reporting in general emerged later and picked up at a slower pace. Moreover, the interest was primarily on the potential financial relevance of sustainability, while reporting on the various sustainability impacts organisational activities received less attention. This showed also how GRI never achieved similar popularity in the United States as it did elsewhere. The swift uptake of the SASB standards in the late 2010s illustrated, however, that there was also an appetite in the US market for standardised sustainability disclosures, provided they were geared towards the interests of the financial markets.

In the early 2020s, the Securities and Exchange Council (SEC) engaged in work to develop some mandatory reporting requirements for firms. After a series of public consultations, exposure drafts and comment periods, in early 2024, SEC eventually published reporting requirements, which would make specific climate-related disclosures mandatory for a substantial number of firms in the US market. The underlying logic of the regulation is the pursuit of comparable and standardised information, which would fulfil the needs of investors as they consider the risks and opportunities arising from climate change going forward. Such requirements can be perceived to be a potentially major step in the US capital markets, within which sustainability disclosures had previously received limited attention. Throughout the legislative process, however, SEC's authority to require disclosures beyond the traditional financial matters has been contested, and given the major political divides and strong sentiments on sustainability in the United States, the eventual implementation and fate of the SEC climate-rule remains unclear. It does nonetheless provide an indication of the direction of travel, with many in the capital markets perceiving reliable climate-related disclosures as important when making assessments of firm risks, opportunities and future prospects.

In addition to the national level, there are in the United States also state-specific regulatory demands that are relevant to consider. The most notable would be California which has set regulatory demands for different aspects of sustainability. They were among the first to set reporting requirements concerning supply chains with the California Transparency in Supply Chains Act (CTSCA), which focuses on tackling modern slavery and human trafficking by requiring retailers and manufacturers operating in California to provide disclosures on their supply chain practices. More recently, California has set up legislation known as the Climate Accountability Package, which requires public and private US companies operating in California to prepare disclosures on various climate-related matters from the year 2026 onwards. In addition to expecting firms to report on climate-related financial risks in accordance with the TCFD framework, the key requirement is that firms are expected to annually report on their carbon emissions, covering scopes 1, 2 and 3 in line with the GHG Protocol (see Chapter 9). Further, these disclosures should also be assured, with the expectation of moving from limited assurance to a more demanding reasonable level in the future. While there are size thresholds and hence not all businesses are impacted by the regulation, these requirements affect a sizable number of firms in California and beyond, and the package has caused considerable stir in the US market. Other states have also followed California's lead and worked on introducing similar or other sustainability reporting requirements in their state laws. This again highlights the swift evolution sustainability reporting is currently going through.

More generally the number of regulatory instruments concerning corporate sustainability disclosures has expanded swiftly around the globe, a development described in more detail in the useful Carrots and Sticks report focusing on sustainability reporting regulation (see Chalmers et al., 2024). As mentioned above, these instruments vary substantially in terms of their nature and scope, with some setting exact reporting requirements on issues such as particular environmental substances, while others take a more generic approach and require non-financial information to be provided for interested parties. It has also been noted that alongside governments such requirements have been increasingly set by other institutions, such as financial regulators and stock exchanges (Chalmers et al., 2024). Such a development has in many cases a lot to do with the investment market, as it has become increasingly evident that in addition to financial information, corporate long-term success is dependent on how they deal with various elements of sustainability. As such, investors are actively seeking to gain access to corporate sustainability information and learn to understand organisations' sustainability performance as well as its relationship with financial performance. We will return to this in more detail later on in Chapter 7.

### 5.4.6 Summary of reporting standards and frameworks

We have highlighted through this selective discussion of standards and frameworks that there are a number of institutions and collectives which seek to influence different aspects of corporate sustainability reporting for various reasons. However, it is also worthwhile recognising that these standards and frameworks overlap and influence each other. For example, the GRI has had influence on the CSRD reporting requirements, TCFD guidelines are explicitly relevant for IFRS Sustainability Standards and the CSRD, and much information that corporations produce through the GRI or SASB reports are included in the CDP database. The interconnections and implicit competition between the various institutions were clearly visible during the intensive stages of evolvement in the field, as the institutions developing and promoting specific frameworks often came out with memorandums of understanding and statements of interoperability (see "Focus on practice"), highlighting how they were seeking to collaborate and find common ground, despite often having different aims and targeting different audiences. The landscape nonetheless remains fragmented, and as sustainability reporting practices continue to become increasingly mainstream, the range of audiences interested in such information grows, and the reporting frameworks mature, it is likely that there will be further shifts amongst the organisations developing and promoting reporting.

We should also bear in mind, and as we raised earlier, that the different sustainability standards and frameworks are also political in the sense that they serve different purposes, have different priorities and emphasise the views of different stakeholders and interest groups. There is hence in this area inherent competition between reporting frameworks regarding which one has the strongest following and the most companies applying them, as these help the framework providers strengthen their institutional position and potentially provide momentum in the policy discussions concerning what sustainability reporting will look like in the future. This political nature of the standards and frameworks has an effect on our next topic, the ongoing debate concerning the regulation of sustainability reporting.

**Focus on practice: Interoperability, Connectivity and Transition planning**

With various standards and regulations happening at pace, it is perhaps not surprising that reporters are seeking clarity and additional guidance on several aspects. Most notable are perhaps three aspects:

**Interoperability.** Interoperability in this context relates to the similarities and differences across the reporting frameworks. This is a key issue for reporting companies who might be required to report under both ESRS and ISSB standards. They want to know where disclosure requirements are aligned, and where they might need to report similar information in different ways. There is an underlying concern here of duplication and unnecessary disclosure burden. This has led to a range of guidance from the standard setters as to interoperability, including a joint guidance document from EFRAG and IFRS on ESRS-ISSB Interoperability (2024), as well as other guidance which relates to interoperability between GRI, TCFD and others.

**Connectivity**. Connectivity is concerned with the connectivity between financial reporting and sustainability reporting. This is again where approaches to materiality have an effect with IFRS noting that their financial materiality perspective and approach to developing standards mean that connectivity is embedded (IFRS, 2023). While perhaps a bit more complex given their double materiality approach, from the EU context, EFRAG too is working on a project on the connectivity (EFRAG, 2025).

**Transition Planning**. While target setting towards carbon emissions reductions and net zero has been common for some time, there is now much more focus on how to get there – that is, how to achieve the carbon or sustainability targets outlined in numerous corporate policies. This has led to what has become widely known as transition planning. Transition planning disclosure requirements feature in much of the guidance and the Transition Plan Taskforce Disclosure Framework (2023) is a key document in setting out practice in this area.

## 5.5 Regulating sustainability reporting: An ongoing debate

Throughout the development of sustainability reporting into its contemporary form, there have been ongoing discussions as to whether the practice of sustainability reporting should be regulated. Further, as the urgency of global sustainability efforts is getting more tangible, and the reported sustainability information is recognised to have value for investors and financial market participants, there have been increasing attempts to create structures that would standardise the provision of sustainability disclosures, or parts of it, for these users with claims that this should enhance the comparability of the sustainability information. Hence, debates surrounding the regulation of sustainability reporting relate to two aspects: is a set of international standards for sustainability reporting needed, and if so, which (or whose) standards should constitute these?

The question of "whether sustainability reporting should be mandatory" is substantially more complex than it initially seems. First of all, given the complexity and potential diversity relating to sustainability discussed above, perhaps the question is not "should an organisation have to provide sustainability disclosures?", but rather "on which sustainability issues does an organisation need to report?" What results is that, while there are some regulatory instruments that require an organisation to provide a certain type of sustainability disclosure on a regular basis, it is more common that regulators have put in place instruments that mandate organisations to publish information on particular aspects of their operations, such as greenhouse gas emissions, water, employee-related aspects as well as questions of anti-corruption and bribery. And there are of course materiality considerations here. Given the underlying role materiality plays in all frameworks, it is unlikely that any organisation will report on all sustainability issues, instead following the materiality guidance, and depending on the perspective taken, a selection of the most material issues will form the basis of disclosure.

Yet another question that arises here is whether the regulatory instrument mandates or otherwise should give specific instructions about how the information should be provided. Some of the established sustainability reporting standards include very detailed guidance on how an organisation should collect, compile and disclose information on particular aspects. With regulatory instruments, this sometimes can be the case, but often the requirements are set in such a way that an organisation can still choose how and in which form it will publish the information.

And what will be the effect of such guidance on, for example, innovation and development of the practice.

There is a strong argument against making a particular sustainability reporting practice mandatory not just from those who wish to avoid reporting, as you might expect, but rather from those who believe that we have not yet reached a position where we know the best way to report. In other words, "best practice" has not been achieved in the reporting of sustainability. They suggest that by setting some current practice as the one everyone needs to follow, regulators would also limit innovation. Within sustainability reporting, we have come a long way from the fledgling environmental reports published in the early 1990s. The market environment has become increasingly global and complex, data collection and processing capabilities have developed extensively, and the general interest in sustainability matters has grown in societies overall as well as in the business world. As such, by not mandating a particular model and by leaving organisations space to imagine and innovate, it is possible that they will come up with new and alternative ways of producing and presenting sustainability accounts and reports, which could help in tackling the complexity of sustainability. Relatedly, reporters have needed to find diverse ways to engage stakeholders, collect information and report given novel configurations of stakeholders, contexts and sustainability issues. Will mandatory requirements result in more or less relevant disclosures given the complex nature of sustainability? Of course, this is perhaps a risky strategy relying on corporations to report and develop reporting practices. Chapter 8 relates to this point and you might find it useful as you seek to develop your own position in relation to the regulation of sustainability reporting.

Finally, as with the setting of any stipulation, it is relevant to ask how the governments or other authorities check whether the regulatory instruments are being followed, and whether there are any sanctions or other consequences for non-compliance. In general terms, many of the instruments are still fairly novel, and as such they are not enforced with similar severity as, for instance, financial accounting regulations are. One of the common approaches thus far has been the "comply or explain" approach, which means that should the organisation not be able (or willing) to comply with the set regulatory requirements, it has to provide in its disclosures an explanation on why it is not doing so at the moment, sometimes followed with a statement regarding how it intends to become compliant in the future. Overall, however, the consequences for non-compliance have been limited.

In addition to, and alongside, these debates as to whether or not sustainability reporting should be regulated practice is the second aspect noted above. This relates to who should regulate such a practice. Like the first aspect, this is a complex and nuanced debate. As we have highlighted, there are numerous global institutions each with, or developing, a set of standards for the practice. These, as we have illustrated are diverse, with varying perspectives on key issues such as materiality and users of such information. Likewise, while all those institutions are likely to share the same goal, that of reaching a sustainable society, there are arguably significant differences in the underlying implicit assumptions regarding, for instance, what sustainability entails, what is required to get there and what kind of structures will be the most helpful in this quest. As such, if sustainability reporting practice is to be regulated, then the follow-on question becomes, who should be those to set the standards? With each of the main players discussed above (GRI, ISSB and CSRD) each staking a claim to such a role at either a global or regional level this is, as Adams and Abhayawansa (2022) highlight, a contested and political question. And if there are multiple regulators, which is likely and the situation with the long standing practice of financial reporting, what are the consequences for sustainability reporting, its users and the transition to sustainability more broadly.

## INSIGHTS FROM RESEARCH: WHAT DO WE KNOW ABOUT SUSTAINABILITY REPORTING?

Sustainability reporting has been developing swiftly in recent years, no matter whether we speak of regulatory environment providing structures for reporting, the stakeholder groups interested in the reported information, the practices organisations draw on when preparing the reports, or the discourse on sustainability reporting, non-financial information, ESG data and sustainability-related financial disclosures more generally. Similarly, the academic research seeking to shed light on these questions has expanded quickly. With so many scholarly publications on reporting out there, it can be challenging to find a good starting point to engage with this work.

Henry Friedman and Gaizka Ormazabal offer an insightful access point for one area of research with their paper. They discuss the current knowledge and open questions related to sustainability reporting through what they call a supply and demand framework. The authors argue that there is a "gap between social and investor interest, on the one side, and firms' provision of ESG information, on the other" (p. 1576), and proceed to consider recent research on sustainability reporting standards, regulatory initiatives, ESG ratings and use ESG metrics for performance measurement. In an accessible way, Friedman and Ormazabal go through theoretical and empirical work, including a good number of working papers emerging in this space, and provide a structured discussion seeking to summarise what we currently know, and what we do not know. For the latter, they conclude with a list of open questions as examples of areas requiring further work, thereby helping others to get started.

It is important to recognise, however, that while Friedman and Ormazabal (2024) provide a very good access point, especially when read together with Christensen and colleagues' (2021) review on mandatory sustainability reporting, it should be seen as an access point to a specific research literature, that being scholarship interested primarily at the role of sustainability reporting in the marketplace. This work also comes with specific underlying assumptions concerning information, stakeholders and social dynamics, as well as accountability and sustainability. Moreover, this literature is more recent and tends to have limited connection to the long-standing tradition of scholarly work which has been exploring environmental, social and sustainability reporting practices for several decades. Drawing on a more diverse disciplinary basis, this literature continues to provide insights into the role of sustainability reporting in society (see Andrew and Baker, 2020; Larrinaga and Bebbington, 2021; Rodrigue et al., 2024), extending to themes beyond the market-oriented approach Friedman and Ormazabal (2024) focus on. Likewise, the underlying assumptions between these literatures are in general not similar, with for instance the assumed pathways of how sustainability can be achieved and what sustainability transition will require from organisations, economies and societies being substantially different.

Overall, sustainability reporting research continues to expand quickly, as scholars seek to understand why practices develop in a certain way and what kind of implications those practices might have in various contexts. Simultaneously, academic work in the area specialises, with streams of literature focusing on exploring particular questions from particular viewpoints. All this underscores the importance of being mindful and going beyond the abstract when reading academic work in this area: think about the assumptions being made, look at the context and data and consider potential proxies made use of. And, in particular, reflect on the meaning of sustainability in a given study, what kind of a role it plays, and what it is assumed to entail (see Adams and Abhayawansa, 2022; Milne and Gray, 2013).

**Friedman, H. L. and Ormazabal, G. (2024). The Role of Information in Building a More Sustainable Economy: A Supply and Demand Perspective. *Journal of Accounting Research, 62*(5), 1575–1609.**

## 5.6 Conclusion

In this chapter, we have provided an overview of the sustainability reporting landscape. At this point, it should be evident that, while in the 1990s, one could still talk of sustainability reporting as a marginal phenomenon, the role and relevance of sustainability reporting is widely established. At the same time, we are still dealing with an evolving practice, which implies that despite considerable and fast-paced development, much of the structures and institutional settings are still developing, and indeed need to develop if they are to take sustainability issues seriously and assist organisations in addressing them.

Furthermore, the development of different standards is not a panacea for sustainability reporting. It is essential for organisations to understand their specific context and what kind of information their stakeholders are interested in. The various reporting standards aid in making disclosures easier for organisations and they can also make the information produced more comparable and understandable. At the same time, however, it needs to be highlighted that the disclosure standards are by their very nature compromises. This implies that these standards very rarely, if ever, make the organisations disclose information that would highlight that their activities are endangering substantially the global pursuit of sustainability. To be sure, the information may be useful for some stakeholders, say to provide decision-useful information about environmental risks and thereby help investors make better financial decisions in the short term. Whether this suffices in the face of the looming global sustainability challenges is a whole different matter. This takes us back to the questions regarding the role of sustainability reporting in societies, as well as to how we understand organisational accountability – something we address specifically in the next chapter.

## References


Adams, C. and Abhayawansa, S. (2022). Connecting the COVID-19 Pandemic, Environmental, Social and Governance (ESG) Investing and Calls for 'Harmonisation' of Sustainability Reporting. *Critical Perspectives on Accounting*, *82*, 102309.

Andrew, J. and Baker, M. (2020). Corporate Social Responsibility Reporting: The Last 40 Years and a Path to Sharing Future Insights. *Abacus*, *56*(*1*), 35–65.

Buhr, N., Gray, R. and Milne, M. (2014). Histories, Rationales and Future Prospects for Sustainability Reporting. In Unerman, J., Bebbington, J. and O'Dwyer, B. (eds), *Sustainability Accounting and Accountability* (2nd edn). pp. 51–71. Routledge.

Burchell, S., Clubb, C. and Hopwood, A. G. (1985). Accounting in its Social Context: Towards a History of Value Added in the United Kingdom. *Accounting, Organizations and Society*, *10*(*4*), 381–413.

Chalmers, A. W., Klingler-Vidra, R., van de Wijs, P. P., Lysenkova, M. and Van der Lugt, C. T. (2024). *Carrots & Sticks: 2024 Annual Report*. University of Edinburgh, King's College London, Global Reporting Initiative (GRI), and the University of Stellenbosch Business School (USB).

Christensen, H., Hail, L. and Leuz, C. (2021). Mandatory CSR and Sustainability Reporting: Economic Analysis and Literature Review. *Review of Accounting Studies*, *26*, 1176–248.

EFRAG (2025). About Connectivity. Available at https://www.efrag.org/en/financial-reporting/about-connectivity (Accessed 7 May 2025).

EFRAG and IFRS (2024). ESRS-ISSB Standards: Interoperability Guidance. Available at https://www.ifrs.org/content/dam/ifrs/supporting-implementation/issb-standards/esrs-issb-standards-interoperability-guidance.pdf (Accessed 25 February 2025).

Ernst and Ernst (1976). *Social Responsibility Disclosure*. Ernst and Ernst.

Friedman, H. L. and Ormazabal, G. (2024). The Role of Information in Building a More Sustainable Economy: A Supply and Demand Perspective. *Journal of Accounting Research*, *62*(5), 1575–1609.

Gray, R., Adams, C. and Owen, D. (2014). *Accountability, Social Responsibility and Sustainability: Accounting for Society and the Environment*. Pearson.

Guthrie, J. and Parker, L. D. (1989). Corporate Social Reporting: A Rebuttal of Legitimacy Theory. *Accounting and Business Research*, *19*, 343–352.

IFRS (2023). Connectivity – What is it and What Does it Deliver? Available at https://www.ifrs.org/news-and-events/news/2023/03/connectivity-what-is-it-and-what-does-it-deliver/ (Accessed 7 May 2025).

IFRS (2024a). International Sustainability Standards Board. Available at https://www.ifrs.org/groups/international-sustainability-standards-board/ (accessed 19 December 2024).

IFRS (2024b). Who We Are. Available at https://www.ifrs.org/about-us/who-we-are (accessed 25 February 2025).

IFRS (2024c). ISSB: Frequently Asked Questions. Available at https://www.ifrs.org/groups/international-sustainability-standards-board/issb-frequently-asked-questions/ (accessed 27 February 2025).

IFRS (2024d). IFRS Sustainability Standards Navigator. Available at https://www.ifrs.org/issued-standards/ifrs-sustainability-standards-navigator/ifrs-s1-general-requirements/ (accessed 19 December 2024).

International Integrated Reporting Council (IIRC) (2021). The International <IR> Framework. https://integratedreporting.ifrs.org/wp-content/uploads/2024/08/IntegratedReporting_Framework_061024.pdf (accessed 25 February 2025).

KPMG (2020). *The Time Has Come: The KPMG Survey of Sustainability Reporting 2020*. Available at https://assets.kpmg/content/dam/kpmg/xx/pdf/2020/11/the-time-has-come.pdf (accessed 2 December 2020).

KPMG (2024). *The Move to Mandatory Reporting. Survey of Sustainability Reporting 2024.* Available at https://kpmg.com/xx/en/our-insights/esg/the-move-to-mandatory-reporting.html (accessed 17 December 2024).

Larrinaga, C. and Bebbington, J. (2021). The Pre-history of Sustainability Reporting: A Constructivist Reading. *Accounting, Auditing & Accountability Journal, 34*(9), 162–181.

Milne, M. J. and Gray, R. (2013). W(h)ither Ecology? The Triple Bottom Line, the Global Reporting Initiative, and Corporate Sustainability Reporting *Journal of Business Ethics, 118*(*1*), 13–29.

O'Dwyer, B., Humphrey, C. and Rowbottom, N. (2024). From Institutional Integration to Institutional Demise: The Disintegration of the International Integrated Reporting Council (IIRCS). *Critical Perspectives on Accounting, 99*, 102699.

O'Dwyer, B. and Unerman, J. (2020). Shifting the Focus of Sustainability Accounting from Impacts to Risks and Dependencies: Researching the Transformative Potential of TCFD Reporting. *Accounting, Auditing and Accountability Journal, 33*(*5*), 1113–1141.

Rodrigue, M., Tregidga, H. and Cooper, C. (2024). The Fragments and Traces of Integrated Reporting that Prevail: On the Importance of a Sustained Critical Perspective on Reporting. *Critical Perspectives on Accounting, 99*, 102726.

TCFD (2021). Task Force on Climate-related Financial Disclosures: Implementing the Recommendations of the Task Force on Climate-related Financial Disclosures. Available at: https://assets.bbhub.io/company/sites/60/2021/07/2021-TCFD-Implementing_Guidance.pdf (Accessed on 7 May 2025).

Transition Plan Taskforce (TPT) (2023). Disclosure Framework. Available at: www.ifrs.org/content/dam/ifrs/knowledge-hub/resources/tpt/disclosure-framework-oct-2023.pdf (Accessed on 25 February 2025).

Tregidga, H. and Laine, M. (2021). Standalone and Integrated Reporting. In Bebbington, J., Larrinaga, C., O'Dwyer, B. and Thomson, I. (eds), *Handbook on Environmental Accounting.* pp. 108–124. Routledge.

## Additional reading and resources

Belal, A. R., Cooper, S. and Roberts, R. (2013). Vulnerable and Exploitable: The Need for Organisational Accountability and Transparency in Emerging and Less Developed Economies. *Accounting Forum, 37*(*2*), 81–91.

Cho, C. H., Michelon, G., Patten, D. M. and Roberts, R. W. (2015). CSR Disclosure: The More Things Change…? *Accounting, Auditing and Accountability Journal, 28*(*1*), 14–35.

Dechow, P.M. (2023). Understanding the Sustainability Reporting Landscape and Research Opportunities in Accounting. *Accounting Review, 98*(*5*), 481–493.

European Sustainability Reporting Standards (EFRAG): www.efrag.org/en/sustainability-reporting.

Global Reporting Initiative (GRI): www.globalreporting.org.

Hummel, K. and Jobst, D. (2024). An Overview of Corporate Sustainability Reporting Legislation in the European Union. *Accounting Forum, 21*(*4*), 320–355.

International Financial Reporting Standards (IFRS): www.ifrs.org.

Lin, Y., Shen, R., Wang, J. and Julia Yu, Y. (2024). Global Evolution of Environmental and Social Disclosure in Annual Reports. *Journal of Accounting Research, 62*(*5*), 1941–1988.

SASB Standards: sasb.ifrs.org.

Sellhorn, T. and Wagner, V. (2024). The Forces that Shapes ESG Reporting. In T. Kuntz (Ed.), *Research Handbook on Environmental, Social and Corporate Governance.* pp. 269–292. Edward Elgar.

CHAPTER

6

# The sustainability reporting process

## Key influences, debates and discussions

In this chapter, we examine multiple decisions made through the process of producing and preparing a sustainability report. We do so not only to help understand the practice but also to consider its multifaceted and complex nature. While many of these decisions and processes are highly influenced by the context within which a reporting company is situated, most notably the regulatory context (see our discussion in the previous chapter), we will illustrate that, even within a context of increased regulation, there is value in reflecting on the production of a report and the various processes therein. Various decisions include, why does an organisation report, to whom is the reported information directed, what is reported on, how is the report compiled, and is the report assured. We ground this discussion, not only in relation to the reporting standards and frameworks but also in relation to accountability which is the overriding perspective taken in this book.

Like the previous chapter, we mainly focus on reporting by corporations, and in particular large corporations. This is for the same reasons stated in Chapter 5. The sustainability reporting practices of corporations (in particular large corporations) arguably have more prominence and visibility not only because of their size, but also their impacts and, due to them being the main focus of scholarly research, our knowledge of them is substantial. While the sustainability reporting processes of other types of organisations, for example, public sector and not-for-profits, will follow some of the process outlined below, some aspects will be different.

By the end of this chapter you should:

- Understand some of the key stages in the reporting process as well as the decisions that are made along the way.
- Understand the implications of various decisions within the reporting process and their implications, including in relation to accountability.
- Have an awareness of sustainability reporting assurance practices.
- Have critically reflected on the role of sustainability reporting in the transition towards a more sustainable society.

DOI: 10.4324/9781003533207-8

## 6.1 Stages in the sustainability reporting process

To provide a context for our presentation of the process of organisational sustainability reporting we focus on five stages[1]:

1. Why does the organisation report? What are the motivations for providing sustainability information?
2. To whom is the reported information directed? Who are the stakeholders addressed in the report?
3. What information is reported on? What issues are material for the organisation, as well as what information do the targeted stakeholders need and are interested in?
4. How is the report compiled? In what form and format is the information disclosed and communicated?
5. Is the report assured? What is the scope of the assurance?

We consider each of these stages in the reporting process below, focusing on key decision points and their implications. It should be noted that, while we discuss each of the stages separately, decisions at one stage affect subsequent stages (e.g. whom the report is directed to can affect what is reported) and as such should be considered in relation to one another.

## 6.2 Why does the organisation report?

The first stage in the reporting process relates to the question, why does an organisation produce a sustainability report? This stage concerns an interest in why many organisations commit what can be substantive resources (time and money) into producing a report. Here we need to consider several things. The regulatory environment is an obvious factor here. As we discussed in the previous chapter, sustainability reports are increasingly subject to regulation, and this will obviously be a key driver in the decision to publish a report. However, it would be remiss to assume that this is the only consideration. It is useful to recognise, and as we discussed in Chapter 5, sustainability reporting has a long history and many organisations have chosen to produce a report, often committing significant resources to it, prior to any such regulation. Furthermore, it is also useful to remember that not all organisations are covered by existing regulation and as such many decide to produce a report on a voluntary basis.

Organisational motives to engage in sustainability reporting have been found to be diverse. Research has identified a variety of reasons, both for the initiation of reporting in the first place as well as for continuing with the practice. We acknowledge that some argue that motivations are less important than the act of reporting itself – that is, what matters most is whether or not an organisation produces a report rather than the question of why. However, as we note above, decisions in the reporting process are interlinked, and hence different motivations lead to different kinds of reporting practices. In other words, the motivations behind the production of a report also affect the other stages of the reporting process. Even when a company is required to produce some disclosures, how they disclose, and as we expand on below, the extent of disclosures and reported topics can be determined by the organisation's overall motivation and view of the role and purpose of the report. In considering this question, it might be useful to consider two extreme positions, that is reporting for strategic reasons or reporting for broader perspective underpinned by ethical reasoning.

Quite simply, and perhaps at one end of a continuum sustainability, reporting can be undertaken for economic and profit motives. Organisations reporting for these reasons are likely to perceive their accountabilities to be first and foremost to their shareholders and to the fulfilment of increasing shareholder wealth. From this perspective, sustainability reporting is seen as a tool to gain, retain or maintain the support of those stakeholders that have power to affect the corporation's goals. As such, the motivation of reporting from this perspective is for these strategic reasons.

At the other end of the spectrum lies a broader consideration likely driven by a more holistic view of accountabilities. From a broader accountability perspective, the motivation to prepare a report can relate to the felt responsibility to be transparent, to discharge the accountability relationship and also to provide the means by which accountability relationships can be established. Motivations from this perspective can also relate to the aim of transforming the companies' practices so that they are more socially, environmentally and economically sustainable.

These polar ends of a continuum are obviously simplifications, and the reality in organisations is much more complicated. There might, for instance, be very different views within an organisation. With the risk of reinforcing stereotypes, we could foresee a sustainability group of an organisation positioning more towards the holistic accountability end of the continuum, with the finance group finding their views of sustainability reporting to be closer to strategic accountability. Such positioning is also likely to be influenced by the standards and frameworks followed. As we have discussed the International Sustainability Standards Board (ISSB) takes a financial materiality perspective while the Global Reporting Initiative (GRI) and Corporate Sustainability Reporting Directive (CSRD) are much broader. But even here, standards only play some of a role with flexibility in their application as we discuss below. Furthermore, while regulatory requirements often cover only some aspects of sustainability, organisations have tended to extend their reporting beyond the minimum requirements.

It is thus evident that there are various reasons which can affect organisational decisions here. We can think of an organisation's culture and values, which may outline what kind of a role the organisation seeks to play in society. Likewise, we should consider how the organisation is positioned within the value chain, as for instance the sustainability policies of key customers may set expectations on those in the supply chain to engage in sustainability reporting. The most obvious and perhaps common example here is organisations seeking scope 3 emissions data from their supply chain. We should also recall that sustainability reporting is not a new phenomenon, and many larger organisations may have a long history of producing such reports, resulting in internal practices, traditions and expectations evolving in specific ways, thereby likely also having an effect on why reporting is conducted in the present day.

Again, it is essential to recognise that in many organisations there are likely to be various motivations in play. The motivation to produce a report in the first place may be different from the motivation to discuss (or not) particular issues within the report. Moreover, there may be different motivations to discuss particular issues in particular ways at particular points in time. From an organisational point of view, this underscores the importance of having regular internal dialogue regarding the role sustainability reporting is seen to have for the organisation. If the approach is not clear and shared internally, the organisation risks having various groups sending mixed messages to stakeholders. This also underscores the relevance internal sustainability reporting champions may have on how sustainability reporting develops in an organisation. Such key individuals can be highly influential in setting the tone for the reporting practice in an organisation.

Overall, it is important for us to consider the motivations organisations have for reporting sustainability information in particular ways. This links us to the purpose of sustainability disclosures. To what extent is sustainability reporting approached as a strategic practice, in which the broader aim of these disclosures is seen as being to help the organisation maximise its shareholder value and manage sustainability-related risks? Alternatively, given the increasing regulation in many jurisdictions, does the organisation perceive sustainability reporting primarily as a compliance exercise, and thereby focus on fulfilling the mandatory requirements without dedicating excessive effort and resources to it. Or, to what extent are the reports intended to discharge a broader and potentially more holistic accountability, which would include considering sustainability disclosures as a key mechanism through which an organisation could transform and move towards social, environmental and economic sustainability? Organisations always have some rationale behind their activities, and while the rationales can at times be fuzzy, unclear or simply assumed, the motives are not trivial. In this case, they affect the next stages of the reporting process.

**Focus on practice: Sustainability reporting infrastructure**

In discussing sustainability reporting, we have thus far focused primarily on two aspects. First, in Chapter 5, we discussed the various external frameworks and standards, both mandatory and voluntary, which are a major influence in shaping how sustainability reporting has developed and continues to do so. Second, in the present chapter, we focus on the organisation and discuss the various stages of the reporting process and highlight different questions and choices the organisation should consider when preparing its disclosures. Both of these are obviously significant elements of the sustainability reporting infrastructure. At the same time, there are also several other actors that we should not forget when thinking of the reporting infrastructure as a whole.

One way to think about the actors involved is to divide them into those playing a role in the production of information and those using it. On the production side, we of course have the organisations who report. Producing a sustainability report requires considerable effort however, and hence organisations might turn to consultancy services and communications firms specialising in sustainability reporting for expertise. There are also sustainability assurance services, the relevance of which is steadily increasing as the expectations for comparability, quality and trustworthiness grow. Moreover, we should also consider the various software providers, which develop software that organisations can use for collecting and organising data needed for the sustainability reports. Such software providers can in fact be quite powerful and influential, as the way the software is set up may dictate or at least have an effect on how data gets collected, reported and visualised. The software also relates closely to the digitalisation of sustainability reporting through digital tagging, which is becoming a feature of all major reporting standards.

On the user side, we obviously have those directly interested in making use of the reported information, be that individual citizens or major institutional investors. This is only one part of it, however. Instead of going through individual reports, many users prefer having aggregated information, or perhaps someone providing options to help with comparing firms. Hence, there are in the marketplace various data providers who compile information from the reports organisations produce, package it, and offer users the opportunity to access information via databases or other types of services. Further, as is the case with financial data, not every user is interested in crunching the data and numbers themselves but would instead like to have someone else do it. This brings in different providers offering sustainability analytics, including for instance ratings and other types of services providing users with additional value by going beyond the original raw sustainability information included in the report. At the same time, we should bear in mind that the data providers and analytics services can also be quite influential, as for instance data aggregating and analysis involves making choices and prioritisations, as does the way information is subsequently presented and visualised. These choices are then likely to impact how the users perceive the data and make decisions based on it, which then has potential implications also on sustainability.

Overall, as the interest in sustainability has grown across societies, also the relevance of sustainability information has fast increased. Further, with the proliferation of big data, digitalisation and AI, we are going to have much more sustainability data available for businesses and societies to use in the coming years. Given how the current sustainability reporting infrastructure has emerged only recently, it is quite evident that more actors will join this space in seeking to develop and promote new innovations that could potentially help us produce better data and make better use of it, hopefully also contributing to making our societies less unsustainable.

## 6.3 To whom is the reported information directed?

Every organisation has a plethora of stakeholders each with their own needs, wants and preferences. As we have made clear, no organisation can satisfy all its stakeholders with the sustainability disclosures provided – at least within one written report. Choices are needed and made, either implicitly or explicitly. Moreover, the perspectives on accountability presented above in the decision to produce a report have an impact on who an organisation sees as the key target for the disclosures.

The reporting standards an organisation is following provide a clear starting point here. This applies both in situations where the reporting organisation is required to report given jurisdictional requirements as well as when the decision to apply a particular framework has been made voluntarily by the organisation. As we discussed in the previous chapter, various regulators and standard setters have different approaches and emphases when it comes to who the primary users of the sustainability information are expected to be. In simple terms, whereas the ISSB and Sustainability Accounting Standards Board (SASB) standards are developed with the interests of the financial stakeholders in mind, the GRI and ESRS standards are set up with a broader stakeholder perspective. The structure, guidelines and underlying assumptions of these reporting frameworks have an impact on whom the sustainability reporting is targeted to, no matter whether the organisation makes an active decision on this matter.

The importance of financial markets for sustainability reporting practices should also not be underestimated, especially when we consider larger organisations. The long-term value relevance of sustainability for corporate success is becoming increasingly evident, and as such the prominence of environmental, social and governance (ESG) considerations in the investment community is growing steadily (see Chapter 7). This has clear implications for the form and content of corporate sustainability reporting. Financial markets are often found to be most interested in sustainability-related risks, as well as those elements which could have long-term financial implications for the corporation. As noted, these considerations are also reflected in some of the key standards and guidelines, such as ISSB, SASB and Task Force on Climate-Related Financial Disclosures (TCFD), as well as other recommendations provided on sustainability reporting by interest groups, stock markets and other institutions in the financial markets. At the same time, this kind of emphasis might imply that the focus of reporting moves away from issues that other stakeholder groups would be interested in.

In general terms, should the organisation perceive sustainability reporting through a narrower and more strategic accountability, as a mechanism to enhance the achievement of the organisation's financial goals, the disclosures are more likely to be catered for the needs of those stakeholders with the greatest influence on this outcome. Despite the impact of the reporting standards, this does not imply that all the disclosures would be similar, however, since the needs and expectations of financial stakeholders vary and the most important stakeholders for achieving the strategic aims of the organisation can be varied. For example, some companies are highly dependent on individual corporate customers in a supply chain and, as such, may use the report to seek to emphasise how they are following all the necessary ethical guidelines and how they manage this key stakeholder relationship. An organisation operating in an industry requiring a regular renewal of environmental permits from the government would likely steer their disclosures according to this. An organisation that relies upon a highly skilled workforce is likely to be in competition with other companies for relatively scarce highly skilled employees, with this stakeholder group being economically powerful in such an organisation and sustainability disclosures targeted accordingly. So, while each of these companies would be seeking to achieve strategic ends with their reporting, the content of their sustainability reports would be different.

In the case where the organisational motive to engage with sustainability reporting falls more towards the broader end of the accountability continuum, the company is more likely to consider a much wider range of stakeholders and the expectations they might have. While many of these groups may not have any immediate impact on the organisation's activities nor on its financial success, providing sustainability disclosures that speak also to the needs of these stakeholders is considered a duty that the organisation should nonetheless fulfil. This would not always be straightforward, since it may require substantial effort from the organisation to figure out the variety of stakeholder needs and expectations. Following reporting standards geared towards broader stakeholders will be helpful as they provide stepping stones on how an organisation can identify which groups would be interested in their sustainability reports and what elements they would be most interested in. The standards only provide a template and general direction however, and hence organisations can utilise stakeholder engagement processes for this purpose to engage in dialogue with the various groups.

### 6.3.1 Determining what stakeholders are interested in

As discussed in Chapter 3, stakeholders and their needs vary. Each NGO, community and investment bank, for example, is different and has different information needs. Likewise, each organisation is different and is located in a specific geographical, social and economic context. This implies that there are no categorical answers as to what a particular stakeholder group expects or wants to know about a particular organisation in relation to sustainability.

Furthermore, organisations can obviously target multiple stakeholders with their sustainability reporting. Given however that the needs and expectations of various stakeholders vary, a single uniform message does not often suffice. Organisations can also use various disclosure media to emphasise different elements of their activities, policies and intentions, with the aim of receiving positive reactions across multiple stakeholder groups. For instance, an organisation might include what it believes to be the most financially material sustainability issues in its annual financial report to cater primarily for investors and financial markets, while at the same time preparing a more wide-ranging sustainability report for its broader stakeholder groups and making use of social media to provide sustainability information for consumers as well as the communities near its facilities. Moreover, it is also important for the organisation to clarify the primary audience of its sustainability reporting, as this choice has implications on how the reporting is undertaken. It is perhaps worth highlighting some general features of the groups most often included as potential users of corporate sustainability disclosures, keeping in mind that not all possible, nor all relevant, stakeholder groups are included in Table 6.1. We can make some general points about each group, which helps us to take into account the different considerations when it comes to who to direct information to.

## 6.4 What information is reported on?

What information is reported on is obviously key when it comes to sustainability reporting. As we have demonstrated, the possibilities here are seemingly endless. Again, the reporting standards a firm follows, either due to requirements or by choice, have an important influence here. Again however, these are only the starting point, as the standards leave plenty of scope for the organisations. Similarly to other stages of the reporting process, what information is reported on is influenced by the accountability perspective taken in an organisation. Taking a narrower accountability perspective focusing primarily on some specific (financial) stakeholders means the scope of the report is likely to be less extensive than that of one prepared from a more holistic or broader perspective. Not only is the number of stakeholders the report is being directed to likely to be smaller but also the overriding purpose of the report means that the information included will be focused on the potential financial

**TABLE 6.1** Common Stakeholder Groups and Their Common Interests

| Common Stakeholder Group | Potential Stakeholder Interests | Other Points to Consider |
|---|---|---|
| Shareholders and investors | Risk management<br>Financial impacts and dependencies related to sustainability | Expect high-quality information in a concise and comparable form<br>Familiarity with reading corporate reports |
| Banks and insurers | Risk management (e.g. Equator principles: framework for managing social and environmental risks)<br>Consider ESG matters in making decisions regarding financing of major investment projects<br>Carbon: declining interest in many markets to be involved with businesses dependent on coal and oil | May expect private reporting instead of relying on publicly available sustainability information only |
| Employees and trade unions | Have been a key target group for sustainability reporting<br>Social matters, working conditions<br>Sustainability in the supply chain<br>Public reporting used by top management to send messages and motivate employees | Often have access to internal reporting and communication as well as reports prepared for external purposes. For example, sustainability reports can be aimed at attracting high calibre recruits. Reports geared primarily towards financial stakeholders might not fulfil these needs |
| Supply chain or business-to-business consumers | Financial performance and/or sustainability performance may be the focus | Those with power and influence in the supply chain may also expect private reporting or attempt to influence the nature of the report |
| Consumers | Variety of concerns and interests among this stakeholder group which may not be aligned<br>Political interest, viral campaigns.<br>Information spreads fast<br>Instead of general policies and broad sustainability reporting, often focused on single incidents or particular products | Seldom read reports, but use social media<br>Reporting may require faster reactions from an organisation. However consumers might obtain information through NGOs who do use sustainability reports |
| NGOs | Often proxies for stakeholders who cannot raise their concerns: nature, human rights, future generations<br>Also complex topics, such as tax avoidance<br>Challenge the organisation | Some NGOs read sustainability reports, but critically<br>May compare sustainability reporting with information from other sources (possibly to produce counteraccounts) |
| Local community (including vulnerable communities) | Often localised issues and controversies related to particular production sites and areas<br>Often divergent views within this stakeholder group | May not read corporate reports but instead demand information via other channels |

implications and risks deriving from the sustainability impacts and dependencies the organisation has identified. However, even in these situations, determining what to report on is likely to need careful consideration. Whatever the perspective, the reporting organisation will need to decide on what information to include and how much detail should be provided. Here the concept of materiality and the materiality assessment process introduced in Chapter 3 become important.

### 6.4.1 Deciding report content: Materiality and stakeholder engagement

In Chapter 5, we highlighted how sustainability reporting has developed as a mostly voluntary practice in which corporations have had substantial control over which issues they are reporting on, in what form they provide the information and how detailed they wish to be in their disclosures. While the reporting standards have evolved and become increasingly established, the situation arguably remains in many ways, giving organisations substantial leeway in their reporting choices. Thus far, experience shows that some organisations have been very careful and meticulous in their approach to such choices, whereas others have appeared to be more flexible and do not seem to follow any particular plan. Here, it is relevant to understand that the choice of content is inherently related to some of the other decisions discussed above: what the organisation seeks to achieve in the first place, including how the organisation perceives its accountability, why it is producing sustainability information and which stakeholders are the principal target groups for the reported information.

Obviously, whether the corporation is following particular standards or guidelines has a significant influence on the disclosures. This shows both in the topics chosen to be reported upon in the first place, as well as in how the information is then provided. The various standards and guidelines, such as ISSB, GRI, ESRS and other influences such as the UN SDGs, all have different approaches and influences when it comes to choosing the aspects that should be reported upon, depending, for instance, on which group is considered to be the presumed target audience for a report. Likewise, the level of detail requested and recommended in the standards varies substantially. On a general level, it is safe to claim that all corporations need to make choices when it comes to what they are willing to report and how they are going to do it. Given the vast array of topics falling within the umbrella of sustainability, it is beyond any corporation to report all the details on all the issues to everyone out there. This is where materiality considerations come to play an important role.

### 6.4.2 Materiality assessment

Materiality assessments, often referred to as materiality determination exercises, are an essential aspect of the sustainability reporting processes. In essence, materiality assessment means the identification of the most significant sustainability issues for reporting purposes. While sounding rather straightforward in the first instance, such assessments can prove highly challenging. In sustainability reporting, there is no clear single way of performing the assessment, and the definitions of materiality also differ across reporting standards. For example, focusing on financial materiality, the IFRS Sustainability Disclosure Standards start from the premise that the reported sustainability-related information should be useful to primary users of general purpose financial reports. From this perspective, materiality is defined by asking whether information could reasonably be expected to influence the decisions of those primary users. This is entity-specific, and hence each organisation needs to consider what is material for themselves. The SASB standards, associated with the IFRS Sustainability Disclosure Standards, could prove helpful, as in SASB materiality is defined based on the industry a corporation is a member of, therefore starting from the assumption that material issues are likely to be similar for firms operating in the same industry.

A contrasting approach, impact materiality, is presented by GRI. Here, the organisation should seek to identify the actual and potential impacts its activities have given the operating context, and subsequently assess the significance of these to determine which would be most significant impacts to report on. While the IFRS Sustainability Disclosure Standards focus on potential financial impacts on the organisation, the GRI standards expect the organisation to identify and assess its impacts on the economy, environment and people. Throughout, the organisation should engage with relevant stakeholders and experts to ensure their perspectives are taken into account in the process. In slightly simplified terms, the EU Corporate Sustainability Reporting Directive (CSRD), through the ESRS standards, attempts to combine these two different approaches to materiality by highlighting a double materiality perspective, which covers both impact and financial materiality. This means that reporting should follow both financial materiality to the extent that it includes material information about the organisations' risks and opportunities related to sustainability matters, as well as impact materiality so that the report should provide material information concerning the organisation's impacts on people and the environment. In combination, this double materiality approach would result in both financial and other stakeholders to understand the relevant impacts of the company's operations from their respective perspectives, as the reports should include information which is determined to be material from the impact materiality perspective, the financial materiality perspective or both of them.

The reporting standard-setters provide detailed guidance on conducting materiality assessments. Still, in practical terms, these processes can prove quite complicated and are unlikely to result in clear-cut answers as it comes to what exactly should be reported on. There are hence choices to be made. From an organisational perspective, it is thus relevant to perceive these as learning processes and ensure that they have been documented appropriately with sufficient detail, as the assessments should be revisited regularly to ensure that the most material issues are covered in reporting. Furthermore, it is again worth pointing out that the reporting infrastructure continues to evolve, and we still have only limited experience of how the materiality assessments expected by, say, ISSB and ESRS are eventually conducted by organisations. The practices are thus likely to evolve as organisations gather more experience and the reporting standards become more mature. We should also note again that while the reporting standards offer different perspectives on reporting, materiality and prospective users, organisations can in their reporting follow several standards simultaneously. As such, their reporting choices may not come down to how materiality is defined in a specific reporting standard, but they could combine approaches in seeking to ensure that their sustainability reporting achieves the goals they have set for it.

One approach organisations can use to approach and communicate the determination of material issues is a materiality matrix. While these materiality matrices differ, we provide a simple example in Figure 6.1 to illustrate. A matrix is

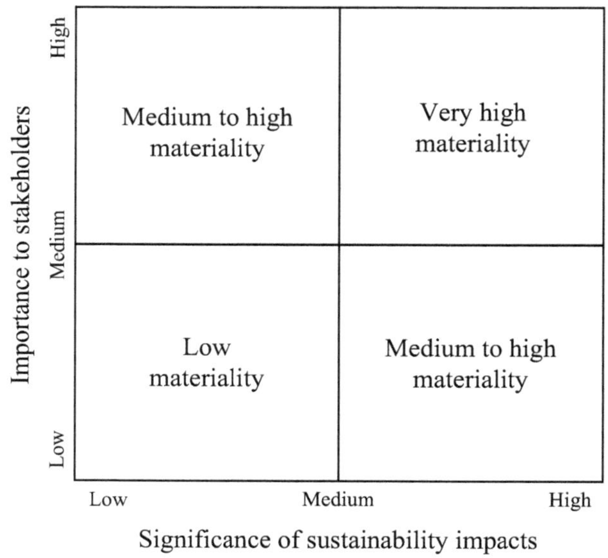


**FIGURE 6.1** Materiality Matrix

used to plot various issues in relation to two dimensions. The dimensions represented in Figure 6.1 relate to the importance of the issue to the stakeholders and the significance of the impact; however, these can vary. For example, some matrices include a consideration of the amount of control that the organisation has on an issue, while others set impact materiality and financial materiality as their two dimensions. It is important to consider what dimensions are included when looking at an organisation's materiality matrix as they do make a difference to what is considered material and hence what may be reported.

The views of the stakeholders are seldom unified. In assessing materiality, the organisation also has to make choices with regard to which stakeholders it considers to have the most relevant or significant views. A materiality assessment is likely to turn out differently depending on who places the issues in the above matrix, the company or the stakeholders themselves. Essentially, materiality is by no means an objective thing, but it is something an organisation defines via judgements at a particular place and point in time. Not surprisingly, materiality and materiality practices have been subject to extensive research, including how materiality is understood and approached differently in different organisations and how it is not as straightforward as it may first seem (Bolt and Tregidga, 2023; Jørgensen et al., 2022; Oll et al., 2025; Puroila and Mäkelä, 2019).

**Focus on practice: Materiality assessment processes and materiality matrices**

To help understand this process of materiality determination for sustainability reporting, it would be useful to consider a practical example of this. Should an organisation follow a reporting standard, as many do, they are generally expected to discuss how they have considered materiality and determined which issues are they have assessed to be material. Oftentimes, included in the materiality assessment process, organisations also include in their sustainability report (or a link therein) a copy of a materiality matrix, which can usefully visualise the different dimensions that have been considered in making reporting choices. We recommend you return to the report you looked at earlier, although a simple internet search of materiality matrix will bring up examples from some large corporations too (e.g. Nestlé, H&M, Danone and Unilever all have comprehensive examples available online).

Find the materiality matrix in the report and reflect on the following questions: what issues do they include, and which ones are considered to have the most/least significance? Are there any issues that you would expect to see that are not included?

As noted, many of these matrices are accompanied by a description of how the materiality determination process was undertaken. We suggest you also read and reflect on this statement in light of this chapter. For example, has the organisation included stakeholders, and does it name the stakeholders included in the materiality process? Do they appear to take a broad or a narrow view of the stakeholders of the company?

We can learn a lot from these materiality exercises, and they directly affect what is included in the report, so can be worth taking some time to consider.

### 6.4.3 What level of detail is required?

Once an organisation has identified the most material aspects, it still needs to decide which information it is going to report on that aspect, how much detail it is going to provide and how in general the information will be presented. In comparison to financial statements, which typically follow a unified structure and format across organisations, in sustainability reporting variation is to be expected. And yes, this remains the case even though the reporting frameworks have become widely applied and more established. Organisations continue to have the space to decide the balance between: qualitative and quantitative information; use of pictures, graphs and infographics; provision of aggregated information or more specific details. There can also be thematic variation: an organisation may decide to use its sustainability report this year to discuss its approach to climate change and carbon performance in more detail while reducing disclosures on other issues to a minimum. Major incidents can also have an impact: BP, for instance, following the Deepwater Horizon oil platform accident in 2010, used a large part of its sustainability report in the following year to discuss the incident, and Volkswagen paid plenty of attention to ethical questions and internal processes after the Dieselgate emission scandal in 2015 highlighted in Chapter 3.

Accordingly, we do not engage in further discussion regarding the details of the information provided here, as the substantial variation inherent in sustainability reporting defies any boilerplate explanations or simple checklists. You will note, however, that we will return to this theme throughout the rest of the book. We will touch upon the contents of sustainability reports when discussing both financial markets and counteraccounts in the two chapters that follow. Likewise, in presenting key sustainability topics in Part III of the book, we will also discuss how those key questions, such as climate, biodiversity and human rights, relate to and feature in sustainability reporting.

## 6.5 In what form and format is the information communicated?

To this point, we have concentrated our discussion on sustainability reports. But there are different potential communication channels organisations can choose to use for disclosing sustainability information.

As highlighted in Chapter 5, corporate sustainability disclosures emerged in traditional (corporate) reports, first within the annual reports and later on as separate standalone reports. The notion of account is however much broader than a traditional report. Press releases on important developments and incidents, as well as leaflets to nearby residents, for instance, have been used by organisations for a long time in seeking to communicate sustainability matters to specific stakeholders. Furthermore, organisational accounts are not necessarily provided in writing, and as such speeches and presentations given by corporate spokespersons in public events or private settings are also a mechanism of providing an account to others.

As technologies have developed, sustainability information alongside other types of disclosures has spread. In addition to website disclosures, social media has been used as an avenue for organisations to reach a broad public – including those who would never consider reading a traditional organisational report. It also gives interested stakeholders an opportunity to engage with the organisation by asking questions and providing public feedback, thus requiring organisations to adapt to a faster pace and topics not entirely under their control. Moreover, social media also gives individual citizens and other stakeholder groups, typically NGOs, a platform through which they can provide their own viewpoints of an organisation, its activities and the disclosures it has provided. We will discuss these counter accounts in more detail later on in this book in Chapter 8. AI would seem to have potential here too, enabling information to be tailored on demand to specific user needs based on their preferences and expectations. Indeed, it is difficult to consider all of the effects of AI on reporting as it is so swiftly developing.

Still, while other forms of accounts have risen in importance, corporate reports remain relevant and have specific roles for the organisations and organisational stakeholders. These regularly published reports are carefully crafted documents, over which organisations have full editorial control. They offer users of these disclosures an opportunity to compare the information over time, giving a better view of trends and developments, as well as across companies and sectors, helping to see how different organisations fare against one another. Granted, a problem for comparability has been the fact that sustainability reporting has been a voluntary exercise, giving organisations the freedom to choose not only whether they report at all but also the topics they wish to discuss, the format used, as well as types of information and metrics used in the disclosures. The maturing of the reporting infrastructure and the key reporting standards is providing some help here, although as we have highlighted above, this is far from straightforward.

Alongside establishing standards for reporting content, all the key sustainability reporting frameworks also come with specific digital taxonomy, known as digital tagging, which is developed to facilitate the use of digital technology, spur comparability and make the use of reports easier and more efficient. In essence, this means that the standard-setters have constructed structured frameworks, which help to organise the reporting content allowing consistent digital reporting using a specific reporting standard. Such tagging helps many stakeholders access and use sustainability data, as the information can be read and analysed more efficiently with digital technology.

## 6.6 Sustainability assurance

As long as there have been some kind of social, environmental or sustainability reports by corporations, there has been scepticism about their contents and credibility. This is not very surprising, given that some organisations have been found to use these reports in a self-laudatory manner. One solution offered to help improve credibility and perceived reliability of the sustainability disclosures is external verification, known as sustainability assurance. The decision to assure a report is an important part of the sustainability reporting process and as such we cover it here.

### 6.6.1 Sustainability assurance and financial auditing practices

In financial accounting and reporting, a regulated audit function is used to provide some assurance that the financial information provided by the organisation provides a true and fair view of the organisation's activities and financial situation. With sustainability reports, the setting is quite different.

Unlike financial accounting and reporting, assurance for sustainability accounting and reporting is only starting to be subject to mandatory regulations. For example, companies reporting under CSRD in the EU will be required to obtain independent assurance. It will however take several years as the practices in the field will evolve and find their form, as the assurance requirements related to CSRD are being phased-in with companies initially required to have limited assurance with requirements potentially developing over time. ISSB does not require mandatory assurance for reports prepared following the IFRS Sustainability Disclosure Standards. In fact, ISSB notes that it does not have the mandate to require assurance, but highlights that it is up to the jurisdictions to decide if assurance will be required. The standards have nonetheless been designed so that the reports would be assurable, and hence it is likely that assurance requirements will emerge at least in some contexts. Another factor here is that the sustainability assurance industry remains less established when compared to the financial audit sector. However, again this is likely to change. With the number of companies being required to prepare reports under both the standards identified above, along with those who voluntarily report in line with standards or otherwise, we can anticipate fast-paced growth. We should also recall at this point that similarly to sustainability reporting, sustainability report assurance has been increasing prior to regulation. KPMG's (2024) study found that 69% of largest global companies obtained independent assurance by 2023. This figure has steadily increased since the survey began monitoring assurance in 2005.

Key to the development and quantity of sustainability report assurance will be the growth of the workforce and skills in this area. For a long time, sustainability assurance services have been offered by both the major multinational accountancy firms as well as some smaller players, including consultancies and NGOs. While assurance processes and practices can vary, including an assurance statement from an external independent party can help to signal credibility, and hence can improve the perceived trustworthiness of disclosures. Moreover, several frameworks now exist to aid reporting organisations, assurance providers and interested stakeholders to agree on how the assurance of a sustainability report could be conducted, what it could entail and what kind of conclusions such assurance facilitates. This is not to say, however, that assured sustainability disclosures are entirely reliable or that they would have a status similar to audited financial statements, as we will discuss in more detail below.

### 6.6.2 Frameworks for sustainability assurance

Assurance services started to develop alongside the early environmental reporting practices, even though the take-off was not very rapid. There was substantial variation in the practices, as in the 1990s and early 2000s, there were no standards or frameworks in place that service providers could have drawn upon. As sustainability reporting continued to grow in popularity, and the demand for assurance services increased, different standards began to emerge for the assurance.

In general terms, it is possible to divide the assurances into two broad types: the accounting type, that is those drawing more on the financial audit function and the idea of compliance, and the consultancy type, which tends to be oriented more towards stakeholders. This distinction is also visible in the two most common frameworks that have been used in assurance, the International Standard on Assurance Engagement Standard 3000 (ISAE 3000), developed by the International Auditing and Assurance Standards Board (IAASB) of the International Federation of Accountants (IFAC), and the AA1000AS, an assurance standard developed through a multi-stakeholder process led by Accountability, a UK-based consultancy firm.

ISAE3000 is more closely related to the financial accounting and auditing practices. It was established by IFAC, which is the international body issuing accounting and auditing standards. The first version was issued in 2003, with a subsequent revision in 2013. While the scope of ISAE3000 is not only about sustainability reporting, as it includes various kinds of assurance engagements other than audits or reviews of historical financial information, it has been used by accounting firms in their efforts to provide assurance for sustainability disclosures. Assurance engagements under ISAE 3000 (Revised) can be performed as either reasonable assurance or limited assurance with the former relating to the consideration of the design and execution of procedures and the latter, reasonable assurance, being similar to a statutory audit opinion in financial accounting and is the highest level of assurance. ISAE also provides specific subject matter assurance standards relevant here. These include ISAE 3410 Assurance Engagements on Greenhouse Gas Statements.

As the sustainability reporting landscape has evolved swiftly, it has become evident that amongst the report users the expectations of credibility and comparability have increased, and as such the expectations regarding sustainability assurance have also grown. To answer such needs, IAASB published in late 2024 a new ISSA5000 standard on sustainability assurance, with the full name of the standard being International Standard on Sustainability Assurance 5000. Being dedicated to the assurance of sustainability reporting, the standard is substantially more detailed than ISAE3000, as the latter has been a generic standard covering a range of issues beyond the financial statements. ISSA5000 also has more detailed coverage of specific themes that have proven to be important for sustainability reporting assurance, such as questions of materiality, forward-looking information and ethical requirements concerning assurance providers. An important feature of ISSA5000 is that it has been designed to be agnostic with regard to both profession and reporting frameworks, which means that it could be used by both accounting and non-accounting professionals offering assurance services for reports developed according to any reporting framework. This is hoped to enhance the previously somewhat fragmented marketplace and thereby improve the perception users have for sustainability assurance. Users have been provided some lead time to shift to ISSA5000, as it will be effective for reporting periods starting in December 2026 onwards, although earlier use is also permitted. Until then, users can continue to use ISAE3000 and ISAE3410 for their sustainability assurance.

The standards mentioned above fall under the so-called accounting-type assurance, drawing on the financial audit function to develop sustainability reporting assurance practices. A long-standing contrast to this approach is provided by AA1000AS, which was originally issued in 2008, with the latest update, v3, published in 2020 (AccountAbility, 2025). With AA1000AS, the focus of the assurance engagement is very different from the ISAE3000 and forthcoming ISSA5000 in that here the assurance provider evaluates the nature and extent of the organisation's adherence to four AA1000 AccountAbility Principles, inclusivity, materiality, responsiveness and impact (see Table 6.2). The aim is to provide stakeholders information on how the organisation in focus manages its sustainability performance and how this is communicated in the sustainability reporting. AA1000AS has two different types of assurance engagements, of which the first type does not include taking a stand on the reliability of reported information, while the Type 2 assurance assignments include the assurance provider also evaluating the reliability of the information, in addition to looking at the elements mentioned above.

The expectations set for sustainability assurance in the marketplace have also set demands for AA1000AS, with the interest of the financial markets together with the proliferation of sustainability-related risks and opportunities affecting the expectations users have for sustainability assurance. Acknowledging such developments, as well as the fragmentation and confusion caused by differing terminologies and methods, AccountAbility has been working to clarify its position by providing additional guidance and documentation related to how the approach and terminology used in AA1000AS compares with those presented in the ISAE3000 (AccountAbility, 2025). These standards, which have been available and in use side-by-side since the early 2000s, are indeed different and employ different terminology. Perhaps the key point here is that while both are used to provide sustainability assurance, they derive from

**TABLE 6.2** AA1000 AccountAbility Principles

| Principle | Definition | Explanation |
|---|---|---|
| Inclusivity | People should have a say in the decisions that impact them. | By engaging stakeholders, organisations can better understand their concerns and integrate their feedback into sustainability strategies. |
| Materiality | Decision-makers should identify and be clear about the sustainability topics that matter. | Materiality ensures that organisations focus on the sustainability issues that have the greatest impact on both the business and its stakeholders. |
| Responsiveness | Organisations should act transparently on material sustainability topics and their related impacts. | Responsiveness requires organisations to respond to stakeholder concerns in a transparent and accountable manner, addressing key sustainability issues identified through the materiality process. |
| Impact | Organisations should monitor, measure and be accountable for how their actions affect their broader ecosystems. | Impact emphasises the importance of measuring and reporting on the real-world effects of sustainability initiatives, ensuring organisations remain accountable for their actions. |

Source: AccountAbility (2025).

different assumptions and to an extent serve different purposes. Looking at the standards and associated documentation side-by-side can hence be a useful exercise when thinking of what exactly we are trying to achieve with sustainability assurance. Before proceeding to discuss some issues and challenges related to sustainability assurance, a brief look inside the sustainability assurance process is in order, presented in the "Insights from research" textbox below.

**INSIGHTS FROM RESEARCH: WHAT LIES BEHIND A SUSTAINABILITY ASSURANCE STATEMENT?**

When you read the assurance statements published within sustainability reports you might be wondering what happened behind the scenes, what were the processes and interactions that took place? Bouten and Hoozée (2025) usefully shed light on this through their examination of three SA engagements.

With the aim of unravelling "the SA work concealed behind SA statements", Bouten and Hoozée (2025) gain unique insights into the largely hidden process of SA. Their study examines both sides of the sustainability assurance engagement by conducting interviews with the main actors involved both at the Big Four assurance providers and at the client firms. Utilising a sensemaking perspective they build on previous research and knowledge about sustainability assurance work "on the ground" by analysing multiple interactions that take place through the course of an SA engagement. Specifically, they consider interactions amongst the audit team and how the members of the team arrive at either diverging or shared meanings of SA work and how such interactions shape the actual work undertaken. They also analyse interactions between assurors and the clients on aspects such as the scope of the engagement and how these also shape SA.

This research helps us understand not only the process of SA but also the implications. Key insights include how interactions (or organisational socialisation) are needed to create shared meanings allowing work to take place and how, while all assurance teams conducted their work in accordance with ISAE 3000, processes unfolded differently, also considering how these differences were reflected (or not) in the SA statement.

**Bouten, L. and Hoozée, S. (2025). How Sustainability Assurance Work Gets Done: Assurors' Sensemaking, Socialization and Interactions with Clients. *Accounting, Auditing and Accountability Journal, 38(1)*, 143–173.**

## 6.6.3 Sustainability assurance issues and challenges

Even though assurance practices have developed over time, the phenomenon is not without challenges. In general terms, the underlying idea of assurance relates to enhancing the credibility and reliability of the sustainability disclosures. As such it is worth asking, for instance, whether and to what extent the assurance providers aid in ensuring the reliability of the reported information, or whether an assurance statement tells us if the most pertinent issues have been covered in a report. In other words, in this context, there is a major difference between asking "Are these numbers right?" and "Are these the right numbers?" The challenge here is that a positive assurance statement given by, say, a major global Big4 accountancy firm, has substantial symbolic power, as it can signal credibility and indicate trustworthiness.

One of the key challenges relates to the scope of the assurance engagements. In many situations, and as regulation here is coming into force, it is up to the reporting firm to decide the scope of the engagement – that is which parts of the report or reporting process will be subject to assurance. As such assurance can be limited to a relatively minor part of the report, implying that in some accounting type engagements the assurors might only have looked more closely into a particular topic area and the information provided therein. Still, a casual reader can easily be left with an impression that the whole report would have been subject to an assurance process, and that the level of said assurance would have been similar to that used in the financial auditing function.

Being under the discretion of the reporting firm's management entails another issue, the assurance provider's independence. While the financial auditors are in principle serving the firm's shareholders, the owners, the sustainability assurance providers are primarily responsible to the senior executives of the firm. That is, the firm's senior executives can outline the scope and the characteristics of the task. Moreover, should the assurance providers come up with a negative report, it could be considered possible that the firm's senior executives would no longer turn to the same providers next year. The independence of the assurance providers was also a question IAASB paid attention to in developing the forthcoming ISSA5000 standard. Further, the International Ethics Standards Board for Accountants (IESBA) published additional guidance and ethical requirements for sustainability assurance engagements in early 2025, seeking to enhance the trust and transparency of sustainability reporting and assurance practices in the marketplace.

Another aspect that perhaps needs to be considered here is the different perspectives on considering materiality by assurors in financial and sustainability assurance (Moroney and Trotman, 2016). Materiality for sustainability assurance is more complex, requiring additional considerations, if this difference is not understood, then there is potential for confusion. These challenges have also been identified by IAASB, which has in the ISSA5000 standard sought to provide further guidance and requirements for assurance providers when it comes to considering materiality in sustainability assurance engagements. The differences in assessing the materiality of financial and sustainability information will nonetheless remain relevant, and hence we consider the current differences further in the "Focus on practice".

**Focus on practice: ISAE 3000 (revised) and materiality**

As should now be apparent, when it comes to sustainability accounting and sustainability reporting in particular, the concept of materiality is a fundamental one. This is also the case for sustainability report assurance. As outlined by ICAEW (2025), while The International Standards on Auditing do not explicitly define materiality for financial reporting, they do provide reference through several statements and as such provide context for what materiality for financial information means. These relate to where misstatements or omissions could reasonably be expected to influence the (financial) decisions of the user. However, when considering materiality for sustainability reporting and ESG-related subject matter, there are additional considerations relating to economic, environmental and social aspects. These include:

- "The varied and complex nature of the subject matter criteria;
- The impact of auditing forward looking information;

- The impact of the information on the decision-making of a broad set of stakeholders; and
- The accompanying narrative does not omit or distort the information" (ICAEW, 2025).

Furthermore, the ICAEW notes that what needs to be assessed is both the relevance (report materiality) and accuracy (element materiality) of the information.

Source: ICAEW (2025)

## 6.7 The role of sustainability reporting and its limits

A critical question to ask in regard to sustainability reports, sustainability-related disclosures and sustainability information more generally is what role do these reports serve, and do they contribute to attempts to take societies towards less unsustainable trajectories. Sustainability reports command a lot of interest and substantial time and energy are put into preparing and producing them, but we are still largely in the dark when it comes to their role and relevance in societies. Would it be better if both the organisations as well as sustainability-minded individuals across societies focused their efforts on something else, like performance metrics, management systems and sustainability innovations? Would we be better to focus more on actions, not words?

As reporting practices remain a predominant and highly visible activity, several debates are ongoing in search of solutions: how do sustainability reports develop in the future? Will the emphasis be more on a broader level, discharging accountability by providing information to various stakeholder groups with varying needs and wants? Or, as the emphasis in recent years has been, do organisations continue to narrow the focus, mainly serving the investors and fulfilling the information needs this community has? The latter model has gained prominence through, for instance, the establishment of ISSB and the publication of the IFRS Sustainability Disclosure Standards. At the same time, it still appears that stakeholders make limited use of the sustainability reports organisations produce. Before reading this book, had you looked at a sustainability report?

It is much more likely that you will have received sustainability disclosures from companies by other means like social media. While the traditional medium of producing an annual static report of sustainability activities still prevails, social media offers organisations the opportunity to report on activities on a more instant basis, and also to interact with its stakeholders. Likewise, stakeholders can more easily than ever ask questions, make comments and state demands to organisations, and these interactions can swiftly become viral and raise attention to unprecedented levels. Increasing digitalisation, AI tools and new communication channels will also likely have an impact on organisational mechanisms to provide information to stakeholders in the future.

On a social level, sustainability reporting standards are a form of private governance. Instead of nation-states establishing regulations that organisations would be mandated to follow, private organisations operate as de facto standard-setters, in this case with standards such as GRI and IFRS, which organisations then follow. How does such a development fit with democratic processes? Who gets to decide what kind of information organisations are expected to disclose, and in what form?

## 6.8 Conclusion

In this chapter, we have focused on the process of sustainability reporting by discussing the different stages and various choices organisations go through and make as they develop and publish their sustainability reports. We discussed how a key choice relates to the approach to organisational accountability an organisation takes. Sustainability reporting can be approached in a more strategic manner focusing on a narrower group of stakeholders and their respective expectations regarding sustainability information, oftentimes emphasising potential financial implications, risks and opportunities sustainability might have for the organisation. Alternatively, at the other end of a continuum, the organisation can base its accountability on broader ethical considerations regarding a duty to provide sustainability information to a wider group of organisational stakeholders. We have then highlighted key questions in the reporting process, why does an organisation report, to whom is the report targeted, what information is reported on, how is the reporting conducted, and whether the report is subject to assurance. We discussed how the accountability approach an organisation takes, as well as whether it is following specific reporting standards, has implications on choices throughout these stages.

While a range of concluding thoughts could be emphasised, we will limit ourselves to just two. First, we have throughout this chapter and the previous one highlighted the diversity of sustainability reporting in organisations. At the same time, this means that one should avoid simplistic conclusions regarding such reporting. In simple terms, we should neither assume that organisations by definition engage in sustainability reporting purely to pursue private interests and make all their reporting choices accordingly, nor should one put faith in how enhanced reporting will solve global sustainability problems by providing the financial market with sufficient information to make efficient resource allocation in economies. Instead, we wish to emphasise that sustainability reporting practices should be approached with a critical mindset and without taking simple explanations at face value.

This is particularly important in the current day and age, when sustainability reporting, often identified as non-financial reporting, appears to be more prominent than ever. New regulations and frameworks are becoming established, sustainability information is a mainstay in the business media and the perceived relevance of sustainability information in the financial markets has grown swiftly. Remarkable changes have taken place in a very short period of time, and the practices continue to evolve. All this is very significant. Still, we wish to emphasise that it is important to consider the implications such developments have for organisational accountability. The inherently interconnected nature of sustainability, as evidenced for instance by the SDGs, implies that sustainability challenges cannot be tackled without focusing sufficiently on the needs and expectations presented beyond a narrow group of financial stakeholders. We recommend you keep these concluding thoughts in mind as you proceed through the remaining chapters of the book.

## Note

1 In presenting these questions and discussing the five stages we are drawing on the hierarchical staged process model on sustainability reporting originally proposed by Deegan and Unerman (2011). We subsequently developed the model further in the third edition of this book. While we only make limited reference to the model itself here given that its processual nature might be somewhat straightforward for the contemporary context, the proposed stages and associated questions remain helpful for understanding the various decisions concerning sustainability reporting in an organisation.

## References

AccountAbility (2025). AA1000 AccountAbility Principles. Available at www.accountability.org/standards/aa1000-accountability-principles (accessed 27 February 2025).

Bolt, R. and Tregidga, H. (2023). Methodological Insights "Materiality Is …": Sensemaking and Sensegiving through Storytelling. *Accounting, Auditing and Accountability Journal, 36*(1), 403–427.

Bouten, L. and Hoozée, S. (2025). How Sustainability Assurance Work Gets Done: Assurors' Sensemaking, Socialization and Interactions with Clients. *Accounting, Auditing and Accountability Journal, 38*(1), 143–173.

Deegan, C. and Unerman, J. (2011). *Financial Accounting Theory*. London: McGraw-Hill.ICAEW (2025). What Assurance Opinions Can Be Given on ESG Metrics under ISAE 3000 (Revised)?Availableatwww.icaew.com/technical/financial-services/esg-assurance/assurance-opinions-on-esg-metrics-under-isae-3000-revised (Accessed 27 February 2025).

Jørgensen, S., Mjøs, A. and Pedersen, L. J. T. (2022). Sustainability Reporting and Approaches to Materiality: Tensions and Potential Resolutions. *Sustainability Accounting, Management and Policy Journal, 13*(2), 341–361.

KPMG (2024). *The Move to Mandatory Reporting. Survey of Sustainability Reporting 2024.* Available at https://kpmg.com/xx/en/our-insights/esg/the-move-to-mandatory-reporting.html (accessed 17 December 2024).

Moroney, R. and Trotman, K. T. (2016). Differences in Auditors' Materiality Assessments When Auditing Financial Statements and Sustainability Reports. *Contemporary Accounting Research, 33(2)*, 551–575.

Oll, J., Spandel, T., Schiemann, F. and Akkermann, J. (2025). The Concept of Materiality in Sustainability Reporting: From Essential Contestation to Research Opportunities. *Sustainability Accounting, Management and Policy Journal, 16*(2), 321–350.

Puroila, J. and Mäkelä, H. (2019), Matter of opinion: Exploring the socio-political nature of materiality disclosures in sustainability reporting. *Accounting, Auditing & Accountability Journal,* 32(4), 1043-1072.

## Additional reading and resources

Adams, C. A. (2002). Internal Organisational Factors Influencing Corporate Social and Ethical Reporting: Beyond Current Theorising. *Accounting, Auditing and Accountability Journal, 15(2)*, 223–250.

Adams, S., Hall, M. and Xiao, X. (2024). Styles of verification and the pursuit of organisational repair. The case of social impact. *Accounting, Organizations and Society, 113*, 101478.

Cho, C. H., Laine, M., Roberts, R. W. and Rodrigue, M. (2015). Organized Hypocrisy, Organizational Facades, and Sustainability Reporting. *Accounting, Organizations and Society, 40*, 78–94.

Larrinaga, C. and Senn, J. (2021). Norm Development in Environmental Reporting. In Bebbington, J., Larrinaga, C., O'Dwyer, B. and Thomson, I. (eds), *Handbook on Environmental Accounting*, pp. 137–150. Routledge.

Michelon, G. (2021). Financial Markets and Environmental Information. In Bebbington, J., Larrinaga, C., O'Dwyer, B. and Thomson, I. (eds), *Handbook on Environmental Accounting*, pp. 165–178. Routledge.

Reitmaier, C., Schultze, W. and Vollmer, J. (2024). Corporate responsibility and corporate misbehavior: are CSR reporting firms indeed responsible? *Review of Accounting Studies*. https://doi.org/10.1007/s11142-024-09850-8

She, C. and Michelon, G. (2019). Managing Stakeholder Perceptions: Organized Hypocrisy in CSR Disclosures on Facebook. *Critical Perspectives on Accounting*, *61*, 54–76.

Unerman, J. and Zappettini, F. (2014). Incorporating Materiality Considerations into Analyses of Absence from Sustainability Reporting. *Social and Environmental Accountability Journal*, *34*(*3*), 172–186.

CHAPTER

7

# ESG and financial markets

Escalating global sustainability challenges bring increased risks and impacts not only to organisations but also to social, environmental and economic systems more broadly. Financial markets are an example of such a system, and one in which the awareness and significance of sustainability has grown swiftly, as our discussion of the sustainability reporting frameworks in Chapter 5 already showed. In this chapter, we take a closer look at financial markets, risk management and investments from the perspective of sustainability. We present and discuss the increasingly visible practice of what is commonly labelled environment, social and governance (ESG) investments and risk management. Specifically, this chapter discusses not only what ESG investments are, but also how sustainability accounting information and accountability relationships are interconnected with the financial markets and increasing ESG investment activity. This includes how sustainability issues can affect the financial performance and success of an organisation, as well as reflecting on how the financial markets can influence the social and environmental activities of organisations. While understanding the sustainability impacts of organisations is important, this chapter also highlights how accounting for dependencies can be very significant in the context of financial markets.

By the end of this chapter, you should:

- Have considered and reflected upon how and why financial markets are increasingly interested in sustainability.
- Understand how sustainability is a key element in an organisation's attempts to understand future uncertainties and manage associated risks.
- Be able to identify how sustainability performance is intertwined with financial performance, and why pinpointing the exact nature of this relationship has proven to be challenging.
- Understand how financial investors engage with organisations on sustainability matters and have critically reflected on what kind of implications this may have on sustainability.
- Be able to identify and critically reflect on the implications of the higher interest in ESG in financial markets for accounting and accountability.

DOI: 10.4324/9781003533207-9

## 7.1 Introduction to financial markets and sustainability considerations

As we discussed in Part I, different sustainability concerns at both local and global levels have implications on the operating contexts of organisations. The implications of these sustainability issues vary by industry, region and in time, and they can be challenging to understand, estimate and foresee. Financial markets, the system within which capital is allocated to different types of organisations, projects and activities through various financial instruments, are a key element in contemporary societies and are affected by sustainability concerns (Jouffray et al., 2019).

In this chapter, we discuss how sustainability has become, and is likely to continue to be, a highly relevant component for the evaluation of both risk and return, which are the fundamentals of financial markets. Before proceeding, we should point out that while there may be a tendency to speak of investors and financial markets in a fairly general sense, financial markets and systems are complex and include a wide range of investor types and investment arrangements. Investors come in many forms, including for instance private individuals, pension funds, hedge funds, large investment banks, (often large) state-owned equity funds and so on. Likewise, while financial markets are global and interconnected, there are differences in how sustainability and ESG are perceived and valued in different regional and national marketplaces. Furthermore, financial instruments used in financial markets to facilitate capital allocation are also broad and diverse, from the relatively straightforward corporate shares to more complex derivatives and emerging instruments like green bonds and social bonds.

As with many topics covered in this book, it is simply not possible for us to cover all aspects in one chapter, and as such we have had to be quite narrow in our inclusion. Our aim is to provide an introduction to the topic and the key aspects related to our area of focus – sustainability accounting and accountability. As such, rather than a comprehensive coverage we introduce and examine various core concepts. While an attempt has been made to include some diversity, in some of our discussion we have primarily chosen to focus on investment in corporations specifically, rather than, for example, investment in projects or investment by financial institutions which can be influenced by institutional standards and agreements (e.g. the long-standing Equator Principles, see O'Sullivan and O'Dwyer, 2009). However, many of the topics illustrated in this discussion are also relevant for other investment forms and types and some readings and resources are provided at the end of this chapter for those interested in looking further into the topic in more depth.

### 7.1.1 Financial markets, risk and return: How sustainability blends into the mix?

In finance and investment markets, there is a wide range of different methods used to value an investment target, like a corporation. We are not going to go into those valuation models here, as for our purposes, it suffices to say that in virtually any financial model, there are two key elements to be considered when valuing a financial instrument: risk and return. In this context, risk relates to how much risk is involved in the investment whereas return is concerned with the (usually financial) return of the investment. However, if we want to understand how sustainability is associated with the risk and return from the perspective of the investor or the markets more broadly, we also need to consider how sustainability risks manifest at the organisational level.

For organisations, understanding the implications of sustainability in relation to organisational risk has become increasingly relevant. This is especially with regard to making long-term strategic choices that would help the organisation to succeed in the changing operating context. The importance of considering how sustainability affects organisational risk and long-term strategic decisions also has implications on the information managers need in their decision-making. For instance it raises the need to account for various types of dependencies and to understand what types of social and environmental resources, services and aspects are critical for the organisation's long-term success. Relevant questions include, for example, how exposed is the organisation to the various effects of climate change, or what kind of implications do biodiversity loss and the weakening of ecological services in a given region potentially have for the organisation? Likewise, there is a need to learn to evaluate, assess and account for different types of events, developments and scenarios related to sustainability, and subsequently to seek to assess what kind of financial implications these would have for the organisation.

The same applies to investors and the wider range of actors in the financial markets. Similar to organisations, investors try to understand and take into account how sustainability will affect the value and future outlook of the various organisations and other investment targets. That is, a consideration of how various sustainability issues affect the risk and potential returns associated with an investment. In some cases, sustainability has the potential to bring about a range of opportunities which, for example, could help the organisation grow substantially into new markets or product segments. Green tech companies can be considered here as they may be able to leverage off addressing or responding to environmental issues. For others, however, the consequences of sustainability might be more adverse. An increased risk of regulatory intervention, which would lead to higher costs or, in more extreme cases, even require abandoning the current business model, is a situation that illustrates this point. For example, an organisation might be highly dependent on a particular environmental resource, making its financial outlook highly vulnerable. An obvious instance here would be those companies that rely on fossil fuels. However, as the previous chapters illustrate, it is not only fossil fuel companies that are exposed to the risks associated with sustainability, so such concerns are important more broadly.

The sustainability context is therefore important in thinking about ESG investments and risk management which we will discuss in the remainder of this chapter. We will next discuss how sustainability features in the context of risk and financial markets with a brief overview of key concepts in the area. From there, we will consider the organisational level and provide an overview of the relationship between sustainability and risk management. This will then serve as a backdrop for a discussion which explores how sustainability has become a highly significant issue in financial markets through the proliferation of the ESG considerations. We consider here how market actors seek to make sense of the relationship between sustainability, risk and financial returns. Throughout, we will consider what kind of implications all this has for sustainability accounting and accountability.

**Focus on practice: Principles for Responsible Investment**

The Principles for Responsible Investment (PRI) is based on a set of voluntary investment principles concerning how ESG issues can be included in investment practices. Founded in 2006, the aspirational goal behind the Principles is the development of a more sustainable global financial system, which is believed to benefit both the natural environment and societies as a whole. The Principles, originally developed by the investor community, have been signed by a broad range of major professional asset owners, financial service providers and investment managers. The PRI has since the beginning been supported by the United Nations (UN), but it is the organisation that is neither a part of the UN nor associated with any government.

PRI seeks to advance responsible investment and sustainable markets in various ways. They engage in policy work with global policymakers, they develop tools for investors who seek to incorporate ESG factors into their decisions, and they engage in the development and publishing of data and knowledge on responsible investments, ESG and the sustainability of global financial markets. In addition to collaborating with policymakers and the investment community, the PRI also engages with academics in seeking to create more scientific research on responsible investment and sustainable financial markets, and to stimulate interaction between academics, policymakers and the investment community.

## 7.2 Financial markets and ESG

The relationship between financial markets and sustainability has recently gone through major changes, with the dynamics continuing to evolve swiftly amidst increasing understanding of the global sustainability issues, the polarised political atmosphere in many societies, and major geopolitical shifts in the 2020s. Before delving into the present, it is however worth having a quick look at the history, as awareness of past developments will help understanding the present and putting current trends into context.

Until perhaps the early 2000s, there was a fairly common view in the marketplace that by putting emphasis on social, environmental or ethical considerations, the investor could in effect be losing out on opportunities to create financial returns. Sustainability activities were considered to potentially have a negative effect on the financial performance of an entity and any potential return to the investor. This was largely due to them being considered an additional, and for many unnecessary, cost or expense.

In fact, amongst institutional investors, fund managers and pension funds, the polarisation of views surrounding sustainability-related costs and expenses was even stronger. On the one hand, a niche investment market had existed for a long time, with both pioneering ethical investment funds as well as some pension funds actively engaging with social, environmental and ethical considerations. On the other hand, it was often argued that fund managers had a fiduciary duty to take care of the funds handed over to them in a way that created the best possible financial returns, and taking into account social, environmental or ethical aspects through personal values or otherwise secondary considerations would be in conflict with the fund manager's primary duty. These arguments are still present and have featured fairly prominently in the politically loaded conversation in the US market, but in general terms, the discussion has shifted substantially in recent years. There are likely to be a range of reasons for this change, but we can identify two key drivers here.

First, as we have outlined elsewhere, there is now a widespread understanding that in addition to financial resources, organisations and their managers have responsibilities for social and environmental resources and impacts. As such, and as discussed in Chapter 3 in relation to organisational legitimacy and the social contract, an organisation's performance is no longer seen to be based solely on financial performance. Alongside this, and as an organisation's financial returns are associated with this broader understanding of an organisation's performance, the financial performance of a firm is more closely intertwined with its sustainability performance. Second, given the increasing awareness of the likely impacts of sustainability on organisations, for example due to dependencies on the social and environmental context creating potential sustainability risks, rather than being perceived as a cost or expense, managers' careful consideration of sustainability can be seen as an investment towards the long-term success of the organisation. This is perhaps further amplified with prevalent narratives concerning how taking care of sustainability matters is also good for business. This is known as the business case for sustainability. Taken together, these aspects can increase confidence in an organisation and send positive signals to some investors.

At this point, it is worth noting that, as outlined in Chapter 2, sustainability is understood in various ways within the context of financial markets and risk management. This results in a range of terms being referred to. We have defined some of the key terms in this area in the "Pause and reflect" below. However, in this swiftly evolving field, we acknowledge that these terms are not always used in a very coherent manner and can at times be used relatively flexibly and interchangeably.

**PAUSE AND REFLECT…**

Before going further let's take a moment to acknowledge the terminology that you are likely to come across in this area. As you read through them, and before we discuss some of them further below, we suggest you take some time to reflect on the similarities and differences across the different terms used.

**Sustainable finance**: An overarching term used to describe market practices, financial products and ways of thinking, which seek to incorporate sustainability into how the markets operate. The term escapes an exact definition and it is used and understood in varying ways. European Commission in its overview defines sustainable finance as referring to "the process of taking environmental, social and governance (ESG) considerations into account when making investment decisions in the financial sector, leading to more long-term investments in sustainable economic activities and projects" (European Commission, 2025).

**ESG**: The term we use in this chapter is used in different ways and in combination with other terms (e.g. ESG-investing) to indicate that environmental, social and governance issues have in some way been considered. You are likely aware of various ESG investment funds, the market of which has grown rapidly, and which are now available for retail investors in great numbers. It is important to be aware however that the label ESG does not specify how environmental, social and governance factors are considered, as there are numerous ways of doing so. It is also pertinent to note that the term ESG is used more extensively in the context of financial markets and investments than the term "sustainability", despite the overarching term "sustainable finance" being widely used.

**Negative screening**: Implies processes in which investors pre-screen possible investment targets based on some pre-defined characteristics. Common examples are excluding companies dealing with, say weapons, gambling or pornography from the portfolio. This means companies in these industries are excluded altogether from investment regardless of potential returns. Characteristics used in the screening process vary and can change over time. Recent examples would be coal, which more and more investors are seeing as a "non-investable" activity, while the geopolitical tensions of the 2020s have resulted in some investors removing conventional weapons from their negative screening lists.

**Socially responsible investing (SRI)**: SRI is another common term. SRI tends to be used as a broader label to indicate investment approaches trying to diminish the social and environmental impacts of investment targets. At times SRI is used interchangeably with ethical investing and sustainable investing. We note however that these later terms can have more specific meanings.

**Ethical investment**: One of the early terms used in the area. Traditionally used to refer to investment strategies following certain values or ethical beliefs, implying for instance the exclusion of particular industries via screening. You may have heard of ethical investment funds, for example. These funds are set up to assist investors who want to balance financial returns with ensuring they direct their investment into ethical (or at least not problematic) activities. While you can continue to see the term used in this way, it is today also used interchangeably with other terms, such as ESG-investing, to indicate to more generic meaning.

**Impact investing**: Impact investing is when investors use the investment or the allocation of capital in seeking to achieve other outcomes beyond financial returns. Impacts might for instance refer to social goods or environmental improvements, which do not bring direct financial returns to the investor. Impact investing does not, however, imply the provision of concessionary capital, even though these are at times associated together.

### 7.2.1 Types of ESG investing

When reading the business press or following social media, it has become increasingly hard not to notice how sustainability and financial markets are frequently tied together. The picture given is sometimes filled with simplifications, in which the diversity in this area gets lost as everything is lumped together in producing catchy headlines or simple checklists. In addition to providing definitions for some key terms in the above "Pause and reflect", it may be useful to provide further signposts regarding some key categories in the financial markets. We will do this by outlining three commonly discussed types of ESG investing, that is, ways in which questions of sustainability are taken into consideration in investment decisions (see Crifo et al., 2019). We will provide more nuance to these overviews as we proceed with this chapter.

The traditional way to take sustainability into account in the financial markets would perhaps be value-based investing. Value-based investing essentially implies designing one's investment portfolio according to one's values, beliefs and norms. Typical examples here would include investing in projects, companies or industries which are seen to align with one's values; for example, those producing environmentally responsible products or organisations known for having good social performance. As a private investor, you may well be aware of some value-based or ethical investment funds, a range of which have been available since the 1960s. Value-based investment also often means excluding investments into particular industries, such as tobacco or gambling, or the decision to divest from particular organisations should the company engage in something the investor thinks is in contradiction with their own value position. Here, value-based decisions are often superior to considerations of risk and return, meaning that the investor is willing to bypass some financial opportunities due to social, environmental or ethical reasonings.

Currently, the biggest stream of ESG investing is arguably the approach of ESG integration. ESG integration starts from the idea of improving the risk-return characteristics of one's investments through a careful consideration of ESG factors. Again, there is a range of styles, approaches and principles used by investors. In general, the investors do not rule out investment opportunities categorically based on some characteristics. Instead, the ESG factors, foreseen opportunities and potential risks would be assessed in various ways and these considerations are embedded in the evaluation of the investment's risk-return characteristics. Perhaps it is useful to consider an example. The car industry provides us with a range of things that could be considered here. ESG concerns in the car industry could involve the investor carefully considering the range of models a given manufacturer has developed, the new technologies it has invested in, as well as the company's social and environmental performance and its relative position within the industry, perhaps as assessed by some third-party industry expert. In essence, in this approach, the investor is acknowledging that the world is changing and hence aims at developing one's investment process and appraisal methods to take this change into account in the investment decisions.

A third area of ESG-investing worth mentioning here is the different forms of impact investing (see above for a definition). Within impact investment, the logic of the investment appraisal is again different as, in addition to the risk-return considerations, the investor is also seeking to create other types of impacts, mostly in the form of social or environmental goods. These impacts would not benefit the investor directly, but would benefit some other groups, communities, geographical areas or the society in general; for example, through the reduction of income equality or slowing of deforestation and regional loss of biodiversity. It is also possible that the investor gets some indirect benefits via, for instance, increased stability of an area or improved reputation. These indirect benefits are unlikely to be the key element here, however, as it is relevant to note that impact investment is not the same as charity or donations, and the investment is nonetheless expected to bring a financial return to the investor.

A practical example of impact investing would be the various opportunities to invest in the production and distribution of solar panels in Sub-Saharan Africa. There might be other, financially more attractive investment options available, but for an impact investor such solar panels could offer a possibility to both receive financial return and contribute positively on various SDGs. From the corporate sphere, we could use the example of Novo Nordisk, a Danish pharmaceutical company. Novo Nordisk established, through its holding company in 2018, the REPAIR Impact Fund. This fund invests in early stage companies and start-ups in seeking to address resistant micro-organisms, such as bacteria, which are a growing global sustainability problem. As was the case with the solar panels, the REPAIR Impact Fund is not about philanthropy, but it operates according to usual principles of venture capital. The key for Novo Nordisk and the Fund, however, is that such investments can potentially contribute to alleviating a substantial global health issue. Within climate tech, the activities of the Breakthrough Energy would fit this mould, as core mission behind its investments is seeking to accelerate climate work and help societies avoid climate catastrophe.

**Focus on practice: Green bonds**

In addition to the equity market we mostly focus on in this chapter, ESG integration is becoming more prominent also in the debt market. Green bonds are an example of the new types of financial instruments emerging as the financial markets are increasingly engaging with sustainability. In simple terms, a green bond is an instrument used to raise capital for environmental projects. Such projects can be aimed at achieving different types of environmental outcomes, such as environmentally friendly technologies, sustainable agriculture, energy efficiency and mitigation of climate change, to name but a few.

The market for green bonds has expanded swiftly since they were introduced in the late 2000s. This relates to the increasing need for both the private and public sectors to find capital for projects needed to help organisations and societies tackle sustainability challenges, mitigate sustainability risks and harness opportunities that arise. The attractiveness of green bonds for investors is often related to tax incentives or other types of government subsidies associated with them. Green bonds also offer investors reputational benefits and can help them satisfy potential requirements set by states or other actors concerning allocating some of their assets to climate-friendly or environmental investments.

Despite their increasing popularity, the standardisation and regulation of green bonds remain somewhat scattered. However, international voluntary process guidelines and standards do exist, such as the Green Bond Principles published by International Capital Market Association ICMA, and the Climate Bonds Standard published by the Climate Bonds Initiative. There are now also a range of national standards and guidelines, including, for instance, China Green Bond Principles, set in 2022, Brazil's Sovereign Sustainable Bond Framework, established in 2023, and Indonesia's Green Bond and Green Sukuk Framework, going back to 2018. In Europe, the EU introduced in 2024 the EU Green Bond Standard, which is a voluntary label for the issuance of green bonds. In setting the standard, the EU is aspiring to facilitate finding finance for the investments needed for low-carbon transition and to reduce greenwashing creating problems in the marketplace. The EU Green Bond Standard is closely linked to other EU sustainable finance initiatives, and it draws on the criteria of sustainable economic activities set out in the EU Taxonomy.

## 7.3 An organisational perspective: Risk, future uncertainty and sustainability

The variety and increased popularity of ESG investments increases the demand for information as all the types of ESG investment decisions outlined above require additional information beyond simply financial performance. Furthermore, such information required by ESG investors cannot come solely from external assessments or sources. Indeed, ESG investment decisions need to be supported with a considerable amount of information deriving from inside the investment target, be that an organisation, a project or any other type of entity. This is directly connected to the fast evolution of sustainability reporting practices in recent years, as well as the grown interest of financial market institutions to be involved in shaping sustainability reporting frameworks. Further, we should also bear in mind that the information does not simply appear in a report, but it must originate from somewhere. As such, the growth in demand for sustainability information means that accounting and other information systems in organisations are key. While our earlier discussion of the role of sustainability management accounting and control systems in organisations in Chapter 4 is relevant in this context, we extend that discussion here with a further look into the relevance of risk and risk management in organisations from a sustainability perspective.

### 7.3.1 Identifying risks related to sustainability

For the managers of an organisation, one of the key elements through which sustainability gets approached is through a consideration of uncertainty. While organisational managers have always had to deal with uncertainty and different types of risks, be that in relation to abrupt political changes, currency fluctuations or sudden natural catastrophes like earthquakes or flooding, the escalating and intertwined social and environmental challenges have brought an additional layer of complexity to the consideration of uncertainty and risks.

Furthermore, it is widely understood that the uncertainties associated with sustainability are going to grow further, and likely in ways which are challenging to understand, foresee and control. To make it even more complicated from an organisational perspective, sustainability-related risks are typically beyond the organisation's control. An organisation's actions per se might not be causing the materialisation of the risk, but perhaps the actions or cascades of interconnected actions by several other groups in society trigger a flow of events, eventually affecting the company and its operating context. We can think of the risks associated with climate change here. This uncontrollable and unpredictable nature of sustainability for individual organisations and its associated impacts has also brought in a shift in many organisations' approach to it. While previously many organisations may have looked more into preventing and stopping potential impacts (e.g. reducing carbon emissions as part of addressing climate change), it has now become more commonplace to also focus on how the organisation can adapt its operations and become resilient to a range of changes and risks. The significance of this approach is illustrated by how the guidelines put forth by the TCFD quickly gained a prominent position among organisations and the business world, and how the identification, assessment and disclosure of climate and other sustainability risks and associated risk management strategies sit at the core of the sustainability reporting standards being set by the ISSB (see Chapter 5).

We should also keep in mind here that the financial markets with their dominant operating logics have an effect on how organisations consider sustainability-related risks. While sustainability risks can materialise in different ways, such risks and their possible consequences are always seen from a particular perspective. In the context of the financial markets, sustainability risks are still often assessed with regard to an organisation and its activities through a financial lens. In essence, we are focusing on an outside-in perspective, which looks at the kind of financial implications sustainability could have on a particular entity or activity. It is not uncommon that corporate executives follow a similar logic when considering how the organisation is exposed to potential sustainability risks. This approach of assessing with priority given to financial implications, i.e. focusing on financial materiality, tends to ignore or devalue a range of other types of risks and consequences associated with the organisation's accountability relationships. Typically, these would not affect the organisation but some other groups, like vulnerable communities, incommensurable or intangible values or some species without a direct economic value associated to them. In other words, the inside-out perspective of sustainability, which would be the focus of impact materiality, is in general paid less attention to or not considered to be as significant.

### 7.3.2 Illustrating increased uncertainty: Climate change

When thinking about the range of implications sustainability has for an organisation, it is necessary to consider organisational risks on various levels and on different timescales. Let's consider some examples related to climate change to illustrate various sustainability-related risks. We will here approach risks through three categories – physical risks, transition risks and liability risks – which illustrate different types of implications that climate change can have on organisations and the financial system more broadly (see Carney, 2015).

Physical risks are perhaps the easiest place to start from. At local and regional levels, organisations need to be aware of, for instance, the likelihood of more weather-related risks caused by the higher occurrence of adverse weather conditions due to climate change. If production facilities are in vulnerable locations, for example, logistics could be affected. Such risks can be sudden and have substantial material effects on the short term. Think of seasonal wildfires in California and the seasonal floods in Bangladesh, both of which appear to be growing in severity due to climate change. Moreover, as many organisations, in particular large corporations, are dependent on long supply chains spread out over a large geographical area, the risk could be challenging to avoid entirely.

Climate change and changing weather patterns are also a significant factor when it comes to the availability of resources. Both long-term droughts and extensive rains are expected to be more common, which poses new types of risks for companies dependent on crops from particular areas. Take global cocoa production, much of which takes place in a small area in Western Africa. In early 2020s, crops in this area were severely affected by adverse weather patterns, which are seen to be at least partly caused by climate change. The climate risks have hence materialised, resulting in low supplies and hiking prices, leaving organisations dependent on supply chains in this region with substantial problems in finding alternative solutions. This on-going development has already incentivised some companies to diversify their supply chain and in particular trying to ensure that their raw materials are sourced from multiple geographical locations. However, this is not possible for all organisations, especially those that are much smaller in size or those which operate mainly in the local context.

It is the longer term in particular which makes climate change an important driver for organisations to develop their risk management systems and processes. At the macro level, there is a consensus that climate change will impact societies and economies in different ways. At the same time however, it is hard to pinpoint how, when and in what ways exactly this will happen. We can here refer to transition risks, which include financial risks potentially following from the transition to a low-carbon and less unsustainable economy. It is likely that there are going to be public policies and regulations, related for instance to the use of natural resources and consumption. Likewise, market demand and consumer preferences can change substantially, partly due to new public policies and taxation, but also due to a pressing need to do things differently. Such changes can happen over a longer period, or they might be rather abrupt and sudden. Furthermore, environmental degradation in a given region may give rise to social unrest and make societies less stable, which again can cause significant challenges to organisations operating in those regions or being dependent on resources sourced there. Taken together, such changes in policy, technology and social structures may result in substantial changes in how assets are valued, as impacts, dependencies, costs and opportunities become more visible and better understood. Such transition risks can be significant for both individual organisations and the financial markets more broadly.

Furthermore, in addition to such transition risks, we should also acknowledge the potential liability risks climate change brings about. While the most apparent risks arising from climate change could concern the physical environment and hence cause physical risks for organisations, it is important to note how such physical changes can also create substantial liabilities for organisations in the long term. For example, individuals, communities or societies could seek compensation for the damages or losses they have suffered due to climate change from those parties that are considered to be responsible. While this may seem far-fetched in the first instance, it would not be the first time something like this has happened. Think about asbestos, which was widely used as a building material across the globe. After the substantial health risks associated with asbestos became understood, its use has been banned or heavily restricted in numerous countries. Individuals suffering from serious health issues caused by asbestos, such as cancer or other asbestos-related illnesses, have sought compensation from the companies involved in the production or use of asbestos, for instance on the grounds that these organisations knew about the dangers, and did not act to remedy them or provide sufficient information for those exposed in the workplace. Given that many of the asbestos-related illnesses take years or decades to develop, the liabilities have also incurred slowly, providing an example of a long-tailed liability. Court cases and frequency of climate litigation in relating to corporate liability for damages associated with climate change is increasing, with high profile cases often involving oil and gas companies. The potential for substantial long-term liabilities is hence recognised in the corporate sphere and it is having tangible consequences for organisations and the marketplace. Increasing insurance costs associated with some organisations, regions or activities is an example of such consequences, as insurance companies can charge higher premiums for those considered to be increasingly exposed to climate related risks.

The above illustration is not an exhaustive list but intends to provide examples of the types of uncertainties arising from a particular issue, in this case climate change. Other sustainability issues have different types of implications. It is significant to keep in mind here that sustainability issues are interconnected, as the SDGs aptly visualise, and hence they should not be considered and treated as isolated things. Climate change, as discussed above, is connected with the availability of water, food and nutrition, equality and human rights, social stability and biodiversity, to name but a few other sustainability issues. Some of these connections are more immediate, whereas others can materialise only over a longer period.

### 7.3.3 Risk assessment

Identifying and evaluating sustainability-related risks is not an easy task for any organisation. Still, this does not mean that organisations cannot, and should not, take steps to prepare, learn and eventually act in ways which take the uncertainties into account. The emergence of novel sustainability reporting frameworks, such as TCFD, ISSB and CSRD, also means that considerations of sustainability risks have become mainstream in major organisations, since the frameworks require firms to assess sustainability risks and subsequently disclose the principles and approaches they follow. At the same time, the multifaceted nature of sustainability implies that these assessments can be complicated, and sometimes firms may resort to a tickbox exercise and be content with boilerplate disclosures. Properly understanding the complexity of sustainability and associated risks may require stepping outside a traditional mindset, however, and understanding that the intertwining impacts and dependencies may require new types of competencies, skills and ways of working.

Accounting has a key role in this process as it is influential with regard to various types of assessments and evaluation in organisations. Once the possible risks and opportunities have been identified, organisations will need to assess and understand their relevance. Given that sustainability risks can affect an organisation on multiple levels, on varying timescales, and in unforeseen ways, such assessments are likely to need to go beyond traditional risk assessment dimensions looking at the likelihood of occurrence and the severity of potential impacts.

There are a wide range of options when it comes to how risks can be evaluated. Qualitative risk assessments and evaluations are perhaps the most common approach. These can be used to gain an initial understanding of a situation, to estimate the scale of risks and opportunities and to provide a starting point for further analysis. A commonly used example here would be a risk matrix (see Figure 7.1), on which the potential sustainability risks are plotted. The axes of such a matrix would typically focus on the likelihood of impact, ranging from very unlikely to very likely, and the significance of the impact, ranging from negligible to extensive. Visualising potential risks through such a matrix can provide an easily understandable overview of the situation, and thereby prove useful also as a communication tool to different stakeholders.

Oftentimes, however, some quantitative figures, in the form of financials or otherwise, are needed for one to be able to compare different alternatives. Here, we are facing similar challenges to those discussed in Chapter 4 in regard to quantification

| Likelihood of occurrence \ Significance of impact | Negligible | Minor | Moderate | Major | Massive |
|---|---|---|---|---|---|
| Very Probable | Low | Medium | High | Critical | Critical |
| Probable | Low | Medium | High | High | Critical |
| Moderate | Low | Medium | Medium | High | High |
| Unlikely | Very low | Low | Medium | Medium | High |
| Very Unlikely | Very low | Very low | Low | Medium | Medium |

**FIGURE 7.1** Risk Matrix

and commensurability. In addition, to understand how uncertainty can unfold and impact the organisation in the longer term, different scenarios and alternative paths can be created, modelled and evaluated. Here, it is relevant to acknowledge that inaction can be costly. Sustainability changes societies and operating contexts in substantial and significant ways – it is unlikely that any organisation can simply remain as they are.

No matter what type of models and estimation tools are being used, assessments are dependent on the information that is available. Here, the different sustainability accounting tools are relevant, as this information helps the organisation to understand both what kind of sustainability-related impacts its activities have as well as which sustainability aspects, issues and services it is the most dependent on. Moreover, to supplement the organisation's own information systems, having healthy dialogue with different stakeholder groups is often essential. This can help foresee some silent signals and forthcoming trends which could have an impact on the organisation's activities.

### 7.3.4 Decision-making and communication

Assessments will have limited relevance unless they are both integrated into the organisation's decision-making process and communicated to those external parties interested in the organisation's decisions.

Internally, taking sustainability into account in decision-making and long-term forecasting will require the development of new heuristics. Despite quantitative modelling and various scenarios, one might still not be able to compare alternatives directly. For this, constant modelling and follow-up is needed. Furthermore, and as the knowledge and understanding of sustainability develops and affects the prepared scenarios, their likelihoods and possible impacts over time need to be constantly updated. Moreover, it is also important to consider how sustainability is incorporated into an organisation's remuneration and compensation schemes. That is, integrating relevant sustainability targets into the compensation schemes of the managers and employees responsible for achieving those goals can help by providing incentives for them to take action, and hence guide decisions.

In addition to integrating risk assessments into decision-making, there is also a need to communicate those evaluations to external stakeholders. As we discussed in Chapters 5 and 6, sustainability reporting takes many forms and can contain a variety of information directed to interested parties, including the financial markets and various investors. There are different approaches to sustainability reporting depending on preferences and materiality assessments. A report can be intended to cater to a broad mix of stakeholders, seeking to provide sufficient information to satisfy the differing expectations such groups have. Alternatively, a report can be aimed at a narrower audience by focusing on issues and types of information some specific stakeholder groups are more interested in. Disclosures prepared according to reporting frameworks such as the SASB, TCFD and ISSB would often be such examples, as these would typically be catering to investors and financial stakeholders.

At the same time, the investors might not consider the information included in an organisation's sustainability report as sufficient for their evaluation of the company. Despite an organisation putting its best effort into producing a report, the expected information might still not be available, it might be provided in a form that the investor cannot readily make use of, or there might be concerns regarding the credibility and accuracy of the report. Hence, investors, especially large investors and investment funds, can approach companies and request supplementary information or meetings to gain a more comprehensive understanding of the potential implications the sustainability risks and opportunities may have for the company. While the evolution of standardised sustainability reporting targeting the financial markets is likely to improve the transparency and comparability of publicly available information, it remains unclear whether the quality of these disclosures will satisfy the needs of investors. The role of private sustainability disclosures is likely to change however as reporting becomes increasingly mandated and thus subject to regulatory demands more akin to those associated currently with financial reporting.

Moreover, as the financial markets are often considered to be the most powerful stakeholder, the requests and expectations of investors can also have implications on questions of accountability (see Andrew and Cortese, 2013). Does the management prioritise the expectations and viewpoints of the more powerful stakeholders, and thereby for instance ignore or downplay demands stated by some vulnerable groups? Does the information demanded by powerful stakeholders override other concerns? Do the expectations of financial stakeholders have an effect on how an organisation develops its assessment and accounting systems in regard to sustainability, and how this information is taken into account in decision-making processes? Sustainability, ESG and corporate responsibility are seen in different ways by different groups, and this can have implications on the identification, assessment and communication of risks. Indeed, the investor community is an important influence on sustainability accounting and accountability, having the potential to influence the form it takes. This relates closely to the perspective taken: are potential risks considered primarily through a financial materiality, placing the emphasis on the outside-in view and the question of what kind of risks sustainability can bring to firm financials and future outlook, or are risks also considered through an impact materiality viewpoint with an inside-out focus looking into the potential sustainability risks firm activities might be causing or accentuating? The recent evolution in the sustainability reporting landscape has clearly moved the emphasis towards the former.

**Focus on practice: EU Taxonomy and Sustainability Finance Disclosure Regulation**

Since the early 2020s, the EU has been working to develop the continent following the European Green Deal. The Green Deal consists of a wide-range of actions, initiatives, fundings elements and regulatory changes seeking to make EU more resource-efficient and climate friendly. Sustainable finance has been one the areas for policy development as the EU has sought to find ways to support finance to take into account environmental, social and governance factors, and thereby assist in achieving the environmental and climate objectives of the Green Deal. This has resulted in various initiatives, such as the European Green Bond Standard (discussed below) and the EU regulation on ESG ratings. And, of course, sustainability reporting regulation, the Corporate Sustainability Reporting Directive (CSRD) and European Sustainability Reporting Standards (ESRS) discussed in Chapter 5.

Alongside the CSRD, there are also two other related regulations relevant in the context of the financial markets, namely Sustainable Finance Disclosure Regulation (SFDR) and the EU Taxonomy. The SFDR focuses on financial markets in particular, and stipulates how various financial market participants, such as asset managers and financial advisers, should communicate sustainability information to prospective investors. The implications of the SFDR can be visible for private investors as well, since alongside other disclosure requirements it includes requirements to provide sustainability information on the product level. Known as articles 6, 8 ("light green") and 9 ("dark green"), these categories should, in simple terms, distinguish products which promote sustainable characteristics, but do not have sustainability as the key goal (article 8), and those that have sustainable investment objectives and target sustainable investments as a primary goal (article 9), from the non-sustainable funds which do not integrate sustainability into the decision-making process and should not be considered to be ESG funds (article 6).

EU Taxonomy is a classification system which seeks to facilitate sustainable investments by helping investors and other market participants better identify potential opportunities, with the goal being directing financial flows to more sustainable alternatives and activities. The classification is based on prescribed criteria and environmental objectives, which an activity has to fulfil in order to qualify. These classifications are also applied within the CSRD and SFDR, as those reporting need to consider how the activities are aligned with the EU Taxonomy's classification of sustainable economic activities.

Together with the CSRD, the SFDR and EU Taxonomy are expected to assist EU with the sustainability transition, as they are expected to help companies, investors and the financial markets with making more sustainable investment decisions by having more consistent, reliable and comparable information available for them. The effects of increased requirements and expectations of transparency became tangible in December 2022 and January 2023, when numerous market participants downgraded various ESG funds from Article 9 to Article 8. This illustrates how these EU regulatory initiatives can have an effect on what kind of an investment or a fund can be called or marketed as sustainable.

## 7.4 How sustainability features in financial markets

Having discussed what kind of implications sustainability has on organisations' consideration of risk and uncertainty, we now move to the broader landscape and start discussing how sustainability features in financial markets. In so doing, we also shift our perspective: while in the previous section we focused on the organisation, in the following, our emphasis is on looking at the questions from the viewpoint of the investors or the markets more broadly.

As highlighted above, the basic principle for investors and any analysis for investment purposes relates to evaluating the risk-return characteristics of the investment target. Corporate finance, for example, has developed a wide range of models which can be used to deconstruct the financial information provided by a company as well as to analyse how the various companies in the marketplace are positioned in comparison with one another. A key requirement for this is the comparability of the statutory financial disclosures. Companies covered by financial reporting regulations are required to deliver the financial information in a particular way, following strict guidelines and according to specific schedules. While the financial disclosures might not be perfectly comparable, they are nonetheless close enough to allow the markets to digest the information through standard procedures.

The sustainability setting remains different. While there are different types of sustainability reporting guidelines, standards and frameworks (see Chapter 5), and while some of those are primarily geared towards the investors and the financial markets, the information provided by companies on these matters continues to be very different from the financial information. This is caused by considerations of materiality, for example, as sustainability in general is much more context dependent than financial measures. The same items, questions and issues cannot be assumed to be material in a similar manner for all companies. Moreover, even if the material questions were identified to be similar, different companies may use different indicators, they might collect the information in different ways, and they might communicate and emphasise different aspects. As such, investors cannot use standard processes and models in a plug-and-play fashion, and they hence need to learn how to take ESG and the various ESG-related information into account in their analysis.

For many, a key question through which a variety of sustainability factors are analysed in financial markets still boils down to looking into how they could affect the financial performance and future cashflows of the company. That is, for many investors, especially institutional investors, the primary concern remains the financial dimension with sustainability often primarily considered in relation to its ability to affect financial performance and future prospects either negatively or positively. With regard to sustainability, the challenges faced by investors when analysing this information are similar to those faced by the organisation. How are uncertain effects, impacts and dependencies assessed and valued over varying timeframes, given in particular the fact that the information available might not be in a standard form?

The concept of materiality continues to have relevance here. Differing possibly from other stakeholders' viewpoints, from an investor's point of view the materiality of ESG information is evaluated from a financial standpoint. It is hence possible to find situations and contexts in which some aspects of sustainability might be highly topical and perhaps discussed in the public sphere, but they might still not be considered relevant for the investor. Clearly, it might not always be that simple to identify which would be the sustainability issues that become the most relevant in the near future. The SASB standards seek to tackle this very issue in their framework for sustainability reporting by providing industry-specific lists which, according to their criteria, would be the most material aspects for each industry. It is worth remembering from Chapter 3 however that materiality is not something absolute, as the relative importance of issues differs based on the observer, the timeframe and the value judgements made.

As mentioned above, sustainability information seldom comes in a form which can be readily inserted into existing and well-established financial models. Instead, after identifying the material questions and topics, the investor needs to assess the value of different types of qualitative and quantitative ESG information and then integrate this evaluation into the financial decision-making process. Given that ready-made solutions are limited, each investor has to come up with their own approach. This is further complicated when we keep in mind that different investors have different values and aims motivating investment decisions. In addition, the process of identifying, collecting and analysing the necessary sustainability information requires considerable resources and skillsets, which might not be available even for many institutional investors. As such, the power of the various ESG rankings and sustainability rating schemes is substantial as investors seek to find some tangible, and apparently objective, basis for their estimations.

### INSIGHTS FROM RESEARCH: UNBURNABLE COAL AND STRANDED ASSETS

"Accounting disclosures are critical to the effective functioning of stock markets" (Bebbington et al., 2020, p. 2). Not only is this a statement made explicitly on page two of this research paper by Bebbington et al., but also it is a central proposition running throughout the paper on fossil fuel reserves and disclosures, unburnable carbon and stranded assets.

Unburnable carbon is a term used to signal carbon reserves (e.g. oil and gas, and coal) that exist but are unlikely to be able to be combusted due to various constraints. These constraints can be financial – the expense required to access the reserve makes them uneconomical – as well as constraints related to the increasing scientific understandings of the climate emergency and the global agreements which restrict global warming activities.

To investigate the issue of unburnable coal and its implications, Bebbington et al. conduct a literature review, interview market commentators and participants, review reporting requirements for fossil fuel companies and review disclosure practices of firms from 35 companies from seven countries with substantive fossil fuel listings on their stock exchanges.

They find the presence of what can be termed "unburnable coal" in the stock market and note that this has potential, although largely unknown, implications for the financial market. They state:

> On the one hand, data in annual reports and accounts quantify fossil fuel reserves and resources, and financial markets ascribe value to reserves and resources because they imply a future revenue stream. In contrast, global climate change science (alongside regulatory regimes in this area) suggests that not all fossil fuel reserves and resources currently identified will be combusted because to do so would lead to greenhouse gas emissions targets not being met (hence the phrase "unburnable carbon").
>
> (p. 2)

They ultimately note that the scientific understandings of climate and carbon develop separately from the financial market considerations and note that there is a potential carbon bubble in the stock market. Their interviews suggest that there is a "common belief" that at some time carbon constraints will have an impact on firm valuations which will have an effect on the stock market. However, when looking at company disclosure they found only a "small number of direct references in mandatory or voluntary reports to stranded assets", and hence conclude that "the issue of unburnable carbon is not currently considered a material item" (p. 12).

This research highlights both the way in which sustainability has the potential to affect organisations and stock markets, as well as demonstrates the uncertainty as to how we might account for them. Furthermore, if accounting disclosures are important for the functioning of the stock market, and required by investors to make investment decisions, it also bodes the question as to why this value relevant information is not disclosed by many of the large fossil fuel companies included in this study. While the sustainability reporting frameworks have taken major steps since the publication of this paper, particularly from the investor perspective, it is unclear whether corporate disclosures have evolved in a way that would make the findings of a similar study any different today. A significant consideration here would be time, and the question of whether markets consider any potential major disruptions to be so far in the future that they are not worth considering in the present time.

**Bebbington, J., Schneider, T., Stevenson, L. and Fox, A. (2020). Fossil Fuel Reserves and Resources Reporting and Unburnable Carbon: Investigating Conflicting Accounts. *Critical Perspectives on Accounting, 66,* 1–22**

## 7.5 The role of ESG-scores, ratings and ranking lists

The complexity inherent in the assessment and evaluation of sustainability factors has paved the way for the emergence of different types of aggregated metrics and rating schemes. These metrics and rating schemes aim to help those interested in taking sustainability into account in their decision-making in the financial markets. Some of these resemble labels one can see in a supermarket: if an investment target, be that an organisation or a bond, fulfils particular criteria, it receives a label signalling it. At the simplest, this could entail for instance an NGO including a company on a list of signatories committed to protecting some type of wildlife in its investments, or alternatively on a negative list of companies, which have not publicly committed to reducing their emissions according to the most recent climate accord.

Other powerful examples would be stock market indexes such as the Dow Jones Sustainability World Index and the FTSE4Good. Both of these indexes include an annually updated list of companies which have been selected on the basis of varying sustainability criteria. Many companies consider these indexes to be important and are keen to highlight their membership as a signal of their commitment and achievements in sustainability (see next "Focus on practice" for more details).

On a more advanced level, there are various ranking lists which are based on more complicated scoring systems of organisational activities. Examples of these include CDP's A-list, focusing on corporate transparency and climate action, and Corporate Knights Global 100 listing what they label the most sustainable companies in the world. Likewise, scores and ratings are available via prominent financial media companies, such as Bloomberg, major financial market companies, such as MSCI, Refinitiv and Morningstar Sustainalytics, as well as the leading rating firms, such as

Moody's and S&P Global Ratings (or just S&P). In some of the rating schemes companies are given exact scores, while in other cases rankings are handed out in tiers. Oftentimes, however, the exact mechanism used to produce the scores is not presented publicly or is only vaguely discussed, even when the rating provider publicly claims to be committed to high transparency. In other words, those seeking to use the information have limited capability to evaluate how the scores have been put together and which items have been given emphasis. This is also relevant as the scoring systems used by different providers result in discrepancies in scores (Berg et al., 2022), which together with the limited transparency can cause challenges for those seeking to make use of this information. Some regulators are seeking to enhance the transparency, with the EU ESG rating regulation serving as an example. Finally, it also worth noting that many of the rating organisations are also businesses, and hence they use their scores, scoring systems and ratings to compete for market share against their own peers.

**Focus on practice: Sustainability in stock market indexes**

You may have noticed that in stock markets across the world, be that in Tokyo, Shanghai, Sydney or Sao Paolo, there are indexes which refer to including companies based on various sustainability, ESG or CSR criteria. While these indices may look similar and have similar names, the criteria used to include companies differ substantially. To illustrate these differences, we will here present two alternative approaches.

In the London Stock Exchange, sustainability indices come under the FTSE4Good-series. FTSE4Good was one of the world's first ESG indices when it was launched in 2001. Today, there are some 300 indicators across 14 themes that can be used to evaluate each company. To be included in the index, the company must reach a minimum threshold score set on an annual basis. This implies that there is no set amount of companies from a particular industry that will be included. FTSE4Good also has some exclusion criteria, stipulating that companies from particular industries will not be included. In addition to industries such as tobacco and controversial weapons, which have been excluded for a longer time, the exclusion also includes a more recent addition in coal. There have however been controversies about the latter, since the criterion only excludes companies which have coal as their main business area, which implies that major coal producers can still be included, should they be conglomerates or have substantial operations in other business areas.

The New York-based Dow Jones Sustainability World Index (DJSWI) is probably the most widely known ESG index in the world. Launched in 1999, it was the world's first sustainability index used in stock exchanges. DJSWI differs from FTSE4Good in that it follows a best-in-class approach in its inclusion. This implies that after the potential companies have been evaluated and scored, the companies receiving top sustainability scores in each industry will be included in the index. The number of included companies varies between 10% and 30% of evaluated companies depending on the type of index. There are no direct excluding criteria in DJSWI, which means that the index includes leaders from industries some may have a hard time considering sustainable, such as tobacco, gambling and firearms. There is a mechanism however to evaluate and exclude companies that are associated with controversial activities or are considered to be major risks on the composition of the indices.

Again, these differences illustrated in this example highlight the need to be mindful that variations in practices exist, and that there is often the need to stop, consider and evaluate the various practices and their implications.

For example, by not excluding any type of industry or corporate activity, but instead applying the best in class principle, the Dow Jones Sustainability Index includes the companies receiving the highest scores of the applied criteria from any industry. This type of an approach presupposes a particular worldview: economic growth and technological innovations will solve any social and environmental challenges. Moreover, this also implies that some companies operating in industries with severe sustainability challenges, like oil and gas, can boast their reputation by highlighting how they are members of the sustainability index. Such a label can be used to gloss over controversial decisions. A prominent and high-profile example from the past would be Shell, which at the same time as being included in the Dow Jones Sustainability World Index was under scrutiny due to, for instance, environmental degradation and human rights violations in the Niger Delta.

The popularity of ESG in the financial markets can also be problematic. It could, for example, send a signal that complex sustainability problems could after all be solved without having to give up too much and by continuing on the path of economic expansion with some green twist.

Such rating schemes can be highly influential in societies. Explored from the perspective of media coverage and societal discussion, leading companies can receive praise and good publicity due to their commitment to sustainability, and thereby come to set a benchmark for others regarding what it means to be a leading company. Again, such examples can be seen in a positive light, as they can stimulate others to compete and improve. However, they can also be interpreted more pessimistically as some of these praised examples fall far from what is required for a sufficient transition to sustainability.

The implications are also substantial from the perspective of capital allocation and financial markets. An increasing number of major institutional investors and investment funds, such as mutual and pension funds, can have sustainability criteria embedded in their investment choices. While many investors conduct their own sustainability assessments, there are a substantial number of those who rely on a particular rating scheme in their decisions. A similar situation is evident for many private investors: while many would like to take sustainability into account when making their personal investments, very few have the knowledge and capability to conduct such an analysis. It can also lead to controversial situations for some individuals, who may only later find out that the green investment fund they have saved in can invest in companies included in the DJSWI, and as a result the individual ends up investing in, say, British American Tobacco, a mainstay on the indices almost since they were established.

## 7.6 Financial markets, ESG, accounting and accountability

As highlighted above, to function the markets require information, and not only any type of information, but something that could be decision-useful and have relevance for investors in their decisions regarding investment allocations. This can have highly significant implications on how we perceive sustainability accounting and accountability, and how sustainability accounting and accountability develop over time. Here, we consider two aspects further, the link between ESG and financial performance and investor engagement. We discuss these in relation to our key focus, accounting and accountability.

### 7.6.1 ESG and financial performance

So, how does taking ESG considerations into account affect the investors? The link between sustainability and financial markets, and in particular the effect on investor value creation, has attracted substantive interest and debate. Questions such as: "does sustainability create higher returns?" or "do ESG considerations imply that the investor will need to accept lower returns?" are questions which are often posed in the media, popular books and in the classroom. Likewise, in the scholarly literature, one can find an increasing volume of studies looking at these themes, at times presenting contradicting findings. However, such questions are perhaps too simple, and risk representing the complex relationship between sustainability and financial markets and returns in an overly straightforward manner. They also risk reducing the ESG investment to financial concerns, something that we have established would be too narrow as broader accountability considerations are relevant here too.

Overall, there does seem to be some evidence that companies with better ESG ratings are associated with higher future returns. Now, several caveats are in order here. First, these results are likely to be dependent on how the ESG rating is compiled and what kinds of proxies are used in the analysis, or in other words what is used as a measure of ESG performance. For example, is the rating based on disclosures, some particular element of performance, or perception-based reputation? Second, it is important to consider what timeframe is being investigated. In general terms, sustainability-related issues, in particular at the macro level, will have effects over an extended period, and might not be captured on a shorter timeframe. Considering such timeframes is important from a risk/return perspective. Third, how is the financial performance or return being measured? Some studies look at stock markets and investor returns, whereas others focus on accounting-based performance metrics like return on investments or return on assets (ROI/ROA). Different measures of financial performance and their influence on findings are important, but are often not explicitly considered. Fourth, it is relevant to look at how the comparisons are made and what kind of assumptions there are in regard to the control groups used. For instance, is the comparison being made with the entire corporate universe, or is it perhaps limited to companies in a given industry or of a particular size. Finally, it is essential to acknowledge that context can have a substantial influence. While ESG-considerations were a key talking point in the financial markets in the early 2020s, the context was very different only ten years before.

Both companies and investors are now doing things differently and are likely to do things differently again in the foreseeable future. The availability of information has increased both in terms of breadth and depth, implying that there is a wider range of more in-depth information about investment opportunities and the contextual developments that investors can draw on in making decisions. As such, it is essential to avoid making hasty conclusions based on single studies or research reports, no matter by who and where it is published.

### 7.6.2 Investor engagement

Investor engagement is another element of financial markets' interest in how corporations deal with sustainability. In this context, engagement entails that investors are not only making investment decisions and allocating capital from a distance, but that they get actively involved with the organisation in different ways with the aim of achieving some changes or reinforcing some types of decisions. Investor engagement should be distinguished from shareholder activism, a primarily US-based phenomenon, where shareholders seek to use their voting power to make particular initiatives visible in the corporate annual meetings, and possibly to initiate changes in corporate practices (see Michelon et al., 2020).

Major institutional investors engage regularly with companies already in regard to their traditional investment analysis as they try to gain deeper insights into how each particular company seeks to prosper in the future. As the relevance of sustainability for the future financial outlook of companies is becoming more broadly understood, investor engagement focusing on ESG matters is becoming a more widespread practice. Given the complexity and uncertainties related to sustainability, such engagements provide opportunities for both the company and the investors, although the dynamics and their potential value creation remains relatively poorly understood. From the company's point of view, investor engagement offers opportunities to learn of the concerns this stakeholder group has, to gauge their views on how particular ESG policies can work, and to receive more nuanced feedback on whether the information provided in the corporate disclosures appears to be sufficient for the marketplace.

Moreover, investor engagement can also provide opportunities to enhance internal processes. The internal information flows, decision-making practices and sharing of responsibilities can all be scrutinised to ensure coherence towards the investors. For the investors, there are the obvious benefits of gaining a deeper understanding of how an organisation and its key personnel perceive sustainability, whether they appear to understand and have planned for the uncertainties and potential risks related to key impacts and dependencies, and also to evaluate how well the external reporting seems to correspond with the actual policies and practices. Moreover, there are also clear opportunities to learn internally as the interlinkages between financial analysis and sustainability become more elaborated. As such, ESG analysis can shift from a peripheral add-on to a key element in investment analysis.

At the same time, however, such investor engagement can be approached critically from a broader societal perspective. As the investors are getting more say in which elements of sustainability are the most important, and emerge as the key stakeholder in this area, there is a risk that broader systemic sustainability concerns get dismissed, or are overtaken by the interests and emphasises given to the ESG metrics that financial markets and institutional investors are focusing on. More often than not, this would be the financial implications of sustainability, instead of some social and environmental consequences. For example, prioritising financial materiality, the IFRS Sustainability Reporting Standards and TCFD recommendations discussed in Chapter 5 place attention on the financial implications of the climate emergency for organisations, rather than putting front and centre the concern of climate change itself as well as the significant physical implications that follow for communities and ecosystems. Moreover, despite all the talk of long-term opportunities and broad scenarios, the financial markets still tend to be geared towards the shorter term. As such, the markets could also be seen to drive development towards sub-optimal solutions, which might not be beneficial for the broader sustainability.

As we have stressed several times in this book, it is beyond organisations to assess, measure and report on all possible forms of sustainability. Choices have to be made, and as a result some elements and viewpoints are emphasised, while others get omitted. Here, it is evident that the information needs of different stakeholder groups are different. As we know that the financial markets are a highly powerful player in society, it is worth asking what kind of implications their growing interest in sustainability has on how organisations assess, account for and report on sustainability. There are several possibilities here. One obvious one is the development of different sustainability reporting standards. As we have discussed, the GRI Standards, with a broad stakeholder focus and emphasis on impact materiality, have for long been the most widely used guidelines. While the GRI remains popular, there are signs that the landscape is shifting towards a more investor-minded approach, with the frameworks and standards developed by TCFD, SASB and eventually ISSB emerging as prominent options explicitly targeting investor communities. And there is nothing wrong with that as such. However, it does impact how activities, entities, risks and opportunities are evaluated.

## 7.7 Conclusion

As we have now established, sustainability has become a feature in financial markets and investment considerations. The question then becomes what we are to make of it? Why is this relevant? What are the implications? Does the growing interest of financial markets and powerful investor groups enhance the well-being of vulnerable communities, enhance social cohesion, justice and democracy, and help societies stay within the planetary boundaries by slowing down climate change, biodiversity loss and other environmental problems?

It is clear that the ESG considerations are no longer seen as an anomaly or a short-term fad which will disappear from the radar as fast as they have emerged. Sure, ESG might be discussed differently in the public sphere, as the political tensions around ESG investments have become increasingly prominent in specific regions, such as the United States in particular. Nonetheless, many of the world's largest investment funds and asset management houses indicate that ESG considerations are now an integral part of their investment processes, and that they cannot be ignored should an investor wish to take care of their portfolio. Moreover, continued discussion of ESG in major financial media outlets and leading marketplaces means that ESG is constantly gaining visibility, which is important for their consideration.

At the same time, it is worth asking whether the prominence of ESG in the financial markets, high-level indices and ESG criteria actually help steer the global societies away from sustainability challenges. Does the high popularity also create an impression signalling that things are "under control now that major investment funds and the financial markets are using their wisdom to steer societies towards some better goals?" That is, the logic of the markets is based on the fundamental belief in their power to process information and to find effective solutions. The solutions, however, are dependent on the information that is being used.

While we recognise our discussion here only provides an introduction to the very broad and complex topic, it should now be clear that to function, financial markets require information, which has highly significant implications for accounting. With the growing awareness of the impacts of sustainability on organisations, including their financial performance, ESG investment and risk management are areas of great importance. The investment community is a powerful stakeholder with considerable influence, so how the financial market responds to, or is leveraged for, sustainability has implications.

## References


Andrew, J. and Cortese, C. (2013). Free Market Environmentalism and the Neoliberal Project: The Case of the Climate Disclosure Standards Board. *Critical Perspectives on Accounting, 24(6)*, 397–409.

Bebbington, J., Schneider, T., Stevenson, L. and Fox, A. (2020). Fossil Fuel Reserves and Resources Reporting and Unburnable Carbon: Investigating Conflicting Accounts. *Critical Perspectives on Accounting, 66*, 1–22.

Berg, F., Kölbel, J. F. and Rigobon, R. (2022). Aggregate Confusion: The Divergence of ESG Ratings. *Review of Finance, 26(6)*, 1315–1344.

Carney, M. (2015). Breaking the Tragedy of the Horizon – Climate Change and Financial Stability. Speech delivered at Lloyd's of London, 29 September 2015. www.bankofengland.co.uk/speech/2015/breaking-the-tragedy-of-the-horizon-climate-change-and-financial-stability (accessed 30 November 2020).

Crifo, P., Durand, R. and Gond, J.-P. (2019). Encouraging Investors to Enable Corporate Sustainability Transitions: The Case of Responsible Investment in France. *Organization and Environment, 32(2)*, 125–144.

European Commission (2025). Overview of Sustainable Finance. https //finance.ec.europa.eu/sustainable-finance/overview-sustainable-finance_en (Accessed 8 January 2025).

Jouffray, J. B., Crona, B., Wassénius, E., Bebbington, J. and Scholtens, B. (2019). Leverage Points in the Financial Sector for Seafood Sustainability. *Science Advances, 5(10)*, eaax3324.

Michelon, G., Rodrigue, M. and Trevisan, E. (2020). The Marketization of a Social Movement: Activists, Shareholders and CSR Disclosure. *Accounting, Organizations and Society, 80*, 101074.

O'Sullivan, N. and O'Dwyer, B. (2009). Stakeholder Perspectives on a Financial Sector Legitimation Process: The Case of NGOs and the Equator Principles. *Accounting, Auditing and Accountability Journal, 22(4)*, 553–587.


## Additional reading and resources


CFA Institute and UN PRI (2018). Guidance and Case Studies for ESG Integration: Equities and Fixed Income. www.unpri.org/download?ac=5962 (accessed 28 August 2020).

Garcia-Torea, N., Luque-Vilchez, M. and Rodriguez-Gutiérrez, P. (2024). The EU Taxonomy, Sustainability Reporting and Financial Institutions: Understanding the Elements Driving Regulatory Uncertainty. *Accounting Forum, 48*(3), 427–454.

Krueger, P., Sautner, Z., Tang, D.Y. and Zhong, R. (2024). The Effects of Mandatory ESG Disclosure Around the World. *Journal of Accounting Research, 62*(5), 1795–1847.

Michelon, G. (2021). Financial Markets and Environmental Information. In Bebbington, J., Larrinaga, C., O'Dwyer, B. and Thomson, I. (eds), *Handbook on Environmental Accounting*, pp. 165–178. Routledge.

Nyström, M., Jouffray, J.-B., Norström, A., Crona, B., Søgaard Jøgensen, P., Carpenter, S., Bodin, Ö., Galaz, V. and Folke, C. (2019). Anatomy and Resilience of the Global Production System. *Nature*, *575*, 98–108.

Principles for Responsible Investment: www.unpri.org.

The Equator Principles: https://equator-principles.com/.

van Duuren, E., Plantinga, A. and Scholtens, B. (2016). ESG Integration and the Investment Management Process: Fundamental Investing Reinvented. *Journal of Business Ethics*, *138*, 525–533.

Young-Ferris, A. and Roberts, J. (2023). 'Looking for Something that Isn't There': A Case Study of an Early Attempt at ESG Integration in Investment Decision Making. *European Accounting Review*, 32(3), 717–744.

CHAPTER

8

# Counter accounting

Counter accounting is generally understood as accounting which is prepared to counter an existing account. Early references to counter accounting, often by a different name as we discuss below, were undertaken by those external or outside of the entity for which the account related and by those who wished to make visible problematic impacts of an entity and expose organisational accountabilities when the organisation failed to do so. While still used in this way, counter accounting is also increasingly being used to provide accounts and expose accountabilities at a broader level, for example, at an industry, government or regional level.

Himick and Vinnari define counter accounts in this way as "alternative representations of the activities of organisations, industries or governance regimes" (2023, p. 349). As such, it can be useful to think about counter accounting as an umbrella label for a myriad of practices of accounting by a range of groups and individuals not usually considered accounting entities. In this chapter, we will be discussing the various practices as they are relevant to sustainability accounting and accountability. We begin by introducing the phenomenon, including a short history of its emergence, before considering the main motivations and rationales for the practice. We then consider some of the various information sources used in the production of counter accounts before discussing the main counter account producers and their audiences. Some of the critiques or limitations of the practice are then outlined. While this chapter provides further context for later discussions in the book, it also presents a form of accounting which challenges some of our taken-for-granted assumptions about accounting practices. Ultimately, counter accounting encourages us to think critically about accounting tools and practices and accountability relationships through a consideration of how they could be different.

By the end of this chapter, you should:

- Understand the practice of counter accounting.
- Understand the motivations and rationales for counter accounting.

DOI: 10.4324/9781003533207-10

- Be able to distinguish between various information sources for counter accounting and understand their differences.
- Be aware of the different groups that might produce counter accounts.
- Have a critical awareness of the critiques and potential of counter accounting.

## 8.1 A brief note on terminology and focus

Before we proceed further, a short note regarding terminology and our focus in this chapter is in order. First, as noted above, we use the term counter accounting to refer to the range of practices which involve forms of accounting produced by those external (i.e. outside) to the entity for which they are providing the account. While a number of other possible labels exist and are used (e.g. external accounting, social accounts, anti-accounts), we have chosen to use counter accounting as it has arguably emerged as the main term used when referring to these practices. Furthermore, while external accounting is a term that defined much of the earlier practices with its focus on the external accountant being situated external to the organisation for which it was providing an account, this term can also be quite confusing. This is mainly due to external accounting being increasingly used with reference to accounts and reports organisations produce for external stakeholders (to contrast with reports for internal purposes). As such, counter accounting perhaps avoids such conceptual confusion. There are also some specific forms of counter accounting which carry particular labels, for example, shadow accounting, silent accounting and social audits. We discuss some of these specific examples below.

In order to assist us in identifying and delineating the practice of counter accounting, throughout this chapter, we draw not only on practice from the field but also on accounting research which helps us understand and reflect on this practice.

## 8.2 Counter accounting practices and their emergence

Counter accounting at the most general level can be defined as the practice of providing an alternative account of an entity or industry to which they are referring. Counter accounts can be financial or non-financial in nature. However, as you will see below, within the sustainability accounting and accountability field, they tend to focus on the non-financial. While using the term *external accounting*, Dey and Gibbon (2014, p. 109) provide a clear explanation and consideration of the audiences of the practice:

> In general terms, external accounts are a form of social accounting produced by external individuals and/or organizations, including campaigning NGOs, on *their* representation of the social and environmental impact of others. The intended audience for such external reports is not simply the accounting entity associated with the problematic impacts, but may also include political institutions, civil society, the media and sections of the general public.

Importantly, counter accounts can be used to make visible such environmental, social and/or economic impacts of an organisation that might not have been included and be visible in the organisation's own disclosures. We will return to a discussion of who the main producers of counter accounts are, and indeed could be, later in this chapter; however, it is perhaps useful to note before we proceed that producers are generally those that hold less power, and less resources, than those that they usually seek to provide accounts on (e.g. large corporations and governments).

While the forms counter accounting takes and the motivations for producing such accounts are also discussed below, we first outline the emergence and development of counter accounting practices. In doing so, it is important to recognise that what we refer to in this chapter as counter accounting is not a new practice. It is, however, one that is on the rise. This rise has perhaps been fuelled by the increase in access to information in the public domain through the internet and social media in particular, as well as the use of such channels to disseminate information. The increase in counter accounting practices is also likely to be the result of the increase in civil society awareness and action in relation to sustainability issues. Labelling these practices as a form of accounting by accounting academics and researchers is also important to recognise here. This labelling helps position these practices within the sphere of accounting and recognises them as a practice of giving an account, thus highlighting the importance of considering counter accounting within the broader spectrum of sustainability accounting and accountability practices.

What we now refer to as counter accounting has had many different names as it has developed over a period of time. We present a history of counter accounting (see also Dey and Gibbon, 2014) focusing on the concept of accountability, given this is a key focus of this book, and also, as we have argued, a key concern for sustainability accounting. Tracing the history of this practice not only is useful to highlight the array of various aspects and approaches to counter accounting but also helps understand such things as the various terminology used as noted above. This history also helps contextualise the practice, including some of the motivations for the practice discussed below.

### 8.2.1 Early examples and development

Social audits and Counter Information Services (CIS) Anti-Reports produced from the 1970s and 1980s are often the first forms of activity identified when referring to counter accounting. Medawar (1976) outlines the social audits produced in the UK by Social Audit Ltd., essentially the publishing of information on various organisations in response to the perceived absence of accountability disclosures. That is, there was a demand for organisations to provide information to various stakeholders, yet, the organisations themselves were not meeting those demands.

As discussed in Chapter 5, the 1990s saw a rise in corporate environmental reporting. During this period a focus of many, including accounting academics, NGOs and other civil society organisations, was on improving the sustainability-related disclosures of companies. The emerging reporting practices were seen as a sign that corporations and other organisations were beginning to respond to the demand for information. Accordingly, many focused their efforts on promoting and facilitating the emerging practice, increasing the number of organisations reporting, and subsequently on enhancing the quality of that reporting.

However, despite this rise in practice, there remained (indeed, still remains) dissatisfaction with corporate-led sustainability reporting. Not only did the number of reporting organisations remain low for a number of years, but there was also dissatisfaction with the quality of the reports that were being produced. Again, organisations were seen to be failing to meet the accountability demands of those outside the entity. They were perceived by many to be producing reports that appeared to focus on emphasising positive issues while downplaying any broader concerns or negative developments.

While many social movements and NGOs had been steady critics of organisations for years, their leaflets and other material had seldom focused on providing comprehensive accounts of organisations, or alternatively these had not spread widely beyond the local contexts. This began to change in the early 2000s, when building on the earlier Social Audit and CIS Anti-Reports several counter reports, such as Friends of the Earth's "Failing the Challenge: The Other Shell Report" (Friends of the Earth, 2003) and Action on Smoking and Health's "British American Tobacco – The Other Report to Society" (ASH, 2002) attracted attention (see "Focus on practice" below).

Around the same time, some academics engaged with social and environmental reporting were also looking for ways to contribute in developing the practices. Perhaps as a response to the perceived lack of progress, a group of academics introduced the practices of silent and shadow reporting and conducted a practical example of how such counter accounting could be done, although they referred to as external accounting (see Gibson et al., 2001). These practices are outlined in more detail below, but essentially, they again highlighted the potential for such reports to produce information on a company's impacts and accountabilities when the organisation failed to do so.

In later years, while a focus on counter accounting in the form of preparing reports has continued, other aspects have also become a focus. For example, increasing attention has been placed on highlighting issues or industries and accountabilities that arise. In these occasions, counter accounts can be used to move beyond a specific company and seek to turn the focus on problematising and challenging for instance a dominant discourse around a given industry or corporate practice. Thereby, as counter accounting has become more commonplace, the practices can be seen to have extended to cover a range of different aspects. While we continue to have counter accounts targeting specific (corporate) accounts or presenting countering narratives on a given issue, we also see counter accounts prepared in what could be called to fulfil the watchdog function in society. These counter accounts take place online or through reports providing alternative information, or simply providing information in the first place in situations where there is absence of publicly available information or potentially a failure to provide sufficient information on something. We discuss examples of these further below.

Prior to doing so, however, we should highlight that in the contemporary era of social media, artificial intelligence and alternative truths, it is important to acknowledge that all information should not be considered an account, and that considering the veracity and reliability of any counter accounts is significant. We will return to these considerations throughout this chapter, and also discuss the challenges these aspects present to the potential of counter accounting.

**PAUSE AND REFLECT...**

Before proceeding further, it may be useful to take a look at counter accounting examples. This includes some of the historical examples we identified above.

There are a range of counter reports that one can look at online. The reports produced by and available from the Friends of the Earth (2025) as well as the various reports available from CIS's Anti-Report (2025) allow taking a look at the interesting historical developments and evolution of this practice. Take the Unilever's World CIS Anti Report No. 11 (CIS, 1975) as an early example. In this dense report extended over 100 pages, CIS highlights the vast size of the firm and subsequently questions the minimal amount of information there is about the multinational in the public domain. In particular, the report focuses on the often unseen influence Unilever has on societies, as well as outlines the social and economic impacts its practices have around the world, including dependent nations in the Global South serving as sources for raw materials. As another example, the widely recognised "The Other Shell Report" by the Friends of the Earth (2003) responds to the Shell Corporation's report of 2003 in which the company encouraged people to respond to their progress on sustainable development through a "Tell Shell" Campaign. In this counter account, the Friends of the Earth and others compiled their report in a format resembling a standard corporate report, providing an alternative account of Shell's practices. Containing a director's report, summary of past performance and a range of case studies on Shell's practices in various locations, this report provides the reader with an alternative view of Shell's social and environmental performance than is provided in their own reporting.

Online counter accounting practices are also useful to consider. Two examples include BankTrack and the Oil Spill Monitor. BankTrack (2025) is an online platform run by an international organisation seeking to challenge commercial banks globally for their (in)action on climate change, destruction of nature and violation of human rights. Through its actively maintained website, BankTrack seeks to make public and shed light on how banks finance high impact business sectors, companies and projects, which have substantial negative impacts on people and planet. The organisation also seeks to benchmark potential commitments banks are making and subsequently engage with these financial institutions in trying to have such commitments strengthened. A more regional example would be The Nigerian Oil Spill Monitor (2025), which is essentially a public account of oil spills that have taken place in Nigeria. Run by a government agency, the website combines data received through regulatory requirements from oil companies and observations gathered when visiting sites of oil spills. Citizens are also encouraged to get involved and report oil spills they observe. While the information included on Oil Spill Monitor is not complete, the website nonetheless can be seen to provide a counter account on the oil industry in Nigeria, visualising the extent of social and environmental impacts oil industry has in the area.

We encourage you to take some time to look at these examples – perhaps one from each (i.e. one report and one website). Furthermore, when looking at them, it is useful to consider the reports of the companies involved, for example, the Shell report of 2002 and 2003 for comparison to the counter account produced by Friends of the Earth or their more recent reports when it comes to a consideration of the material on the Oil Spill monitor and what is reported in the corporate reports of the companies who work in this area. Questions that you might find useful to consider include: how do these counter accounts compare to the sustainability reports of the corporations they refer to or other corporate sustainability reports you have looked at (i.e. what are the similarities and differences between the accounts produced)? Who do you think are the potential audiences of these various counter accounts? And do you think that they are useful in providing accounts and/or highlighting accountability? We encourage you to keep these reflections in mind as you continue with this chapter.

## 8.3 Motivations and rationales to produce counter accounts

It is perhaps clear from the above discussion that one of the key motivations for the production of counter accounts is a dissatisfaction with organisational reports, and specifically with the information presented on sustainability, again primarily those from large corporations. This is not only the case for the early counter account producers, but also for those producing counter accounts today. While both the amount and quality of sustainability reporting have increased over the past years, it is still perceived to be limited or insufficient by many. There are two aspects of this motivation for counter accounting that are useful to highlight.

First, counter accounting can be motivated by a lack of reporting by organisations. While, as was discussed in Chapters 5 and 6, the practice of corporate and other organisational sustainability reporting has increased, there is still dissatisfaction with this reporting. For example, the number of organisations that produce a sustainability report which might be considered comprehensive is still not considered sufficient, especially when we go beyond the largest corporations. That is, while the large and "visible" companies often produce reports there can be limited reporting by small- or medium-sized firms. And, when reporting does exist, there can be some limitations in relation to the extent and nature of that disclosure. Here, in this context of a lack of organisational reporting or lack of comprehensive reporting, counter accounting can be motivated by an attempt to fill a gap by preparing information when an organisation fails to do so or when the information disclosed is considered insufficient. Many of the counter accounts focusing on corporate tax avoidance, such as ActionAid's (2010) report on SABMiller discussed below, are typical examples here, as corporations generally remain silent on their tax planning practices and potential use of tax havens.

Second, counter accounting can be motivated by insufficient or unbalanced information reported by organisations. Here counter accounting attempts to balance the information provided by including information that is not covered in the official accounts. Counter accounts can be used to provide additional information that is either absent from the organisation's own reports, or where the counter accountant considers this information to be misleading. The Friends of the Earth (2003) report in the above "Pause and reflect" textbox is an example of this. Given that many of the counter accounts we see in practice seek to target an organisation that already undertakes some form of sustainability reporting, it could be argued that it is the latter of the two motivations that appears to motivate much of the existing counter accounting practices.

In short, when it comes to the practice of organisational sustainability reporting, weaknesses in current practices remain and, despite improvements, the need for additional and/or alternative information identified by Social Audit Ltd and CIS in the 1970s and 1980s still exist today. However, a dissatisfaction with sustainability reporting is not the only motivation for the production of counter accounting and its rise. A range of other motivations exists.

In relation to the concept of accountability, counter accounts can also be used by producing groups or individuals to call an organisation or industry to account or to highlight where an accountability relationship exists. For example, a counter account can be used to highlight an issue where the counter accountant perceives the organisation or industry to be responsible and accountable. An example from accounting research is useful to illustrate this point. Laine and Vinnari (2017) in their study demonstrate how animal activists use counter accounting practices in an attempt to hold the pig farming industry to account. The activists use counter accounting practices to provide visibility to aspects of animal production which the industry prefers to omit from their own accounts. Similarly, Denedo and colleagues (2018), in their consideration of Nigerian Oil Spill Monitor and the counter accounting related to oil and gas production in the Niger Delta, highlight the importance of accountability relationships associated not only with the oil and gas industry, but also with the public sector organisations and authorities tasked with regulating and overseeing the industry.

Relatedly, counter accounts can also be produced with the aim of education. In this sense, they can be motivated by the aim of increasing awareness about impacts or accountability relationships. This can be seen as a major goal for those who have produced counter accounts focusing on corporate tax avoidance. The following "Focus on practice" discusses this further.

Counter accounting can also be motivated by the will to get alternative voices heard (Himick and Vinnari, 2023). Again, while practices in relation to stakeholder engagement have developed and arguably improved over recent years, some stakeholders can still find themselves excluded from the organisational-driven process. In this situation, individuals or groups can be motivated to produce a counter account in order to get their perspectives heard. For example, social movement groups or activist organisations who may not be considered to be a legitimate stakeholder by an organisation, and therefore excluded from stakeholder engagement discussions, may use counter accounting as a way of having their voice heard and represented (see Tregidga, 2017). We can also consider this in relation to the discussion above. Counter accountants can perceive it as important to express their views and be heard in order to balance the information available in the public sphere.

### Focus on practice: Counter accounting and corporate taxation

For a long time, taxation was widely seen as a technical, complex and really boring topic. Corporate taxation was something that accountants and lawyers dealt with and it seemed that no one else was very interested. Things changed in the 2010s, however, and all of a sudden taxation was getting broad media attention and social media limelight. Reports of how major multinationals, such as Apple, Google and Starbucks, engaged in a range of sophisticated tax planning schemes featured in mainstream media outlets. But why? Where did this sudden interest emerge from?

Counter accounts on corporate taxation played a key role in raising public awareness and putting a spotlight on these complex practices. One of the first counter accounts gathering broad attention was entitled "Calling Time: Why SABMiller Should Stop Dodging Taxes in

Africa", published originally in 2010 by ActionAid, an international development NGO headquartered in South Africa. The report combined information collected from published financial reports and interviews, as well as some undercover research, to discuss in detail a range of tax planning schemes SABMiller was using to minimise its taxes. While SABMiller denied the allegations and maintained that it did pay a fair share of taxes and contributed substantially to the development of African economies, the report attracted international attention and was one of the building blocks for the emerging international debate regarding corporate taxation as well as its relationship with corporate accountability and social responsibility.

Taxation is a complicated topic, and in practice, there tends to be a grey area between tax avoidance, which is legal, and tax evasion, which is illegal. Companies, in seeking to improve their profit margins, are interested in finding innovative ways to minimise their tax obligations. Individual organisations are not the only active player in this area, however. Major accountancy firms, for instance, actively offer their services to help clients optimise their taxation (i.e. pay less tax). Nation states are not idle either. There are some well-known tax havens, such as the Cayman Islands and the Bahamas, which offer both minimal tax rates and high secrecy jurisdiction, making them attractive locations for companies to domicile or establish subsidiaries. Perhaps less well-known, but nonetheless highly influential, are countries such as the Netherlands, Switzerland and Ireland, as well as regions such as Delaware in the United States and Jersey in the UK, all of which have public policy features resembling tax havens. On a more limited scale, in many regions, there are so-called Special Economic Zones, the rules of which feature substantial tax breaks and other concessions to organisations residing in or making investments there. Oftentimes, governments and authorities use such tax policies in attempting to attract and spur economic activity, although other reasons also exist.

We will return to taxation in more detail in Chapter 13, including how high-profile multinational governance initiatives led by the OECD are impacting the practices of both businesses and governments, as we discuss how accounting relates to economic inequality. Meanwhile, we refer to some insightful books which shed light on the complexity of taxation, such as Shaxson's (2011) *Treasure Islands*, Obermayer and Obermaier's (2016) *Panama Papers* and Michel's (2021) *American Kleptocracy*.

Lastly, it can also be argued that it makes sense that those external to an organisation provide an account on sustainability-related issues and therefore such accounting can be motivated by what could be considered logical and practical reasons. With regard to financial reporting, we could well argue that it makes sense for corporations and other organisations to provide their own financial accounts. Given that an organisation has access to information on the financial position and performance of the entity, it is perhaps best placed to collate and communicate it. When it comes to sustainability or non-financial information, which relates to the social, environmental and economic impacts and dependencies of the entity, it could be argued otherwise. Here, we could consider that those who feel the effects (those who are impacted) or those who understand such dependences (e.g. scientists) are best placed to provide the account on those impacts and dependencies. What could be labelled stakeholder prepared counter accounts would therefore seem appropriate. This is not to dismiss the need for organisational disclosures (again there are disclosures for which the company is best placed to provide the information) but if, for example, we are discussing the impact on communities and workers, why not get the communities and workers/unions to provide the account? Moreover, there is substantial evidence from several industries, such as tobacco and pesticides, highlighting that corporations with vested interests to protect their business may seek to use various types of reporting and public relations activities in an attempt to shape the general opinion and public policies (e.g. Oreskes and Conway, 2011). This can be seen to supplement the need for counter accounts to be produced.

So, while the practice of counter accounting seems to have emerged as an attempt to counter information or fill the gap in relation to the lack of information resulting from inadequate organisational reporting, it has since expanded in scope and practice and is now an important topic in the field of sustainability accounting and accountability. The overall value of such accounting is its ability, and potential, to increase the amount of information in the public domain, especially as this information can assist in understanding accountability relationships that exist in relation to individual entities or on an issue more broadly. These accountability relationships may have been masked through more traditional forms of accounting. In this sense, counter accounts are understood to have the ability to expose and challenge power relations.

## 8.4 Sources of information for counter accounting

While it is outside of the scope of this chapter to outline all forms of counter accounting practices and their differences, in this section, we provide some definitions of the most common practices distinguishing between how the information within them is obtained or produced. This discussion also illustrates the varied practice. Perhaps partly due to their sporadic development discussed above, the terminology surrounding counter accounting practices is not always clear. Indeed, counter accounting practices, while not labelled as such or being considered a form of accounting, have occurred in civil society for a very long time and research on various activities has been undertaken intermittently, making the field somewhat difficult to delineate. However, there are some common terms with some general understandings which are useful to distinguish between. Again, as noted above, we draw on both the practice of counter accounting as well as the research which analyses it in our discussion.

Silent accounting, the first form we will discuss, is where a counter account is produced by compiling information from various corporate or organisational disclosure channels. Organisations produce a myriad of different information using a diverse range of communication channels. For example, in addition to their sustainability report, organisations disclose information related to their sustainability performance in their annual reports, websites, advertising campaigns and through press releases. Silent accounting involves the collection of this alternative information and preparing an account from it. When it is done to expose the inadequacies in an organisation's sustainability reporting, this can be seen as using their own information against them.

To help illustrate, let's consider an example. An airline company may disclose in their sustainability report their commitment to reducing their carbon footprint and express a strong commitment to climate action. However, that same company may, in their annual report, discuss their growth strategy, their intent to increase their number of aircraft, flight paths and total flight miles. These two disclosures, in two different channels of communication, are hard to reconcile. In one, the company is committing to reducing emissions, while in the other, they are clearly outlining a strategy which would, necessarily, lead to increased emissions which would call their commitment to emission reduction into question. A silent account preparer could use the information from the company's annual report to expose this tension. Given this form of counter accounting uses the organisation's own disclosures and information, it can be termed an unofficial account. When this form of accounting is published in report form, a format similar to a corporate sustainability report, it is often labelled a silent report.

A related, but slightly different practice is shadow accounting. Here the counter account consists of relevant information that is produced independently of the organisation. While originally conceived as consisting of the collation of information available in the public domain, for example media reports, court and other legal documents (see Gibson et al., 2001), it has also been used to describe counter accounting practices whereby those producing the account collect their own data or provide narrative from their own perspective. Again, when it takes the format of a report, it is commonly referred to as a shadow report.

Shadow reports have been a relatively common device used by NGOs and social movement groups. "Failing the Challenge: The Other Shell Report" we discussed above is an example of this (Friends of the Earth, 2003), as is the more recent "Uncovered: Unilever's complicity in the plastics crisis and its power to solve it" (Greenpeace International, 2023), for which the Greenpeace International combined research reports and other publicly available information with Unilever's reports to challenge the company's vocal commitments of reducing plastic use. Some of these reports are very comprehensive and serious in tone while others can use parody and satire in an attempt to present their alternative view. Some of the latter are referred to as "mock" reports. The format and style of such reports is perhaps important in relation to how the reports are received by an audience, a point we discuss further below.

## 8.5 Producers and audiences of counter accounts

The practice of counter accounting takes several forms, and as the practice continues to increase it is likely that new forms and styles will emerge. The continued impact of changing social media is likely to influence this, as it helps in the preparation and dissemination of counter accounts by making the collection of information easier and by providing cheaper and faster access to a broader audience. Indeed, you might find it useful to think of your own social media activities and whether you can recognise practices which you think might constitute a counter account. Likewise, the changing levels of trust in society will also play a role, especially in situations where citizens for some reason lose their confidence in politicians, authorities, media (including social media) or other major organisations. These factors are an important consideration for the various producers and potential audiences of counter accounts. We turn to a discussion of this next.

### 8.5.1 Producers of counter accounts

There are many different individuals or groups who produce counter accounts. And, as consideration of the practice of counter accounting develops, we see the variety of different counter account preparers developing alongside new forms of counter accounting.

Early research on counter accounting, that which largely considered silent and shadow accounts as above, noted several similarities in relation to counter account producers. First, as we identified earlier, producers are usually external from the entity to or for which they are providing the account, seeking accountability, or seeking to expose accountability relationships. The counter accountants were also noted to be less well-resourced than those that they sought to target. However, research has moved to consider counter accounts more broadly, and this has included expanding the focus of counter account producers. Here, we will briefly consider some of the main producers of counter accounts.

NGOs, social movements and civil society groups are key producers of counter accounts, and some groups have a relatively long history of producing counter accounts in the form of shadow or counter accounts. We have mentioned several times Friends of the Earth. This developed into a series of what they call "alternative" reports of Shell's performance over several years. The other example we have noted is Action on Smoking and Health's "British American Tobacco – The Other Report to Society" which also followed by a long-term, sustained counter accounting campaign, the diversity of which is discussed in more detail by Thomson et al. (2015). Concurrently, in some regional settings, such reports can emerge from dedicated national NGO's, such as Swedwatch in Sweden and Finnwatch in Finland, which investigate corporate activities and publish reports focusing on specific companies or issues as they seek to promote responsible business practices through raising awareness and engaging in public discussion.

In addition to these well-known and relatively large NGOs, a range of similar kinds of examples can be found both at the international and national levels. Tregidga (2017), for instance, analyses the shadow report of a national social movement that sought to prevent the expansion of a local coal mine in New Zealand. The producers here were a small social movement group. Such research shows how various groups of different sizes have used counter accounts in various ways to get an alternative voice or perspective heard.

Counter accounts produced by some civil society groups are not necessarily focused on individual companies, as the example of BankTrack we highlighted in the "Pause and reflect" above illustrates. BankTrack is an online platform which is dedicated to monitoring and disclosing practices of global financial institutions. Instead of a one-off report, BankTrack provides an extensive resource made up of counter accounts of financial institutions' practices, while also indicating how technology and online collective activities can be used in the counter accounting process. The Oil Spill Monitor in the Niger Delta also noted above and discussed by Denedo et al. (2018) is another example of this. Here a range of groups, including those located in and working with the communities affected, maintain a monitor, tracking oil spills in the region – essentially a counter account of the oil industry's performance in the Niger Delta region. A different type of example is discussed by Laine and Vinnari (2017), who analyse the counter accounting practices of animal rights groups seeking accountabilities in relation to the treatment of animals in Finland. In this case, no organisation or group was formally identified as the counter accountant. Instead, a collective of individuals produced accounts of meat production on a regular basis over a period of several years, leading to a sustained public debate involving politicians, corporations, farmers and the general public.

While NGOs and civil society groups are probably the most active with counter accounts, they can also be produced by others. Labour unions have for instance taken part in producing counter accounts, or alternatively provided active support in collaborative efforts seeking to make visible some problematic practices concerning labour rights, health and safety issues, or other employee-related questions. Sometimes counter accounts originate in investigative journalism, perhaps in the areas of financials, corruption and taxation in particular. Here it is worth noting that there is sometimes a fine line between whether we should be talking about journalism or counter accounting. At the same time, however, the roles might not always be that clear cut. For instance, sometimes stories appearing in the press have been written by activists serving as freelance journalists, or large reports can be outputs of a broader collaborative effort between various groups. It can be discussed whether events like the Panama Papers or LuxLeaks, both of which included releasing vast amounts of previously classified information to the public domain, should be categorised as counter accounts or not (see Obermayer and Obermaier, 2016).

Accounting practitioners and academics can also be producers of counter accounts – indeed, some of the earlier examples seemed to highlight the potential role accounting academics can have here. Accounting practitioners and accounting academics, alone or with others such as NGOs or other stakeholder groups, hold particular knowledge which could be utilised to produce counter accounts. While examples are perhaps not as common as may be expected, there are nonetheless some exemplars reporting how academics have engaged in counter accounting, at times with important impacts. An example of this is provided by Cooper and colleagues (2005) and their accounting practices in relation to student hardship in Scotland. Cooper and colleagues drew on a large survey and their own knowledge of accounting to provide an account of how some university students seeking to study full time were prone to be exploited, as they were essentially forced to accept any part-time work to ensure their livelihood. The account Cooper and colleagues produced was also used in the political debate concerning the funding of higher education in Scotland. Similar examples can also be found in other contexts including Spain where a number of accounting academics engaged in an intervention which challenged a legislative reform which affected Spanish industrial relations (Archel et al., 2022).

As can be seen, counter accounts are produced by a range of different individuals and groups. With the emerging attention on this practice, developing technologies enabling the practice, and also, as we will discuss in the chapters that follow, the emerging global and local movements expressing concern in relation to sustainability-related issues (e.g. climate, biodiversity and inequality), it is likely that counter accounting practices will continue to grow. A key consideration when producing a counter account is an audience. We turn to this aspect now.

**PAUSE AND REFLECT...**

Let's take a moment to pause and reflect on the possible preparers of counter accounts for sustainability-related issues and where it would seem useful to have counter accounts. We have given a few examples above but let's think about this a little more.

For example, in relation to accounting for income distribution and its effects, that is the payment of a living wage, Skilling and Tregidga (2019) posit that the workers, those that are impacted, are perhaps the best placed to provide the account. Or, at the least, an account. But are there other areas where an employee would also make a good counter accountant – health and safety for example?

Take one sustainability-related issue (perhaps one of the SDGs) and consider the potential counter account preparers and the type of things they could include in their counter accounts. You might like to think of a specific company to make this easier. For example, who would be some possible counter account preparers for Coca-Cola and SDG 6 Clean Water and Sanitation, or McDonald's and SDG 3 Good Health and Wellbeing?

As you work through the chapters of this book, consider who is best placed to produce an account. Is it the organisation/corporation? And furthermore, does this change when we consider different types of questions? You might also like to think of examples when a counter account might not be appropriate or useful, for example, where misinformation is used.

### 8.5.2 Audiences

As we have discussed, counter accounts are prepared from various information sources, have various authors, and can be prepared for various purposes. It is also quite clear that there are multiple potential audiences for a counter account.

It is perhaps fair to assume that for many counter accountants the target entity, often a corporation, is the intended audience for the counter account produced. Given that some motivations for such practice are related to accountability and calls for organisations to be more accountable, it is possible to assume that the counter report is produced in the hope of receiving attention from the entity itself, potentially spurring some subsequent changes in the organisation's practices. There is even the possibility that counter accounts lead into a conversation between the organisation and the counter accountants, although quite often the target organisation's public response to such external attention garnered through counter accounting has appeared to be more about denial than active collaboration. There are exceptions, however, such as in cases where a counter account has highlighted problems deep in an organisation's supply chain, which the organisation for some reason had previously not been aware of. On these occasions, the targeted organisation may acknowledge the counter account together with a commitment to collect further information and pursue necessary actions.

Other potential audiences exist, however, and it would be too narrow to just consider the target corporation as the audience for such accounts. For example, in the examples mentioned above other audiences are evident. In Cooper et al.'s (2005) study on student hardship, the target audience of the counter account created was likely to include government and other decision-makers. While individual organisations could clearly help address the issue by paying higher wages to student workers, the systemic nature of the issue is likely to require institutional level actions and as such government was likely to be a target audience for this counter account. Tregidga (2017) in her study of a particular shadow report targeted at a coal mining company found that journalists and civil society in general (that is the general public) were the intended audience. While the counter account clearly targeted a specific entity, the social movement group noted that their intent was to raise awareness of the issues and the corporate's actions amongst the general public. They therefore sent the report to, among others, journalists and used it as a tool for education and encouraging support for their movement. In similar terms, the counter accounts produced in the long-term campaign ASH are running against the tobacco industry have targeted a number of audiences, including both civil society and policy makers (see Thomson et al., 2015).

Clearly, the targeted audience is connected with the aims the producer of a counter account has set. When counter accounts are intended to raise attention to a particular corporate practice, the counter account may primarily be meant for the attention of relevant authorities or other civil servants. For instance, a civil society group may have become frustrated by a lack of oversight at some organisation's production facility, and as a result put together a counter account concerning how the organisation neglects the requirements set upon it in an environmental permit. At the other end of the spectrum, when a counter accountant is seeking to raise awareness of an industry or systems level issue or accountability relationship, the counter account could be seeking to reach a large audience by targeting the general public through for instance social media. Think about a civil society group, which tries to raise awareness of widespread corruption amongst large state-owned companies and the ruling elite in an authoritarian state. In such cases, the counter accountants could try to raise awareness and spur action, which would challenge the currently dominating individuals and organisations in that given context.

A counter account can also seek to achieve several goals and hence target several audiences. The detailed counter accounts on corporate tax planning, such as ActionAid's (2010) report on SABMiller discussed above, serve as a good example here. These kinds of counter accounts can aim at making an organisation change its practices, at challenging politicians to take a critical look at the tax policies, regulation and potential loopholes, and also at educating the general public of the main features of corporate taxation and the implications a particular tax policy in a given society may have.

### INSIGHTS FROM RESEARCH: LABOUR ISSUES IN THE CHOCOLATE INDUSTRY

"So, how does your chocolate taste now?". This is the question posed by Stephanie Perkiss and colleagues in the introduction to their paper which examines human rights issues around labour, and in particular child labour, in the international chocolate market.

Some readers might be familiar with the issues that relate to the production of chocolate. Like bananas, another common food item with well-known negative social and ecological impacts, the production of cocoa is often highlighted in the media and elsewhere. If not, Perkiss et al. outline what they refer to as "three sticky problems with chocolate", namely: (1) demand exceeds sustainable farming (it is relevant to note here that most of the world's cocoa is grown in the Ivory Coast or other developing countries, yet consumed by industrialised countries); (2) to keep prices low farmers are poorly paid, with some below the poverty line; and, (3) again, due to low prices paid to cocoa producers "most resort to using child labour and even slave child labour" (pp. 1–2).

In their paper, they explore how companies operating in the cocoa supply chain attempt to justify their operations. They focus on one of the large companies in this sector Nestlé, and analyse both their own discourse in relation to labour and child labour, as well as counter accounts from groups that seek to challenge the industry by exposing their practices and highlighting accountabilities in this space. In engaging with these issues the paper addresses many of the points discussed in this chapter and throughout the book.

For example, the sticky problems noted above relate to discussions regarding supply chain responsibilities for organisations, and how they should be mindful of, for example, low-cost production and supply. Nestlé, the authors point out, is a signatory to the 2001 Harkin-Engel Protocol. This protocol seeks to eradicate the worst forms of child labour, including slavery. Being a signatory to this Protocol, the company has expressed commitment to this, and as such, the public commitment enables NGOs and others to highlight where they fall short. The case illustrates how counter accounts are a way that is often used by such NGOs and social movements who wish to expose such accountabilities.

Lastly, another important aspect raised by Perkiss et al. that we have sought to highlight throughout the book is that of change. They ask "Has the discourse brought about change?" (p. 21). While they note some evidence of progress, some reduction in the statistics about child labour as well as an indication that the counter accounts have had some positive effect on the farmers, there is much more to be done. They note not only the responsibilities of the corporation, Nestlé, but also the systemic issues, the financial and the political, at play here. Human rights are complex and multifaceted, yet fundamentally important.

**Perkiss, S., Bernardi, C., Dumay, J. and Haslam, J. (2021). A Sticky Chocolate Problem: Impression Management and Counter Accounts in the Shaping of Corporate Image. *Critical Perspectives on Accounting, 81,* 102229.**

## 8.6 Some limits and the potential of counter accounting practices

Thus far, we have focused on describing the variety of counter accounts as well as on discussing the key characteristics of this practice. However, as with most practices, counter accounting is not without its problems. We will now move on to cover some of the main issues and critiques of counter accounting practices before looking at a key area where such accounting practices appear to offer us potential in our transition towards sustainability.

### 8.6.1 Some critiques of counter accounting practices

Counter accounts have been critiqued for being as narrow and as biased as corporate accounts. That is, just as the corporate account which is often the target of the counter account is limited and written from a particular perspective, so too are counter accounts.

For example, the counter accounts produced by environmental NGO groups may fail to consider all environmental aspects, let alone social and economic ones. The animal rights activists discussed by Laine and Vinnari (2017), for example, based their counter accounts on pictures and video material they had collected by secretly entering farms at night without permission. The counter account the activists produced focused on animal rights, but at the same time, they were accused of paying less attention to other issues, for example, the potential animal health risks related to how they collected the video material at farms, or the potential social consequences their actions had for farmers, such as the mental health issues and weakened capability to work individuals reportedly experienced after activists had entered private farms at night. How the narrow or biased nature of the counter accounts impacts how they are perceived by audiences is perhaps not clear. Spence (2009) makes an interesting point on this when he considers this aspect of counter accounts (although Spence primarily uses the label anti-accounts). He identifies that counter accounts are an alternative truth, but argues, often the preparer of the counter account knows this, whereas the corporate accountant might not be aware of the partial or biased nature of a corporate account.

Another potential issue or problem with counter accounts, or for counter accountants, relates to problems with having the account read and more particularly having the account "heard". Think about the corporate report. Do you ever question the legitimacy of the corporation to produce this account? The role and legitimacy of the account provider is something that is brought to the fore when we consider counter accounting practices, and it is likely to affect their potential to, for example, raise accountability concerns. But, as we raise briefly above, the logic of who is best placed to provide accounts could be considered from other perspectives. Accounting takes for granted the legitimacy of the entity to provide the account. Perhaps when it comes to the financial aspects internal to the firm, this makes sense – the entity does after all know what happens internally better than those who lie outside the organisation (although, of course, we recognise problems here with quality and transparency). However, when it comes to accounting for the impacts of the entity on those both internal and external to the organisation – the range of stakeholders discussed in Chapter 3 – this legitimacy to provide the account could be called into question. However, would we consider all groups in society to carry a legitimate voice – a legitimate position to provide an account? And what forms would we consider to be counter accounts? Such questions remain and perhaps will be the subject of consideration moving forward.

Some have also questioned the ability for counter accounting to effect change often referring to those who claim that such practices have emancipatory potential (see Li and McKernan, 2016; Tweedie, 2023). While it is unlikely that all counter accounts will have a direct and visible impact on, for example, the target corporation or particular policy or regulatory initiative, as we have discussed above in relation to the intended audience and motivation, this is not necessarily the intent nor expectation. The impact may be much more subtle, nuanced, even more long-lasting than this (as would be the case in those seeking to highlight a particular issue). So while it is important to critically reflect on, the potential of such practices, and take care not to overstate their "impact", it is useful to also consider how counter accounts may also have had indirect influence in societies or concerning specific questions. This includes their ability to challenge the understandings of conventional accounting. A topic we consider next.

### 8.6.2 How counter accounting challenges conventional views of accounting?

Counter accounting challenges conventional understandings of accounting, for example encouraging us to think both who are (and should be) account providers and what the nature of an account is. These aspects are important issues which have implications. On the positive side, challenging accounting and our taken-for-granted assumptions about what accounting is and what it should be is likely to be useful in fostering our thinking and enabling us to see accounting differently. However, is there a danger of seeing everything as an account? This is perhaps a discussion that would be useful to be had, and something that you might like to reflect on. While we have in this chapter noted the relevance of social media and highlighted the possibilities it offers, we would be wary of perceiving all social media posts on the various platforms as counter accounts. Fundamental to accounting however is the act of giving an account and the presence of an accountability relationship (whether or not such a relationship is accepted by both parties).

Overall, counter accounting encourages us to think critically about accounting tools and practices and accountability relationships through a consideration of how they could be different. Perhaps as you have been reading this chapter you have considered how you could use counter accounting practices (as an individual or in collaboration with others) to advance a sustainability issue that you are particularly interested in. In a world where global ecological boundaries are transgressed, social justice constantly challenged, and democracy increasingly undermined, counter accounting presents a potentially powerful example of a practice which emphasises the importance of accountability and highlights power inequalities. This is essential if we are to take seriously the question of what is required of accounts and account providers if we truly hope to transition to a more sustainable society.

## 8.7 Conclusion

Counter accounting can be understood as an umbrella label for a myriad of practices of accounting by a range of groups and individuals not usually considered accounting entities. Counter accounting is an important area of sustainability accounting and accountability, as practical examples from a variety of local and international contexts have shown how counter accounts have the potential to establish accountability relationships, challenge power structures and diversify public debate by bringing more voices to the conversation. Counter accounting is likely to develop, expand and grow in importance in the future. This is likely to be helped with enhanced technology, development of artificial intelligence and growing social media platforms which make the collection and dissemination of information essential for counter accounting practices more accessible, efficient and effective. In addition to facilitating the production of counter accounts in general, digitalisation has also paved the way for various online collaborative platforms (such as Banktrack and the Oil Spill Monitor mentioned above), which appear to have considerable potential in enabling multiple perspectives to be collated and more comprehensive accounts produced. At the same time, the advancement of digitalisation and proliferation of artificial intelligence entails that assessing the reliability and authenticity of information becomes both more important and increasingly challenging, presenting novel questions for accounting, counter accounts and accountability relations.

As we proceed through the next chapters of the book, those that make up Part III and which focus on accounting in relation to some key contemporary sustainability issues, we would encourage you to think about where counter accounting practices could be used to help inform this transition and re-imagine new ways of accounting and accountability.

## References


ActionAid (2010). Calling Time: Why SABMiller Should Stop Dodging Taxes in Africa. www.actionaid.org.uk/sites/default/files/doc_lib/calling_time_on_tax_avoidance.pdf (accessed 2 December 2020).

Archel, P., Carrasco, F., García-Benau, M.A. and Larrinaga, C. (2022). Intellectual Engagements of Accounting Academics: The 'Forecasted Losses' Intervention. *Critical Perspectives on Accounting, 86*, 102359.

ASH (2002) *British American Tobacco – The Other Report to Society*. www.cqct.qc.ca/Documents_docs/DOCU_2006/BRIE_02_06_00_ASH_BAT_OtherReportToSociety.pdf (accessed 28 August 2020).

BankTrack (2025). Home. https://www.banktrack.org (accessed 4 February 2025).

Counter Information Services (CIS) (1975). Unilever's World. CIS Anti Report No. 11, produced in collaboration with SOMA (Amsterdam); and in co-operation with The Transnational Institute. https://www.anti-report.com/LIBRARY (accessed 4 February 2025).

Counter Information Services (CIS) (2025). Anti-Reports. https://www.anti-report.com (accessed 4 February 2025).

Cooper, C., Taylor, P., Smith, N. and Catchpowle, I. (2005). A Discussion of the Political Potential of Social Accounting. *Critical Perspectives on Accounting, 16*(7), 951–974.

Denedo, M., Thomson, I. and Yonekura, A. (2018). Accountability, Maps and Inter-generational Equity: Evaluating the Nigerian Oil Spill Monitor. *Public Money and Management, 38*(5), 355–364.

Dey, C. and Gibbon, J. (2014). External Accounts. In Bebbington, J., Unerman, J. and O'Dwyer, B. (eds), *Sustainability Accounting and Accountability*, pp. 108–123. Routledge.

Friends of the Earth (FoE) (2003). *Failing the Challenge: The Other Shell Report 2002*. Friends of the Earth. www.foei.org/resources/publications/publications-by-subject/resisting-mining-oil-gas-publications/failing-the-challenge-the-other-shell-report# (accessed 28 August 2020).

Friends of the Earth (FoE) (2025). Publications. https://www.foei.org/friends-of-the-earth-international-publications/ (accessed 4 February 2025).

Gibson, K., Gray, R., Laing, Y. and Dey, C. (2001). *The Silent Accounts Project: Draft Silent and Shadow Accounts 1999–2000*. CSEAR: Glasgow.

Greenpeace International (2023). Uncovered: Unilever's Complicity in the Plastics Crisis and Its Power to Solve It. https://www.greenpeace.org/international/publication/63935/unilever-uncovered/ (accessed 4 February 2025).

Himick, D. and Vinnari, E. (2023). Counter Accounts, Accountability and Governance. In Carnegie, G. and Napier, C. (eds), *Handbook of Accounting, Accountability and Governance*, pp. 349–368. Edward Elgar.

Laine, M. and Vinnari, E. (2017). The Transformative Potential of Counter Accounts: A Case Study of Animal Rights Activism. *Accounting, Auditing and Accountability Journal, 30*(7), 1481–1510.

Li, Y. and McKernan, J. (2016). Human Rights, Accounting, and the Dialectic of Equality and Inequality. *Accounting Auditing & Accountability Journal, 29(4)*, 568–598.
Medawar, C. (1976). The Social Audit: A Political View. *Accounting, Organizations and Society, 1(4)*, 389–394.
Michel, C. (2021). *American Kleptocracy: How the U.S. Created the World's Greatest Money Laundering Scheme in History*. St.Martin's Press.
Obermayer, F. and Obermaier, F. (2016). *The Panama Papers: Breaking the Story of How the Rich and Powerful Hide Their Money*. Oneworld Publications.
Oil Spill Monitor (2025). Nigerian Oil Spill Monitor. https://nosdra.oilspillmonitor.ng (accessed 4 February 2025).
Oreskes, N. and Conway, E. (2011). *Merchants of Doubt: How a Handful of Scientists Obscured the Truth on Issues from Tobacco Smoke to Global Warming*. Bloomsbury.
Perkiss, S., Bernardi, C., Dumay, J. and Haslam, J. (2021). A Sticky Chocolate Problem: Impression Management and Counter Accounts in the Shaping of Corporate Image. *Critical Perspectives on Accounting, 81*, 102229.
Shaxson, N. (2011). *Treasure Islands: Tax Havens and the Men Who Stole the World*. Vintage.
Skilling, P. and Tregidga, H. (2019). Accounting for the "Working Poor": Analysing the Living Wage Debate in Aotearoa New Zealand. *Accounting, Auditing and Accountability Journal, 32(7)*, 2031–2061.
Spence, C. (2009). Social Accounting's Emancipatory Potential: A Gramscian Critique. *Critical Perspectives on Accounting, 20(2)*, 205–227.
Thomson, I., Dey, C. and Russell, S. (2015). Activism, Arenas and Accounts in Conflicts over Tobacco Control. *Accounting, Auditing and Accountability Journal, 28(5)*, 809–845.
Tregidga, H. (2017). "Speaking Truth to Power": Analysing Shadow Reporting as a Form of Shadow Accounting. *Accounting, Auditing and Accountability Journal, 30(3)*, 510–533.
Tweedie, J. (2023). The Emancipatory Potential of Counter Accounting: A Žižekian Critique. *Critical Perspectives on Accounting, 95*, 102505.

## Additional reading and resources

Adams, C. A. (2004). The Ethical, Social and Environmental Reporting Performance-Portrayal Gap. *Accounting, Auditing and Accountability Journal, 17(5)*, 731–757.
Andrew, J. and Baker, M. (2020). The Radical Potential of Leaks in the Shadow Accounting Project: The Case of US Oil Interests in Nigeria. *Accounting, Organizations and Society, 82*, 101101.
Corporate Watch (2014). Investigating Companies: A Do-It-Yourself Handbook. https://corporatewatch.org/wp-content/uploads/2017/09/Investigating-Companies-Corporate-Watch.pdf (accessed 4 February 2025).
Gallhofer, S., Haslam, J., Monk, E. and Roberts, C. (2006). The Emancipatory Potential of Online Reporting: A Case of Counter Accounting. *Accounting, Auditing and Accountability Journal, 28*(5), 846–874.
George, S., Brown, J. and Dillard, J. (2023). Social Movement Activist's Conceptions of Political Action and Counter-Accounting through a Critical Dialogic Accounting and Accountability Lens. *Critical Perspectives on Accounting, 91*, 102408.
Harte, G. and Owen, D. L. (1987). Fighting De-industrialisation: The Role of Local Government Social Audits. *Accounting, Organizations and Society, 12(2)*, 123–142.
Unerman, J. and Bennett, M. (2004). Increased Stakeholder Dialogue and the Internet: Towards Greater Corporate Accountability or Reinforcing Capitalist Hegemony? *Accounting, Organizations and Society, 29*(7), 685–707.

PART

III

# Issues in accounting for sustainability

CHAPTER

9

# Accounting for climate

Discussions of climate change and concerns about its catastrophic effects are everywhere. It is, without doubt, a sustainability issue of critical importance. While concerns over rising global temperatures have been present for some time now, the urgency surrounding the issue is at an all-time high, with the scientific community and international bodies such as the United Nations (UN) emphasising the critical need to act fast. This urgency can be seen in the media and on the streets where we are seeing global movements protesting against governments, industry bodies and large corporations on the issue of climate change. The need for action, that is the need to do something beyond recognising climate change as an issue, can also be seen in the framing of the UN Sustainable Development Goal related to climate. Goal number 13 titled "Climate Action" represents that not only is climate one of the 17 goals needed to be achieved in relation to sustainability, but also that we need action on the issue – and urgently. At the same time, there are forces slowing down climate action through, for example, drawing attention elsewhere. For instance, challenges associated with a focus on short-term economic growth, national political developments and increased geopolitical tensions can lead both voters and politicians prioritise other issues ahead of climate.

In this chapter, we discuss climate change focusing specifically on why climate is an issue for organisations and, more specifically, for accounting and accountants. As such, after providing a brief overview of climate change and its consequences to frame our discussion, we locate the issue in relation to organisations, accounting and accountability. We then consider accounting practices in relation to accounting and climate and the various accountabilities that arise. We conclude by discussing a number of areas which are useful to reflect on as we consider the overall role of accounting in addressing the climate emergency.

By the end of this chapter, you should:

- Understand climate change and why it is a key issue of critical importance.
- Understand why climate change is important to organisations and accounting.

DOI: 10.4324/9781003533207-12

- Have developed an awareness of current accounting practice in relation to climate change and various accountabilities that arise.
- Have reflected on the limits of current practices in relation to accounting for climate.

## 9.1 Climate change: An issue of critical importance

### 9.1.1 Climate change: A brief introduction

Climate change refers to any long-term change in temperature and weather patterns over time – whether from natural causes or human activity. Climate change leads to more extreme weather events such as extended heatwaves, droughts and floods. Climate experts are in general agreement that we are experiencing a period of global warming and that this warming is being driven by human activity, in particular the build-up of heat-trapping greenhouse gases (GHGs) in the atmosphere.

While many products and processes have become more energy-efficient and hence less carbon-intensive, such relative improvements have been outpaced by economic growth. Alongside the high carbon-intensive lifestyles of many in what can be referred to as high-income countries, as well as the ultra-carbon-intensive lifestyles of the elite, the rise of industrialisation and improved standard of living in some low- and middle-income countries, while often helpful in reducing global inequality, have increased emissions. It is also important to recognise that the consequences of climate change are not felt consistently across the globe, with the Global South, in particular low-lying developing countries, feeling the major effects of the changing climate first (Perkiss, 2024; Scobie et al., 2024). Overall, the interconnections between economic growth, social justice and the reliance on fossil fuels across the world make climate change both political and complex.

While we briefly outline some key points below, we won't engage in extensive discussion here about climate science and what the various levels of warming mean for the planet and for our societies. This is beyond the scope of this chapter and is covered in depth elsewhere. We would encourage you to look further into the literature and discussions on this, noting also that we have found it beneficial to explore how the topic is discussed in different scientific disciplines, e.g. natural science, political science, technology and economics, as well as by different actors in society, such as business front-groups, activists and political insiders (e.g. Hawken, 2017; Loach, 2023). In doing so, however, we would caution you to reflect on the information and the sources of the information that you are engaging with as this is an area where misinformation exists. Indeed, debates can be muddied (intentionally or otherwise) with confusion. As such, we must take care to ensure that we access information from credible sources and that we reflect on that information. A good source of information is the Intergovernmental Panel on Climate Change (IPCC) – the UN body established to assess the science related to climate change (see the "Focus on practice" below).

**Focus on practice: The Intergovernmental Panel on Climate Change**

The Intergovernmental Panel on Climate Change (IPCC) is a body formed by the UN in 1988 with the task of assessing climate change science. Its aim is to help policymakers by consolidating and synthesising scientific evidence about climate change and the impacts it has on societies.

The IPCC has published six assessment reports, with the seventh assessment cycle beginning in July 2023. Each report is produced by hundreds of scientists who come together to evaluate the most recent scientific knowledge available. The reports also assess scientific knowledge regarding the potential social and economic impacts climate change might have in the coming years.

The IPCC reports have been highly influential in helping societies understand climate change and the impacts that might follow, as well as the evolving scientific knowledge concerning it. They are considered the most comprehensive scientific reports about climate change, despite constant attempts by contrarians to discredit them. In addition to the assessment reports, the IPCC also contributes to global climate governance by producing special reports and technical papers used in the climate treaties negotiated through the UN, including the Kyoto Protocol and the Paris Agreement discussed further below.

### 9.1.2 Climate change: The consequences

It is useful in framing our discussion below to outline some of the well-documented consequences that will result from a warming climate. Indeed, consequences are being seen now and are therefore not something "that will happen in the future" – although they are expected to get worse.

While the melting polar ice caps and the resultant sea level rise affecting low-lying regions is well-known, there are a range of current and expected consequences of the changing climate. The IPCC (2018) outlines a range of potential impacts and associated risks in its "Special Report on Global Warming of 1.5 Degrees Celsius (1.5°C)". This 1.5°C, a figure you will often see mentioned in discussions on climate, is the aspirational goal set out in the 2015 Paris Agreement on climate change (see "Focus on practice" below) which aims to limit warming to 2°C above pre-industrial levels, and pursue efforts to limit it to 1.5°C. It is worth noting that the warming effect of many GHGs lasts for decades, and research and current warming trends suggest that the climate is warming much faster than initially anticipated and that the climate will warm by 1.5°C even if we reduce our carbon footprint to zero from today.

The IPCC states that climate models project differences in how global warming of 1.5°C will impact different regions. These include increases in the mean temperature of most land and ocean regions, hot extremes in most inhabited regions, heavy precipitation in several regions and a high probability of drought and precipitation deficits elsewhere. Major impacts on biodiversity and ecosystems are also noted including greater species loss and extinction as well as impacts on terrestrial, freshwater and coastal ecosystems. The IPCC also identifies climate-related risks to health, livelihoods, food security, water supply, human security and economic growth. Some of these impacts are discussed further in the following chapters where we cover water, biodiversity, human rights and economic inequality respectively.

The effects of climate change occur even with only a few degrees of warming. So, while you may be thinking that a few degrees warmer would be nice – just a few degrees will have, indeed are already having, significant consequences. Climate change has been an issue for some time; however, it is widely recognised that more urgency is needed at both global and local levels. This urgency is being generated through the work of climate scientists, climate activists and a range of other national and international groups, including some businesses. The climate crisis is impacting organisations and the next thing this chapter discusses is what the climate crisis has to do with organisations and with accounting.

### Focus on practice: Global attempts to address climate change

Climate change is a truly global issue. While there may be some more localised impacts of air pollution (e.g. respiratory health), emissions from a country, city or individual organisation do not just affect that country, city or organisation – they affect everyone. Given both the global nature and severity of the issue, there have been multiple attempts at the global level to tackle climate change.

The most widely known global governance regime related to climate change and attempts to address it is the UN Framework Convention on Climate Change (UNFCCC), a framework that structures and guides international talks on tackling climate change.

The first phase of the UNFCCC was adopted at the 1992 Rio de Janeiro Earth Summit. From the beginning, the UNFCCC set a fairly ambitious goal of stabilising GHG concentrations "at a level that would prevent dangerous anthropogenic (human induced) interference with the climate system". The UNFCCC is tasked with achieving this stabilisation in a timeframe that allows "ecosystems to adapt naturally to climate change, to ensure that food production is not threatened, and to enable economic development to proceed in a sustainable manner" (UN, 1992, p. 4).

Given the different interests and contrasting political positions of national leaders, the UNFCCC has been a ground for many disputes and political struggles. These have occurred over, for instance, how societies should react to climate change, whether consumers or producers should be held responsible for GHG emissions, how country-level targets should be set and how different types of climate actions should be measured, reported and verified. More recently, a key debate has focused on climate finance and what is known as loss and damage, referring to debates as to what extent more developed countries should provide financing for the more vulnerable nations to help them adapt to climate change as well as to cover the losses climate change is already causing.

In 1997, the UNFCCC adopted the Kyoto Protocol which set ratifying countries binding targets for reducing GHG emissions. Due to its flexibility mechanisms allowing a range of practices to be used to reduce emissions, it may also be considered one of the stepping stones towards international cap and trade systems and the creation of carbon markets. The Kyoto Protocol would eventually be ratified by over 190 countries, but this did not ensure that the subsequent negotiations would proceed smoothly, as annual meetings

(COPs; Conferences of the Parties) often ended with only minor refinements as global political consensus on key issues proved hard to reach.

The Paris Agreement adopted in 2015 marks the latest evolution of the global climate governance regime. The Paris Agreement can be considered an important milestone, as the signatories agreed to "intensify the actions and investment needed for a sustainable low carbon future". The often repeated central aim of the agreement is to keep the increase in global temperature below 2°C above pre-industrial levels during this century and to pursue efforts to limit that increase to 1.5°C. However, the Paris Agreement continues to be affected by national and global politics. While the most prominent example is the back-and-forth of the United States' withdrawal from the agreement since 2017, there are political parties in various countries advocating for taking the agreement less seriously, with the key argument often being (short-term) economic costs of carbon reductions.

### 9.1.3 A note on terminology

Before proceeding further, it is perhaps useful to make a few points about terminology and how we use various terms in this chapter. Climate change, the term you will likely be most familiar with, relates to the changing climate as outlined above. The term carbon is often used to refer to GHG emissions in a general sense, as a kind of shorthand. This is because GHG emissions are often converted into their so-called carbon equivalents through a process of commensuration. We explain this further below. In accounting, the common terms are carbon accounting and GHG accounting. While you might also see climate accounting or climate-related disclosures used at times, carbon accounting is perhaps the most widely recognised. In this book, we use the terms as noted above, however also refer to accounting for climate to signal where practices go beyond a consideration of carbon emissions to broader practices, for example disclosures, relating to the general sustainability issue of climate change, including the financial risks associated with a changing climate.

When looking at the topic of climate and climate change from a technical or natural science perspective, it is important to distinguish between different GHG emissions. However, when discussing accounting and accountability in organisations, referring to the general term *carbon* is usually sufficient. This does not mean that GHG emissions and processes of commensuration are not important; however, indeed, we might argue that better terminology in accounting would be beneficial to address this sustainability challenge.

## 9.2 What has climate change got to do with organisations and accounting?

It is probably already quite clear that climate change has significant implications for organisations and accounting. In this section, we will examine in a little more detail three aspects which help us understand these connections and provide more of a context for the discussion of specific accounting practices and related accountability relationships.

### 9.2.1 Regulation, co-ordination and collaboration

Let's begin by underscoring that climate change is not something that only relates to national governments and large corporations in the most polluting industries. Instead, and really quite simply, all organisations affect and are affected by climate change. These impacts are at different scales and the effects will show in different ways and on different timescales, and they might not always be tangible and immediate, but the climate emergency impacts organisations across the board in both subtle and very clear ways.

National and local governments, as well as international governing bodies such as the UN discussed above, all play an important role in climate. There is much that needs to be done at these levels given the international and transboundary nature of climate. International bodies and both national and local governments are key organisational structures through which national and local climate initiatives, strategies and policies are managed. Climate change also affects national and local governments in relation to the resources needing to be allocated for handling the immediate impacts of climate change. Consider, on the one hand, government responses in the short term to impacts caused by extreme weather events, for example, provision of shelter and aid, and on the other hand, decisions needed for adapting to the impacts over the longer term, for instance, through developing new types of infrastructure and innovative urban planning in cities.

For-profit organisations of all sizes are also clearly affected by climate. Organisational strategy (e.g. decisions on locations, international growth strategies); planning (e.g. emergency planning, adaptation); supply chain management (e.g. access to raw materials); staff management (e.g. staff wellbeing); investment appraisal (e.g. costs of carbon); and attracting investment (e.g. risk profile) all have climate considerations. Similarly, climate change is a significant question for many non-governmental organisations (NGOs). Some NGOs and a myriad of civil society organisations work explicitly on aspects of the climate change agenda, and they often target policymakers and prominent businesses with their campaign work. At the same time, NGOs have their own climate impacts, which they need to consider.

Climate change is complex, and we cannot expect the challenges to be solved by a single industry. A large-scale response will require changes to behaviour, including the behaviour of all organisations. It will also require co-ordination, co-operation and a range of governance regimes to incentivise and coerce. Likewise, it is not reasonable to expect that a solution for the climate challenge will be found in any one action or response. For example, while new technologies are likely to assist in the reduction of emissions and new forms of cleaner energy are being developed, these actions alone will not be enough. The IPCC stresses that a range of responses are required and large-scale change is needed.

Still, government authorities often need to impose rules in seeking to reduce societies' impacts on climate. New regulations on climate change, together with potential changes in the social and political landscape, can potentially have major implications for organisations. Think about the example we discussed in Chapter 3 from Germany, where a major utility company, Uniper, started operating a large new coal-fired power plant in early 2020, having delayed its intended launch date of 2011 partly due to mounting social pressure against coal-fired power plants. From an investment perspective, one would normally assume this type of power plant asset would run for 30–40 years or longer. However, Germany's national climate plan means an exit from coal is currently scheduled to take place by the year 2038, implying a significant reduction in the asset's useful life. So the case of Datteln 4 highlights the impairment risks organisations now face from increasing climate regulation. A similar phenomenon can be seen taking place in the car industry. The EU, for instance, has since 2009 aimed at reducing emissions by setting emission limits and targets for new cars and car manufacturers. The requirements have become stricter over time, with the EU-wide fleet targets for carbon emissions again phased downwards from 2025 onwards. This mechanism has direct implications for car manufacturers, who need to take this into account when designing the fleet they offer.

What these examples demonstrate is that organisations need to adapt and plan ahead as various regulations and views of acceptable practices change in societies. Responding to climate change will also likely involve increased levels of co-ordination and collaboration given the complex nature of the issue and the urgency of the response needed. These examples also highlight the interconnections between climate, social infrastructure, regulation, organisational decisions and accounting. Different types of connections exist, relationships are complex, and policies made in one area will have consequences elsewhere. Accounting practices will have to adapt to adequately support the changes needed.

### 9.2.2 Impacts and dependencies

When thinking about the relationship between climate change, organisations and accounting, the first thing we often think about are the impacts. That is, how much GHG does the organisation emit and is this particular industry among the more carbon-intensive ones. This is clearly relevant, as all organisations currently create emissions through the course of their activities and therefore impact the climate. While some organisations have greater impacts – large multinational corporations operating directly with coal and oil for instance – all organisations produce emissions. Moreover, as societies have become more cognisant of the climate emergency, there is also an increasing need for carbon information, and hence organisations are increasingly being held accountable for their climate impacts.

However, impacts are only part of the equation. When considering the relationship between climate and organisations and their accounting and accountabilities, it is also useful to think about dependencies. Organisations are dependent on the climate for operations and their long-term survival. Likewise, many of the decisions we outlined above, be that in regard to strategic choices, product development, supply chain or investments, are strongly connected to climate change and hence show how the organisation's activities and future success are dependent on climate. As with the impact on climate, the recognition of climate dependencies has also affected the demand for and nature of information. For example, financial markets and investors are increasingly interested in the climate-related financial risks of organisations, which is reflected in the emerging reporting regulation discussed in more detail below.

Given the importance of, and longer-term focus on, impacts, many of the accounting and accountability practices relating to the climate we discuss in this chapter focus on the impacts that organisations, processes and products have. However, the recognition of how organisations are dependent on the environment is also recognised. Specifically, in relation to accounting for climate and climate change, there is an increasing understanding of the organisation's dependency on a stable and functioning climate. A prominent example of such thinking relates to risk and risk management as discussed in Chapter 7 and returned to below.

**PAUSE AND REFLECT...**

The climate crisis is relevant for all organisations no matter their size, geographic location or operations. And, as we have mentioned, this relevance relates both to impacts and dependencies.

When it comes to impacts on climate it is hard, if not impossible, to think of an organisation that does not have any climate impacts. Technology companies, for example, previously considered low emitters, have impacts in relation to the production of the technology and its operations (e.g. as a result of energy consumption). Indeed, with increasing attention on artificial intelligence (AI), together with discussions of its unleashed future potential and the associated vast investment needs, it is not surprising that the energy consumption and climate impacts of AI use are being increasingly discussed. However, when it comes to organisations that have the greatest impact, the results are quite staggering. A 2024 Guardian headline read "Just 57 companies linked to 80% of greenhouse gas emissions since 2016" (The Guardian, 2024, see InfluenceMap, 2024). These oil-, gas-, coal- and cement-producing corporations were both state-controlled corporations and shareholder-owned multinational corporations.

Dependencies are perhaps a little bit harder to identify, but we suggest it is useful to take a few moments to consider how various organisations are dependent on the climate and a functioning climate regulation system. An obvious starting point would be agriculture, where recent examples of such dependencies include the olive harvests in Spain and orange harvests in Brazil and Florida being impacted substantially by climate-related weather patterns in 2023 and 2024, leading to substantial economic consequences for many firms. Whether it is for the sourcing of raw materials, exposure to extreme weather events or the reliance on a healthy and productive workforce or customer base (all things affected by climate change), it again becomes hard to identify an organisation for which the climate is not a material sustainability issue.

### 9.2.3 Direct and indirect emissions: The three scopes of carbon accounting

The concept of scope relates to discussions of direct and indirect emissions. It is a highly relevant topic for carbon accounting, accountability and reporting, as it has major implications on how we measure and report the emissions of an organisation, and subsequently understand the responsibility an organisation has.

As is the case with many aspects of sustainability accounting, when assessing and understanding carbon emissions of a particular product or process it is relevant to look at the different stages of its production and use. While some of the activities and impacts of an organisation take place directly at a facility owned and controlled by the organisation, a major part of them often happens elsewhere in a more indirect fashion. This relates to organisational boundaries discussed in Chapter 3, as well as to questions concerning how far downstream and upstream in a supply chain an organisation's accountabilities and responsibilities reach.

While in some areas of sustainability accounting, there can be flexibility in such boundary setting, there is in carbon accounting a need to be more precise. This relates for instance to situations where a uniform measure of the quantities of carbon emissions is needed, such as for emission trading schemes or where emissions are needed to be disclosed in reports covered by regulation, both instances discussed below. Likewise, given the climate emergency, there are a range of carbon reduction targets at international, national and organisational levels, some of which have been put in place through regulation or set via binding agreements. In order for such schemes and agreements to function, there is a need to have some clarity when assessing and reporting carbon emissions.

In carbon accounting, the idea of different scopes is used to classify direct and indirect emissions resulting from the organisation's activities into three categories. We discuss the scopes of carbon accounting in more detail in the "Focus on practice" below.

**Focus on practice: The three scopes of carbon accounting**

In carbon accounting, three different scopes are used to define operational boundaries in relation to direct and indirect GHG emissions. These have been discussed in more detail by the World Resources Institute (2006), GHG Protocol (2013) and ACCA (2011). In brief, the three scopes are as follows:

Scope 1: Direct GHG emissions

- Includes direct emissions caused by the activities of an organisation, in other words occurring from sources owned or controlled by the organisation. Typical examples include emissions from a factory or exhaust fumes from a company-owned car.
- Scope 1 emissions are more straightforward to assess and measure as the number of sources is typically limited and well-known.

Scope 2: Indirect GHG emissions from electricity

- Includes emissions caused in the generation of electricity the organisation has used. These emissions take place where the electricity is produced, e.g. a power plant.
- For the most part, assessing Scope 2 emissions is not complicated. Electricity production takes place through standardised processes, the emissions of which can be assessed. The organisation also has exact information regarding how much electricity it consumes at a given facility over a given time period.

Scope 3: Other indirect GHG emissions

- Includes all other indirect emissions which result from the activities of the organisation but take place elsewhere at sources which are not owned or controlled by the organisation.
- This implies that Scope 3 emissions should account for the entire supply chain of a product, including for instance the raw materials of products, the use of those

products, as well as any transportation related to both products and people. GHG Protocol's Corporate Value Chain Accounting and Reporting Standard identifies in total 15 categories of Scope 3 activities.

- The range of Scope 3 is very broad, and the Scope 3 emissions of an organisation are often much higher than those of Scopes 1 and 2 combined.
- Assessing Scope 3 emissions is substantially more complicated than those of Scope 1 and 2.

Organisations are not always clear as to how they have assessed GHG emissions. Sometimes organisations only refer to Scopes 1 and 2 when for instance highlighting their achievements in climate-friendly initiatives. The emerging regulatory requirements are hoped to bring some clarity to such disclosures.

At the same time, it is important to avoid double-counting when analysing the emissions of a given location, supply chain or otherwise across organisations. Given how the scopes span organisational boundaries, Scope 2 and 3 emissions of a particular company are by definition also Scope 1 emissions of another organisation.

Finally, we should mention Scope 4 emissions, which you may also note being discussed at times. Referring to "avoided emissions", Scope 4 is used to assess and discuss emissions reductions that result from the use of a particular product or service rather than an alternative one. For example, if a meeting took place online rather than in-person, one could argue emissions were avoided due to not needing travel. These could be calculated and recorded as Scope 4. As you can imagine, accounting for such avoided emissions is quite complex, as it can be challenging to estimate the cause and effects as well as the counterfactuals that are required for completing such calculations. And again, when we are thinking about what matters when it comes to climate, it is not the emissions avoided, but the absolute emissions.

In establishing the scopes for carbon accounting, an important role has been played by The Greenhouse Gas (GHG) Protocol. The GHG Protocol was established in 1998 by the World Resource Institute (WRI) and the World Business Council for Sustainable Development (WBCSD). They recognised an increasing need to create standards for GHG accounting and reporting which at the time was still in its infancy. The two parties joined forces and created, in collaboration with companies and some environmental NGOs, the first edition of the GHG Protocol's Corporate Standard in 2001. Since then, the GHG Protocol has developed additional standards on assessing emissions from purchased energy and also an organisation's value chain, as well as a range of sector-specific and technical guidance. Currently, the GHG Protocol Corporate Accounting and Reporting Standard is the most widely used standard for climate-related accounting in organisations, while its Corporate Value Chain Accounting and Reporting Standard continues to be the only available standard for calculating and reporting the Scope 3 emissions of an organisation.

As we progress through our discussion, it is useful to keep in mind these scopes and reflect on the scope of emissions that organisations are accounting for, or recognising accountability in relation to. We would also encourage you to reflect on the implications for climate change of adopting a broad or narrow scope.

## 9.3 Carbon accounting and accountability practices

Given the long-term awareness and the critical nature of climate change, a range of initiatives have emerged to govern behaviour related to climate change. These occur on different levels and include global and national agreements for example, as well as frameworks which guide practices at both the industry and organisational level. Many of these initiatives have implications for accounting and accountability.

International agreements such as the UNFCCC Paris Agreement and the SDGs discussed above create accountabilities for carbon emissions and action in relation to climate change. They require the measurement and reporting of emissions in order to meet targets, or at least to evaluate progress towards meeting targets. At the organisational level, there also needs to be a range of tools and techniques to measure, report and help manage emissions – both internally and externally for internal and external accounting and accountability reasons. As such, applications of carbon accounting take place on many levels, such as the national and regional level (e.g. how have the emissions of a country changed year-by-year), organisational level (e.g. corporation-level emissions on an annual basis), project level (e.g. comparing different manufacturing processes) and product level (e.g. carbon footprints of food items). Accounting is also done for different purposes: disclosures, internal decision-making, for compliance with regulations as discussed above and so forth. While these purposes can intertwine – for example measurement of emissions for an emissions trading scheme can form the basis of a company's climate-related disclosures, and therefore relate to the same accounting process – this is not always the case.

In this section, we outline some accounting and accountability practices in relation to climate. We discuss carbon financial accounting, climate focused management accounting and control, and climate and carbon disclosure and reporting. We have had to be selective in our coverage. As expected with a complex and long-term sustainability issue, the number of initiatives, frameworks and organisational practices we could have included is large. It should also be pointed out that, like many other areas of sustainability accounting, many aspects of carbon accounting and reporting continue to be primarily voluntary activities. While some carbon accounting activities are required by law in different jurisdictions, many others remain at the discretion of the organisation. The landscape is developing, as the climate emergency is prompting societies and stakeholder groups to set higher expectations regarding organisational accountability on carbon. Carbon and climate change accounting and accountability are highly diverse and fast-developing, which is needed given the scale of the challenge faced.

### 9.3.1 Carbon financial accounting

In the field of carbon accounting and climate change, financial accounting is a significant area. There are perhaps a number of reasons for this, including the fact that, for some time now, carbon emissions have had to be recorded for the purposes of things such as carbon emissions trading schemes or to meet local and national regulations. In this section, we discuss various accounting and accountability practices relating to the area of financial accounting.

#### 9.3.1.1 Emissions trading schemes

As discussed, carbon emissions are global in the sense that no matter where they are produced they all affect the same atmosphere. In an attempt to control the rise of GHG emissions and create mechanisms to govern them, the international community has looked to market mechanisms. The most common examples of these are the various emissions trading schemes, also known as cap and trade models. The European Union Emission Trading System (EU ETS) is one of the most widely recognised, but similar systems are in place elsewhere on both national and regional levels. For example, after experimenting with regional pilot schemes since 2013, China initiated in 2021 a national emission trading system. While this scheme initially covered only the power sector (still making it substantially larger than the EU ETS in terms of GHG emissions governed), there are plans to expand its scope.

Emissions trading is essentially a market-based solution aimed at reducing emissions. The institution (usually a government body) running the scheme sets a cap for emissions over a certain amount of time (often a year) and then creates emission allowances to match the amount of emissions allowed. Organisations involved in the scheme must then account for their emissions and obtain allowances to match their emissions over the time period. Depending on the chosen policies, the governing body running the scheme can either allocate permits to organisations for free or alternatively auction them on a regular basis. The economic incentive is formed through the ability of firms to trade the allowances to each other. Some companies find it easier and/or cheaper to reduce emissions, potentially allowing them to sell their excess allowances to the market, while others buy additional allowances to fulfil their requirements. This mechanism, together with the limited overall number of emission allowances available in the marketplace, sets the market price for emission allowances and thereby aims to drive emissions lower with the aid of the market mechanism.

A fundamental need in emissions trading schemes is to transform different types of GHG emissions, such as carbon dioxide, methane and hydrofluorocarbons, into a commodified unit called carbon dioxide equivalents ($CO_2e$). This enables a price for emissions to be established. Accounting has a key role to play because in order for such a market system to function, a robust basis of processes related to assessment, accounting, assurance, valuation and reporting of emissions is needed. In other words, instead of opting for carbon taxes or binding rules for targeted emissions reductions in certain industries, many have adopted a view that markets can help reduce emissions or have seen emissions trading schemes as a solution to political stalemates on how GHG emissions should be mitigated.

In principle, market mechanisms are an effective way of allocating resources and directing economic activity. The challenge, however, is that how the market functions is strongly influenced by the various assumptions, structures and settings underlying the market mechanism. This includes how the rules of the market are set, which GHG emissions are included in the system, how different types of emissions are converted into a common unit and subsequently accounted for and how broadly the market covers the economy (e.g. are industries such as agriculture included in such mechanisms?). Moreover, if the emissions trading scheme is intended to reduce total emissions, the governing body may need to implement a mechanism which lowers the overall number of allowances available in the system. In the EU ETS, for instance, the total number of emissions available during 2024–2030 is lowered annually by 4.3%–4.4%, which should help lower the overall emissions and further incentivise firms to innovate in less-carbon-intensive practices. Likewise, the regulator needs to consider the possibility of carbon leakage, which can occur if carbon-intensive production is moved to countries with more lax carbon policies, or if carbon-intensive imports replace production covered by the ETS. In the EU, the risk of carbon leakage was originally diminished by distributing free emission allowances, which are from the year 2025 onwards being replaced by a dedicated Carbon Border Adjustment Mechanism (CBAM), aiming to make imports subject to a similar carbon price that EU ETS sets to production within the EU.

The first decade of the EU ETS illustrates the consequences from how the market is set up. For example, the price of the carbon emissions stayed very low throughout the scheme's early years from 2005. This caused many to say that the expensive system was doing nothing to help the environment. There were several reasons for the low price. Most notable was the fact that participating organisations had received vast amounts of carbon allowances for free and there was hence simply an excess of supply in the market for the price to turn into anything meaningful. It was only in late 2017 that the price started to increase due to both some changes to the system as well as an increased awareness in the business sector of the scale of the climate challenge. Developments since the late 2010s highlight that emission trading systems have become to play a key role in EU's strive to lower its emissions. As a part of its "Fit for 55" legislative package, EU is establishing a separate emission trading system ("ETS2"), which will cover emissions from fuel combustion in for instance buildings and road transport. This ETS2 is planned to be fully operational in 2027, with a transition period designed in the implementation to help the system achieve a smooth start.

#### 9.3.1.2 Climate change, valuation of assets and consideration of risks

In considering the financial accounting practices and accountabilities in relation to climate and carbon, it is useful to return to our discussion in Chapter 7 on ESG and financial markets on the effects of climate on financial markets.

In Chapter 7, we discussed the study of Bebbington et al. (2020) and how the fossil fuel industry oil and gas companies account for and report on the amounts of fossil fuel resources they have in their possession, that is, how much oil and gas a company is still able to produce from its existing reserves. We noted how the financial markets ascribe value to these reserves since it is supposedly going to bring cash flows to the company in the future. Remember the catch, however. If we put together all the fossil fuel reserves currently accounted for and burned them, we would not meet the warming targets of the Paris Agreement, indicated as needed by the IPCC.

Bebbington and colleagues (2020) elaborate on this phenomenon of "unburnable carbon" and discuss what such a situation might mean for organisations, accounting and the financial markets. The setting is interesting from the perspective of financial markets and stock prices since the investment community is often considered to be fairly effective in regard to how the share price of a particular company gets set in the marketplace. It is also important from a climate perspective.

Looking at climate change and carbon reserves, there seems to be a mismatch due to the interconnections between financial accounting and climate change not being considered. Should the reserves be valued at a lower price, or perhaps not valued at all, as they cannot be burned without devastating climate impacts? Or, is it accepted by their accounting treatment that the global climate targets are not going to be met as burning of the existing reserves would take us beyond the thresholds identified by the scientific community and agreed upon in many of the international agreements? Or perhaps, are the markets betting on technology developing at a rate that we can keep burning fossil fuels but get rid of the emissions via some form of carbon storage or other abatement mechanism? While many would like to be optimistic about the latter option, it is clear that such technologies are very unlikely to be available at a scale and cost to make them effective in the timescale required. This example provides an illustration of how financial accounting practices are having to adapt and respond to the climate emergency and how "conventional" approaches might no longer be suitable.

The second aspect of climate and financial markets concerns the financial implications of climate change, and the emerging financial accounting practices able to recognise such implications. This relates closely to a discussion of the difference between impacts (i.e. how the organisation's actions affect the local and global societies and ecosystems), and dependencies (i.e. how the organisation is dependent on particular aspects in societies and ecosystems). In general terms, organisations for a long time have failed to report on, or even understand, the financial implications of climate change. In 2017, KPMG noted that a majority of companies did not acknowledge climate change to be a financial risk for them in their annual reports (KPMG, 2017). Practices have evolved quickly however. KPMG (2024, p. 67) found 72% of the largest companies in the world are now not only recognising the financial risk of climate change but reporting on these. The Task Force for Climate-related Financial Disclosures (TCFD), discussed in earlier chapters and returned to below, is a clear influence here.

It has long been noted that climate change will bring major disruption to how societies and economies function. It has been argued how having only inadequate or limited information available can affect how investors and markets evaluate the risks and opportunities of companies. This then leads to the potential misallocation of capital and mispricing of assets in the marketplace. In other words, the information available influences how the markets perceive the companies and their potential in the future, which then affects which organisations are considered to be successful and therefore have more resources available to them. The study by Bebbington and colleagues (2020) illustrates the substantial questions that may arise when organisational disclosures do not necessarily reflect the full financial climate-related risks.

The availability and quality of information has begun to change swiftly from the late 2010s onwards, however. This is due to increased investor interest, leading first to the establishment and recommendations of the TCFD and the Network for Greening the Financial System (NGFS), an initiative by Central Banks and Market Supervisors aiming at supporting the involvement of the financial sector and mainstream finance in sustainability transition. As also discussed in Chapter 7, the TCFD was launched with the aim to improve the quality of organisations' financial disclosures which it believed would enable societies in general and financial markets in particular to better understand how organisations and the financial system more broadly are exposed to climate-related risks. Subsequently, the publication of the inaugural IFRS S2 Climate-related Disclosures Standard can be seen as a direct continuation on the TCFD's work. The underlying premise of these frameworks is that once the financial markets have better information more readily available to them, the markets and market actors will be more equipped to assess, price and manage climate-related issues, opportunities and risks appropriately. On this note, it is worth emphasising that such disclosures and potential financial impacts are not only about challenges and downside risks, but will also include substantial opportunities for many organisations which manage to play a role in societies' transformations to less-carbon-intensive economies (O'Dwyer and Unerman, 2020).

Alongside the IFRS Sustainability Disclosure Standards, we are also seeing quickly evolving climate disclosure requirements in various jurisdictions. One prominent example is the United States, where the Securities and Exchange Council (SEC) adopted in 2024 rules aimed at enhancing and standardising climate-related disclosures by public companies. While the SEC rule was swiftly challenged and put on hold for the foreseeable future, the emergence of such requirements in general makes it clear that in the coming years, the amount of carbon information available for market participants will be considerably higher. At this point, however, it remains unclear how all this information will eventually affect the market dynamics over the short-, medium- and long term. Perhaps more significantly still, it remains to be seen whether and to what extent such "financially material outside-in" information is going to help societies mitigate the climate crisis and adapt to its implications.

### 9.3.2 Climate focused management accounting and control

Management accounting and control refers to the various types of calculations, assessments and systems which are used in different contexts, organisations and processes to provide information for internal decision-making and control (see Chapter 4). When related to carbon and climate, this is a very wide-ranging area as there is a range of settings where such carbon and climate accounting is needed and used. It is also an area that is developing swiftly given the wide interest and need for new knowledge.

To a major extent, the use of carbon accounting in organisational decision-making is similar to what we discussed in Chapter 4, and sustainability management accounting and control more broadly. Organisations have different needs and operate in different contexts, and hence the approaches used in internal management and decision-making vary. Accounting systems are also needed to make sense of the complexity of carbon accounting with many organisations needing to adapt systems to meet their needs (Gibassier and Schaltegger, 2015).

However, despite the varying needs of organisations, due to increasing demand for carbon accounting, assessment and reporting tools, there have been attempts to establish international standards in the area. The influential International Organization for Standardization (ISO) has, for instance, produced several standards related to carbon. One of these is ISO 14064, which specifies the principles of quantification and reporting of GHG emissions and removals at the organisational level. It details the requirements that are set for the design, development, management, reporting and verification of an organisation's GHG inventory. This ISO standard has also been used as a basis of other guidelines and instructions. More recently, ISO published ISO 14067, an attempt to establish an international standard for assessing the carbon footprint of products.

**Focus on practice: Scope 3 emission reduction**

Many major organisations have made commitments to reduce their carbon emissions across their entire value chain. One such example is UPM, a Finnish biomaterials company, which is known as one of the largest forest, pulp and paper companies in the World. In addition to having committed to reducing carbon emissions from its own operations, UPM announced in 2022 that it would also seek to decrease its value chain emissions by 30% from 2018 levels by 2030.

In launching the programme, UPM highlighted that this would be a challenging endeavour not only in terms of the practices but also in terms of having sufficient data on which to make decisions. While the firm has over the years gathered substantial experience of dealing with environmental issues, it noted that the carbon footprint calculations are complicated and emphasised how more information would be needed to understand the environmental impacts of its products.

Secondary data often used for carbon footprint and emissions calculations can serve the purposes of reporting, but given its inherent shortcoming such data is not always very helpful for internal decision-making, and thus in making decisions which would allow the company to meet its climate targets and ambitions. Therefore, as UPM started its supply chain decarbonisation programme, it also announced that it would engage with its over 20,000 suppliers to start collecting emissions data in a systematic way. This is hoped to provide the company a strong foundation to assess, monitor and reduce carbon emissions across the value chain.

Given the scale, this project is obviously not a small feat for either the UPM or the suppliers. To assist its business partners, UPM developed their own product carbon footprint calculation guidelines as well as provided the suppliers with further resources to help them get started. Here, we should perhaps note that for a vast multinational like UPM, its suppliers include a variety of different entities, ranging from fellow multinationals with considerable resources to smaller companies in countries like Uruguay, Indonesia and Finland. These suppliers would hence clearly have different capacities to take part and reply to such data requests. The challenges are obviously considerable also for UPM. Setting up the systems that would allow the smooth collection of this data from the suppliers requires some effort, as will the subsequent processes that are needed before this carbon data will emerge into usable form. In addition to financial resources, the firm also needs to have enough skilled personnel with carbon knowledge to ensure there is sufficient capacity to push the project through. Overall, UPM's supply chain decarbonisation programme and the associated data collection aspirations illustrate the role and significance of carbon data and accounting as businesses seek to reduce their emissions (UPM, 2025).

#### 9.3.2.1 The role of assumptions in carbon accounting and decision-making

When using carbon accounting in organisational decision-making, it is important to consider the assumptions that have been used in producing the assessment, measurement and/or indicator. This is again consistent with what we have discussed earlier with regard to sustainability accounting in general. A few words concerning the significance of underlying assumptions in carbon accounting and decision-making are nonetheless useful to illustrate this further.

First, the role of scopes (discussed above) is important. How are the boundaries of the system set when it comes to the assessment of a particular product or process? Are all the upstream emissions, those taking place before the production of an item, and downstream emissions, those taking place when the item is used after the production, included in the assessment? These choices will have a major impact on the results. Moreover, if such assessments are to be used to compare products or services, it is essential to know how the assessments have been conducted. With some products, most of the carbon emissions take place upstream, and hence it is essential to include Scope 3 for an assessment to have much relevance. For an organisation, however, this also indicates that the assessment becomes more complicated and likely more resource-intensive. The aim of the carbon accounting exercises also needs to be considered.

Decisions regarding system boundaries and the associated inclusion of different scopes in the assessment are not the only assumptions that can make a big difference. Given that we often cannot measure carbon emissions directly, as it would be either too burdensome, expensive or outright impossible, many assessments rely on indirect information or various data sources, such as government- or industry-produced information on the emissions profile of energy used. These choices will obviously have an impact on calculations and the eventual outcomes.

Likewise, there is also the question of how emissions are allocated to different products and services in, say, a manufacturing process. In a sense, this is not that different from traditional management accounting. The choices made in regard to allocating GHG emissions to different items and over different time periods are similar to allocating costs, i.e. we can allocate costs differently and get different results. It is again relevant to consider what the aim of engaging with carbon accounting is. From an external standpoint, and when attempting to establish accountability for carbon emissions, the fact that we do not always know how a particular carbon assessment has been conducted creates challenges. Having limited information of the underlying assumptions limits how users are able to use such comparisons or make decisions based on emissions profiles. At times, incompatible carbon accounting assessments have also been used in comparative settings, which can lead to misleading results either on purpose or by accident.

#### 9.3.2.2 Internal carbon pricing to assist organisational decision-making

Monetisation, placing a monetary value on carbon, is a relatively standard method in organisations trying to incorporate considerations of carbon into their decision-making. In addition to broader emission trading schemes set by governments, some organisations have set up their own internal practices to set a price for carbon, thereby creating a price signal that can be taken into account in internal decision-making.

These internal approaches to monetising carbon come in different forms. Some organisations set what are termed shadow prices for carbon on the basis of forward-looking scenarios. They then include this price as a cost in, for instance, investment appraisals. Shadow prices are based on an assumption that there is likely to be a higher price for carbon in the future and using a shadow price for it at the current time is a way to ensure that the investment stays profitable at this higher price. Shadow prices can also be used to stimulate environmental thinking in organisations, for example, to avoid more environmentally ambitious projects getting sidestepped based on higher current (but not necessarily future) costs. Here, an organisation can set a price for carbon which effectively causes projects with higher carbon emissions to face increased costs. This does not mean that there would always be real cost implications; shadow pricing can be used only when assessing alternatives and making decisions, without having any project or business unit pay something in real money.

However, sometimes internal carbon pricing is associated with real financial consequences and transactions. One such example is Microsoft, which has had an internal carbon fee in place since 2012. In Microsoft, the internal carbon fee is charged from each business unit based on actual carbon emissions, and paid inside the company to fund sustainability improvements. Having business divisions actually pay for their carbon emissions is noted to have tangible impacts, as managers and units have incentives to decrease their energy use and improve overall efficiency. In 2022, the internal carbon fee was 15 USD/ton $CO_2e$. The company used the collected funds to run a support system providing resources for those seeking to come up with innovative ways to further improve the organisation's sustainability performance. In 2020, Microsoft announced that it would further expand its internal carbon fee system, which earlier covered all Scope 1 and 2 emissions as well as Scope 3 travel emissions, to include all Scope 3 emissions. Such a move has substantial accounting implications as assessing carbon emissions throughout supply chains is a complex task.

### 9.3.3 Carbon and climate disclosure and reporting

The third category of accounting and accountability practices we discuss are those related to disclosure and reporting. As we outlined in Chapters 5 and 6, sustainability reporting is a prominent practice in many organisations. Reporting on carbon and climate change is a common form of disclosure in these reports. With the increasing awareness of climate change in both private and public sectors, the volume of reporting has increased. Different types of organisations, including corporations, public sector organisations and entities such as cities, produce carbon disclosures and other climate-related disclosures on a regular basis. Like other types of sustainability disclosures, these too have been evolving swiftly and include considerable variation across organisations and sectors.

Given the relative importance climate change has on the global sustainability agenda, most of the contemporary accounting and reporting initiatives, frameworks and emerging reporting regulation include reference to carbon accounting and disclosures. This includes, for example, the GRI, ESRS, IFRS and the range of national and industry-specific initiatives reporting standards we discussed in Chapter 5. While we provide a brief overview of the current climate reporting practices next, we are not going into much detail at this point, since for the most part climate reporting can be discussed in similar terms as sustainability reporting in general. As such, we recommend you take another look at Chapters 5 and 6. Likewise, it is important to recognise that the regulatory requirements, reporting frameworks and organisational practices in this space and discussed in those chapters continue to develop swiftly, and hence it can be helpful to take a look at the most recent developments from appropriate sources.

### 9.3.3.1 Carbon self-reporting by organisations

As mentioned, providing some degree of carbon disclosures has for some time been relatively commonplace among organisations that publish broader sustainability reports. With the advent of mandatory reporting requirements, the landscape of carbon reporting has evolved and an increasing number of organisations engage in reporting by following the regulation applicable in a given jurisdiction, such as the ESRS framework in the EU or the IFRS Sustainability Disclosure Standards in countries that have applied them. As such, a range of disclosures can occur as part of a sustainability report, annual report, separate climate/carbon report or a dedicated section of an organisation's website focusing on climate change.

A common starting point for climate accounting and disclosures is emissions. Here, the focus is on how emissions should be assessed, disaggregated and reported to provide stakeholders sufficiently detailed information on the organisation's climate-related activities. Such emissions disclosures are covered by various regulating bodies and institutions (including GRI, CSRD and IFRS). While emission information is a good start, it only provides a limited view on climate-related questions, and hence other aspects should also be considered. In addition to management approach disclosures which present a discussion of the organisations general approach to climate change, among the most common are disclosures relating to the risks, opportunities and financial implications related to climate change and disclosures on policies, targets and transition plans. However, practices are constantly evolving. GRI, for example, is revising the standards related to climate change during 2023–2025. They have considered it important to broaden the scope of climate-related disclosures to reflect its contemporary significance for organisations and societies. This implies focusing on the social aspects of climate change, including just transition, as well as incorporating disclosures on questions such as carbon credits, GHG removals and adaptation plans.

As we have discussed, the improved recognition of the financial risks and opportunities related to climate change has led to the need for more standardised disclosures which would potentially fulfil investor needs and expectations in this area. TCFD set the tone in this area by recommending firms to report on 11 disclosure items, focusing on governance, strategy, risk management as well as metrics and targets. These recommendations were published in 2017, and they were soon widely followed by major companies. While the TCFD completed its work and was disbanded in 2023, the disclosure recommendations remain significant as they now form a core element of the IFRS Sustainability Disclosure Standard (IFRS S2).

The IFRS S2 Climate-related Disclosures are about to become a core reference point in many jurisdictions. Since their publication in 2023, these disclosures have been quickly picked up by organisations globally, in addition to which several jurisdictions have progressed with plans to adopt the IFRS Sustainability Disclosure Standards or otherwise make use of them in their national reporting requirements. Here, it is again important to recognise that the scope of IFRS S2 Climate-related Disclosures is considerably narrower than that of the GRI or ESRS for instance, with the IFRS S2 applying only to such climate-related physical and transitional risks and opportunities which can reasonably be expected to affect the organisation's future (financial) prospects. Obviously, and given in particular the range of implications climate change is going to cause, defining which risks should be included within this scope is not going to be exact and clear-cut, and therefore we will learn about the eventual interpretation as the standard becomes applied in practice.

As mentioned above, at the same time as the International Sustainability Standards Board (ISSB) was developing its reporting standard, the Securities and Exchange Council (SEC) progressed in the United States with its own initiative for climate reporting. The final rules known as "The Enhancement and Standardization of Climate-Related Disclosures" were adopted in early 2024, with the aim to help investors assess certain climate-related risks by improving the quality of information available to them. In addition to climate-related risks that are likely to have material implications on the organisation's business and financial outlook, firms are expected to disclose for instance their scope 1 and 2 emissions as well as potential transition plans or scenario analyses that have been undertaken in an attempt to mitigate or adapt to material climate-related risks. As with the IFRS Sustainability Disclosure Standards, the eventual outcomes of this SEC rule will only become evident in the coming years, taking also into account the fact that such initiatives can become the subject of political debate, evidenced by how the SEC rule was swiftly challenged after its adoption and subsequently put on hold for the foreseeable future.

Despite detailed guidance provided by regulators and other standard-setters, challenges concerning the quality of carbon disclosures remain. As is the case with sustainability reporting in general, questions of comparability, consistency and accuracy of reported carbon information can be an issue, given that there is still substantial variation in how organisations approach, assess and report on carbon. In other words, many of the challenges discussed in relation to sustainability reporting in general, such as their potential use for greenwashing or the possible gaps between talk and action, are relevant here. Assurance can potentially be helpful, although it may take time before the practices, institutional structures and required professional competencies develop to a sufficient level in order to have a significant influence.

#### 9.3.3.2 Disclosures to CDP

The challenge related to consistency and comparability of self-reporting is one of the reasons why some investors and other groups have attempted to find alternative ways of collecting carbon information from organisations in a more standardised form. The most prominent example of these would be CDP (formerly known as the Carbon Disclosure Project, see Chapter 5). CDP has collected carbon information since the early 2000s. Over the years, it has managed to reach a broad number of organisations and thereby build what it claims to be the world's largest online database of carbon information. As such, CDP's database has become a prominent source of carbon information.

Each year, CDP sends out questionnaires to thousands of organisations in an attempt to gather information about the current state of carbon-related organisational policies and practices. This includes information on how carbon accounting and reporting are conducted. CDP's database is collected by having organisations answer a range of pre-set questions, which also include guidance on how particular concepts are understood and what types of metrics and measurement practices should be applied. Using such a standardised approach aims at having all organisations provide the information in a fairly similar way, which would potentially improve the quality of the data in terms of accuracy, consistency and comparability.

CDP's platform and the reports it publishes offer an opportunity to see how carbon policies and practices in organisations as well as carbon accounting and reporting have evolved over time. However, despite the ongoing efforts to accurately measure and collect carbon data some issues remain. Among others, the usual challenges regarding self-reported data apply, especially since the information provided by organisations is not always subject to assurance or audit by external parties. Further, while assurance on carbon reporting might, more or less, enhance the credibility on the reported data, it might not cover all of the reported carbon information and might primarily focus on the final numbers rather than the more fundamental and challenging processes of measurement and data collection. Likewise, participation in CDP's questionnaire is voluntary, meaning that the collected database has gaps, which can also cause some bias in the reports compiled on the basis of the organisational responses. Finally, CDP has understandably developed their approach over the years by making changes to the questionnaire and the suggested methodologies. This has affected the consistency and comparability of the data reported at different points of time, while obviously being important to ensure the database includes currently relevant information. An example of such a step was the inclusion of IFRS S2 Climate-related Disclosures into the CDP's questionnaire in 2024. Overall, despite the shortcomings, the CDP database provides a valuable access point to carbon practices in organisations, and the range of reports produced by CDP are accordingly widely followed.

Overall, climate disclosures and reporting have been key areas of accounting practice. However, just as with sustainability reporting in general, concerns remain as to the value of such reporting in attempts to address the climate crisis. While such reporting clearly has value in relation to organisational transparency on their carbon impacts and climate dependencies, and ideally acts as a mechanism for organisations to both understand and act upon such impacts and dependencies, the adequacy of such practices in ensuring the needed transition to a more sustainable future is unclear, despite the increased attention climate reporting is receiving globally. We reflect on concerns such as this next.

## 9.4 Accounting and the climate emergency: Some key issues requiring further consideration

In this chapter, we have introduced accounting's role in how organisations and economic activity more broadly take climate into account. Despite being on the agenda for a long time and accounting's considerable engagement with the issue, it is still quite clear, at least to us, that current accounting practices are insufficient to address climate change. Much more is needed, and fast, in assisting organisations and societies to understand the issue of climate as well as their accountabilities in relation to the climate. Further, in addition to creating this understanding, new accounting systems and processes, tools and techniques are needed to urgently transition towards climate stability. A range of issues could be highlighted, but we will focus on four here.

### 9.4.1 Discussing carbon emissions in relative and absolute terms

With many sustainability topics, it is significant to understand the difference between absolute and relative terms, be that regarding metrics, comparisons or targets. Climate change and carbon emissions are no different.

For many aspects of social activity, we strive for efficiency – that is, creating more with less. We can perhaps make more decisions at a meeting, making it a more effective use of everyone's time, or you might be in better shape by being more effective with the time you use for physical exercise. In these examples, the time used for meetings or exercise would not change, although we would get more results. With climate change and carbon emissions, however, there are substantial problems with such an approach. That is, the climate does not care about relative improvements and efficiency. The only thing that matters here is the absolute amount of GHG emissions flowing to the atmosphere (or more precisely the warming potential of those emissions over time). And, for the aim of limiting global warming to 2°C and pursuing efforts to limit it to 1.5°C, as outlined in the Paris Agreement, the IPCC notes we must curb global emissions to net-zero by 2050. This creates a significant challenge for societies, which have been built to require substantial growth in resource use and economic activity, resulting simultaneously in growing amounts of absolute emissions.

The same challenge of absolute and relative terms applies also on an organisational level. Most organisational managers, and those in businesses in particular, run their organisations with a pursuit of growth, which usually implies more activities, increased use of resources and higher outputs, including emissions. Clearly, there is also often an attempt to be environmentally friendly. What this implies then is a critical question. In terms of climate change, we can ask whether the organisation is seeking to improve its climate performance in relative terms, that is, creating less GHG emissions per unit of output, or if it is striving to reduce its emissions in absolute terms, that is, creating less emissions in total. This is an important consideration from an accounting and reporting perspective. Are the assessments, metrics and reporting baselines set in such a way that they are focusing on relative or absolute indicators? Think about an airline company which highlights that it seeks to reduce its carbon emissions by 20% per seat-mile. A commendable target perhaps, but it does not necessarily mean that the absolute carbon emissions would be any lower if the number of flights and hence seat-miles continues to grow.

We should also consider how organisations discuss their absolute and relative GHG emissions in the sustainability disclosures, as these are often used for making statements regarding both past accomplishments as well as future policies and initiatives. Here, we should pay specific attention to carbon-reduction targets, given how the IPCC reports and the Paris Agreement emphasise the need for substantial emission reductions in the near future. Companies have, for a long time, set carbon reduction targets. Common here are claims to achieve net zero or carbon neutrality (see below). However, over time, the nature of this target setting, and the attention it receives, has increased. Much more attention is paid to the target-setting process, for example, The Science Based Targets initiative (SBTi) is a "corporate climate action organization" which provides guidance on target setting and reduction targets (SBTi, 2025). And in addition to simply setting carbon reduction targets, there is increased emphasis on how an organisation plans to achieve those. Transition planning (see Transition Plan Taskforce, 2023) is the focus here. What are the organisations plans in the short, medium and long terms to meet their targets?

### 9.4.2 Implications of commensuration and marketisation

The second major issue in accounting for climate change we discuss here concerns the increased use of commensuration and monetisation. As carbon emissions have become increasingly mainstreamed, new accounting tools and mechanisms have emerged, often related to the aim of making carbon emissions more comparable. Commensurated figures are needed for instance in all emission trading schemes, and the idea of carbon offsetting we discuss below is also closely associated with setting a price for emissions.

Such commodification of climate is promoted by saying that it helps various actors to make decisions and thereby enhances the efficiency of the markets. That is, there is a strong underlying assumption that by setting a price for things, societies can trust the markets to find a balance and ensure efficient allocation of resources. The complexity of the underlying mechanisms as well as the long timeframe, however, set substantial challenges for the market. Most GHG emissions stay in the atmosphere for decades implying that current emissions continue to affect the climate for an extended period of time. Such commensurated figures, by focusing on $CO_2e$, fail to consider the different types of GHG emissions underlying them, all of which have various life cycles and impacts on climate change (i.e. the commensurated figures may make it harder for organisations to determine the nature of their emissions profile and on which areas to focus efforts). Likewise, in commensurating and aggregating different GHG emissions, we may end up omitting specific types of significant GHG emissions due to various reasons, as is the case with methane with which the challenges related to measuring and monitoring emissions in a sufficiently accurate way across diverse locations are well acknowledged. There can also be a tendency in the marketplace to underestimate the future consequences, which appear to be far away and their relevance diminished by excessive discount rates. Furthermore, the ecological systems and their interconnections are extremely complicated, and we do not understand all these implications. As such, the assumption that markets will provide a solution can be contested (see also Lohmann, 2009).

At the same time, creating a marketplace also changes the nature of particular environmental issues. In principle, once a market is established, actors have the possibility to buy themselves the right to emit. That is, there is no longer a duty to cut emissions and try finding ways to do so at each organisation. Moreover, having a price for carbon can be seen to have an impact on accountability relations: instead of being accountable to society at large for the emissions, the organisation is now accountable to the market and to the providers of financial capital.

### 9.4.3 Carbon offsetting

The third issue we consider is carbon offsetting. In simple terms offsetting means that the emissions created by an activity are mitigated through a reduction of emissions elsewhere, such as through the planting of trees. There is an increasing appetite for offsetting solutions, which are used to lower the net carbon emissions of an organisation, activity or product. These aims can relate to sustainability reporting or to advertising in more general terms. You may have seen such campaigns highlighting carbon neutrality or even carbon-negativity! Offsetting can also be used to support some regulatory processes which require organisations to achieve a particular level of emissions with a particular calculative mechanism (see the "Focus on practice" below).

The field of offsetting is growing quickly and an increasing number of alternative solutions exist. As such, an entire industry has evolved offering different options of carbon offsetting for individuals, companies and even government authorities. An individual going for a holiday can be encouraged to pay a voluntary carbon offset fee to the airline or an NGO specialising in offsetting, which would then use the money for projects reducing carbon. Not surprisingly, the vocabulary can get muddy, and hence it might be hard for anyone without considerable expertise to understand what exactly expressions such as "emission avoidance", "net zero emissions" or "carbon neutral growth" mean.

Two often used concepts in this area are those of carbon neutral and carbon zero. Both of these are sometimes used ambiguously and can hence cause confusion. In simple terms, carbon neutral refers to a situation in which the carbon emissions caused by a product or a service are offset with carbon emission reductions elsewhere. Such reductions could for instance include natural carbon sinks or specific carbon credits acquired through emission reduction programmes or organisations. In other words, this means that some carbon emissions are generated in the process, but after the reductions are taken into account, the net amount would be zero. The other concept, carbon zero, generally refers to a product or service which causes no carbon emissions in its use. Environmentally friendly buildings can sometimes include technologies and designs enabling them to be called carbon zero, if the building for instance generates all the energy needed through solar power. The challenge with both carbon neutrality and carbon zero is that these ideas are used rather flexibly, and at times intentionally so when seeking to represent something in a positive light. Moreover, the very logic of carbon neutral implies that the product or service might not have low carbon emissions: even a very carbon-intensive product can be claimed to be carbon neutral with substantial carbon offsetting.

### Focus on practice: Airlines and carbon emissions

For years, civil aviation has been at the centre of climate discussions. It is often emphasised that flights cause a substantial amount of the carbon emissions and reducing flying is included as a key suggestion in most guidelines on how consumers can reduce their personal impacts on climate.

Airlines were for many years excluded from requirements set in international climate treaties. This was due to the alleged complexity of calculations and their importance in the global economy, for example. Towards the end of 2010s, however, many airlines began to emphasise their commitment to the environment and discuss how they were going to cut their emissions. Among those was EasyJet, which in late 2019 announced that all its flights would soon be carbon neutral. This was to be possible via carbon offsetting, which would be used to reduce the net carbon emissions to zero, as the emissions of the flights themselves were not changing.

One driving force behind the swift increase in the interest to offset is CORSIA, which is an acronym for Carbon Offsetting and Reduction Scheme for International Aviation run by the International Civil Aviation Organization (ICAO). ICAO is a special agency of the UN, which plays an important role in managing and governing international civil aviation. To put it simply, with CORSIA, it is hoped that international civil aviation could reach carbon-neutral growth from the 2020s onwards. In essence, this means that any carbon emissions above the set baseline need to be offset elsewhere.

In itself, the goal here is commendable: the net GHG emissions from flying would not increase, and in fact would slightly decrease as ICAO in 2024 dropped the CORSIA's baseline to 85% of 2019 emissions as for the period of 2024–2035. Further, it is emphasised that offsetting should be seen as a short- and medium-term solution, as carbon reductions through technological development, operational efficiency and infrastructure improvements continue to be actively sought (IATA, 2024).

At the same time, airlines provide a good illustration of the challenges and open questions related to offsetting discussed in this chapter. How is the baseline set, how are emissions calculated, how are reductions assessed and where do all those required offsets come from are all questions that need to be addressed as there are numerous ways to go about them. Moreover, there is the question of communication, as organisations may have a temptation to make their activities look better and more climate-friendly than they actually are. Indeed, major airlines, including EasyJet, received in 2021 negative publicity for using unreliable carbon credits to ostensibly offset their emissions.

Finally, there is also the elephant in the room: to limit global warming, we need to reduce the absolute global emissions substantially, as highlighted in the Paris Agreement and IPCC reports. Even if all companies adhered to CORSIA, and if all the related offsets were actual and properly accounted for, the GHG emissions of flying would only fall modestly by 2035, which does not go together well with the target set in the Paris Agreement. Assuming the volume of aviation continues to grow, this leaves major ground to be covered through technological innovations. The requirements are well-illustrated by EasyJet netzero roadmap, as the company has committed to an ambitious plan to reach netzero by 2050 (EasyJet, 2025).

Offsetting is often an appealing alternative for an individual or an organisation as it can seem like you can reduce emissions in an easy and cost-effective way. Especially compared to developing the activity itself or giving up on doing it altogether. There are however a range of associated questions here, many of which have to do with accounting. How can we avoid double-counting or double-crediting, for instance, in the sense that the same offsets are not counted in favour of several organisations or projects? How do we create processes that ensure that the offsetting activities have lasting carbon mitigating effects? How is time taken into account: planting trees is an often-used example, but trees take time to grow. There is also the issue of counterfactual baselines against which emission reductions are compared to claim that with a particular technology or action an organisation avoids a certain amount of GHG emissions. The challenges have also been reflected on the global carbon offset markets, where the real carbon reductions of several major projects have turned out to be orders of magnitude smaller than they had been presented and marketed, despite being certified by leading organisations. These developments have resulted in many market participants and the broader public losing confidence in the offset market. While COP29 reached in 2024 an agreement concerning the rules required for setting up a global voluntary carbon market led by the UN as laid out in the Paris Agreement, this initiative will continue to face the challenges outlined above.

Finally, there is one last point to highlight – and probably the most important point here. It is very unlikely that we can mitigate a large amount of real carbon emissions with offsetting, let alone the amount required to reach the goals set in the Paris Agreement. In other words, while offsetting can be useful, it is important to keep in mind that what matters here are the absolute GHG emissions. It is therefore important to consider the role carbon accounting and reporting tools play in positioning and facilitating offsetting.

### 9.4.4 Consumers, carbon footprints and product labels

Our fourth issue brings us to the level of individual citizens and consumer practices. While often overlooked in discussions of climate accounting, individual practices are important and accounting and accountability practices can influence these in many ways. You might find it useful to think of your own consumption habits and values as we explore this point.

For example, while many consumers are highly price-driven in their consumption, there are an increasing number of people who include environmental elements in general, and climate change in particular, in their consumption decisions. For this to happen, information is needed. You may have seen how some grocery products have information regarding their carbon footprint printed on the packaging. Or how, when you are booking a flight, some airlines, travel agencies and online search engines provide the amount of carbon emissions of the option next to its price. Still, the evidence of the impact of such information is mixed.

If we look at our example above, we might be able to see that a direct flight route causes less emissions than one with a layover. But this does not say whether the carbon emissions of the direct flight are high or low compared to, for example, driving or taking the train. Instead of exact figures, it could be argued that products should come with climate labelling, making such criteria easier to understand for everyone. There have also been suggestions that contemporary IT systems and data processing capabilities could allow the application of personal carbon budgets. This would give each of us a limit for annual consumption. At the same time, a critical view can be taken on such labels in general. Given that extensive GHG emissions and climate change are systemic issues, critical voices argue that by developing more detailed carbon footprinting and by flirting with personal carbon budgets, the blame gets cast on the individuals, simultaneously shifting the focus away from broad system-level social and economic changes that are needed. For instance, when highlighting that an individual can now pick the lowest emission flight, the question of whether one should take the flight in the first place is actively put aside. Furthermore, this discussion gets increasingly complex when we consider that there are substantial emissions linked to our everyday lives that remain largely hidden. An example would be the massive energy use of datacentres that are required to process and transmit all the data needed in the increasingly digitalised societies where AI is becoming increasingly prevalent.

### INSIGHTS FROM RESEARCH: CARBON FOOTPRINTS AND CONSUMER CHOICES

We have throughout this book highlighted how sustainability information can have a role in affecting decisions across societies. Moreover, as we noted in Chapter 4, the form of the information matters, as those using it can perceive, for instance, qualitative, quantitative and monetary information differently and subsequently make interpretations and decisions.

This study by Bianca Beyer, Rico Chaskel, Simone Euler, Joachim Gassen, Ann-Kristin Großkopf and Thorsten Sellhorn delves into such themes by exploring how carbon footprint information affects consumer choice, making use of an experimental research design in a large dining facility, a university restaurant in less fancy terms. In this fascinating study, the researchers in collaboration with the restaurant, manipulated the measurement units and visualisations of carbon footprint information on food labels and subsequently looked into the effects this information had on the customers' food choices consisting of 22,000 meals over a ten day period.

One of the key insights Beyer and colleagues report was that any type of carbon footprint information reduced food-related $CO_2e$ emissions of the customer choices. This is particularly interesting given that the associated survey the researchers collected showed that the customers had only limited concerns about their food-related ecological footprint. Another interesting observation was that effects on meal choices were strongest when the carbon footprint information was expressed using monetary units and signalled with a familiar traffic-light colour scheme. In simple terms that is, there is a lot of nuance in the findings reported in the paper.

Why is this relevant then? Well, for one, a core feature of contemporary policy relates to belief in transparency, shown for instance through how organisations are expected to provide sustainability disclosures on their activities, and how other stakeholders are subsequently expected to make choices based on this information. This applies not only to investors but also to citizens across societies, as it is hoped that, with sufficient information, people will make informed choices for the better of sustainability. Moreover, the study provides food for thought as it shows how the way individuals process and interpret information varies depending on the format the numbers are presented in. We hence recommend you to have a look at this paper. While it can seem technical in places, the context makes it relatable and thereby easier to understand. What can be learnt from this study in relation to not only information that informs our own personal consumption but also decision-making within organisations?

**Beyer, B., Chaskel, R., Euler, S., Gassen, J., Grosskopf, A.-K. and Sellhorn, T. (2024). How Does Carbon Footprint Information Affect Consumer Choice? A Field Experiment. *Journal of Accounting Research*, *62(1)*, 101–136.**

## 9.5 Conclusion

Climate change is an issue of critical importance for society and organisations and it is clear that our current ways of organising are insufficient if we are to prevent the Earth from warming to catastrophic levels. Given the role organisations play in all aspects of society, and given the carbon impacts of large corporations, there will continue to be increased calls for accountability in relation to climate change.

Accounting and accountability tools and practices will be important in both understanding the impacts and dependencies of our organisations on climate as well as in incentivising and managing the reduction of this impact.

Even though the recent advent of mandatory reporting requirements and disclosure frameworks such as ISSB, SEC and ESRS implies that societies, markets, organisations and individuals are in the near future bound to have much more information at their disposal, this does not mean that things can be considered to have been solved. Instead, the swift evolution of the landscape underscores the need to subject the frameworks, associated reports and actors developing them to substantial scrutiny (Rodrigue et al., 2024). As the challenges discussed in the previous section highlight, it is also important to realise that with complex issues like climate change we must ask some fundamental questions. We need to regularly ask ourselves: what is being accounted for, why is it being done in a particular way, for whom and for what purpose are accounts prepared, is accountability being considered and so forth? Moreover, there is a real urgency to develop new accounting and accountability tools and practices in relation to climate, which will make sure that investors and organisations are incentivised to make climate the priority it deserves, instead of considering it an obligatory passage point that has limited impact on eventual decisions. Accounting and accountability can play a very important role in societies' struggle with climate change, but only, as we hope we have made clear, if approached with sufficient critical scrutiny.

## References


ACCA (2011). *The Carbon We're Not Counting Accounting For: Scope 3 Carbon Emissions*. www.accaglobal.com/uk/en/technical-activities/technical-resources-search/2011/april/scope-3-carbon.html (accessed 26 February 2025).

Bebbington, J., Schneider, T., Stevenson, L. and Fox, A. (2020). Fossil Fuel Reserves and Resources Reporting and Unburnable Carbon: Investigating Conflicting Accounts. *Critical Perspectives on Accounting, 66,* 1–22.

Beyer, B., Chaskel, R., Euler, S., Gassen, J., Grosskopf, A.-K. and Sellhorn, T. (2024). How Does Carbon Footprint Information Affect Consumer Choice? A Field Experiment. *Journal of Accounting Research, 62*(1), 101–136.

EasyJet (2025). Our Destination Is Net Zero. https://www.easyjet.com/en/netzero (accessed 27 February 2025).

GHG Protocol (2013). Technical Guidance for Calculating Scope 3 Emissions. https://ghgprotocol.org/sites/default/files/standards/Scope3_Calculation_Guidance_0.pdf (accessed 26 February 2025).

Gibassier, D. and Schaltegger, S. (2015). Carbon Management Accounting and Reporting in Practice: A Case Study on Converging Emergent Approaches. *Sustainability Management, Accounting and Policy Journal, 6(3)*, 340–365.

Hawken, P. (ed.) (2017). *Drawdown: The Most Comprehensive Plan Ever Proposed to Reverse Global Warming*. Penguin Books.

InfluenceMap (2024). The Carbon Majors Database: Launch Report. https://carbonmajors.org/briefing/The-Carbon-Majors-Database-26913 (accessed 28 February 2025).

International Air Transport Association (IATA) (2024). Corsia Fact Sheet, December 2024. https://www.iata.org/en/iata-repository/pressroom/fact-sheets/fact-sheet-corsia/ (accessed 27 February 2025).

IPCC (2018). Summary for Policymakers. In Masson-Delmotte, V., Zhai, P., Pörtner, H.-O., Roberts, D., Skea, J., et al. (eds), *Global Warming of 1.5°C: An IPCC Special Report on the Impacts of Global Warming of 1.5°C Above Pre-Industrial Levels and Related Global Greenhouse Gas Emission Pathways, in the Context of Strengthening the Global Response to the Threat of Climate Change, Sustainable Development, and Efforts to Eradicate Poverty*, pp. 1–24. World Meteorological Organization.

KPMG (2017). The Road Ahead: The KPMG Survey of Corporate Responsibility Reporting 2017. https://assets.kpmg.com/content/dam/kpmg/xx/pdf/2017/10/kpmg-survey-of-corporate-responsibility-reporting-2017.pdf (accessed 26 February 2025).

KPMG (2024). *The Move to Mandatory Reporting. Survey of Sustainability Reporting 2024.* Available at https://kpmg.com/xx/en/our-insights/esg/the-move-to-mandatory-reporting.html (accessed 17 December 2024).

Loach, M. (2023). *It's Not That Radical: Climate Action to Transform Our World.* DK.

Lohmann, L. (2009). Toward a Different Debate in Environmental Accounting: The Cases of Carbon and Cost–Benefit. Accounting, Organizations and Society, 34(3–4), 499–534.

O'Dwyer, B. and Unerman, J. (2020). Shifting the Focus of Sustainability Accounting from Impacts to Risks and Dependencies: Researching the Transformative Potential of TCFD Reporting. Accounting, Auditing and Accountability Journal, 33(5), 1113–1141.

Perkiss, S. (2024). Climate Apartheid: The Failures of Accountability and Climate Justice. Accounting, Auditing and Accountability Journal, 37(7/8), 1761–1794.

Rodrigue, M., Tregidga, H. and Cooper, C. (2024). The Fragments and Traces of Integrated Reporting That Prevail: On the Importance of a Sustained Critical Perspective on Reporting. Critical Perspectives on Accounting, 99, 102726.

SBTi (2025). https://sciencebasedtargets.org/ (accessed 28 February 2025).

Scobie, M., Norris, E. and Wilson, H. (2024). Intergenerational Accountability in the Times of Just Transitions. Accounting, Auditing and Accountability Journal. https://doi.org/10.1108/AAAJ-04-2024-7046

The Guardian (2024). Just 57 Companies Linked to 80% of Greenhouse Gas Emissions since 2016. Available at www.theguardian.com/environment/2024/apr/04/just-57-companies-linked-to-80-of-greenhouse-gas-emissions-since-2016 (accessed on 28 February 2025).

Transition Plan Taskforce (2023). TPT Disclosure Framework. Available at www.ifrs.org/sustainability/knowledge-hub/transition-plan-taskforce-resources/ (Accessed 28 February 2025).

UN (1992). *United Nations Framework Convention on Climate Change (UNFCCC).* https://unfccc.int/resource/docs/convkp/conveng.pdf (accessed 26 February 2025).

UPM (2025). Scope 3 Emissions Reduction. https://www.upm.com/sustainability/supply-chain/emissions/ (accessed 27 February 2025).

World Resource Institute (2006). Hot Climate, Cool Commerce: A Service Sector Guide to Greenhouse Gas Management. www.wri.org/publication/hot-climate-cool-commerce (accessed 26 February 2025).

## Additional reading and resources

Ascui, F. and Lovell, H. (2011). As Frames Collide: Making Sense of Carbon Accounting. Accounting, *Auditing and Accountability Journal*, 24, 978–999.

Busch, T., Johnson, M. and Pioch, T. (2022). Corporate Carbon Performance Data: Quo vadis? *Journal of Industrial Ecology*, 26(1), 350–363.

Cadez, S. and Guilding, C. (2017). Examining Distinct Carbon Cost Structures and Climate Change Abatement Strategies in $CO_2$ Polluting Firms. Accounting, *Auditing and Accountability Journal*, 30, 1041–1064.

Charnock, R.J. (2025). Civil Society as a Quasi-regulator: Coordination in Financial Regulation on Climate Change. *Contemporary Accounting Research*, 42(2), 837–865.

Charnock, R., Brander, M. and Schneider, T. (2021). Carbon. In Bebbington, J., Larrinaga, C., O'Dwyer, B. and Thomson, I. (eds), Handbook on Environmental Accounting, pp. 353–364. Routledge.

MacKenzie, D. (2009). Making Things the Same: Gases, Emission Rights and the Politics of Carbon Markets. Accounting, *Organizations and Society*, 34, 440–455.

Mikes, A. and Metzner, M. (2023). Lightening the Carbon Load: Using Management Control Systems to Manage Decarbonization Strategies. *Journal of Management Accounting Research*, *35*(3), 121–151.

Tomar, S. (2023). Greenhouse Gas Disclosure and Emissions Benchmarking. *Journal of Accounting Research*, *61*(2), 451–492.

Transition Pathway Initiative (2025). https://www.transitionpathwayinitiative.org

CHAPTER

10

# Accounting for water

You are likely to have noticed discussions about water in the media. Sometimes there is a shortage of water, as is the case with local or regional droughts. Other times, there is too much water due to intensive rains, flash floods or melting snow and glaciers. Water issues are important as we are dependent on water in several ways. We need access to clean water and sanitation, as the title of the SDG6 highlights and as we were reminded during the COVID-19 pandemic. Water and implications relating to water are also interconnected with other sustainability issues, such as hunger, human rights and equality. Many species and ecosystems are also dependent on water, including a steady cycle of drought and flooding. As climate change impacts the usual deviation of hydrological cycles, these species may have challenges to adapt to the rapid changes taking place. This not only has impacts on nature but also has various social and economic consequences for communities and societies.

In this chapter, we provide some background regarding why water is a matter of critical importance for the well-being of societies and life on the planet. As was the case with climate change in the previous chapter, we do not delve too deep into the natural sciences but focus our attention on discussing why water is a critical issue for organisations, accounting and accountants. We outline the key global, national and industrial institutions and frameworks relating to water. In the latter part of this chapter, we discuss current accounting practices in the area and consider what kind of a role accounting has in seeking to address the challenges related to water.

By the end of this chapter, you should:

- Have a basic understanding of water and why it is a critical sustainability issue.
- Understand why water is important to organisations and accounting.
- Be aware of global, national and organisational level institutions and frameworks in relation to water and water accounting.
- Be aware of current accounting and accountability practices in relation to water.
- Have considered some of the limits of current practices in relation to water accounting and accountability.

DOI: 10.4324/9781003533207-13

## 10.1 Water as an issue of critical importance

Species, flora and fauna, rely on water for their survival and wellbeing. Fresh water is vital for human life and well-being. We humans need water for drinking and cooking. It is crucial for sanitation and hence a key element of health. Water is needed for growing crops and raising livestock.

**PAUSE AND REFLECT….**

Access to water and sanitation is considered to be a human right. But what does this mean? OHCHR, UN Habitat and WHO (2010) outline this as follows:

> The right to water entitles everyone to have access to sufficient, safe, acceptable, physically accessible and affordable water for personal and domestic use.
>
> The right to sanitation entitles everyone to have physical and affordable access to sanitation, in all spheres of life, that is safe, hygienic, secure, and socially and culturally acceptable and that provides privacy and ensures dignity.

Many people take these rights for granted. But they shouldn't. In the 2024 edition of the World Water Development Report (UNESCO, UN-Water, 2024), it is highlighted that in 2022, 2.2 billion people continued to lack access to safely managed drinking water, and 3.5 billion people lack safely managed sanitation. These numbers are substantial.

Take a moment to reflect on your own use of water and its availability. Do you have sufficient water available for your daily use? Is the quality of the water satisfactory throughout the year? How would your daily rituals be different if your access to water was different in terms of quantity and quality – that is, if you did/did not have access to sufficient clean water and sanitation?

The importance of water is underscored by the United Nations (UN) which has recognised access to water as a basic human right. Water features in the UN's SDGs as Goal 6 Clean Water and Sanitation: "Ensure availability and sustainable management of water and sanitation for all". This SDG includes targets related for instance to access to safe and affordable drinking water, water quality and water scarcity.

Similar to other key sustainability issues discussed in this book, questions related to water resources and use have become increasingly important over the past few decades. As societies have grown to have more people with higher levels of income, there has been an ever-growing demand for water across the globe. Water reserves have been stretched to their limits (or beyond), as more water is needed for drinking and sanitation, for agriculture and for production. At the same time, there is an increasing risk of pollution of water sources. We have seen an increasing number of local water crises. Many are likely to associate lack of water with extensive droughts such as those experienced in Darfur in the 1980s and in other regions of Africa. In the late 2010s, taps ran dry in major cities like Chennai and Cape Town, in addition to which there have been recurring major challenges regarding both quantity and quality of water in regions like California and the Canary Islands. Water crises are not limited to arid regions, however. On a global scale, predictions made on the basis of current trends estimate that water demand is going to greatly exceed sustainable supply by 2030, illustrating the extent and swiftly increasing water challenges societies are facing.

It can be easy to think that water is plentiful. And no wonder given that water covers more than 70% of the planet (WWF, 2023). However, freshwater, the water we drink, irrigate and use for sanitation purposes, is not as abundant as you might think. WWF (2023) notes that only 0.5% of the world's water is fresh and available for use. In addition to the significant amount of people worldwide who lack access to water altogether, nearly half of the world's population encounters severe water scarcity for at least part of the year (UNESCO, UN-Water, 2024). The implications of a lack of clean water and sanitation are large, including poor health, exposure to diseases as well as higher inequality (WWF, 2025; SDG 6).

In addition to economic growth, increasing consumption and higher population in water stressed areas, climate change is also putting pressure on water supplies. Ecosystems have adapted to certain ecological conditions, including typical patterns of rainfall. Swift climate change is now undermining the long-term stability of the water cycle and weather patterns, causing challenges to many living species and ecosystems. There are an increasing number of extreme weather events, such as torrent rainfall or long spells of drought. There is also less regularity and predictability, which has implications on both ecological systems dependent on seasonal rainfall, such as monsoons, and human societies. To mitigate these challenges, many communities and organisations may need to resort to energy-intensive measures to ensure a steady water supply, through for instance pumping water from further locations, going deeper to collect ground water or using more treatments to make lower quality water usable. At the same time, some communities and organisations are forced to turn to costly and energy-intensive procedures to manage and remove flood waters they encounter with increased regularity. None of these solutions are more than temporary fixes, and they often also bring other side-effects, such as increased inequality through rising water prices.

Water crises are not just about inconvenience. A shortage of water has profound implications on food security, public health and socio-economic development. If there is no water for agriculture, crops will fall, leading to malnutrition and potential famines. If someone has to use several hours each day to obtain water, they are less able to work or achieve education, which has personal effects alongside implications for socio-economic development. If there is no water for drinking, cooking and sanitation, people's overall health weakens and many diseases spread easier, again hindering the capabilities of people and communities. And the list goes on.

### 10.1.1 Sustainable water management

Overall, tackling global water stress requires broad changes across societies. Water cannot be looked at in isolation from other sustainability questions, such as biodiversity, climate change and human rights, as we have illustrated above. Political decisions regarding the allocation of resources to competing water uses will take place in different contexts, and it is evident that changes to practices are needed from all actors (e.g. governments, organisations and individuals).

Water is a shared resource, which means that action aimed at sustainable water management needs to be based on collaboration and collective action. We will return to this point and its importance throughout this chapter. Discussions regarding the role of water in societies will continue. While some will call for increased privatisation of water to help more effective allocation and use of this critical resource, therefore taking a market-based approach to water management, others are adamant that the role of water as a fundamental element for human life means that it has to be kept under public control and stewarded through public mechanisms. Nonetheless, and whatever the approach, organisations have to be increasingly prepared for potential changes and challenges related to water.

### 10.1.2 The importance of context

Another key characteristic of water, and again one that we will return to throughout our discussion below, is the importance of context. Water is very unevenly distributed geographically across the globe. In some locations, there is an abundance of water, while elsewhere there is constant scarcity. While for those living in Scotland, Indonesia, parts of India or the Netherlands, rain might seem like a nuisance, in a range of other locations every drop of water is greeted with joy. This implies that using a particular amount of water could be considered somewhat irrelevant in one context while being highly significant with profound implications in another. At the same time, we should avoid making generalisations based on such classifications: an individual living in a water-rich country might not have access to safe and affordable water and sanitation due to for instance reasons of economic inequality (see Chapter 13).

The same applies for time, as there can be major seasonal variability in water sources. In one location there can at times be a shortage of water, as is the case with local or regional droughts, while at other times there can be too much water, or perhaps too much water gathering in the wrong places from the perspective of individuals, organisations or communities. As a result, sometimes an urgent water emergency can be a fairly local or regional and short-term event.

The dynamics are similar for water quality and water discharges. The local context and the prevailing social and ecological characteristics have an effect on what kind of implications certain water discharges would have. Some contexts are more vulnerable than others, while others might be substantially resilient.

When discussing water, it is worth recognising different sources of water and the related aspect of water quality. Beyond rainfall, surface water in rivers and lakes is the most visible, and probably the one most people associate water with. Potential floods and droughts can be seen by looking at river flows and water levels in lakes and ponds. Beneath the surface, the other key type of water is ground water. Many individuals, organisations, communities and, in fact, entire societies are built and depend on ground water. Groundwater supplies are less visible than the nearby river, but are of great importance. While these replenish over time, the increased demand and water extraction has lowered the level of ground water in numerous locations and regions. This causes substantial challenges to many social groups, as extracting water from deeper underground requires more resources and hence often causes social inequality. In addition to overuse, both surface water and groundwater are also prone to pollution, which can cause a water source to become of a lower quality or outright unusable.

Finally, we also have oceans, which cover most of our planet. Oceans are seldom discussed in this context however, since the salinity of the water either stops it from being used for many of the purposes humans or organisations need water for, or makes the use prohibitively costly. Healthy oceans are nonetheless of high significance for human societies, for instance through their role in planetary water cycle, global ecosystems and climate regulation (see Österblom et al., 2017).

### 10.1.3 Water is a complex and multifaceted issue

Overall, questions of water are complex and multidimensional. With water, some challenges are more immediate, such as flooding, although they might be impacted and become more severe due to long-term trends, such as climate change. Other issues, such as the depletion of ground water quality, might be caused by a short-term incident, but still cause long-term problems for a particular community.

The contextual nature of water noted above adds to this mix. Increased demand of some water-intensive crops or livestock, such as avocados or meat, can cause water overuse in a vulnerable region producing them if farmers seek to quickly increase their production without paying attention to sustainable water management and the potential consequences to water availability in the area. The global and local contexts also intertwine in different ways when it comes to water. For example, the overuse of ground water reserves in a given location is not necessarily related to the major changes of weather patterns caused by the global climate change in the short term, but these patterns might nonetheless reduce rainfall and impact the functioning of the aquifers, subsequently slowing down the replenishing of a particular local ground water reserve. Such complex relationships might seem far removed from accounting but they do have implications on water accounting, accountability and reporting, as you will see below.

Meanwhile, to bring clarity to these intertwining issues around water, we provide short descriptions of some of the key questions in Table 10.1.

**TABLE 10.1** Some Examples of Different Water Issues

| Term | What Does It Mean? | Examples of Issues and Implications to Consider |
|---|---|---|
| Water scarcity | People or communities do not have access to the water they need. Could be due to physical shortage of water, lack of infrastructure or failure of social institutions, for example | Intense and long-lasting water scarcity can lead to mass migration as living conditions in regions fall. WRI (2023) reports that one-quarter of the population face extreme high water stress each year, and at least 50% of the world's population (approx. 4 billion), live under high water stress for at least one month a year |

*(Continued)*

**TABLE 10.1** (Continued)

| **Term** | **What Does It Mean?** | **Examples of Issues and Implications to Consider** |
|---|---|---|
| Water stress | Related to water scarcity. Occurs when the demand for water exceeds its availability. Could be either short-term or long-term | Fresh water resources can deteriorate as a result, which can manifest for example through issues of quantity (drying aquifers and riverbeds) or water quality (pollution, increased salination) |
| Water overuse | Increased population and economic activity can cause water demand to increase and exceed availability. Can be short term, or potentially lead to more chronic water stress | Lack of water can have major implications on the health and well-being of a community if not addressed early. Worth considering whether overuse is related to low efficiency or water allocation (e.g. excessive amounts of water used for tourism and golf courses) |
| Water quality | Available water is not of sufficient quality for the purposes it is needed for. Can be either short-term or long-term | Multiple potential reasons. Could be related to water stress and overuse, particular incidents, constant inflows to ground water basin, or to excessive amounts of water, e.g. flooding |
| Water cycle disruption | Changes to hydrological flow and cycle of water. Climate change causes long-term changes in weather patterns, which can lead to regions receiving substantially higher or lower amounts of rain. Large discharges of water can also affect water cycles | Has impacts on ecosystems through changing the conditions to which flora and fauna of a given region are accustomed to |
| Water accessibility | Individuals or communities do not have access to water. Water might be available, but physical or economic reasons preclude access | Potentially caused by water scarcity, but occurs also for other reasons, such as lack of infrastructure, failing institutions or social inequality |
| Excess of water | There is too much water in a given location over a certain period of time. Can be either short-term, such as flooding, or long-term, such as increased rainfall, changing river flows, rising sea levels | In addition to climate change, could be caused by other reasons, such as major dams. Can harm the quality of water supplies. Potential impacts to agriculture and housing over short and long term |

**PAUSE AND REFLECT...**

At the beginning of this chapter, we prompted you to consider what it means for water to be a human right and your own experiences of water. We have also noted how water is a topic where context matters and how the issue of water is complex and multifaceted. Let's elaborate on this by considering this further.

It is important to recognise the stark realities of the global population who lack access, or sufficient access, to usable water. These can be defined as highly water stressed countries where water use really matters. The WRI reported in 2023 that 25 countries, housing one-quarter of the global population, face extremely high water stress (WRI, 2023). They report the six most water-stressed countries to be Bahrain, Cyprus, Kuwait, Lebanon, Oman and Qatar. Countries given their low supply of water which we might expect to appear on such lists. However, they also note how other countries such as England, India, Iran, Mexico and South Africa who are among 25 countries which currently use over 80% of their renewable water supply for irrigation, livestock, industry and domestic needs. This can mean that even short-term droughts can cause problems (WRI, 2023) – as we noted earlier was the case with South Africa where regions suffered from extreme water shortage. This report demonstrates that it is not easily identifiable as to which areas/countries fall into the water-stressed category and one must be careful not to make assumptions.

Indeed, an earlier report by the WWF (2006) titled Rich Countries, Poor Water also is worth keeping in mind. This report shows how, while water is often considered an issue for the poorer nations, for some time has been a key issue for wealthy nations. They highlight how in many parts of the world, including what we would consider "rich countries", available water is decreasing and the quality is worsening. They identify a range of countries and regions (e.g. Europe, the United States, Australia and Japan) and also note common water problems for the developed world such as exhaustion of water supplies, water-related conflict, degraded landscape functioning and economic burdens. And in data from 2023 collected by Water Witness International (Chapagain and Mekonnen, 2023), Fair Water Footprints (2023) report that high-income nations like the UK, the United States, Japan and the Netherlands are "dependent on water from beyond their borders to produce their goods", tracing "these water footprints to areas of the Global South facing extreme water insecurity".

Hence, as you proceed with the following discussions and the role of accounting in the area of water, we suggest you keep this in mind. These two aspects highlight how water might be a critical and urgent issue for some – but it is an important and potentially emerging issue for all.

## 10.2 What has water got to do with organisations and accounting?

The broad and complex nature of water issues has major implications for organisations. Growing water stress in many regions, for instance, is going to affect organisations and accountability for water use and impacts on water are likely to grow. But we cannot expect all organisations to be affected in the same way. When it comes to water, particular industries are affected more, and as we have already noted, location matters as well.

### 10.2.1 Impacts and dependencies

As is the case with many other sustainability issues, we can approach the relationship of organisations and water through a consideration of both impacts and dependencies. As heavy users of water in many locations, organisational activities and practices have impacts on watersheds and ground water reservoirs. Impacts take place through various mechanisms, but the key ones would relate to water use and water discharges.

An organisation can, for instance, contribute to the over-consumption of the water sources at a specific location, thereby impacting everyone's access to water. The impacts of an organisation on a catchment area from water use can be wide-ranging, from direct consequences on natural life and ecosystems to social and economic impacts on local communities. Through discharges, an organisation can for instance cause the quality of a particular water source to deteriorate. This can happen in the short term, through for example a one-off accident letting harmful chemicals flow into a river, or over a longer period of time, such as through leakages of dangerous toxic substances to the ground water basin, which can as a result become compromised.

Impacts are not the only relevant aspect here; dependencies are also important. Organisations in various industries are dependent on having access to sufficient and secure water supply. However, water stress can imply that water might no longer be readily available. Or there might be other causes of limitations in its use, for example the quality of the water might not be what is needed, or, if the water source has been privatised or made difficult to access, it might not be economically viable. As access to a safe and stable water source may have been taken for granted by many organisations, they might not have considered such dependencies very carefully. In such cases taking a risk perspective is potentially helpful.

### 10.2.2 Water risks

In thinking about how significant a question of water is for an organisation, it can be useful to think about the potential challenges and risks that an organisation may face due to a diverse range of water issues.

Both impacts and dependencies cause risks for organisations. There can for instance be a range of operational risks, varying substantially across industries and geographical contexts. It is relatively easy to understand that for food and beverage companies, water availability and quality are absolutely essential. They are not alone, however. Many industries require substantial amounts of water in their production processes for cooling purposes, energy production and the like. Furthermore, organisations also have responsibilities to provide quality water and sanitation to their employees, which need to be considered part of an organisation's operations (see WaterAid, 2018). Reputational risks are also relevant to consider. An organisation might not want to be seen as the owner of a factory which uses excessive amounts of water and causes water shortages in a community, or be perceived to be depleting the water quality in local rivers and ponds. Such reputational considerations can provide organisations an incentive to improve water management practices as well as water-related accounting and reporting systems (see the "Focus on practice" relating to Coca-Cola later in this chapter).

Just like with communities, water-related risks can manifest for organisations in the short or long term. Over the short term, we can think of factors caused by extreme weather events such as flooding or droughts. Such events can weaken access to raw materials, damage production facilities, or cause effects on the workforce meaning they are unable to work. After dealing with the immediate impacts, it might be worthwhile for an organisation to consider whether the situation was likely to be a one-off event, or is it likely that such events will become more frequent, due to, for instance, the changing weather patterns caused by climate change. This is also another example of how climate risks tie together with various other types of nature-related risks for organisations. Accordingly, the increasing probabilities and severity of draughts and floods, for example, require firms to consider the significance of such events also as financial risks. Likewise, such water risks can have tangible consequences also for banks, insurance companies and other financial institutions not only through immediate economic impacts but also with the potential of assets getting stranded. It is noteworthy that despite the growing recognition of water risks in general, CDP (2023) reports that in the financial sector, water risks continue to remain an under-prioritised issue and as a consequence some financial institutions are potentially underestimating their exposure to water risks.

Over a longer period, we could consider such locations or regions in which water stress has become increasingly severe and hence water availability is limited. In short, there might not be enough of water for all those needing it. In these situations, governments or other institutions often step in and use regulatory and other mechanisms to allocate and manage water. These regulatory responses can be significant. Increased water stress may lead to governments implementing new regulation regarding, for instance, water use and allocation, water pricing and effluent requirements. The decisions a government may need to make as well as the questions it needs to consider can be far from simple, however. What happens when a water shortage hits a particular region? Does the government ensure that citizens have sufficient drinking water and to do so order organisations with major water use to shut down their production facilities? Does the government favour particular industries, such as tourism or agriculture, in trying to keep the economy functioning? Here, you may want to consider the island of Tenerife in the Canary Islands, where the local authorities have had to make difficult choices due to continued lack of rainfall and depleting water resources. The local economy is dependent on tourism, but at the same time, one cannot ignore the needs of the local communities. Or, if the water scarcity adds to the vulnerability of a catchment area or river basin, does the government place tougher requirements for the treatment of wastewater discharges? Or something else? For an organisation, these government interventions and regulatory changes might lead to increased costs, or in extreme cases mean that an organisation needs to cease operations, if it as a result no longer has access to sufficient water supply. Regulation surrounding water does not always happen in an organised fashion, however, which can lead to challenges for the organisation and the communities. We return to this point further below.

### 10.2.3 Implications water has for accounting and accountability

From an accounting and accountability perspective, the increased scrutiny of water use will mean more demand for different types of metrics, assessments and reports outlining an organisation's water use practices. The demand comes from various sources. Internally, management needs information to make decisions regarding operational practices for both the short and long term. Within the supply chain, both organisational managers and end-users are interested in knowing how much water is used to produce a particular product. Likewise, investors and other external stakeholders can require organisations to disclose more information on their water policies and practices as well as actual numbers.

These issues are amplified by the nature of water as a shared resource, what is often referred to as a common good. How each individual or organisation uses and manages water supplies has implications for others. As organisations are often heavy users of water in many contexts, it can reasonably be argued that they should be accountable for their practices, policies and intentions. In other words, societies and communities are interested in knowing how much water an organisation is using, where the water is coming from and for what it is used.

## 10.3 Key institutions and frameworks relating to water

As with all the sustainability issues discussed in this book, there are a range of institutions and frameworks, at various levels, that all play an important role when it comes to water. We outline some of the key ones here.

### 10.3.1 The United Nations

Recognising how substantial and widespread water issues are globally, the UN has had water on its agenda for several decades now. At first this was influenced by key international events such as the massive and long-lasting drought in the Sahel region in Africa in the 1970s and 1980s. Since then, and alongside water stress becoming more commonplace across the world, the importance of water on the UN's agenda has grown. In the 2000s, as noted above, the UN recognised access to water and sanitation as a human right, and it is prominently included in the SDGs as Goal 6 "Clean Water and Sanitation".

In line with many other UN programmes, the UN-Water Programme does not have a strong regulatory position. Its key roles relate to gathering knowledge, informing policies and monitoring actions. In addition to the UN-Water, water also features in several other UN programmes and conventions, ranging from key agenda mechanisms such as the Rio Earth Summit to more specific sectoral items, such as the Paris Climate Agreement. As such, like with many of the sustainability issues discussed in this book, the UN are a key institution when it comes to water.

### 10.3.2 Water regulation and governance

Given its context-specific nature, much of the management of water takes place at a country level, often through regulation set at the national, local and/or regional levels. Authorities set different kinds of regulatory demands focusing on water use, allocation, discharges and pricing, to name but a few. These vary across contexts. In some arid contexts with major water stress such regulatory demands can be substantial, whereas in more water-rich contexts, the approach can be more focused on particular elements, such as pollution, discharges or addressing flood risks.

As is often the case, the potential of regulation is limited. Even if authorities want to put in strong measures, their ability to regulate, assess and control water issues varies substantially. It matters here, for instance, what kind of a water infrastructure a given context has as well as how strong and stable the institutions governing it are. If the infrastructure is relatively well-developed and somewhat centralised, it can be easier, and more effective, to set up a system to assess and control both the water quality as well as the quantity of water flowing in and out.

A fragmented infrastructure, where the water management system is disjointed and lacks cohesion, is an important consideration. Such a situation is typical in the rural areas of many developing countries. Here, a centralised water infrastructure either does not exist, or it could be highly unreliable or prohibitively expensive. Hence, communities and organisations can be prompted or forced to turn to alternative sources of water, such as gathering water from a river or using their own wells. Controlling and regulating such a setting is obviously much more complicated. While the authorities can potentially set limits on the installation of tube or bore wells, for instance, as well as control the amounts of water withdrawn from ground water reservoirs, such requirements can often be circumvented, limiting the influence local authorities can effectively have on water use and discharges. Such situations can potentially lead to local conflicts, if for example the level of the groundwater aquifers drops due to extensive use, and hence only richer individuals and organisations with resources have the capability to install deeper wells.

While water is considered a local issue, transnational governance is relevant. The hydrological cycle of water knows no state boundaries, and many watersheds span multiple jurisdictions. For example, major rivers and associated catchment areas have been the focus of several longstanding and well-known debates around water use. Take the Mekong River basin in Southeast Asia. The river has been the lifeblood for many communities since ancient times, serving as a source of nutrition, as a means of transportation and in the production of energy. The river spans across six countries, and there have over the years been constant disputes regarding who has the right to use the water and for what purposes. Similarly to the case of the Nile River in northern Africa, a significant source of controversy on the Mekong is energy production: as countries and organisations upstream build large dams to produce hydro-energy, the countries and communities downstream are impacted through the changing and irregular water flows. While such disputes often take place between national governments, they have both direct and indirect implications for organisations.

### 10.3.3 Other water initiatives

It is unlikely that regulation alone, especially due to the limitations noted above, can solve the range of challenges related to water in different contexts. As such, and similarly to other sustainability issues, different groups have come together to form frameworks and initiatives, with the aim of taking part in addressing water challenges. Such initiatives can serve multiple purposes, ranging from complementing the regulation set by authorities, being of a more general nature and focusing on indicating interest and general goodwill towards recognising the importance of water, or helping to identify and disseminate best practices related to water use and management. The primary goal of these alliances and frameworks varies and may at times be related to the groups that have established them, as some initiatives are being led by NGOs, while others consist mainly of businesses coming together to work on the topic.

An example of an NGO-led initiative would be the WWF Water Risk Filter, which is aimed at bringing together knowledge and tools that help users to examine, evaluate and understand various water risks, and thereby enhance sustainable water management. WWF's Water Risk Filter highlights the importance of businesses to understand the nature and potential significance of their water related business risks, which are split into physical, regulatory and reputational risks. These risks are explained to be due to either the conditions of the water basins, referred to as basin water risks, or how the operational sites are dependent upon and impact water, known as operational water risks. WWF's Water Risk Filter provides firms tools to help them become more aware of and analyse their water risks.

The influential business community World Business Council for Sustainable Development (WBCSD) has included water in several of its programmes, focusing for instance on circular water management, wastewater impact assessment and water-smart agriculture. In addition to emphasising how water is essential for the functioning of all societies and economies, WBCSD also points out how water risks are significant for many major listed companies through them being exposed to water stress across their value chains. To help organisations assess, understand and manage their water-related impacts and dependencies, WBCSD has also developed the Freshwater Accountability Navigator, under which they have collected information on various tools and frameworks organisations can use.

Initiatives can also be formed on the basis of collaboration, as in the case of the Alliance for Water Stewardship (AWS), which is a collaborative effort between international NGOs, businesses and governments. AWS seeks to nurture water stewardship and to emphasise the value of water through the AWS International Water Stewardship Standard. A range of other initiatives also exists, and is also likely to emerge, as the challenges related to global water accessibility mount.

## 10.4 Water accounting and reporting practices

We have in the above text highlighted the complex and multidimensional nature of water, and also emphasised the importance of understanding the role of context when considering water use. These observations connect to how water accounting and reporting in organisations has developed. In general terms, while there are a number of frameworks concerning water accounting and reporting across contexts and industries, none can be considered dominant. As such, water accounting and reporting within organisations continue to be relatively fragmented. This means that instead of there being widely applied uniform tools and techniques, different organisations use different types of tools for different purposes. However, as water issues are becoming more important and urgent, and the value of comparable information is being increasingly recognised, having frameworks in place is likely to be important. As water stress becomes increasingly evident in developed areas, such as California and South Africa, it can be foreseen that the swift development of new frameworks, initiatives and accounting tools will continue.

In this section, we overview current practices in organisations. In so doing, we will present some of the most prominent organisational practices of water accounting and water reporting and the frameworks that guide them.

### 10.4.1 Water measurement and management accounting practices

As the demand for water increases, there is an increasing need to develop better information systems which support organisations' management in their decision-making concerning water. As a result, many water accounting practices focus on the measurement and management of water. However, despite attempts to create some general frameworks, which would influence, and in many cases standardise, how accounting for water is conducted, on an organisational level these practices remain relatively fragmented. This might relate to the context-specific nature of water, which implies that the particular needs organisations have vary significantly depending on geographical location. The need to enhance the conversation around water accounting and to bring some standardisation has been recognised. An example here was an attempt by the World Resources Institute (WRI) and the CEO Water Mandate to develop a Common Water Accounting Framework. They aimed to establish common practices that would have enhanced stakeholders' ability to compare the information provided by different water users. Over the course of the project, the focus of the initiative evolved with understanding that due to climate change water resilience should be given priority, leading eventually to the publication of Water Resilience Assessment Framework in 2021, together with supplementing corporate guidance (CEO Water Mandate, 2025).

While the focus here is on the organisational level, water accounting is also done for other purposes at for instance the governmental or regional level. For countries, the UN has developed a framework called the "System for Environmental-Economic Accounting for Water", intended to help in standardising the way countries, regions and territories calculate and report on water resources as well as water use in societies. At this point it is worth mentioning that the UN has an annual publication called the World Water Development Report. This report looks at the global water situation, providing a range of metrics as well as insights on the global issue of water (UNESCO, UN-Water, 2024).

A more regional-level initiative took place in Australia, in which a Water Accounting Standards Board was established to help create the Australian Water Accounting Standard. The aim here was to generate a framework for General Purpose Water Accounts, which would again aid in collecting standardised and comparable information on water resources, withdrawals and consumption (Tello et al., 2016). While the eventual application of these accounts has been limited overall, the state of New South Wales for instance publishes regular water resource accounts for major inland valleys in the state.

#### 10.4.1.1 Water footprinting

Water footprinting is an example of a practice used for the measurement and management of water in organisations. This is one of the more well-known applications of water accounting. The idea of water footprinting is to calculate all the direct and indirect freshwater used for a particular product, service or activity. This implies that the assessment should include all the stages of the product's supply chain.

Water footprinting, just like other footprint assessments like environmental footprints and carbon footprints, features frequently in the press and on social media, when for instance different types of food products are compared. What is perhaps less widely known, however, is that there are multiple definitions for a water footprint, and also that there are different ways of assessing and calculating one for a product or a service. There is, for instance, the ISO14046:2014 standard called "Environmental management – Water footprint – Principles, requirements and guidelines", and the Water Footprint Assessment which is presented by an NGO called Water Footprint Network. In general terms, these two have a similar approach to assessing water footprints, although while the ISO14046 is based on the Life Cycle Assessment and looks more at the potential water-related environmental impacts, the Water Footprint Network's assessment focuses on quantifying water productivity through mapping green, blue and grey water footprints, each of which is describing a different dimension of water use. Further, while the Water Footprint Network's tool is freely available and perhaps easier to apply, it does not necessarily provide as much detail in its results as a more specific application of the ISO14064:2014 would potentially do.

Without getting into the details of the approaches, it is relevant to acknowledge that different methodologies can exist even for such a popular form of water accounting. This means that it is not advisable to readily compare water footprint figures produced at different locations and by different people without taking a look at the how the assessments were conducted. When a standard methodology is used, water footprinting allows, in principle, an easy and fairly comprehensible comparison of, say, different types of food and beverage products, which include figures describing how a cup of coffee, a serving of cheese, tofu or a steak would require this much water to be produced. Even with a standardised methodology however, the quality of the underlying primary and secondary data is an important factor affecting the usefulness of the calculations.

This is an area where the context-specific nature of water is relevant. Context means that coming up with an accurate number is not without challenges. The most significant question is probably the fact that information on water use from different regions and contexts cannot and should not be directly compared as this leaves out considerations of how significant the water use in a given area is. While different assessment methodologies take the variation of contexts into account to some extent, the assessments are still based on a range of assumptions and simplifications – otherwise the calculation would become too complicated. A report produced jointly by SABMiller and WWF (2009) illustrates the diversity of issues arising depending on the site of production. The report examines the water footprint associated with beer production in two geographical locations, South Africa and the Czech Republic, and highlights the significance of considering and understanding the context when interpreting such quantitative information.

It is important to highlight that the challenges do not mean that water footprinting cannot or should not be used. Unilever, for instance, has applied water footprinting to analyse its water usage for several years, and the company has used the method to develop its products so that they would require less water. Similarly, Raisio, an international food company based in Finland, uses water footprinting to assess the amounts of water its products require. Raisio added a water footprint label to its oat flakes as early as 2009, being amongst the first companies in the world to do so. From an organisational perspective, following such a standardised methodology on a consistent basis can offer a useful tool for assessing and developing the direct and indirect water use of products and services.

## 10.4.2 Water reporting

The second type of water accounting practices we discuss here are those relating specifically to water reporting. As is the case with many other areas of sustainability, companies are increasingly including water disclosures in their sustainability reporting. At the same time, practices are still underdeveloped. The development of the guidance included in the most prominent sustainability reporting frameworks has arguably helped to improve water reporting practices.

### 10.4.2.1 Frameworks for corporate water reporting

In terms of disclosures, Global Reporting Initiative (GRI) Standard 303 Water and Effluents is a relatively well-developed basis for reporting. The GRI published a revised version of its water standard in 2018. The standard emphasises that organisations need to understand the specific nature of water, stemming from it being a shared resource as well as the relevance of the local context for many water-related impacts. The GRI also encourages organisations to prioritise areas with water stress in their actions, as well as to focus on collaboration with other water users in aiming at sustainable water management.

**Focus on practice: GRI Standard 303 Water and Effluents**

The GRI underscores that quantitative indicators are not sufficient for stakeholders, who seek to understand how an organisation manages water-related impacts and develops its water management practices. Therefore, in the area of water and effluents, the GRI guidelines include two specific management approach disclosures. These supplement the more general management approach disclosures requested by GRI Standard 103. Management approach disclosures:

- Disclosure 303-1 Interactions with water as a shared resource
- Disclosure 303-2 Management of water discharge-related impacts

Topic-specific disclosures:

- Disclosure 303-3 Water withdrawal
- Disclosure 303-4 Water discharge
- Disclosure 303-5 Water consumption

The GRI notes that water withdrawal, water consumption and water discharges are closely related. An organisation is therefore expected to report on all of them if it has identified water as a material topic. It is worth pointing out here that the GRI emphasises how reporting only the total amounts used and discharged across all activities and sites of an organisation does not suffice with water, due to the high relevance of the local context as well as the context-specific nature of impacts and dependencies related to water. Instead, while the GRI's disclosure guidelines also include items on total water withdrawal and consumption, organisations are strongly encouraged to break down the numbers to a more detailed level, as well as to provide further narrative descriptions regarding different types of aspects. Such information might be helpful for those reading the reports to form a more comprehensive understanding of the organisation's relationship with water.

Other reporting frameworks also include different types of requirements and guidance regarding water disclosures. In the European context, the ESRS E3 standard on water and marine resources includes disclosure items on water usage and consumption but also asks companies to consider their water policies and anticipated financial effects of water-related impacts, risks and opportunities. From a more investor-focused perspective, organisations making use of the SASB Standards can follow their application guidance to develop water-related disclosures. Depending on the specific industry and the associated materiality of water, firms are expected to report on questions concerning their water usage, water risks and operational strategy through qualitative discussion and quantitative metrics. Following the ethos of SASB standards, the primary aim of these disclosures would be helping investors in their decision-making. Similarly, water could also be discussed when organisations report according to TCFD recommendations or the IFRS S1 and S2 sustainability standards, even though those frameworks do not focus on water specifically. Here, the need to report on water arises from how it intertwines with climate change, and as such water disclosures could be important for investor decision-making in the context of for instance assessment and management of water risks as well as organisational transition plans.

Another arguably influential framework for disclosures comes from the CDP, which conducts large surveys targeting thousands of major companies on an annual basis. In addition to climate and carbon, water is one of CDP's focus areas, and companies are expected to reply to a broad range of questions, including both specific numbers and organisational policies, management of risks, as well as handling of water issues in the supply chain. The reports CDP produces on the basis of the questionnaires provide good snapshots of the current corporate practices concerning water. Given that the CDP surveys companies each year, the questions could also have an influence on corporate practices.

### 10.4.3 Summary of water accounting practices

While a number of different tools, frameworks and methods exist when it comes to water accounting and reporting, it is still reasonable to say that the quality of organisational information systems on water and water reporting practices could be better. Here, being better can refer to several things, such as whether water accounting helps with organisational decision-making, provides tangible economic benefits for the organisation, aids in diminishing potential negative environmental consequences of water use, or communicates water issues and accountability for water more broadly. Moreover, in considering accountability there are a number of issues left unaddressed here. Is accountability for water and water issues sufficiently considered in the above practices? Take comparability, a key accounting principle, for instance. Given the great variability in water accounting practices, the potential for comparison is at times limited from the perspective of both managers and stakeholders. We discuss some of the limits, or unaddressed issues, when it comes to water accounting and accountability next.

**Focus on practice: Coca-Cola water stewardship**

Coca-Cola has for some time emphasised their commitment to water stewardship. The global company, the products of which are available virtually everywhere on the planet, highlights that water is the key ingredient for its beverages, and hence it is clear the organisation is also dependent on having access to safe water supplies. Water is also relevant from a financial standpoint, as any price changes, even minor ones, will have an impact on the company.

There is also a backdrop to the current practices in the company which creates important context for how the company approaches water and the issue of water use. In the early 2000s, Coca-Cola received substantial criticism over how it was using massive amounts of water in its factories located in water-stressed areas, such as Kerala in India. The negative publicity the company received at the time, together with the rising awareness of sustainability within business, prompted the company to make environmental commitments.

Coca-Cola identifies in its reporting the shared nature of water and the company's responsibility to protect water resources. They have also made a pledge to return every drop of water they use, which they aim to achieve through constantly improving water efficiency, replenishing water sources, mitigating water risks as well as recycling treated wastewater. The company has also collaborated with NGOs in developing ways to assess their water consumption as well as to find ways to enhance sustainable water management in their production.

While it is acknowledged that the company has made progress in its environmental commitments, it continues to receive criticism about the claims it is making. For instance, the methods Coca-Cola uses to account for its water use have been claimed to be selective, and its reporting has been accused to focus on bolstering the positive elements while giving some negative aspects less attention.

We would encourage you to look at Coca-Cola's water accounting and reporting. There are various aspects here that will help you understand water accounting and accountabilities relating to water and water use. However, as always, we encourage you to critically reflect on their reporting and practices – considering what they do well, and also where they could improve their practice.

## 10.5 Water accounting and accountability: Some issues going forward

As with all sustainability issues, there is also in this area a need to constantly reflect on and develop our practices. Here, we discuss several topics of discussion and debate to reflect on the potential, as well as the limits, of current practices of water accounting and accountability.

### 10.5.1 General issues concerning water accounting in organisations

From an organisational perspective, developing a solid water accounting system is important for both sustainability and financial reasons. Water extraction, consumption and discharges can have substantial short- and long-term impacts on the surrounding communities and ecosystems, which means that management needs to be aware of them in order to take part in the sustainable water management of a given context. As discussed, organisations are often dependent on a reliable water supply, implying that in areas of increased water stress, the management needs to have high-quality information at their disposal to ensure that decision-making takes water and water-risks into account in an appropriate manner. The same holds from a financial perspective. The increased scarcity of water is driving up prices in many contexts, and this can have major financial implications for an organisation. Consideration of risks is also relevant, and particularly so if an organisation operates or has its supply chains in areas of heightened water stress. Limits to water availability due to either quantity or quality issues may have substantial financial consequences, if for instance operations need to be limited or even shut down temporarily.

However, in considering how water accounting should be conducted, we should reflect on the considerations we have highlighted above. To begin with, the importance of the local context implies that aggregate level figures simply do not make as much sense with water as they would with, for instance, carbon or energy use. Total amounts of water use and discharge can potentially provide some information about trends and production efficiency, for example if analysed in relation to overall scope and volume of operations. Again, and as will now be becoming evident, an important aspect here is the site-specific nature of water. As we have discussed, in terms of water use, this means that consuming a particular amount of water in a water-rich location should not be considered the same as using the same amount of water at a water scarce place. As an example, water use in Sweden where water is abundant and in general of a high quality cannot be directly compared with water use in Morocco, which is regularly a location of water scarcity.

Moreover, the source of the water needs to be taken into account as well. Water can be drawn from ground water reservoirs, or it can be taken from a nearby lake or river, for example. Neither one is by definition better than the other, but for an organisation, it is significant to understand where the water it is using is coming from, whether there are potential short- or long-term risks associated with the supply, and how the organisation's activities are impacting on this supply. The timing of the water extraction is relevant as well: drawing water from a nearby river in the rainy season would not be the same thing as withdrawing the same amount from the same river during the dry season. This then brings us to a link to water being a shared resource, the use of which by someone can have implications on others relying on the same resource. We must consider whether these things are built into the accounting system, and if not, how effective that system is for providing the information needed to understand, say, organisational impacts and dependencies.

As we have also highlighted, organisations are often major water users, and as such their actions can have impacts on communities' and other organisations' ability to use water. In developing water accounting, an organisation would hence benefit from going beyond mere numbers and considering such implications, as this can potentially help in fostering stakeholder relationships, avoiding conflicts, and developing collaborative action needed for sustainable water management in an area. An organisation may well benefit from collaboration with NGOs or consultancies, as these groups are more likely to have the knowledge needed to evaluate the relevance of water use and discharges at a particular context.

While the list above may seem lengthy and gives us a sense of just how complex water accounting is, it should not be taken to mean that water accounting for management purposes is overly complex or outright impossible. Instead, it implies that engaging with water accounting can be highly significant for an organisation, but also that preparing such accounts requires knowledge and expertise and when using them a good level of critical thought and reflection. In order to be useful, water accounting should often be focused on context-bound settings, and any figures derived from it need to be interpreted from this perspective. As we have seen throughout this book, this is not unique to water, but there is nonetheless a contrast with many of the general principles applied in conventional financial accounting, for example.

### 10.5.2 Volumetric water accounting

Let's take a closer look at the issue of measurement in water accounting. In general terms, it is relatively straightforward in most contexts to look at the stocks and flows of a physical thing like water. As such, this is often the level where organisational water accounting takes place: how much water is used, how much of that gets embedded into the products, and how much water flows out after the processes. Managers might also have access to other measures, such as water quality, particularly if there is regulation in place requiring an organisation to regularly monitor these things.

With water, such numbers might not take us very far, however. From an organisational point of view, it is important to understand what such information would mean. Are the volumes significant, potentially to such an extent that it endangers sustainable water supply in the location? Is the quality and quantity of the water discharge at a facility such that it causes potential social and environmental risks to the ecosystem or the local community? How about if we asked the same questions regarding the organisation's supply chain? Or taking a different approach, how water efficient the processes and products are? Or, how does the organisation perform in comparison to other similar organisations?

Answering such questions requires both managers and the water accounting system to go beyond volumetric information. Having access to both absolute and relative information would aid managers in assessing efficiency, identifying trends over time, as well as making comparisons with other organisations or relevant benchmarks. Such information would also help others assess the responsibilities and performance of an organisation in relation to water.

### 10.5.3 Accounting and the pricing of water

In discussions of water accounting and accountability, the focus tends to be on water extraction, water discharges and water consumption, as is the case with the GRI and ESRS disclosures for example. There is however a distinct yet highly relevant water issue which also needs attention: water privatisation and water pricing. Here, the focus is more on the governance of water supplies, as well as on the institutional structures created around water production and related services. This is an area where more traditional financial accounting practices potentially have substantial implications on considerations of sustainability. Moreover, the interconnections of sustainability issues mean that we need to look beyond the SDG 6 Clean Water and Sanitation, and also consider the implications water governance and associated accounting practices have, for instance on SDG 1 No Poverty, SDG 3 Good Health and Well-Being, and SDG 10 Reduced Inequalities.

Water has traditionally been a public good and service, but private organisations have in numerous places shown substantial interest in running water production or wastewater treatment facilities. One significant motivation here relates to the fact that water service is usually a natural monopoly in a given context. There is often only one water grid and hence there would be no competition or alternative services available for customers. While private organisations often emphasise that their involvement would ensure that there would be sufficient resources to maintain and expand water infrastructure, there are obviously critics. Critiques of the privatisation of water often centre around questions such as whether private organisations have sufficient interest in investing in infrastructure to ensure plentiful and/or sustainable supply, whether they would use the position of natural monopoly to make substantial price increases potentially making water unaffordable for some, and whether water services would after privatisation be equally available and accessible to all citizens and social groups. Essentially concerns relate to the ability to control and manage the resource from a profit/business perspective, rather than having water recognised as an essential need which all should have the right to. The overarching and fundamental question asked is whether a shared critical resource such as water should be privatised in the first place (see the "Insights from research" for an example).

### INSIGHTS FROM RESEARCH: SUSTAINABLE URBAN WATER MANAGEMENT IN GHANA

How does sustainability go together with financial efficiency in the area of water management? Matthew Egan and Gloria Agyemang offer insights on this topic in their study examining urban water management in Ghana between 2005 and 2017.

Egan and Agyemang note how in many developing countries governments have over the last decades faced substantial pressure from major supranational funding bodies, the World Bank in particular, regarding a need to focus on financial efficiency in their public policy. At the same time, it is evident that in many developing countries institutions and key infrastructure are lacking. In their study, Egan and Agyemang look at the urban water management in Ghana and discuss the progress and barriers from the perspective of sustainable development.

The availability and accessibility of sustainable water supplies is a significant challenge in many developing countries. In this paper, Egan and Agyemang argue that progress towards less unsustainable urban water management was achieved through greater democratic governance, public accountability and public engagement. The authors maintain that these elements were important for improving knowledge and clarifying the goals in the sector. At the same time, the aim of sustainable water management was countered by the strong supranational lenders, who emphasised the importance of financial efficiency in the sector.

Safe and sustainable water supply is essential for both human communities and ecosystems. Egan and Agyemang show here how it may be beneficial to draw on a wide range of stakeholders in the development of water management, instead of simply following the demands of the most powerful ones with narrow interests. Moreover, the paper also highlights the role accounting figures and financial calculations can have in considerations of sustainable development.

**Egan, M. and Agyemang, G. (2019). Progress towards Sustainable Urban Water Management in Ghana. *Sustainability Accounting, Management and Policy Journal, 10(2)*, 235–259.**

In this context, and in addition to the broader debates about the ethics of water pricing, accounting can be seen to play a major role. For instance, water was for a long time considered to be an ample resource, which was either considered to be free or to have a relatively low price. Obviously, there are substantial contextual variations here: in water scarce locations the price of water is likely to be far higher than it is in places with richer water resources. As the demand for water increases and in many places exceeds the available supply, the pricing of water becomes a significant issue. Key here is the recognition that accounting for water has implications, so we need to consider the consequences of, for example, pricing water.

### 10.5.4 How useful is water reporting?

We discussed above the practice of water reporting and the key frameworks that underlie it. We have also discussed the limits of volumetric measures. But there are other aspects of water reporting worth reflecting on. For example, at present, reporting tends to focus on specific metrics (usually past performance), while reporting on targets and goals as well as the achievement of previous goals is less frequent. Likewise, reporting tends to focus on the organisation itself rather than consider the organisation in relation to its water context.

While limited in practice, looking at impacts and dependencies in reporting would be useful as this would help various stakeholder groups evaluate an organisation's activities. Take investors for example. Many organisations are highly dependent on having access to safe, sustainable and steadily priced water sources, but these dependencies and associated business risks are not often discussed in sufficient depth. As we have noted above, organisational water reporting has been developing and such reports already serve many readers by providing useful information about the water policies and use in a particular organisation. At the same time, it is perhaps appropriate to ask whether such reports are sufficient when we are trying to address the issue of water.

Think about a small river, or a catchment area somewhere. The organisational reports potentially describe how the activities of individual organisations impact such a watershed, as well as how those individual organisations are dependent on water. Being organisation-specific, and focusing on what happens within the boundaries of single entities, these organisational reports are unlikely to be informative when thinking about the local river or ground water basin in general. This level of focus is needed if we are concerned about sustainable water management in a specific context, as it is not individual organisational performance that signals the sustainability of the water supply but a consideration of the water supply itself. We consider this further next.

### 10.5.5 Levels and timing of water reporting

Given the above, it is worth considering whether multiple levels of water reporting are needed in order to understand the issue of water in a given context. That is, in addition to water accounting at the level of the organisation, do we also need other water accounts to understand issues of water and to assist organisations in addressing issues relating to water?

Dey and Russell (2014) ask "Who speaks for the river?" Given the critical role water has for humans, and also how dependent communities often are on a single freshwater source such as a river or an aquifer, it is likely that as the water challenges escalate accounts of water supplies or catchment areas are needed. That is, instead of having an organisation as the reporting entity, such a water report would focus on a different type of an entity and draw on information from various sources. Such an account or report could be used to discuss the state of this water source, but also to discuss the potential impacts this river or aquifer has on human communities and ecosystems, as well as consider how dependant the health of this ecological system would be on particular actions, such as those of human communities, organisations and the broader weather patterns. This type of an approach would potentially help in making the intangible and tangible value of local and regional water systems more visible.

Furthermore, Russell and Lewis (2014) emphasise how it would be beneficial to investigate and approach different types of technologies and accounting tools across different scales, instead of trying to come up with some type of a uniform approach to be applied on for instance the organisational level. Questions of the accounting entity and boundaries are highly relevant with water. It is worth asking how much sense it makes to produce aggregate figures of the water withdrawals and consumption of a multinational organisation with operations across a hundred countries and locations or without an understanding (an account) of the water context.

As we have demonstrated, in water accounting it is important to consider the interactions and interconnections of various groups in society. Here, the shared nature of water interconnects with the hydrological cycle of water within catchments and ground water reservoirs. In most cases, water catchment areas span across national and organisational boundaries. This implies that sustainable water governance requires collaboration, transparency and the creation of trust. Public and private sectors are intertwined, as the actions of one group can have direct consequences for the other, in water-stressed regions in particular. When water is scarce and harder to access, it is often those with more resources who can nonetheless keep accessing the supplies, either by drilling their wells deeper or by paying a premium to ensure constant water flow, while individuals and communities in weaker positions end up struggling to get by with smaller quantities of lower-quality water. Given that access to safe water and sanitation is considered a human right, it is essential that organisations are accountable for their use of this shared resource. Hence, the development of more dynamic, real-time and contextualised reporting approaches based on appropriate water accounting metrics are needed. In this sector, reporting aggregate information on an annual basis might be less relevant than the provision of instant, short-term and localised data, showing how an organisation is taking into account the local and temporal circumstances.

## 10.6 Conclusion

We have provided an overview of water accounting and accountability. As access to safe and sustainable water sources has become increasingly limited across the world, a need to find and establish different types of water accounting and accountability practices has become more urgent. These practices are relevant for organisations and financial institutions, as managers and investors need timely, high-quality and context relevant information to support their decision-making. Such practices are arguably more important for stakeholders, who rely on water and are interested in holding organisations accountable for their water management practices. The shared nature of water amplifies this: in a specific context, most individuals and organisations across sectors are dependent on the same water sources.

Water accounting practices are developing quickly. While some common frameworks and practices are likely to be developed in the near future, the context-specific nature of water makes it probable that accounting practices will remain varied. This underscores the need for anyone producing and using water accounting figures to go beyond volumetric information of stocks and flows. Moreover, both managers and stakeholders need to develop their ability to critically interpret what the available water accounting information actually means. Such knowledge is essential as we try to tackle the range of water challenges facing contemporary societies.

## References


CDP (2023). Financial Institutions Are Valuing Water. How the Financial Sector Is Responding to the Water Crisis. https://www.cdp.net/en/insights/financial-institutions-are-valuing-water (accessed 20 February 2025).

CEO Water Mandate (2025). Water Resilience Assessment Framework. Available at https://ceowatermandate.org/resilience-assessment-framework/ (Accessed 28 February 2025).

Chapagain, A. and Mekonnen, M. (2023). *Understanding Water Footprints of the Global North and Dependency on Water Use in the Global South*. Water Witness International.

Dey, C. and Russell, S. (2014). Who Speaks for the River? Exploring Biodiversity Reporting using an Arena Approach. In Jones, M. (ed.), *Accounting for Biodiversity*, pp. 245–266. Routledge.

Egan, M. and Agyemang, G. (2019). Progress towards Sustainable Urban Water Management in Ghana. *Sustainability Accounting, Management and Policy Journal, 10(2)*, 235–259.

Fair Water Footprints (2023). New Data Reveals Rich Countries' Shocking Reliance on Water Beyond Their Borders. Available at https://fairwaterfootprints.org/2023/03/22/shocking-new-data-shows-50-of-water-use-to-supply-high-income-economies-is-unsustainable/ (Accessed 28 February 2025).

OHCHR, UN Habitat and WHO (2010). Fact Sheet 35: The Right to Water. www.ohchr.org/Documents/Publications/FactSheet35en.pdf (accessed 20 February 2025).

Österblom, H., Jouffray, J.-B., Folke, C. and Rockström, J. (2017). Emergence of a Global Science–Business Initiative for Ocean Stewardship. *PNAS, 114(34)*, 9038–9043

Russell, S. and Lewis, L. (2014). Accounting and Accountability for Fresh Water. In Bebbington, J., Unerman, J. and O'Dwyer, B. (eds), *Sustainability Accounting and Accountability*, pp. 213–230. Routledge.

SABMiller and WWF (2009). Water Footprinting: Identifying and Addressing Water Risks in the Value Chain. https://awsassets.panda.org/downloads/sabmiller_water_footprinting_report_final_.pdf (accessed 20 February 2025).

Tello, E., Hazelton, J. and Cummings, L. (2016). Potential Users' Perceptions of General Purpose Water Accounting Reports. *Accounting, Auditing and Accountability Journal, 29(1)*, 80–110.

UNESCO, UN-Water (2024). *United Nations World Water Development Report 2024: Water for Prosperity and Peace*. UNESCO.

WaterAid (2018). *Strengthening the Business Case for Water, Sanitation and Hygiene: How to Measure Value for Your Business.* WaterAid. https://washmatters.wateraid.org/publications (accessed 20 February 2025).

World Resources Institute (WRI) (2023). 25 Countries, Housing One-Quarter of the Population, Face Extremely High Water Stress. Available at https://www.wri.org/insights/highest-water-stressed-countries (accessed 3 March 2025).

WWF (2006). Rich Countries, Poor Water. Available at https://assets.wwf.org.uk/downloads/richcountriespoorwater.pdf (Accessed 28 February 2025).

WWF (2023). We Have Undervalued Freshwater; We Have Also Undervalued How Much It Matters. www.worldwildlife.org/blogs/sustainability-works/posts/we-have-undervalued-freshwater-we-have-also-undervalued-how-much-it-matters (accessed 18 February 2025).

WWF (2025). Water Scarcity. www.worldwildlife.org/threats/water-scarcity (accessed 20 February 2025).

## Additional reading and resources

Burritt, R. L. and Christ, K. L. (2017). The Need for Monetary Information within Corporate Water Accounting. *Journal of Environmental Management, 201*, 72–81.

Egan, M. and Agyemang, G. (2022). An Exploration of Developing Approaches to Water Accounting. In Adams, C. (ed.), *Handbook of Accounting and Sustainability*, pp. 279–299. Edward Elgar.

Hazelton, J. (2013). Accounting as a Human Right: The Case of Water Information. *Accounting, Auditing and Accountability Journal, 26(2)*, 267–311.

Hoekstra, A. Y., Chapagain, A. K., Aldaya, M. M. and Mekonnen, M. M. (2011). *The Water Footprint Assessment Manual.* Earthscan. https://waterfootprint.org/media/downloads/TheWaterFootprintAssessmentManual_2.pdf (accessed 20 February 2025).

Russell, S. (2021). Water. In Bebbington, J., Larrinaga, C., O'Dwyer, B. and Thomson, I. (eds), *Handbook on Environmental Accounting*, pp. 365–376. Routledge.

Schneider, T. and Andreaus, M. (2018). A Dam Tale: Using Institutional Logics in a Case Study on Water Rights in the Canadian Coastal Mountains. *Sustainability Accounting, Management and Policy Journal, 9(5)*, 685–712.

WBCSD (2025). Freshwater Accountability Navigator. https://archive.wbcsd.org/Imperatives/waterFAN/Freshwater-Accountability-Navigator-FAN (accessed 20 February 2025).

World Resources Institute (WRI) (2021). Toolbox for Setting Enterprise Water Targets. Available at https://www.wri.org/toolbox/setting-enterprise-water-targets (accessed 3 March 2025).

CHAPTER

# 11

# Accounting for biodiversity

Biodiversity, at its simplest, refers to the variety of all living things. It is essential to the wellbeing of the planet, and hence essential to the wellbeing of people and their organisations. Biodiversity is also at serious risk, and biodiversity loss is recognised as a sustainability issue of critical importance. This has resulted in growing awareness of the need to account for biodiversity as well as in increasing consideration of responsibilities and accountability relationships in relation to biodiversity. However, what this accounting might look like, what form it might take, who should provide the account, for what purposes, and to whom, are just some of the questions that need to be considered in seeking to develop accounting that will help in addressing biodiversity loss.

In this chapter, we discuss biodiversity and the related concept of ecosystem services in relation to accounting and accountability. We first outline what biodiversity is and discuss why biodiversity and biodiversity loss are receiving increasing attention in various spheres of society – individuals, organisations and governments. Second, we map key international bodies and frameworks that relate to biodiversity and its protection at the international level. We outline key guidelines and initiatives discussing how organisations can assess and value biodiversity and ecosystem services. Third, we discuss the current practice of biodiversity accounting from the perspectives of reporting, recording and measuring, before considering some key questions we should address in relation to accounting and accountability for biodiversity going forward. Specifically, in the last part of this chapter, we highlight the need to take a critical look at practices relating to accounting for biodiversity and engage in critical reflection as to their implications and consequences in any attempt to move towards a more sustainable state.

By the end of this chapter, you should:

- Understand biodiversity, biodiversity loss and the related concept of ecosystem services.
- Be aware of why biodiversity loss is a key issue of critical importance.

DOI: 10 4324/9781003533207-14

- Understand why biodiversity and biodiversity loss are important to organisations and accounting.
- Be aware of global, national and organisational level initiatives relating to biodiversity.
- Have a critical awareness of current accounting practice in relation to biodiversity and ecosystem services.
- Have considered the potential and limits of current understandings and practices in relation to accounting for biodiversity.

## 11.1 Biodiversity loss as key sustainability issue

Biodiversity, short for biological diversity, refers to the degree of variation of life, or simply, the variety of all living things inhabiting the Earth. While often being represented by images of particular species (especially those with popular appeal in danger of extinction such as the panda or polar bear), it is important to recognise that biodiversity refers to more than just animals. The Convention on Biological Diversity, a key international agreement on biodiversity, defines biological diversity in its Article 2 as "the variability among living organisms from all sources including, inter alia, terrestrial, marine and other aquatic ecosystems and the ecological complexes of which they are part; this includes diversity within species, between species and of ecosystems" (UN, 1992, p. 3). With biodiversity, we are hence referring to several levels (see Table 11.1).

When it comes to biodiversity, it is not just the number of a particular species or the number of species in an ecosystem that matters; rather it is the interactions between them. It is generally understood that the greater the biodiversity in an ecosystem, the more stable and resilient it will be. We can also refer to different levels of biodiversity loss and their implications. For example, if a population living in an area disappears, we say that it has gone locally extinct. Once all populations of a species disappear, the species is extinct. Extinction is irreversible. And this is just one of the reasons why biodiversity is important and why the loss of biological diversity is a cause for serious concern.

### 11.1.1 Biodiversity loss and the sixth mass extinction

Like fluctuations in population size, extinction is part of the natural cycle of life. Within this cycle of life new species develop (although very slowly) with the rate of new species development typically equalling or exceeding what is referred to as the background rate of extinction. As such, biodiversity generally increases over time, with the current biodiversity having developed over millions of years. However, just as at five other times in history, we are currently in a period of mass extinction. The most well-known of the previous five mass extinctions took place in the Cretaceous period when the dinosaurs and about 80% of all other species went extinct (Robertson, 2017). Our current period is commonly referred to as the "sixth mass extinction".

This period of the sixth mass extinction is not only considered to be well underway, but it is also progressing at a rapid rate. Scientists estimate that extinction

**TABLE 11.1** Levels of Biodiversity and Their Relevance

| Level | Definition | Why It Is Important |
|---|---|---|
| Species diversity | The variety of different species | Each species interacts with each other and plays a role. While context is important here, having more diversity within an ecosystem often means it is more stable and resilient. |
| Genetic diversity | The variety of genes within and between species | The size of any population fluctuates naturally, however, the larger the population the greater the ability for it to recover from the negative impacts of such things as droughts, floods, storms or fire. If a population in an area is too small, inbreeding can occur, which weakens the population through the loss of genetic diversity and potential increase of congenital defects and genetic diseases. |
| Ecosystem diversity | The different habitats that exist and their living (biotic) and non-living (non-biotic) components | Enables the maintenance of variety in biodiversity. Different types of ecosystems globally include, for example, forests and deserts. There can be different ecosystems regionally as well, for example, wetlands within urban areas. |

rates have reached hundreds, if not thousands, of times the background extinction rate (Ceballos et al., 2015), which refers to the "normal rate" caused by evolution and the so-called natural cycle of life. This means that species are currently going extinct at a rate not seen in 65 million years! (Robertson, 2017). The global Living Planet Index, a key index run by WWF that monitors biodiversity, shows that "over the past 50 years (1970–2020), the average size of monitored wildlife populations has shrunk by 73%" (WWF, 2024, p. 7). This decline is particularly evident in the tropical subregions of the Americas where a 95% decline is noted – the largest decline of any region (WWF, 2024).

There is an important difference between the previous extinction periods noted above and the one we are currently experiencing that is relevant to our discussion of organisations, accounting and accountability: the impact of humans and human activity. The sixth mass extinction currently underway is closely linked to the expansion of human societies and the growth of economic activity. Key drivers of biodiversity loss can be remembered by the acronym HIPPO coined by conservation biologists. HIPPO refers to habitat destruction (H), invasive species (I), pollution (P), population (P) and overexploitation (O). All of these drivers relate in one way or another to humans and human activity. Again, the effect of humans and human activity on the Earth and on its biodiversity is recognised by reference to the Anthropocene. In brief, the impacts of humans and, as discussed below, their organisations, on biodiversity are multi-faceted and affect all regions of the globe.

### 11.1.2 Ecosystem services

Alongside the growing awareness of the increasing rates of biodiversity loss, there is a growing consideration of the importance of biodiversity to human life. In such considerations, the focus is often on ecosystem services, which are the various services derived from the underlying biodiversity on which humans are reliant. It is worth noting at this point that in discussions regarding the importance of nature for organisations and accounting, there has in recent years been a shift towards focusing on ecosystem services rather than biodiversity as such. This can be noticed also in some of the disclosure recommendations, which have their emphasis on nature-related impacts and dependencies, for instance. One of the reasons for this is probably the fact that biodiversity loss manifests to organisations via weakening ecosystem services, which can subsequently lead to tangible consequences for them. It is important to recognise however that ecosystem services are fundamentally reliant on biodiversity, and hence in this chapter, our focus is primarily on biodiversity. We will return to this point further below.

Ecosystem services are usually considered in relation to four areas, known as servicing streams. We identify these in Table 11.2.

In discussions regarding biodiversity loss and ecosystem services, it is important to recognise the tight interconnections both within the natural ecosystems and also between human societies and the natural environment. Considering the ecosystems in general, while science keeps on making swift progress in accumulating knowledge, there are still plenty of things about biodiversity and ecosystems that we do not know. For instance, we are still largely in the dark in relation to how vulnerable some ecosystems are towards the loss of particular keystone species or changes in weather patterns due to climate change. We do not know for sure what are the specific tipping points that can lead to a rapid decline in biodiversity or particular ecosystem services in a given area or more broadly, but we know those exist and that they are rapidly approaching. This last point is significant when considering the dependence of human societies on the natural environment and the ecosystem services it provides. No matter how urbanised we might get, in the end, all human communities are fully dependent on healthy ecosystem services.

### 11.1.3 Why biodiversity is important

In discussing biodiversity, it is important to recognise how the value of nature can be approached in different ways. For some people, particular landscapes, specific species or nature as a whole might appear as nearly sacrosanct and should be discussed and treated accordingly. For others, the same things can also appear highly valuable, but more from the perspective of how they could be utilised to create something for humans to use. Acknowledging the difference between these perspectives is beneficial when discussing why biodiversity is important. To simplify, we can outline two different perspectives.

**TABLE 11.2** Ecosystem Services

| Type | Example of Services Provided |
|---|---|
| Provisioning services | Food, fresh water, genetic resources |
| Cultural services | Aesthetic, inspirational, educational, spiritual, religious |
| Support services | Soil formation, nutrient cycling |
| Regulating services | Climate regulation, disease regulation, water purification, pollination |

First, biodiversity loss can be seen in line with an anthropocentric viewpoint. This is where biodiversity is considered from a human-centred (preservationist) perspective, and the value of biodiversity and related ecosystem services is primarily considered from how it benefits human societies. Second, biodiversity can be considered from a moral or ecocentric (conservationist) perspective. Here, nature has an intrinsic value. This means that biodiversity or ecosystems are considered to have value in their own right, independent of humans. Let's take an example here – a forest. From a human-centred perspective, this forest could be considered valuable due to its use for timber and recreational purposes. However, from an ecocentric perspective, the same forest has value, but not because it can be used by humans, but rather because it is valued for what it is. These two views can be referred to as anthropocentric – nature has value to human beings – and non-anthropocentric – nature has value in itself. Understanding the difference between these two viewpoints can be useful in many situations, such as when members of an organisation seek to engage its stakeholders in a conversation regarding how a particular area, say a swamp located next to a factory, should be taken into account when planning an expansion to the facility.

Given the above discussion and the increasing understanding of biodiversity and its loss amongst civil society, including the role of humans in that loss, it is perhaps not surprising that biodiversity has emerged over a relatively short time to be a key sustainability issue. But what, you might be asking, has this got to do with accounting?

## 11.2 What has biodiversity got to do with organisations and accounting?

### 11.2.1 Impacts and dependencies

Biodiversity, biodiversity loss and ecosystem health are governmental issues as regional, national and local governments have the ability to influence biodiversity through regulation, for example. However, a wide range of other organisations also have responsibilities and accountabilities when it comes to biodiversity and biodiversity loss. As with the other sustainability issues discussed in this book, business organisations, in particular large corporations, are a particular focus of attention in questions related to biodiversity. To understand the relationship between organisations and biodiversity in more detail, it is again useful to recognise the role of impacts and dependencies.

First, organisations, especially large corporations, can have a significant impact on biodiversity and ecosystems (Lamont et al., 2023). Many current practices of organisations contribute to the loss of biodiversity, as their activities reinforce key drivers of biodiversity loss such as habitat destruction, pollution and over-exploitation. Perhaps the most obvious, but not insignificant, impact that organisations have is their physical footprint. Organisations occupy land and impact biodiversity and ecosystems through their physical presence, the location of their buildings, for example. Many organisations also impact land through various choices, such as supply chain-related decisions. A food producer or retailer for example could have different impacts on land based on how they decide to source their supplies, i.e. producers with operations in highly biodiverse areas.

These potentially large effects have led to increased scrutiny of organisational impacts on biodiversity by governments and the public. There have increasingly been calls for accountability for biodiversity and for organisations to address biodiversity issues. Customers, for example, are becoming more concerned about the biodiversity impacts of the companies they choose to purchase from. A prominent example here is the concern citizens have for sentient beings, such as farm animals, reflected in the growing numbers of people choosing vegetarianism or veganism on ethical grounds or seeking to better understand the lives that animals have lived before they become food. At the same time, it seems to be much harder to attract large interest on pollinator loss, such as bees, an important issue that we return to soon.

Second, organisations are dependent on biodiversity. Organisations and ecosystems are linked and therefore, like humans, all organisations depend on ecosystem services and their underpinning biodiversity for their survival. All organisations rely on the critical provisioning services (e.g. freshwater and food) and regulatory services (e.g. climate regulation, flood control, water purification and waste treatment) they provide. In addition to such general level dependencies, each organisation can have some more specific dependencies regarding particular species or ecosystem services in a given context. Some clear examples here would be a fishing company, which is dependent on the health of fish populations in a given area, or a company offering wildlife tours in an ecological reserve, and as such in need of a healthy and diverse ecosystem. A more complex and far-reaching example would be agriculture, which is in many places having problems due to shortage of pollinators, and hence facing potential major crop losses each year (see Atkins and Atkins, 2016). The potential significance of such biodiversity and more broadly nature-related risks are swiftly becoming better recognised as material issues also from a financial perspective, as highlighted by the emergence of the Taskforce on Nature-related Financial Disclosures (TNFD) and how such questions are being considered by the ISSB in their development of sustainability accounting standards. We return to these initiatives in more detail below.

Pollinator loss is an example of where organisational impacts and dependencies interlink. Monocropping and massively expanded size of agricultural fields have substantially reduced the natural habitats of many species, including pollinators. This has led to the population decline of pollinators, on which these same crops and agricultural practices are often dependent. Pollinator loss also shows how biodiversity loss takes us back to the considerations of an organisation's supply chain, as the biodiversity impacts and dependencies can often feature more prominently outside an organisation's legal boundary. As such, in addition to their core activities, organisations are increasingly being held responsible and accountable for their biodiversity impacts throughout the supply chain, and they also need to consider their potential dependencies from a broader perspective.

### 11.2.2 Biodiversity and accounting

We have demonstrated throughout this book that sustainability issues affect accounting. This is no different when it comes to biodiversity and biodiversity loss. Indeed, for many, the first step required for business and other organisations (including governments) is the need to have tools to assess and understand, and preferably accurately measure, their impact and dependence on biodiversity and ecosystem services.

Accounting and accountants are widely considered to have skills in collecting, organising and reporting data, and as such it is no surprise that the majority of biodiversity accounting practices relate to the recording, valuing and reporting of biodiversity by various kinds of organisations. There are, however, diverse and competing views as to the best way to account for biodiversity with many key issues in need of further consideration and debate – including, fundamentally, whether or not conventional accounting is suitable for accounting for biodiversity in the first place.[1] It is therefore important to recognise the tensions created by the different views discussed above, as well as to acknowledge the potential accounting and accountability problems surrounding different responses to whether we should account for biodiversity, how we might do it, and what kind of implications such accounts would have. Furthermore, we need to consider the role of organisations (in particular corporations) and individuals in that accounting.

Before looking at these issues further through a consideration of practice, we first outline the various institutions and initiatives related to biodiversity and ecosystem services. This overview will provide some context for discussing the accounting and organisational practices and also gives us a backdrop against which we can reflect on the questions and tensions mentioned above.

## 11.3 Institutions and initiatives relating to biodiversity

There is a myriad of global-, national- and organisational-level institutions and initiatives that relate to biodiversity. This is not surprising, given that biodiversity loss has global, national and local causes and impacts. We outline some of the more prominent and/or well-known institutions and initiatives here and, like in other chapters in the book, we highlight those that have the most relevance to the organisational and accounting context.

### 11.3.1 International level initiatives

There have been a number of international initiatives and conventions over the years which have attempted to address biodiversity and biodiversity loss. We introduce four key ones here.

#### 11.3.1.1 The Convention on Biological Diversity

The United Nations Convention on Biological Diversity (CBD, known also as the Biodiversity Convention) has quite a long history and has had varying degrees of success. Signed by 150 government leaders at the 1992 Rio Earth Summit, the CBD came into force in 1993. The convention has three main objectives: (1) the conservation of biological diversity, (2) the sustainable use of the components of biological diversity, and (3) the fair and equitable sharing of the benefits arising out of the utilisation of genetic resources (CBD, 2024a).

**TABLE 11.3** Global Biodiversity Framework: Global Goals for 2050

| Goal | What Does the Goal Entail (Examples) |
|---|---|
| Protect and restore | The area of natural ecosystems is substantially increased by 2050.<br>Extinction rate and risks of all species are reduced tenfold.<br>Genetic diversity within populations of wild and domesticated species is maintained. |
| Prosper with nature | Biodiversity is sustainably used and managed.<br>Nature's contributions to people are valued, maintained and enhanced, supporting the achievement of sustainable development for the benefit of present and future generations. |
| Share benefits fairly | The monetary and non-monetary benefits from the utilisation of genetic resources are shared fairly and equitably.<br>Traditional knowledge associated with genetic resources is appropriately protected. |
| Invest and collaborate | Ensure adequate means of implementation, including financial resources, capacity-building, technical and scientific cooperation, to fully implement the Kunming-Montreal Global Biodiversity Framework are secured and equitably accessible to all. |

Source: Convention for Biological Diversity (CBD) (2024c).

An important aspect of the CBD are the aims set in The Kunming-Montreal Global Biodiversity Framework adopted at COP15 of the CDP in 2023. The overarching vision for 2050 is structured around four long-term goals, which are Protect and Restore, Prosper with Nature, Share Benefits Fairly, and Invest and Collaborate (see Table 11.3). To facilitate the achievement of these goals, the framework also includes 23 action-oriented global targets for 2030, requiring immediate action to achieve the targets by the end of the decade. The 23 global targets are divided into three groups: (1) Reducing threats to biodiversity; (2) Meeting people's needs through sustainable use and benefit-sharing; and (3) Tools and solutions for implementation and mainstreaming (CBD, 2024b). With respect to organisations and accounting, Target 15 specifically highlights the need for businesses to assess, disclose and reduce their biodiversity-related risks and negative impacts.

While targets associated with the Biodiversity Convention have been utilised within the private and public sectors for some time, the awareness of them amongst the general population has however been low when compared to climate change for instance. Moreover, the road to achieving these targets has also proved challenging. This is illustrated by a review conducted by the CBD in 2020, which highlighted that none of the targets set for the period of 2011–2020, known as the Aichi targets, were achieved in full (Secretariat of the Convention on Biological Diversity, 2020). Some countries and regions have made progress, and there are areas in which societies have succeeded to tackle some of the challenges, but overall the review notes that only six of the 20 Aichi targets could be considered to be partially achieved. As a whole, this report highlights the severity of biodiversity loss and associated weakening of ecosystem services, and hence repeats how urgent action is needed from both public and private sectors to reverse the trend of swiftly declining biodiversity and to keep the global goals and targets set in the Kunming-Montreal Global Biodiversity Framework within reach.

#### 11.3.1.2 The UN Sustainable Development Goals

We have discussed the UN Sustainable Development Goal's (SDGs) at various times throughout this book. While biodiversity is a topic that features in many of these goals through interconnections with various aspects such as climate change, no hunger and sustainable cities, for example, there are two goals specifically related to biodiversity: SDG 14 Life Below Water and SDG 15 Life on Land.

As the titles of these goals suggest, SDG 14 is concerned with the world's oceans and marine resources while SDG 15 focuses on terrestrial biodiversity, forests and desertification. These two biodiversity-related goals highlight the importance (and threat to) biodiversity on a macro/global scale, but they are also important at the national level with many governments reporting progress on biodiversity conservation drawing on the goals. The SDGs are also frequently referred to by organisations, as they provide a widely recognised reference point that can be drawn on in reporting or when discussing plans, policies and potential targets concerning biodiversity.

#### 11.3.1.3 The International Union for Conservation of Nature

Established in 1948, the International Union for Conservation of Nature (IUCN) is one of the world's biggest environmental networks, which is recognised as a major authority on global ecosystems and potential measures needed to safeguard them. It has been involved in the establishment of major international environmental agreements, including CBD mentioned above as well as the Convention on International Trade in Endangered Species (CITES), which is an international agreement between governments aiming at ensuring that trade of wild animals and plants does not threaten their survival.

IUCN is known as a comprehensive source of information on the global conservation status of animal, fungi and plant species. This information helps inform a range of conservation decisions, and it is widely used by governments, NGOs, educators and the business community also for other purposes. Amongst civil society and environmental groups, the IUCN is probably most well-known for its IUCN Red List of Threatened Species, or simply the Red List, which identifies those species at risk of extinction. The information provided by the IUCN, including the Red List, is also referenced by the Global Reporting Initiative (GRI) and European Sustainability Reporting Standards (ESRS) in their guidance for biodiversity disclosures discussed further below.

#### 11.3.1.4 The Intergovernmental Science-Policy Platform on Biodiversity and Ecosystem Services

The Intergovernmental Science-Policy Platform on Biodiversity and Ecosystem Services (IPBES) is an "independent intergovernmental body established by States to strengthen the science-policy interface for biodiversity and ecosystems services for the conservation and sustainable use of biodiversity, long-term human well-being and sustainable development" (IPBES, 2024). IPBES brings together expertise from the science and other knowledge communities to inform policies at all levels: governmental, society and private sector.

IPBES categorises its activities as falling into four functions: assessing knowledge on biodiversity and nature, strengthening the knowledge foundations, building capacity, and supporting policy (IPBES, 2024). An example of their work, featured on their website, is a study on pollinators, pollination and food production. Here they demonstrate how their science- and knowledge-based approach to understanding biodiversity and ecosystems is essential in informing policies to address this sustainability issue. Their focus on decision-making and the need for information in decision-making processes also signals the links to accounting and accountability as we discuss in this book.

## 11.3.2 Frameworks and initiatives on assessing and valuing biodiversity

As we have outlined, biodiversity and ecosystem services are important and of high value to humans and organisations. But what do we mean by value? Given the complexity of this issue, it has proven to be substantially more challenging to consider how biodiversity and ecosystem services should be assessed, measured and valued. We will next give an overview of a couple of significant initiatives which have sought to provide guidance and frameworks on how this could be done.

### 11.3.2.1 The Economics of Ecosystems and Biodiversity

The Economics of Ecosystems and Biodiversity (TEEB) is a global initiative focused on drawing attention to the economic benefits of biodiversity. The origins of TEEB are in the late 2000s, when the need for a global analysis of the economic significance of biodiversity was recognised by the environmental authorities of major governments. In particular, there was an interest in understanding how costly the loss of biodiversity would be, as well as what would be the cost of the failure to take protective measures when compared to the potential cost of effective conservation. That is, comparing the cost of conserving biodiversity to the cost of failing to do so.

The objective of TEEB is to highlight the growing cost of biodiversity loss and ecosystem degradation (TEEB, 2024). As the title of the initiative indicates, TEEB focuses on the economics of biodiversity and ecosystems, and as such involves measuring and valuing them. It is worth pointing out here that while TEEB has also provided guidance reports for business and enterprises, its work is now directed more to the macro level, through for instance helping to make more visible the relationship between natural capital and economic growth at the national/country level. One of the practical applications in this area is the System of Environmental Economic Accounting (SEEA), which is an internationally standardised framework for organising and presenting statistics on the environment-economy relationship. Overall, while the most active period of TEEB took place in the 2010s, the approach it promoted served as a catalyst for the development of subsequent initiatives. Similar themes are highlighted in the highly publicised *Dasgupta Review*, written by Professor Sir Partha Dasgupta, which focuses on the economics on biodiversity and discusses how we should account for nature in economics and decision-making (Dasgupta, 2021).

#### 11.3.2.2 Capitals Coalition

TEEB was an important stepping-stone for the establishment of the Natural Capital Coalition. First established in 2012 under the name TEEB for Business Coalition it was renamed the Natural Capital Coalition in 2014. In 2020, The Natural Capital Coalition was further developed, as it was united with Social & Human Capital Coalition to become Capitals Coalition, which continues to work with a broader remit.

The Capitals Coalition is a coalition of organisations – including businesses, accountancy firms and the professional, science and academic, finance, policy and conservation organisations – who share the common vision to broaden the basis on which decisions are made. This is outlined in their ambition statement: "by 2030 the majority of businesses, financial institutions and governments will include the value of all capitals in their decision-making and that this will deliver a fairer, just and more sustainable world" (Capital Coalition, 2025a). One of the key concepts for the Coalition is natural capital, which they define as "the stock of renewable and non-renewable natural resources that combine to yield a flow of benefits to people" (Capitals Coalition, 2025b). The Coalition runs projects, engages in a range of events and produces materials to assist organisations with understanding their impact and dependencies on natural, social and human capitals. The Coalition also has a Framework for Integrated Decision-making which focuses on the significance of considering how natural, social, human, and produced capital are interconnected.

As it comes to nature, an important activity of The Coalition has been the development and promotion of the Natural Capital Protocol. This protocol is essentially a decision-making framework which helps organisations to identify, measure and value their direct and indirect impacts and dependencies on natural capital. The Protocol draws on a number of existing measurement practices and guidance as it aims to broaden both the quantity and quality of natural capital information available. Such information is argued by the Coalition to be essential to allowing organisations to include important natural capital information in organisational decision-making and in processes such as the identification and mitigation of risk, supply chain and material sourcing and product design. From the perspective of accounting, it is relevant to note that the Protocol does not stipulate the choice of tools used for assessing, measuring and valuing natural capital. It also acknowledges limits to the comparability of these assessments. The Protocol and associated guidance do however encourage organisations to engage in measuring and valuing natural capital and biodiversity (often in monetary and/or physical terms). It is worth pointing out here that such practices are still widely debated, as we will discuss in more detail below.

The role of accounting is evident not only in the development and promotion of the Coalition and the subsequent Protocol (e.g. ICAEW is a founding organisation that hosted the scheme) but also in the explicit identification of the role of accountants in using their expertise relating to the measuring and reporting of information to help embed what has become known as natural capital accounting. Some very large and high-profile companies, such as Coca-Cola, Philips and Nespresso, have been involved with Natural Capital Accounting, and the approach has also been implemented by a range of public sector organisations, for example, Forestry England.

#### 11.3.2.3 Taskforce on Nature-related Financial Disclosures

The TNFD is one of the more recent initiatives on assessing and valuing biodiversity and nature in the organisational context. Drawing on the experiences of the climate-focused TCFD, the initiative to set up TNFD was announced in 2020 with the formal launch taking place in June 2021. TNFD is based on the understanding that societies and our economic systems are dependent on nature, biodiversity and the ecological services ecosystems provide. Further, the swiftly deteriorating state of the natural environment is seen to cause growing risks to business and finance across societies. As a market-led initiative, TNFD seeks to develop guidance that will help integrate nature into decision-making, and thereby not only reduce risks and create new commercial opportunities but also contribute positively to reducing and reversing the biodiversity and nature loss we are currently experiencing.

The core idea underlying the TNFD is that better information on nature-related issues makes it possible for businesses to assess nature-related risks and opportunities, and subsequently allow organisations and market participants to incorporate them into strategic decision-making, risk management and asset allocation. To achieve this, TNFD launched in 2023 a set of disclosure recommendations aiming at facilitating organisations to assess, report and act on their nature-related dependencies, impacts, risks and opportunities. Similar to TCFD, the underlying logic is that the availability of such information will have impacts on the capital markets with investors making use of the disclosures, thereby directing financial flows from nature-negative to nature-positive outcomes. Given the influence of the earlier TCFD on climate reporting (e.g. influencing both the IFRS and ESRS climate disclosure standards), we might anticipate a similar role for TNFD in the future as we recognise below.

### 11.3.3 Summary of key institutions and initiatives

As is evident from the above, there are a range of institutions and initiatives that attempt to govern biodiversity and its loss at the global and national levels. While they ultimately all seek to address biodiversity loss and promote conservation they do so in different ways. At times, the approaches overlap, while at others, they go in different directions. Take valuation for example: whether or not biodiversity is assigned with a quantitative or monetary value, and if so, how it is valued, is a key discussion point. We take a closer look at this in the next section where we discuss accounting for biodiversity and consider the practices applied by different organisations.

## 11.4 Biodiversity accounting and accountability practices

While biodiversity accounting practices have not been applied in organisations for as long as, for example, carbon accounting, there are a range of practices currently being undertaken. We provide an overview of some of these now, organising our discussion under three areas which capture much of the practices: reporting, recording and valuing.

### 11.4.1 Reporting biodiversity

Biodiversity reporting is a key way in which a wide range of organisations including governmental departments, cities, regions, NGOs and business organisations engage with accounting for biodiversity. We have discussed the role of the reporting function in relation to sustainability previously in the book, but to consider how it relates to biodiversity it is useful to recap why reporting is the focus of many accounting initiatives attempting to transition organisations towards sustainability.

Reporting is a core part of organisational accountability and stewardship. It is a key mechanism by which things are made visible. In relation to reporting on biodiversity, as well as more specifically on an organisation's impacts and dependencies on biodiversity and ecosystem services, reporting can allow both the report producer (the organisation or other reporting entity) and the reader of the report to understand impacts, dependencies, and relatedly, responsibilities and accountabilities. Similarly to sustainability reporting in general (see Chapters 5 and 6), much depends on how the reporting is conducted. Reporting frameworks and other guidance documents are therefore important.

#### 11.4.1.1 Biodiversity in reporting frameworks

The GRI biodiversity standard (GRI 101: Biodiversity 2024) features in total eight topic-specific disclosures, three of which focus on how the reporting organisation manages its biodiversity-related impacts, with the remaining five focusing on providing more specific information about those impacts. GRI also notes that the topic can also be relevant for disclosures based on other GRI Standards, such as those focusing on water and effluents, rights of indigenous people, and local communities. While the full list of these disclosures can be seen in the "Focus on practice" below, it is useful to acknowledge that these disclosures focus largely on biodiversity and the impacts organisation has on it, with ecological services featuring less. It is also worth noting that in the Standard, GRI makes references to and directs reporting organisations to consider guidance and recommendations provided by several organisations we have referred to above, such as the IUCN Red List on endangered species, the Natural Capital Protocol as well as the TNFD's guidance on assessing nature-related impacts and dependencies.

**Focus on practice: GRI 101: Biodiversity 2024**

GRI published a major revision update to its biodiversity disclosure standard in 2024, when GRI 101: Biodiversity 2024 replaced the earlier GRI 304: Biodiversity 2016. In this revision, the disclosures included in the Standard were updated and expanded. The Standard also aligns with the goals and targets included in the Kunming-Montreal Global Biodiversity Framework discussed in the beginning of this chapter. In the Standard, three disclosures focus on the managing of biodiversity-related impacts and five focus on providing further information the biodiversity-related impacts.

Disclosures included in the GRI 101: Biodiversity 2024 Standard:

- Disclosure 101-1 Policies to halt and reverse biodiversity loss
- Disclosure 101-2 Management of biodiversity impacts

- Disclosure 101-3 Access and benefit-sharing
- Disclosure 101-4 Identification of biodiversity impacts
- Disclosure 101-5 Locations with biodiversity impacts
- Disclosure 101-6 Direct drivers of biodiversity loss
- Disclosure 101-7 Changes to the state of biodiversity
- Disclosure 101-8 Ecosystem services

The EU reporting standards also include biodiversity disclosures. ESRS E4 Biodiversity and Ecosystems includes six disclosure requirements covering general disclosures, impact, risk and opportunity management and metrics and targets. Given the ESRS's double materiality approach, these include requirements relating to both the impact metrics (e.g. the impact that the entity has on biodiversity and ecosystem change) along with financial materiality in the form of assessing the potential financial effects from biodiversity and ecosystem-related risks and opportunities.

While the ISSB does not yet have a disclosure standard focused on biodiversity (instead being covered by IFRS S1), it is anticipated that it will only be a matter of time before one is released. This is especially due to the ISSB noting biodiversity, ecosystems and ecosystems services (BEES) as part of their 2024–2026 work plan where the topic is being researched and the necessity and feasibility for standards considered. In line with their financial materiality approach, we can anticipate the standard focusing on the financial related risks and opportunities to entities from biodiversity and ecosystem services. As above, we might expect the work of the TNFD to influence both the ESRS and IFRS standards in this area.

#### 11.4.1.2 Biodiversity reporting by various organisational types

Given the responsibilities of governments at the national level in relation to biodiversity and its protection (e.g. as outlined in the Kunming-Montreal Global Biodiversity Framework goals and targets discussed above), reporting on biodiversity is often found at the country level. These reports, sometimes entitled State of Nature, usually focus on a country's biodiversity, biodiversity "management" and conservation plans. Such reporting is often undertaken by government departments such as the Department for Environment, Food, and Rural Affairs (DEFRA) in the UK and the Department of Conservation (DoC) in New Zealand.

You will also find disclosures relating to biodiversity in the sustainability reporting of an increasing number of corporations and business organisations. However, it is by no means as common a practice than for instance reporting on carbon and climate change, as many organisations, including many large corporations, do not provide any information on their potential impacts and dependencies on biodiversity nor on their policies concerning it. Previous research discussed in our "Focus on practice" below notes how biodiversity reporting has been far from common, even amongst large corporations. While KPMG's last two surveys on sustainability reporting in 2022 and 2024 demonstrate an increasing awareness amongst large corporations, and a related increase in reporting, it is still not as common as one might anticipate given the seriousness of the issue and its potential effects on organisations. Furthermore, and in addition to concerns regarding the quantity of reporting for biodiversity, it is worth asking whether the quality of biodiversity reporting is what it potentially could and should be. In other words, is the biodiversity information provided by organisations in their reports helpful for those using the reports, including the organisation itself? We return to a discussion of this in the following section of this chapter.

**Focus on practice: Biodiversity reporting by large corporations**

> Almost half (49) of the Fortune 100 mentioned biodiversity in reports, and 31 made clear biodiversity commitments, of which only 5 could be considered specific, measurable and time-bound.
>
> *(Addison et al., 2019, p. 307)*

These were some of the main findings of research by Addison et al. (2019) published in the journal Conservation Biology and featured on the website of the Natural Capital Coalition. This research gives us insight into the practice of biodiversity reporting by some of the largest corporations in the world. And the results do not make for good reading.

Many companies, even large ones, did not provide information on their biodiversity impacts and dependencies. And, those that did provide a variety of different information on how they are managing impacts, restoring habitats or investing in biodiversity, for example. However, this research found that only nine companies provided quantitative indicators, which are arguably needed to assess the magnitude of their activities. Such quantitative indicators would be, for example, area of habitat restored as per the GRI disclosure standards.

Furthermore, this analysis of the Fortune 100 found that "no companies reported quantitative biodiversity outcomes". This, the authors suggest, makes it difficult to determine whether the actions of a business are sufficient to address its impacts.

The KPMG sustainability reporting surveys also shed light on biodiversity reporting by large corporations and changes in reporting practices. They also demonstrate the significant increase in attention and awareness of biodiversity amongst the world's largest companies. Indeed, they report (2024, p. 57) that the "proportion of companies which report on loss of biodiversity and nature as a risk to the business has doubled among the G250 companies from 28 percent in 2020 to 56 percent" in 2024. This doubling is also seen amongst the N100 group where the change is reported as growing from 23% to 49% over the same period.

We encourage you to look at some company reports and websites and see how they are reporting on biodiversity. Danone, Nissui and Unilever are three companies that could be called "best practice" reporters in the area. We encourage you to critically reflect on the practice. Consider what you learn from such reporting, and think about how it could be improved.

## 11.4.2 Recording biodiversity

The second aspect that we will discuss here relates to the processes and practices of recording biodiversity, which in simple terms is concerned with how we might go about recording what biodiversity exists. Recording biodiversity is related to the reporting of biodiversity discussed above as we must have some way of recording biodiversity to be able to report on it beyond general level policy statements and commitments. Furthermore, the recording of biodiversity is important as in order to protect biodiversity or understand biodiversity loss we need a system of knowing what the state (quantity and diversity) of that biodiversity is. Here, we can see a clear role for accounting and accounting expertise in relation to measurement.

Broadly speaking there are two approaches to the recording of biodiversity. These can be defined simply as bottom-up and top-down approaches (see Jones, 2014 for a detailed discussion). These two models of recording biodiversity differ substantially, but as there are examples of both approaches in practice, we briefly outline them here.

#### 11.4.2.1 The bottom-up approach to recording biodiversity

A bottom-up approach attempts to inventory the biodiversity in a particular place. A good example of this relates to the recording of biodiversity by local community groups, such as conservation and enthusiast groups. For example, think about birdwatching groups who record bird species and, in some locations, constitute a comprehensive source of information on bird populations and their trends. We noted above that the reporting of biodiversity often occurs at the national level with many governments worldwide reporting biodiversity within their country context. Biodiversity recording in such cases usually takes a bottom-up approach. At the international level, the most prolific and comprehensive recording of biodiversity is perhaps undertaken by the WWF, which records an array of biodiversity and thereby enables an understanding of possible changes taking place in biodiversity, including also the identification and follow-up of the status of those species that are at risk of extinction (see WWF, 2024). The Red List discussed above is also an attempt at recording biodiversity in this way.

From an organisation's perspective, it may be that engaging in recording biodiversity is best done in collaboration with a group with suitable expertise on the topic. While it might not be reasonable to expect an organisation's managers or employees to engage in recording biodiversity across all its operation sites, there are situations where this practice would be valuable or is needed. Let's consider an example here. A major production facility which discharges water into a shallow gulf nearby and has been identified as the key source of pollution in the area, resulting among other things in substantial loss of biodiversity, can be used for illustrative purposes. As the organisation decides to renew the facility and install new, state-of-the-art technology to clean up the discharges, it would likely be beneficial for it to engage in recording of biodiversity in the area. This would give the organisation first-hand knowledge of the potential benefits of its investment, and subsequently help it make decisions at its other operational sites with similar challenges. Likewise, recording and reporting on such information when the organisation's activities have impacts on a specific endangered species can be useful both the organisation and its stakeholders, as also discussed in GRI's biodiversity disclosure 101-7 Changes to the state of biodiversity.

#### 11.4.2.2 The top-down approach to recording biodiversity

The top-down approach to the recording of biodiversity takes a more ecosystems approach. Rather than building up an inventory of the biodiversity as noted in the bottom-up approach, the top-down approach starts at the level of an ecosystem and then seeks to record the different elements that make up that ecosystem. This top-down approach to recording biodiversity has the potential to help with understanding the biodiversity together with the interconnections which make up the system, and as such it can provide a much more holistic recording. However, it is also more complex. It is perhaps this complexity which means that it is far less evident in practice.

An approach developed by the World Business Council for Sustainable Development (WBCSD) referred to as the Corporate Ecosystem Valuation (CEV) framework is one example that takes such an approach. The CEV attempts to record biodiversity at the ecosystem level, it does so in relation to the organisation, and usually at the level of a single project, product or service. This means that only those aspects of the ecosystem that provide direct benefits to, or are impacted by, the organisation are attempted to be recorded. As such, an organisation utilising the CEV framework, for example a dairy company recording ecosystem dependencies and impacts in relation to their chocolate milk product, is unlikely to provide a comprehensive record of the ecosystem itself. Still, such recording is likely to lead to a greater understanding of the product's dependencies and impacts on the ecosystem, and hence probably be of value for the organisation.

## 11.4.3 Measuring biodiversity

The final aspect of biodiversity accounting practices that we discuss relates to measuring biodiversity. In order to both report on and record biodiversity we must have some way of measuring it. When it comes to measuring biodiversity there are again two main approaches that exist. The first is the use of a simple, usually numerical, count. The second is the "valuation" of biodiversity. Like in financial accounting, this valuation is often undertaken through monetisation, the placing of a monetary value on biodiversity or its ecosystem services. Each approach has advantages and disadvantages, which we will briefly introduce here. This aspect of accounting for biodiversity is also perhaps the most controversial and debated.

### 11.4.3.1 The numerical approach

The numerical or count approach to measuring biodiversity is simple and straightforward. Essentially what is required is the measuring of biodiversity through a simple count – for example, the noting of how many of each species exist. The WWF uses this approach when they, for example, note that only 1,860 giant pandas or 75 Javan rhinos currently exist in the wild (WWF, 2025). Organisations too can use it by noting, for example, how many of a particular species are located in the habitat affected by their operations or planned developments. Such measures are useful as they form a basis for understanding the amount and diversity of biodiversity that exists in general or at a particular context. At the same time, the usefulness of such information for decision-making can be limited. What does it mean, for instance, that there are now six fewer bird species living around a lake, or that there are 1,860 giant pandas in the wild? This disadvantage is perhaps most obvious, or at least most mentioned, within the business context. For businesses, this way of measuring biodiversity can lack relevance. This is one of the reasons why initiatives such as Natural Capital Protocol and TNFD prompt organisations to consider different ways of assessing the value biodiversity and ecosystem services have for them.

#### 11.4.3.2 The valuation approach

The second way in which biodiversity can be measured involves the valuing of biodiversity and/or its services. This measurement of value is often presented in monetary terms. Just like in other areas of accounting where a variety of things are recorded and valued in monetary terms (for example, buildings and property, patents, leases and human labour), a similar approach of monetising can also be utilised when it comes to biodiversity. Here, biodiversity or ecosystem services are translated into a commensurable measure – money. This approach to the measuring of biodiversity is argued to be more useful for decision-making, as it describes biodiversity with a comparable metric which decision-makers are already familiar with (see also Chapter 4).

Within organisational practices the valuation of biodiversity in monetary terms is most commonly seen in the ecosystem services approach discussed above, which looks at the monetary value of the ecosystem and the services it provides to the organisation. Here the question of whose perspective the value is determined from is made clear. That is, the value to the organisation is the key focus, instead of the value to society, the environment or the animal itself, for example.

To make this more concrete, let's consider one practical example we mentioned above, agriculture and pollination. Looking at the value from the organisation's point of view implies that the measurement is concerned with the value pollination provides to the organisation – or put another way, what would the cost to the organisation be if there were no natural pollinators (like bees and other insects) to perform the task. As you should be able to see, this does provide useful information. In most cases for an organisation operating in agriculture, it would be fairly evident that the value of natural pollinators is very high, or perhaps even that the organisation is outright dependent on this ecosystem service. Valuing biodiversity in this way would provide an organisation with a driver to ensure that the pollinators are protected. At the same time, there are also substantial challenges in such valuations, and while the results may appear to be precise and objective, hence apparently providing a solid basis for decision-making, in practice the results are often ambiguous and debateable, implying also that the decisions made on their basis can be contested.

In its Biodiversity Guidance aimed at supplementing the Natural Capital Protocol, the Capitals Coalition highlighted that an organisation should assess and understand the potential advantages and limitations related to the method used in biodiversity valuation (Capitals Coalition and Cambridge Conversation Initiative, 2020). While it was noted in the Biodiversity Guidance that monetary valuation can simplify decision-making and at times make it easier to assess the value of biodiversity alongside other social, economic and environmental considerations, the Capitals Coalition also emphasised that there are aspects of value in biodiversity which it is better to assess with other types of quantitative or qualitative approaches. In addition, in The Biodiversity Guidance, it is highlighted how an organisation should be transparent towards its stakeholders concerning the measurements used and their associated limitations, and it is also underscored how assessments used for internal decision-making should be accompanied with sensitivity analysis to describe how dependent the assessments are on the measurement approaches used.

## 11.5 Key debates surrounding biodiversity accounting and accountability

As we have begun to point out above and will highlight further in this section, biodiversity accounting and accountability is a challenging area. This is not uncommon though as we encounter similar questions in most areas of sustainability accounting and accountability. Indeed, it is hardly surprising that when we seek to extend organisational accounting, accountability and reporting into the interconnected terrain of sustainability, we come across new types of complexities and ambiguities that need to be dealt with. Moreover, while a lot of further development and consideration is still needed in the area, it does not mean that practical applications of biodiversity accounting and reporting should be placed on hold.

While continuing the work to develop the already-existing approaches as well as to create novel ones, it is important to consider some potential consequences of these emerging biodiversity reporting, recording and measuring practices. Below we consider some of the challenges and additional areas that we suggest you reflect on. Again, we divide our discussion into the three areas above, but acknowledge there are additional challenges not captured here. First however, we draw some insights from research addressing this point.

### INSIGHTS FROM RESEARCH: ACCOUNTING AND BIODIVERSITY CONSERVATION

In his commentary titled "Making Accounting for Biodiversity Research a Force for Conservation" Thomas Cuckston (2018) raises an important question. Amongst the rapidly rising number of academic journal papers studying accounting and biodiversity, which ones offer the most potential to develop into a force for conservation? Essentially, Cuckston (2018) highlights the need to consider what kind of research is being done and which approach is the most useful if we wish to address the issue of biodiversity loss, rather than just simply increase or alter accounting practices in the area.

Cuckston (2018) usefully classifies the biodiversity accounting research into two categories:

1. Those that focus on efforts to bring biodiversity into existing social and environmental accountability mechanisms. That is, those that take existing practices, like reporting, and apply these to biodiversity, e.g. extending disclosure indicators to include biodiversity.
2. Those that look at biodiversity conservation efforts and investigate the role of accounting in such efforts. These contrast with the above as the focus here, Cuckston argues, is on conservation first.

While this paper is useful for finding out more about what the research says about accounting and biodiversity, the commentary also provokes us to think about the content, intent and implications of our accounting practices in the area of biodiversity. For example, rather than assuming that reporting in itself is useful or will necessarily lead to improved conservation or positive biodiversity outcomes, Cuckston prompts us to think about what outcomes are needed and what type of reporting would be needed to help achieve these.

We suggest taking the time to read this commentary (at six pages of text it is quite short!). In addition to reflecting on what Cuckston argues in relation to biodiversity accounting, you might also find it useful to ask similar questions about the other topics in this book.

**Cuckston, T. (2018). Making Accounting for Biodiversity Research a Force for Conservation. *Social and Environmental Accountability Journal, 38(3),* 218–226.**

### 11.5.1 What constitutes good biodiversity reporting?

What constitutes good biodiversity reporting is far from clear. Experience from practice has shown that in organisations many reporting processes concerning just about any area can turn into so-called tick-box exercises. That is, they can involve an organisation simply making a disclosure without giving sufficient attention to what is being reported, how it is being reported, and perhaps most importantly why it is being reported. This is an important consideration in relation to biodiversity reporting.

Despite frameworks and guidance such as those presented above, the question of what constitutes "good" biodiversity reporting is still left unanswered. There also remain questions as to the overall value of such reporting, as well as to how far reporting can get us in addressing biodiversity loss and the sustainability challenge it presents. In a way, this is understandable given that biodiversity reporting has emerged alongside other areas of sustainability reporting and does not have an extensive history. At the same time, the urgency of the biodiversity crisis does not leave much time for errors. We need to know a lot more about biodiversity reporting and the role it has or could have in shaping the behaviour of both organisations and organisational stakeholders. The question remains, how does, or can, biodiversity reporting lead to accountability for biodiversity and biodiversity loss? On this point, Bebbington and colleagues (2024) maintain that having more information will not be enough to support nature-positive outcomes, and continue by arguing that disclosures need to be set within wider governance processes, through which companies are expected or nudged by state or other public and private institutions to reduce their impacts or even restore nature. It is clear however that there remains plenty of scope for organisations to improve both the quantity and quality of their biodiversity reporting practices.

Moreover, biodiversity reporting also raises some interesting and thought-provoking matters when it comes to sustainability accounting and accountability more broadly. We have noted that biodiversity accounting raises questions as to whether or not conventional accounting practices translate well into all areas of sustainability. We could here for example consider whether focusing on the conventional organisational entity provides us with sufficient information, or should we alternatively at times look into the networks of companies forming broad supply chains in sectors with high biodiversity risks and impacts, such as global fisheries (see Österblom et al., 2022). Likewise, as was the case with water discussed in the previous chapter, we might again ask whether organisations are in all cases the most useful entity for this type of accounting and reporting, and consider how other accounting "entities" are possible (Dey and Russell, 2014). Furthermore, as above, the recording of biodiversity by local or community groups also highlights the value of those other than the organisation in providing accounts, which we explore further next.

### 11.5.2 How complete are attempts to record biodiversity?

Despite the array of emerging practices and local, national and international initiatives that underpin them, the recording of biodiversity is far from complete. Such approaches, even the most developed, only capture and record a small amount of selected biodiversity or provide a limited recording of the ecosystem and its services.

Again, this is not surprising, given the difficulties of recording biodiversity. Biodiversity is complex, non-static (often seasonal) and requires specialist knowledge. In many cases, the recording of biodiversity relates to a specific species or species type rather than the biodiversity total in a particular location. For example, local birdwatching groups identified above can be a good source for the recording of a bird species or a number of bird species in an area but are unlikely to record any other flora and fauna. Governments often prioritise endemic or icon species which again means incomplete records. The bottom-up approach discussed above is however an interesting way to consider the role of accounting and how it can be extended to provide an account of biodiversity (Siddiqui, 2013).

What is clear from our brief consideration of both methods of recording biodiversity above is that they are, at present, significantly limited. Limitations arise from both a lack of resources and a lack of understanding. That is, no matter how resourced a group, organisation or government department is our knowledge of biodiversity and ecosystems is still limited, hindering our abilities to record. Christian (2014) takes up some interesting challenges and potential in relation to recording biodiversity. He raises the potential of volunteers and local conservation groups in building data on biodiversity and essentially providing accounts of biodiversity. The potential of this form of accounting in relation to the recording of biodiversity, what we have termed counter accounting in Chapter 8, is something useful to consider further. However, we must also consider how we record biodiversity. Does the measure we use record it in a meaningful way?

### 11.5.3 How should we value biodiversity?

As we discussed above, there are several approaches to the measurement and valuation of biodiversity. However, no approach is without its disadvantages and there is no agreement as to the "best" approach. It is an important issue for accounting for biodiversity and one which, like many others discussed in the swiftly developing area of sustainability accounting and accountability, remains far from resolved.

From an accounting perspective the practice of placing a monetary or financial value on biodiversity is an important one that has some support. Monetisation does come with many disadvantages, however. Some of these include abstraction, which means that the monetary value is removed from what is being measured. Furthermore, such valuation is difficult, if not impossible. How would you place a monetary value on, say, the giant pandas and Javan rhinos noted above? From whose perspective do we measure the value? And is it even morally appropriate to measure biodiversity in this way, particularly when we focus on sentient beings?

Valuation and markets are also used in other ways when it comes to biodiversity. For example, in the area of conservation market mechanisms are being trialled. Have you heard of Rhino Impact Bonds? These were well documented in the media in 2019 and are essentially an attempt to use financial instruments (in this case impact bonds) in conservation efforts relating to the black rhino, a species at risk of extinction. Biodiversity offsets are also one approach that is taken. Following the same logic as offsetting practices used in relation to climate, biodiversity offsetting is however much more complex and potentially even more debated (see Tregidga, 2013; Weir, 2019).

Overall, the valuation of biodiversity in monetary terms is a complex matter. Despite the challenges noted above, commensuration and monetisation of biodiversity can be seen as a way to help take biodiversity into account and appreciate its high relevance, and some advocates argue that it has substantial potential for being useful in decision-making (see Dasgupta, 2021). At the same time, monetisation is far from being a generally accepted and widely applied practice. As a comprehensive discussion of this complexity and the debate is well outside the scope of this chapter, we provide a brief summary in the "Pause and reflect" below and would encourage you to consider this important aspect of accounting for biodiversity further.

**PAUSE AND REFLECT...**

There are comprehensive and convincing arguments on both sides of the debate as to whether the placing of a monetary value on nature and biodiversity is the best way in which to measure and ultimately protect it.

Advocates, those who support the placing of a monetary value on biodiversity and ecosystem services, argue that nature/natural capital has value and that value needs to be captured so that it can enter into decision-making. They argue that pricing, valuing, monetarising, and financialising nature is often the best way to do this and focus on improving such practices to communicate the "value" of nature.

Critiques of the practice of valuing nature and natural capital are also well established. The most relevant for accounting are: the problematic nature of the values attached (from a moral as well as practical perspective); the problem with putting the natural world into the financial system and its effects such as unbundling ecosystems rather than considering them as a holistic coherent system; problems with tradability, power and control of valuation; and the recognition that putting a "price on nature" does not necessarily change the relationship between people and nature and can lead to solidifying power of people over nature. Critics also note that this approach to environmental issues has failed in the past – for example, carbon emissions trading schemes discussed in Chapter 9, which are relatively simple compared to biodiversity!

Take a moment to reflect on what your view regarding the monetary valuation of biodiversity is. As this might be a challenging question, it is potentially helpful to consider it through a practical example. You could, for instance, think about how valuable a particular species in a region is if there are abundant populations around the world, and whether you think this value changes if this particular region is the only place this species resides.

### 11.5.4 Summary of key debates

While the development of biodiversity reporting, recording and measuring practices may be driven by a concern to understand and/or protect biodiversity, they may nonetheless lead to problematic outcomes. For example, while reporting on the cute and cuddly (e.g. the panda or polar bear) might have broad appeal, can you envisage a corporate report on cockroaches and soil? Yet the latter might have similar, or greater, biodiversity importance within a particular ecosystem. If the reporting, recording and measuring focuses on the cute and cuddly, does it also mean that the policies and practices end up being geared towards those species, potentially at the expense of some others that would arguably be more significant from the perspective of the ecosystem?

## 11.6 Conclusion

In this chapter, we have discussed accounting for biodiversity. We have highlighted why biodiversity is a key sustainability issue and how it is related to organisations and accounting. We have identified the existence of a large number of initiatives relating to biodiversity and ecosystem services, and how both organisational practices and knowledge relating to accounting for biodiversity are developing at pace. However, we have also identified how these practices are contested. This is perhaps the result of the complexities related to biodiversity and how we might account and be accountable for it, as well as of the topic having received less attention in practice, public discussion and research compared to other sustainability topics, such as climate change. Still, moving forward biodiversity and its loss will, due to its significance, fundamentally change the relationship between organisations and nature. It is therefore a topic that warrants further consideration and attention as we develop the best ways and approaches to account for biodiversity and its conservation.

## Note

1 For example, Jones (2010) outlines six impediments that prevent conventional accounting from being appropriate for environmental and social accounting – all of which are relevant in relation to accounting for biodiversity. He notes: (1) capitalist orientation; (2) business focus; (3) reliance on neo-classical economics; (4) numerical quantification; (5) monetary dependence; and (6) technical accounting practices.

## References

Addison, P., Bull, J. and Milner-Gulland, E. (2019). Using Conservation Science to Advance Corporate Biodiversity Accountability. *Conservation Biology*, *33*(2), 307–318.

Atkins, J. and Atkins, B. (eds) (2016). *The Business of Bees: An Integrated Approach to Bee Decline and Corporate Responsibility*. Greenleaf.

Bebbington, J., Blasiak, R., Larrinaga, C., Russell, S., Sobkowiak, M., Jouffray , J-B. and Österblom, H. (2024). Shaping Nature Outcomes in Corporate Settings. *Philosophical Transactions of the Royal Society B*, *379*, 20220325.

Capitals Coalition (2025a). Our Ambition. https://capitalscoalition.org/the-coalition/our-ambition-capitals-coalition/ (accessed 10 May 2025).

Capitals Coalition (2025b). The Capitals Approach. https://capitalscoalition.org/capitals-approach/ (accessed 10 May 2025).

Capitals Coalition and Cambridge Conservation Initiative (2020). Integrating Biodiversity into NaturalCapitalAssessments.https://capitalscoalition.org/wp-content/uploads/2020/10/Biodiversity-Guidance_COMBINED_single-page.pdf (accessed 26 February 2025).

Ceballos, G., Ehrlich, P. R., Barnosky, A. D., García, A., Pringle, R. M. and Palmer, T. M. (2015). Accelerated Modern Human–Induced Species Losses: Entering the Sixth Mass Extinction. *Science Advances, 1(5)*, e1400253.

Christian, J. (2014). Accounting for Biodiversity: A Deep Ecological Perspective. In Jones, M. (ed.), *Accounting for Biodiversity*, pp. 124–145. Routledge.

Convention for Biological Diversity (CBD) (2024a). Introduction. www.cbd.int/intro/ (accessed 28 November 2024).

Convention for Biological Diversity (CBD) (2024b). Targets. https://www.cbd.int/gbf/targets (accessed 28 November 2024).

Convention for Biological Diversity (CBD) (2024c). 2050 Goals. https://www.cbd.int/gbf/goals (accessed 26 February 2025).

Cuckston, T. (2018). Making Accounting for Biodiversity Research a Force for Conservation. *Social and Environmental Accountability Journal, 38(3)*, 218–226.

Dasgupta, P. (2021). *The Economics of Biodiversity: The Dasgupta Review*. HM Treasury.

Dey, C. and Russell, S. (2014). Who Speaks for the River? Exploring Biodiversity Reporting Using an Arena Approach. In Jones, M. (ed.), *Accounting for Biodiversity*, pp. 245–265. Routledge.

IPBES (2024). Home. https://ipbes.net (accessed 28 November 2024).

Jones, M. (2010). Accounting for the Environment: A Theoretical Perspective. *Accounting Forum, 34(2)*, 123–138.

Jones, M. (ed.) (2014). *Accounting for Biodiversity*. Routledge.

KPMG (2024). *The Move to Mandatory Reporting. Survey of Sustainability Reporting 2024*. Available at https://kpmg.com/xx/en/our-insights/esg/the-move-to-mandatory-reporting.html (accessed 17 December 2024).

Lamont, T. A. C., Barlow, J., Bebbington, J., Cuckston, T., Djohani, R., Garrett, R., Jones, H. P., Razak, T. B. and Graham, N. A. J. (2023). Hold Big Business to Task on Ecosystem Restoration. *Science, 381(6662)*, 1053–1055.

Österblom, H., Folke, C., Rocha, J., Bebbington, J., Blasiak, R., Jouffray, J.-B., Selig, E. R., Wabnitz, C. C. C., Bengtsson, F., Crona, B., Gupta, R., Henriksson, P. J. G., Johansson, K. A., Merrie, A., Nakayama, S., Ortuño Crespo, G., Rockström, J., Schultz, L., Sobkowiak, M., Søgaard Jørgensen, P., Spijkers, J., Troell, M., Villarrubia-Gómez, P. and Lubchenco, J. (2022). Scientific Mobilization of Keystone Actors for Biosphere Stewardship. *Scientific Reports, 12*, 3802.

Robertson, M. (2017). *Sustainability: Principles and Practice*. Routledge.

Secretariat of the Convention on Biological Diversity (CBD) (2020). Global Biodiversity Outlook 5. www.cbd.int/gbo/gbo5/publication/gbo-5-en.pdf (accessed 26 February 2025).

Siddiqui, J. (2013). Mainstreaming Biodiversity Accounting: Potential Implications for a Developing Economy. *Accounting, Auditing and Accountability Journal, 26(5)*, 779–805.

TEEB (2024). Home. https://teebweb.org/ (accessed 28 November 2024).

Tregidga, H. (2013). Biodiversity Offsetting: Problematisation of an Emerging Governance Regime. *Accounting, Auditing and Accountability Journal, 26(5)*, 806–832.

UN (1992). *Convention on Biological Diversity*. UN.

Weir, K. (2019). The Logics of Biodiversity Accounting in the UK Public Sector. *Accounting Forum, 43(3)*, 348–379.

WWF (2024). *Living Planet Report 2024 – A System in Peril*. WWF, Gland, Switzerland. https://livingplanet.panda.org/ (accessed 10 May 2025).

WWF (2025). Home. https://support.wwf.org.uk/ (accessed 10 May 2025).

## Additional reading and resources

Bebbington, J., Cuckston, T. and Ferger, C. (2021). Biodiversity. In Bebbington, J., Larrinaga, C., O'Dwyer, B. and Thomson, I. (eds), *Handbook on Environmental Accounting*, pp. 377–387. Routledge.

CBD (2020). Business Reporting on Biodiversity. www.cbd.int/business/projects/reporting.shtml (accessed 20 October 2020).

Feger, C. and Mermet, L. (2022). New Business Models for Biodiversity and Ecosystem Management Services: Action Research with a Large Environmental Sector Company. *Organization & Environment*, *35*(*2*), 252–281.

Feger, C., Mermet, L., Vira, B., Addison, P. F. E., Barker, R., Birkin, F., Burns, J., Cooper, S., Couvet, D., Cuckston, T., Daily, G. C., Dey, C., Gallagher, L., Hails, R., Jollands, S., Mace, G., McKenzie, E., Milne, M., Quattrone, P., Rambaud, A., Russell, S., Santamaria, M. and Sutherland, W. J. (2018). Four Priorities for New Links between Conservation Science and Accounting Research. *Conservation Biology*, *33*(*4*), 972–975.

Garel, A., Romec, A., Sautner, Z. and Wagner, A.F. (2024). Do Investors Care about Biodiversity? *Review of Finance*, 28(4), 1151–1186.

Gray, R. and Milne, M. (2018). Perhaps the Dodo Should Have Accounted for Human Beings? Accounts of Humanity and (Its) Extinction. *Accounting, Auditing and Accountability Journal*, *31*(*3*), 826–848.

Russell, S., Milne, M. and Dey, C. (2017). Accounts of Nature and the Nature of Accounts: Critical Reflections on Environmental Accounting and Propositions for Ecologically Informed Accounting. *Accounting, Auditing and Accountability Journal*, *30*(*7*), 1426–1458.

CHAPTER

12

# Accounting for human rights

Human rights are the fundamental rights and freedoms to which all humans are entitled (UN, 1948). You perhaps cannot get more of an important social issue than human rights as it goes to the heart of values of freedoms and justice and, in relation to the central themes of this book, sustainability and accountability. Human rights issues are broad and cross-cutting. A close look at the sustainable development goals (SDGs), for example, shows that many of the goals identified relate to, or intersect with, human rights. Furthermore, and as we will outline in this chapter, human rights are an important issue for organisations and the relationship between human rights and organisations is complex.

In this chapter, after briefly defining human rights, we focus our discussion on aspects central to organisations, accounting and accountability. We discuss several human rights protection organisations and regulations that operate at both the global and organisational level before turning our attention to current accounting and accountability practices. Having considered contemporary practice, we seek to reflect on the limits of current practice and consider how accounting might develop or change to better address human rights violations and organisational accountability issues relating to human rights.

By the end of this chapter, you should:

- Be able to define and have an understanding of human rights.
- Understand why human rights considerations are important to organisations and accounting.
- Be aware of the governance regimes which operate at global and organisational levels in relation to human rights.
- Be aware of some current accounting and accountability practices in relation to human rights.
- Have a critical awareness of the limits of current practices and how they could be advanced.

DOI: 10.4324/9781003533207-15

## 12.1 Human rights

As noted above, human rights relate to the basic rights and freedoms to which all humans are entitled. As outlined in the Universal Declaration of Human Rights (UDHR), human rights consist of both civil and political rights and economic, social and cultural rights. Civil and political rights include, for example, the right to life, liberty, and property; freedom of expression; pursuit of happiness; and equality before the law. Economic, social and cultural rights include the right to participation in science and culture, the right to work and the right to education. While some reading this book may take these rights for granted, it is important to reflect critically on the nature of human rights and consider them as a sustainability issue, and in particular given the focus of this book, as an issue with relevance for organisations and accounting.

The UDHR is a key document outlining human rights. Drafted by representatives from across the world, the Declaration was proclaimed by the UN General Assembly in 1948. The UDHR sets out the fundamental human rights to be universally protected. It does so through 30 statements or "Articles". For example, the beginning of Article 1 of the UDHR reads, "All human beings are born free and equal in dignity and rights" (UN, 1948, p. 2).

When prompted to think about human rights you might first think of instances where someone's rights are clearly being taken away. For example, a situation where the right to free speech or political or religious freedom is not possible, or where practices such as forced labour and human trafficking are taking place. It can be too easy to consider these from a Western perspective, which can bring one to assume that human rights are something that happens elsewhere, for example, the Global South. When taking this perspective, you can too easily consider the issue of human rights to be disconnected from your daily life. However, as we will demonstrate, human rights abuses are happening globally. We encourage you to pause and reflect now on both global and local human rights issues.

**PAUSE AND REFLECT ...**

It might be useful at this early point of this chapter to pause and reflect on your own awareness and understanding of human rights. This includes the issues that you are most aware, and perhaps interested in. In doing this, we encourage you to consider both global and local human rights issues.

What thoughts/images does reference to human rights prompt? We mention some of the global issues above in the text, but there are likely to be more local, even personal ones, that are important to make connections with. For example, while global in relevance, local experiences with human rights issues may include rights associated with LGBTQI+, Black Lives Matter (BLM) and climate justice.

Many human rights issues that you may have considered are directly relevant to organisations, and perhaps particularly so for organisations with global supply chains.

Indeed, while the issue of the rights of individuals has been a consideration of all societies there have been several issues or events, especially relevant to the organisational context, that have brought the issue of human rights into the spotlight. We discuss three such issues here in this chapter: Rana Plaza, modern slavery and conflict minerals. We however do so recognising that they are only three issues/ events that are relevant, and many more could have been included.

### 12.1.1 Rana plaza

The collapse of an eight-storey commercial building, Rana Plaza, which killed over 1,000 people and left many more injured in Bangladesh in 2013, was a key moment which exposed human rights issues and, specifically, made visible how human rights issues are intertwined with global corporations and their supply chains.

The Rana Plaza building was part of Bangladesh's large ready-made garments sector, a sector that accounts for some 80% of the country's total export revenue and employs over 4 million people (ILO, 2023). The global supply chain of which workers in the Rana Plaza building were part of also meant that the disaster was not solely a Bangladesh disaster, although they clearly were the most affected. Should the workers have mainly been serving the local markets, there sadly may have been less international attention. With Rana Plaza, however, the global connections became particularly evident when the building was found to house the manufacturing workshops of labels such as Mango and Primark. As pictures of company clothing labels appearing in the rubble of the building were spread by the global media, Rana Plaza came to be recognised as a symbol of the price being paid for low-cost fashion.

In the aftermath of the disaster, many started paying attention to a range of alarming issues that had been part of the daily life of those working at Rana Plaza, including known safety concerns, health hazards, and otherwise poor working conditions. While Rana Plaza was primarily an issue regarding the rights of workers to safe working environments, the tragedy also exposed issues surrounding exploited workers. This takes us to the core of our next issue.

### 12.1.2 Modern slavery

A related human rights issue of increasing interest and significance is the question of *modern slavery*. It is particularly relevant to organisations as it relates to the relationship between the worker/employee and their employer. Someone is considered to be in slavery if they are: forced to work (through coercion or mental or physical threats); owned or controlled by an employer (again through mental or physical abuse or the threat of abuse); dehumanised, for example treated as a commodity or bought or sold as "property"; and/or physically constrained or have restrictions placed on their freedom of movement (Anti-slavery, 2025). Slavery is explicitly covered in the UDHR through Article 4.

Modern slavery might seem distant at first, since it tends to take place somewhat hidden from the public eye. Examples are numerous, however. Think about some restaurants which employ chefs brought in from abroad. The employee might be in a highly vulnerable position, without any networks, knowledge of the local language, or understanding of how the society works. Moreover, the employee may have had to pay something up front to receive the work, in addition to which the employer may have taken away the employee's passport, purportedly to ensure that the employee stays committed for a particular period. In such situations, the hallmarks of modern slavery are often present: the employee is essentially forced to work, for instance as their passport or ID has been confiscated by their employer, is prone to mental abuse, as they do not have connections, is dependent on the employer, and is likely to encounter restrictions on movement or otherwise, as the employer does not want the person to talk with anyone.

Modern slavery is a human rights issue that affects nearly all countries and contexts. However, most commonly, slavery affects people and communities who are vulnerable to being taken advantage of. Facts and figures reported on the International Labour Organization (ILO) website (see "Pause and reflect" below) identify the stark global numbers in relation to this issue. Modern slavery and the human rights abuses it relates to are connected with organisations, their accounting systems, and also have accountability dimensions. We discuss these further below. Meanwhile, we introduce our third illustrative human rights issue spanning the modern economy, conflict minerals.

**PAUSE AND REFLECT ...**

Let's take some time to stop and consider the extent of modern slavery globally. Figures from the ILO (2022) outline the issue through a stark list of facts.

- At any given time in 2021, an estimated 49.6 million people are in modern slavery, including 27.6 million in forced labour and 22 million in forced marriage.
- It means there are 6.3 victims of modern slavery for every 1,000 people in the world.
- Out of the 27.6 million people trapped in forced labour, over 17 million people are exploited in the private sector such as domestic work, construction or agriculture; 6.3 million persons in forced sexual exploitation; and 3.9 million persons in forced labour imposed by state authorities. There are more than 3.3 million children in forced labour.

Global figures are thus substantial. But what does this mean at the local level? Consider the area where you live, the restaurants you eat at, and the various services offered by businesses. Do you think that you could find examples of forced labour, modern slavery or human trafficking in the community? Why/why not? How would your community compare with other towns, regions or countries in this matter? What would be the potential reasons for these differences?

### 12.1.3 Conflict minerals

Many of our modern-day devices such as mobile phones, laptops, gaming stations and jewellery rely on a number of core minerals in their manufacture. Four key minerals are Cassiterite, Columbite-tantalite, Wolframite and Gold, with the three first used to extract Tantalum, Tin and Tungsten, respectively. One, if not the, key region where these minerals are found is in the Democratic Republic of Congo (DRC) and bordering African countries. Several campaigns by NGOs and other civil society groups have been successful in exposing the conditions within which these minerals are being mined. Issues such as forced labour, child labour, human rights abuses and revenues being used to purchase weapons all feature in the industry. Given this, the term *conflict minerals* has been coined to refer to the mining of these minerals in these conditions.

It should be clear that conflict minerals are another example of where human rights issues are at the fore. And again, you are likely to be seeing how this is relevant to organisations, although perhaps a narrower type of organisation, that is electronics and other manufacturers reliant on these minerals in their supply chain. It is also an example of how many human rights issues are unknown or hidden in product supply chains. Were you aware of this issue before reading this? While it is a relatively well-known and long-understood issue, some of you reading this, some of you on your phones, tablets or laptops, are also now likely to be considering the minerals that appear in your devices. How this affects accounting, and has led to particular accounting regulation, is returned to below.

### 12.1.4 Introduction to human rights summary

It is important to restate that the threats and challenges to human rights do not just occur in certain parts of the world, although it is also important to recognise that there are parts of the world where human rights abuses are more shocking and urgent. Human rights are central to the achievement of a sustainable environment, society and economy and as we have mentioned human rights concerns underlie many of the SDGs introduced earlier in the book. The Rana Plaza disaster, modern slavery and conflict minerals discussed here and the human rights issues they expose lead to questions as to the responsibility, and related accountability relationships that result, of organisations at all levels (e.g. government organisations as well as business organisations) and our responsibility as consumers and citizens. We suggest the latter should not be underplayed as the role we can play as citizens (political power) and consumers (purchasing power) is key and likely to be a major (perhaps the only) way in which changes can be brought about. We return to the role of the consumer later after a consideration of the issue in relation to organisations and their systems of accounting and accountability.

## 12.2 What have human rights got to do with organisations and accounting?

As should be clear from the above discussion and our selected examples, human rights issues have considerable relevance for organisations. While there are obviously important moral obligations for organisations in the protection of human rights that require highlighting, we can also identify economic and commercial reasons.

### 12.2.1 Organisational impacts on the rights of humans

While there are, in most contexts, legal duties written into national law which underpin the protection of human rights, there can be instances where these fall short, or are ineffective, in protecting human rights in the workplace. There are expectations on business to be accountable for their impact on human rights. Business organisations can affect the human rights of their employees and contract workers, their customers, workers in their supply chains, communities around their operations and end users of their products or services. Quite simply, they can have an impact – directly or indirectly – on virtually the entire spectrum of internationally recognised human rights.

While such accountabilities for human rights exist for all businesses, they are particularly important when global supply chains exist and when the operations along the supply chain are either located in geographical locations where human rights abuses are known to occur or where conditions are not "visible". Think about the global fishing industry, in which problems of forced labour, human trafficking and other forms of human rights abuse are severe, as workers end up in vulnerable positions on board fishing vessels, often operating in the high seas with limited governance structures overseeing the practices. Further, while it might be more obvious to you that a company with a supply chain that includes countries where child labour is a concern needs to consider human rights, these issues are not isolated solely to these companies. For example, there has been increasing attention on modern slavery within several European countries with concerns in sectors such as the agriculture and hospitality sectors – for example, pickers, hotel and restaurant staff – as cases similar to what we described above have emerged.

In addition, in today's economy, work is increasingly being outsourced. Some of this outsourcing occurs locally. This outsourcing or "contracting out" can create distance between the organisation and the employees through, for example, leaving the hiring of workers and the conditions of their contracts to the contracting company. These forms of arrangements can "hide" human rights concerns. Consider the construction industry where such contracting arrangements are common. While a company might have the overall contract for a construction project, it may only have very few, if any, employees involved in the construction itself. Instead, it organises the project by contracting out aspects of the work. In addition, these contractors may in turn themselves engage subcontractors and so forth. These forms of working relationships can mean that the worker on the building site may be far removed from the company in charge of the project, which is likely not involved in establishing the employment arrangements of contractors and subcontractors. These arrangements raise interesting questions as to the responsibility and accountability of those involved, in particular the responsibility and accountability of the company at the top of the employment chain.

### 12.2.2 Human rights and organisational risk

Like several other topics we have discussed, human rights also represent risk and reputation issues for organisations. Consider the examples above. Fashion outlets that had their clothing manufacturing at Rana Plaza found themselves under immense scrutiny after the tragedy, electronics companies who rely on minerals which may be sourced under conflict are at risk of reputational damage, as too are companies found to be engaged in forced labour, knowingly or not.

The increasing attention on notions of decent and fair work (including but not limited to modern slavery) as well as a range of human rights issues related to the environment – including the increasing claim that corporations, through knowingly causing climate change, are breaching our fundamental human rights – make it an issue of key contemporary concern globally. And as we have identified, human rights issues are not just an issue for companies in, or with operations located in, countries in the Global South. Human rights are an issue for all organisations in all countries.

## 12.3 Human rights protection organisations and regulations

As one would expect, given the nature and fundamental importance of human rights, there are a large number of organisations and various regulations that aim at both promoting and protecting human rights. These are an important part of the context within which organisations and accounting operate. We next outline some key global organisations and thereafter focus on those particularly relevant for the focus of this book, accounting and accountability.

### 12.3.1 The United Nations

The most significant international institution in the promotion and protection of human rights is the United Nations (UN). The UDHR introduced above sets out the fundamental rights to be universally protected and forms the basis on which the majority of discussions surrounding human rights are framed. In addition, the UN has the protection of human rights at the core of its work across all its activities. We briefly introduce three aspects of the UN and its focus on human rights most pertinent to sustainability accounting and accountability.

#### 12.3.1.1 The UN Guiding Principles of Business and Human Rights

Perhaps the most relevant of the UN activities and oversight to organisations and accounting is the UN Guiding Principles of Business and Human Rights. These Guiding Principles are often referred to as the Ruggie Principles or the Ruggie Framework after Professor John Ruggie, who served the UN as a Special Representative for Business and Human Rights in the late 2000s. In his role, Ruggie was tasked to advance discussions concerning the relationship between business and human rights. Ruggie proposed the principles in 2008, and they were later endorsed by the UN Human Rights Council.

The Guiding Principles on Business and Human Rights are a set of guidelines for both states and corporations and make clear that all companies have a role to play in respecting human rights through responsible operations and respecting all relevant national and international laws and standards. They apply to all states and businesses regardless of such things as size, ownership, sector and structure. The Guiding Principles are based on the three pillars of protect, respect and remedy (see "Pause and reflect" below).

**PAUSE AND REFLECT...**

The UN Guiding Principles of Business and Human Rights set the landscape for how business organisations should consider human rights in their operations.

The UN Guiding Principles are grounded in recognition of (UN, 2011, p. 1):

a. States' existing obligations to respect, protect and fulfil human rights and fundamental freedoms;
b. The role of business enterprises as specialised organs of society performing specialised functions, required to comply with all applicable laws and to respect human rights;
c. The need for rights and obligations to be matched to appropriate and effective remedies where breached.

While these three pillars of protect, respect and remedy may seem abstract and somewhat distant from actual business decisions at first, recognising the Guiding Principles has tangible implications on how businesses plan their activities, operate in multiple contexts and make decisions concerning their own employees and various stakeholder groups.

Take a moment to consider what the UN Guiding Principles mean for businesses. You could for instance do a quick internet search to find out whether there has been press coverage concerning potential human rights violations and modern slavery within the country you live in. One area you might look at is the farming industry providing fruits and vegetables. There are several examples across the world showing how labour-intensive agriculture is often dependent on migrant workers, who are often undocumented and in a highly vulnerable position (see Ruiz-Ramírez et al., 2024).

Once you have familiarised yourself with the setting, you could consider the case and agriculture more broadly in light of the three pillars highlighted above. Is there a reason to doubt that the state has respected and protected human rights and fundamental freedoms in the case? Do the companies involved appear to have complied with all applicable laws and respected human rights? Are there attempts to remedy potential human rights breaches, and if so, what kind of implications would such remedies have for the industry, the companies, the operations and the products in question?

McPhail and Ferguson (2016) discuss the UN Guiding Principles of Business and Human Rights and consider their relevance for accounting. They identify that the Guiding Principles represent a "potentially significant" shift in the context within which accounting operates and note that the second pillar of the principles, which outlines that corporations have a responsibility to respect human rights, is particularly important. Still, McVey and colleagues (2023) have pointed out that even though the Guiding Principles have been in place for over a decade, actual corporate practices in this area remain poorly understood, while highlighting that human rights practices in corporate contexts are likely to include negotiations and compromises despite the binding nature of the Principles. We further discuss the role of accounting in this task in the next section of this chapter.

#### 12.3.1.2 The International Labour Organization

The second UN institution we look at here is the ILO, the remit of which is more specifically at the level of the workplace. The founding of ILO in 1919 relates closely to the creation of the League of Nations, the UN's predecessor, the objective of which was the establishment of universal peace. It was however perceived that universal peace can only last if it is based on social justice. As workers were at the time widely exploited across industrialised nations, it was in the pursuit of social justice considered important to form an international institution, the ILO, which would bring together governments, employers and workers in seeking to enhance working conditions and remove hardship. Today, the ILO is a UN agency, which sets international labour standards to advance social justice and promote decent work in the workplace. A key document from the ILO is the Declaration on Fundamental Principles and Rights at Work.

Adopted in 1998, and subsequently amended in 2022, the ILO Declaration commits member states to respect and promote principles and rights in five categories:

freedom of association and effective recognition of the right to collective bargaining, the elimination of forced and compulsory labour, the abolition of child labour, the elimination of discrimination in respect of employment and occupation, and a safe and healthy working environment (ILO, 2025). The original Declaration included the first four categories, while the category of safe and healthy working environment was added in 2022. The ILO Declaration makes clear that these rights are universal and apply to all people in all states regardless of the level of economic development. Mention is also made of groups with special needs, including the unemployed and migrant workers. Importantly, the Declaration recognises that economic growth alone is not sufficient to ensure equality, social progress and to eradicate poverty.

#### 12.3.1.3 The UN Sustainable Development Goals

More recently, human rights issues have been highlighted by the UN in the SDGs. While there is no specific goal on the protection of human rights, it is a cross-cutting issue across the goals, featuring in particular in the targets underlying them. For example, goals relating to poverty, hunger, inequalities, climate and decent work all relate to the issue of human rights. Indeed, several of the targets listed under Goal 8 Decent Work and Economic Growth explicitly mention forced labour and modern slavery. For example, Target 8.7 reads:

> Take immediate and effective measures to eradicate forced labour, end modern slavery and human trafficking and secure the prohibition and elimination of the worst forms of child labour, including recruitment and use of child soldiers, and by 2025 end child labour in all its forms.

As child labour clearly has not been eradicated within the aspired timeframe, the work for achieving these targets continues. Indeed, a review of the SDGs in their entirety demonstrates that human rights are a key consideration within the goals.

### 12.3.2 OECD Guidelines for Multinational Enterprises

Alongside UN, another significant international institution in the context of human rights is the OECD. Specifically, The OECD Guidelines for Multinational Enterprises on Responsible Business Conduct which have an important role in the global sphere. The Guidelines have been multilaterally agreed on by governments and include recommendations to multinational enterprises concerning responsible business conduct. In essence, these non-binding Guidelines spell out how governments expect multinational businesses to carry out their operations. The Guidelines were first established in 1976 and have been regularly updated since. The most recent revision was published in 2023 (OECD, 2023). Human rights have featured more prominently in the Guidelines since the 2011 revision, which also aligned the Guidelines with the UN Guiding Principles on Business and Human Rights discussed above. The most recent updates of the Guidelines in 2023 emphasise the need for organisations to pay specific attention to potential adverse impacts on vulnerable individuals and groups, which could include human rights defenders and indigenous people, and highlight that enhanced due diligence is needed when operating in the contexts of armed conflicts or heightened risks of gross abuses.

The Guidelines cover a range of topics relevant for responsible business conduct, such as consumer rights, bribery and taxation, and they are considered to be a significant international document from the perspective of global governance of businesses in the area of human rights. The Guidelines emphasise that enterprises should follow them in every country they operate in, and, for instance, avoid causing or contributing to adverse human rights impacts, put in place a policy commitment to respect human rights, and carry out appropriate human rights due diligence processes to identify and address potential human rights issues and impacts (OECD, 2023).

### 12.3.3 Governments and national laws

As noted, governments and international and national legal institutions have responsibilities relating to human rights. This responsibility includes the business and other organisational responses to human rights as it is the duty of the state to set and enforce obligations from national treaties into domestic law. National laws therefore include various and differentiated protections against human rights abuses by businesses. Labour laws, health and safety laws, and non-discrimination laws in the workplace are some examples. We not only outline two further examples relating to the phenomena we illustrated above but also remind you that these are just two of many such examples.

#### 12.3.3.1 Modern slavery acts

As modern slavery has received increasing international attention in recent years, governments have taken action to revise their legislation on the topic. As a result, several dedicated acts have emerged globally relating specifically to modern slavery. The California Transparency in Supply Chains Act, which came into force in 2012, is often mentioned as a pioneering example. It requires large manufacturers doing business in California to be transparent regarding their actions to eradicate slavery and human trafficking in their supply chains. On a national level, one of the firsts was the UK's Modern Slavery Act which came into effect in October 2015. The Modern Slavery Act requires companies in England and Wales with turnover in excess of £36 million to ensure that slavery and human trafficking is not taking place in their business and supply chains. The act requires companies to disclose a statement on human trafficking signed by one of the company directors. This brings about a lot of implications for the corporation and the accounting function. Similar acts exist elsewhere such as in Australia, whose Modern Slavery Act came into effect in 2018.

In the EU, the EU Parliament approved in 2024 the Forced Labour Regulation, covering the import of goods and the trade of goods within the EU, as well as the Corporate Sustainability Due Diligence Directive (CSDDD), which requires companies to conduct effective human rights and environmental due diligence on their supply chain. While these requirements continue to be the target of intensive lobbying and political debate, they are nonetheless expected to have implications on modern slavery as they are being transposed to national legislations by 2026 and become applicable through a staggered approach by 2029. We will return to the accounting and reporting implications of these regulations in more detail below.

#### 12.3.3.2 Conflict minerals regulation

In the United States, the Dodd-Frank Act 2010 (or, in full the Dodd-Frank Wall Street Reform and Consumer Protection Act) was passed in response to the 2008 global financial crisis. The Act represented a significant change to financial regulation in the United States. While the Dodd-Frank Act affects many aspects of financial regulation, one key area in relation to human rights is the required disclosure related to conflict minerals, the issue discussed above. The Dodd-Frank Act contains disclosure requirements for companies in relation to their operations in conflict zones and includes a requirement that companies using gold, tin, tungsten and tantalum make efforts to determine if those materials came from the Democratic Republic of Congo (DRC) or an adjoining country and, if so, to carry out a "due diligence" review of their supply chain to determine whether their mineral purchases are funding armed groups in eastern DRC. The rule requires companies to report publicly on their due diligence and to have their reports independently audited.

In Europe, the EU Conflict Mineral Regulation came into effect in 2021. The regulation covers the same minerals and focuses on similar issues as the Dodd-Frank Act discussed above, requiring all EU importers to ensure that the minerals they are dealing with have not been produced in ways which fund conflicts or other related illegal practices. The regulation draws on the OECD guidance on conflict mineral trade, and includes requirements on risk management, independent third-party auditing as well as regular reporting on supply chain diligence.

### 12.3.4 International NGOs

There are many NGOs, social groups and other organisations established to address human rights abuses globally. Many such groups focus on the promotion of human rights in general, as well as on seeking to flag human rights abuses or events and conditions prone to human rights violations. There is however also one additional defining feature for human rights work, which relates to some of the civil and political rights included in the Declaration of Human Rights, such as freedom of expression and equality before the law. There are numerous historical and contemporary examples of situations where governments have not tolerated dissidents or people with otherwise strong views opposing the governing political party or ruler, and as a result have imprisoned or otherwise silenced individuals for their views. In such cases, it is often uncertain that the individual receives a fair trial or is treated equally before the law. International human rights organisations have over the years brought numerous cases to international knowledge.

Amnesty International is a long running and probably the most well-known international organisation focusing on protecting and educating around human rights. Amnesty International seeks to maintain full independence from governments, political ideologies, economic interests or religions, and hence they for instance do not accept any funds for human rights research from governments or political parties. Another well-known international example is the Human Rights Watch, which in its human rights work focuses on governments, armed groups and businesses. Like Amnesty International, Human Rights Watch also refuses government funding and emphasises how it reviews all other potential donations to ensure the independence of its work. In addition to these two, several other major international NGOs, such as Oxfam International, include human rights work within their remit.

### 12.3.5 Summary of human rights protection organisations and regulations

There are a range of various international- and national-level organisations and frameworks operating within the area of human rights. We have mentioned just a few above. These organisations and regulations are major drivers of accounting and accountability processes and practices as they form the context which they relate within, and in many ways respond to.

## 12.4 Accounting for human rights practices

Within the context discussed above, especially the regulatory context, there has been an increase in the number of organisations accounting for human rights or recognising potential accountabilities for human rights and their protection. However, it should be recognised that such practices are not widespread nor as developed as they are in some of the other sustainability aspects we have discussed in the earlier chapters. At the same time, it is necessary to acknowledge that many accounting practices can have significant indirect or direct implications on human rights.

In this section, we will outline some of the key aspects of organisational practices relating to human rights. As with the other topics discussed in the book, we encourage you to critically reflect on both the potential, as well as the limits of the current practices discussed. For example, do current practices enable organisations to be held accountable for their human rights impacts?

### 12.4.1 Accounting for human rights

Human rights is a challenging question for accounting. After all, we may end up asking questions such as: how do you account for humans? Is it possible to measure how human rights are being taken care of? Can you put a quantitative figure or perhaps even a monetary value on human rights? This is not to say that accounting does not have anything to do with human rights. It most certainly does. But the role of accounting is not as obvious as it is with regard to, say, climate and water, as we discussed in the previous chapters.

One of the reasons for this relates to how human rights abuses, violations and incidents tend to take place in the shadows. Consider for instance modern slavery, typical for which is that employees in vulnerable positions might not have formal contracts and oftentimes receive their (low and irregular) pay in cash payments. This implies that such contracts and payments do not show in the formal accounts. Similarly, in global supply chains, production can be outsourced to illicit shadow factories, run with forced labour working in inhuman and unhealthy conditions. In other words, an organisation may need to consider how it accounts for something that may remain hidden, and hence which it might have no information about. As such, accounting features in a different role when it comes to considerations of human rights, as we may, for instance, need to pay more attention to what is not there, or perhaps compare whether some aggregate figures and ratios appear to be within the range that one would expect. Such questions may fall under the remit of management accounting, human rights due diligence or assurance, for example, as we will discuss in more detail in the following section.

This is not to say that there would not be a need for any indicators for human rights. This is also highlighted in Principle 20 of the UN Guiding Principles on Business and Human Rights, which reads

"In order to verify whether adverse human rights impacts are being addressed, business organisations should track the effectiveness of their response. Tracking should: (a) be based on appropriate qualitative and quantitative indicators; (b) Draw on feedback from both internal and external sources, including affected stakeholders".

The reporting frameworks we will return to below provide some guidance for organisations. Focusing specifically on human rights, The UN Guiding Principles Reporting Framework aims at helping companies communicate how they are working with the topics included in the UN Guiding Principles of Business and Human Rights. Moreover, the Global Reporting Initiative (GRI) disclosure standards approach human rights through indicators on training, investments and operations which have undergone human rights reviews or impact assessments, while the EU's European Sustainability Reporting Standards (ESRS) reporting requirements include a range of indicators and datapoints on incidents, policies and corporate practices.

As the significance of human rights for businesses and their supply chains has become more widely acknowledged, there is also an increasing amount of additional guidance available for organisations on such indicators. Some examples could include a number of potential human rights incidents, figures on contracts including human rights clauses, as well as information on regular visits to organisations and facilities in the supply chain. There is also the potential that human rights implicate substantial financial risk for the organisation, and hence it can at times be necessary to consider such potential economic consequences in the financial reporting. It is perhaps worth noting, however, that as International Sustainability Standards Board (ISSB) was in 2024 setting priorities for its research programme on further disclosure standards, human rights were considered but eventually left out for a potential inclusion at a later stage. Elsewhere, following in the footsteps of Task Force on Climate-related Financial Disclosures (TCFD) in the realm of climate change, a group of major public and private organisations established in late 2024 the Taskforce on Inequality and Social-related Financial Disclosures (TISFD), which is set up to develop recommendations and guidance to assist businesses and financial institutions in understanding and reporting on their impacts, dependencies, risks and opportunities related to people.

### 12.4.2 How accounting can enhance accountability for human rights

As we noted above, the fact that human rights issues and violations often take place in the shadows hidden from the public eye sets challenges for organisations in terms of how they can identify potential situations that should be paid attention to. While obviously there are also companies which knowingly take part in human rights violations or questionable practices due to profit motivations, most organisations try to keep their house in order and follow good practices. Nonetheless, there are regular news stories about incidents in which human rights abuses are shown to have taken place in the supply chains of major organisations. Usually, the company highlights how they are committed to human rights and follow best practices and the highest available standards. Still, issues such as complex global supply chains, outsourcing and vigorous cost-cutting can make an organisation more prone to human rights risks. Moreover, even if the organisation was not aware of some illicit actions taking place far beyond its own organisational boundaries, it can still be considered to be accountable for such violations.

#### 12.4.2.1 Human rights due diligence

One of the central features of the UN Guiding Principles on Business and Human Rights is the expectation that business enterprises carry out human rights due diligence processes to help identify, prevent, mitigate and account for their adverse human rights impacts. This requirement also has direct relevance to corporate accountability, reporting and auditing, as having proper and effective due diligence processes requires engaging with and reporting on these issues on an ongoing basis.

In addition to asking for due diligence, The UN Guiding Principles provide companies with guidance on how human rights due diligence processes can be carried out. A key aspect here is that due diligence should focus on both actual and potential adverse human rights impacts. This means that while it is important that a company seeks to remedy any actual impacts, it is equally significant that effort is put into preventing or mitigating any potential future impacts. Adverse human rights impacts are often caused by structural issues, and hence such risks can potentially be tackled (or made worse) more effectively by decisions taken at the earlier stage of an investment process or forming of a supplier contract. The UN Guiding Principles also acknowledge that it may at times be beyond the capabilities of a large enterprise to conduct comprehensive human rights due diligence processes across all their functions, contracts and value chains. In such situations, it is noted that the organisation should aim at setting out general policies on human rights, and focus its resources on carrying out careful due diligence processes in specific operations, contracts or geographical areas, which are considered to have the highest risk for potential and actual adverse human rights risks. In addition to the UN Guiding Principles, organisations can also draw on OECD Due Diligence Guidance for Responsible Business Conduct (OECD, 2018), which provides guidance for conducting due diligence processes on such topics and illustrates the practical relevance of following UN Guiding Principles and other key recommendations.

While the UN Guiding Principles on Business and Human Rights have broad support, the expectations are nonetheless primarily recommendations, and hence it is up to the corporations as to how, and to what extent, they engage with the Principles. While the Principles emphasise that carrying out comprehensive due diligence processes is important from a risk management perspective, and hence provides clear benefits for the organisation, it is evident that engagement with and continuous development of such processes in some companies is partial or non-existent. The reasons for this may be various, such as fear of rising costs, lack of knowledge, or even outright ignorance.

Stepping beyond recommendations, the EU CSDDD establishes a duty for companies to identify and address adverse human rights and environmental impacts of their actions, no matter whether they occur within or outside the EU. In addition to their own operations, organisations were originally required to also consider their subsidiaries and business partners across their global value chains. Set to become effective in a staggered approach by the end of 2020s, this regulation is currently estimated to apply to some 6,000 large EU companies, which have more than 1,000 employees or over 450M EUR turnover worldwide, as well as to some 900 non-EU companies, which have at least 450M EUR turnover within the EU. While SMEs are not directly within the scope of this regulation, such smaller organisations both inside and outside the EU could be affected indirectly should they be part of the value chain of larger entities. It should be noted however that alongside other regulatory elements of the EU Green Deal, the requirements included in the CSDDD continue to be the target of intensive lobbying and political debate, demonstrated by the so-called omnibus proposal European Commission adopted in February 2025. Seeking to simplify EU rules in the name of competitiveness and more favourable business environment, the proposal for instance introduced a delay to the implementation of the CSDDD requirements as well as suggested limiting the extent of due diligence requirements on corporate supply chains to organisations' direct business partners. These amendments illustrate the complex relationships between politics, business, sustainability and economy.

#### 12.4.2.2 Accountants, accounting functions and human rights

Accounting practices can be helpful in diminishing the potential of human rights violations occurring both inside the organisation's boundaries and in its supply chain. An obvious example here relates to internal and external auditing functions. By building up rigorous internal processes regarding supply chains and outsourcing, an organisation can enhance the information it has concerning these activities. The accounting function can play a key role in terms of developing sufficient information systems as well as in collecting and assessing the information. It may well be, however, that in this area, companies could benefit from collaboration with other groups or organisations that have more expertise on human rights or context-specific local knowledge of cultural and social practices. Such knowledge is useful when trying to identify potential high-risk suppliers or areas where human rights violations are more commonplace.

Accountants are also in a good position to use their data-management skills to identify potential irregularities in the information received from suppliers or other organisations with regard to contracts, offers or production reports. In seeking to reduce human rights risks it can be helpful to scrutinise any such information from the perspective of whether the presented pricing information, time commitments or other details raise questions or appear irregular. For instance, such information may show that a supplier commits to delivering an order with a price, the achievement of which would not be possible if the workers were provided fair compensation. If such a situation emerges, the organisational managers may be presented with a decision juxtaposing short-term financial gains with broader accountability for human rights. Therefore, the managers would be in a better position to make the decision should there be clear human rights policies in place indicating how the organisation reacts to and deals with potential human rights issues.

From a different perspective, an organisation should be aware whether its own management systems, incentive structures and accounting practices increase its vulnerability to be exposed to human rights risks. To provide a simple example, putting a supplier under pressure in terms of tight production schedules and low price together with strict penalties for late delivery is likely to increase risks.

Moreover, such situations can be accentuated by internal organisational policies. Consider a situation where the bonus compensations of business group managers are dependent on reaching a very fast schedule or achieving high profit margins. Such accounting practices may create incentives for managers to bypass human rights considerations when attempting to improve their performance on other metrics. As such, in addition to having human rights policies and commitments in place, an organisation may benefit from setting up active processes monitoring internal processes to ensure that such counter-productive incentives do not take over.

### 12.4.3 Human rights reporting and disclosure

As with many sustainability issues discussed in this book, reporting and disclosure has been a key focus of accounting and accountability for human rights. This is perhaps not surprising, given the context discussed above which signals that legislation and guidance reveals a strong preference for reporting and transparency as a way to address various human rights problems relating to organisations. The focus on disclosures and the reporting function highlights the important role that accounting plays in accountability relationships and also the important link between transparency and accountability. Accounting is a key way in which transparency can be achieved as to an organisation's human rights obligations and practices and a key basis in which accountabilities are identified and recognised. However, such reporting can be problematic. We will next discuss the various reporting practices before returning to a discussion of some of the limits of this practice in the next section.

#### 12.4.3.1 Sustainability reporting frameworks

As the most widely used global sustainability reporting framework, the GRI provides important guidance which affects accounting and reporting practices in this area. In the GRI Standards, the human rights disclosures are spread out across several disclosure standards, such as those focused on labor, child labor, human rights assessments and occupational health and safety. In several of these standards, the more detailed topic-specific disclosures relate both to an entity's operations as well as to employee training. This implies that the GRI's reporting guidelines cover both the entity's exposure and involvement in activities which may involve human rights issues in their operations as well as their actions and policies ensuring that staff are aware of and familiar with human rights issues and responsibilities. If you consider this in relation to the materiality discussions we presented in previous chapters, it is evident that for some entities these issues are highly material.

Many of the human-rights disclosures currently included in the GRI Standards (GRI 401–418) date back to an update that took place in 2011. As we have discussed in this chapter, substantial developments have since taken place in the governance of organisations' human rights practice, with the UN Guiding Principles together with its associated reporting framework as well as the OECD Guidelines becoming key reference points globally. Accordingly, when the GRI updated their Universal Standards in 2021, they included a requirement that all organisations using the GRI Standards are expected to report following the intergovernmental expectations for human rights due diligence set by the UN and OECD, which we discussed above. Moreover, the GRI has been undertaking a major review and development project of its labor-related Topic Standards, which includes not only updating the topic-specific disclosures but also to make them aligned with revised Universal Standards, which now have the human rights-based approach and due diligence at their core. GRI's approach to require all organisations to report following the guidance and expectations set by the UN and OECD underscores how human rights are an important consideration for all organisations, no matter whether these questions are specifically identified to be material.

Human Rights are also present in other reporting frameworks. Similarly to the GRI, the EU's ESRS framework aligns closely with the UN Guiding Principles on Business and Human Rights and the OECD Guidelines for Multinational Enterprises on Responsible Business Conduct. The Standards highlight how human rights are relevant across all four social reporting standards, ESRS S1 Own workforce, ESRS S2 Workers in the value chain, ESRS S3 Affected communities, and ESRS S4 Consumers and end-users, and include disclosure requirements in each of them. In SASB, Human Rights are included under several disclosure topic categories, but such items are only considered material for selected industries. As we noted above, the ISSB has thus far not included human rights as an explicit priority in its development of reporting standards, although reporting about them might be applicable through the IFRS S1 General Requirements for Disclosure of Sustainability-related Financial Information should they be considered sufficiently material. The issue of human rights, therefore, highlights how the selection of reporting frameworks can affect organisational disclosures.

#### 12.4.3.2 The UN Guiding Principles Reporting Framework

The UN Guiding Principles Reporting Framework has been developed to bring the topics included in the UN Guiding Principles of Business and Human Rights into corporate communication and practice (Shift/Mazars, 2015). The framework has intentionally been designed to be straightforward and easily approachable. It contains 31 questions touching on areas such as public commitment, impact assessment and tracking of performance, including detailed and practical questions such as "What kinds of human rights issues are discussed by senior management and by the Board, and why?" and "How does the company know if its efforts to address each salient human rights issue are effective in practice?" To keep the threshold low and encourage companies to report on human rights, a company can start following the guidance by replying at the minimum to eight of the questions. Despite companies often following some of the general sustainability reporting frameworks discussed above, you can still see firms referring to the UN Guiding Principles Reporting Framework in their disclosures, illustrating the continued relevance of the UN Principles.

The UN Guiding Principles Reporting Framework also includes guidance in regard to what organisations should take into account when being attentive to and managing human rights risk, as well as subsequently providing information about human rights to stakeholders. The underlying logic here is that companies should "know and show" how they take human rights into account and respect them in practice. In addition to providing guidance to reporting organisations, the framework also includes guidance for assurance providers on how companies' human rights reporting and performance could be evaluated.

### 12.4.3.3 Regulated reporting practice on specific human rights topics

Alongside the broader sustainability reporting framework presented above, dedicated legislation on modern slavery and conflict minerals has affected how organisations are reporting on their human rights policies and practices. This is evident when looking at the various examples from practice of companies reporting according to various legislations.

Marks & Spencer for example produced a modern slavery statement. Their 2023/2024 statement (2024), running 16 pages, is published in accordance with the UK's Modern Slavery Act 2015 and outlines the steps taken by the company to prevent modern slavery and human trafficking in its business and global supply chain. Likewise, Apple produces alongside its environmental report and supplier responsibility report, a specialised disclosure report on conflict minerals (Apple, 2024). This report, available online, responds to the requirements of the US Securities and Exchange Commission (SEC) on the issue of conflict minerals. In Australia, Christ et al. (2019) analysed modern slavery disclosures before the Australian Modern Slavery Act was passed in 2018. They found that some companies were voluntarily disclosing various aspects and interestingly suggested that required modern slavery disclosures from other overseas Acts were related to the voluntary practices in Australia. This demonstrates how local reporting practices can be influenced by global practices.

While reporting practices have been developing, organisations may have been unsure how they should respond to the requirements set in some of the recently introduced legislation. Responding to the developing legislative context, and likely also in response to the demands of the profession seeking to understand how to operationalise the Modern Slavery Act in the UK, the Institute of Chartered Accountants in England and Wales (ICAEW) has actively engaged in the conversation regarding how modern slavery bears relevance for accounting and the accountancy profession, including releasing guidance and viewpoints on what a slavery and human trafficking statement should include (see the "Focus on practice" below). They have identified a range of information a company could include when preparing their reports.

**Focus on practice: What should the slavery and human trafficking statement include?**

"Mainly, organisations must state the steps they are taking to eliminate slavery from their organisations and supply chains, even if this equates to no steps taken, all eligible organisations must publish a statement. The statement should demonstrate a commitment to tackling slavery, exploitation and coercion under its remit.

The following six areas must be covered:

- Organisation structure and supply chains
- Policies in relation to slavery and human trafficking
- Due diligence processes
- Risk assessment and management
- Key performance indicators to measure the effectiveness of steps being taken
- Training on modern slavery and trafficking

> These six areas are a guideline, and the quality of the information presented should evolve over time. Any modern slavery risks that have been identified and mitigated should be disclosed, as well as prioritised in order of most dangerous risk, instead of evaded to avoid detection."
>
> Source: ICAEW (2022)

### 12.4.4 Summary of accounting for human rights practices

In summary, much of the current practice relating to accounting for human rights involves reporting. This relates to the focus of accounting on transparency and the reliance on transparency bringing about accountability. While reporting on human rights is not as widespread and developed as the practices are with some of the other areas of sustainability, it is likely that we will continue to see more focus on reporting on human rights issues as they continue to get more attention and regulation expands into more countries and regions. However, flexibility inherent in the reporting frameworks as well as the considerations we have presented above in regard to accounting and accountability for human rights highlight the potential limits of expecting increased transparency to deliver accountability. So, while it is encouraging to see more legislation and reporting practices relating to accounting and accountability for human rights, there is still a lot that needs to be done to address this issue. This is perhaps also evident in a number of public rankings which seek to complement organisational self-reporting. For example, the Corporate Human Rights Benchmark published by the World Benchmarking Alliance, can potentially serve as a public medium which puts organisations' human rights policies, processes, and practices under increased scrutiny and transparency.

## 12.5 Developing human rights accounting and accountability practices

There can be little doubt that human rights issues are fundamentally important for today's societies and organisations. However, despite the increase in practices relating to accounting for human rights, these practices are far from comprehensive or widespread. While awareness of human rights issues as they relate to corporations, and indeed all organisations, has grown, assisted by the UN Guiding Principles, the SDGs and the OECD Guidelines, there is still much left to be resolved. There also exists an important discussion as to the adequacy of conventional accounting, and current sustainability accounting practices, in addressing the human rights agenda. We will next outline some of the questions we need to consider going forward. To assist us in this discussion we turn to the accounting research on the topic of accounting and accountability for human rights. We do so as, in the context of limited practice, researchers help to highlight areas of relevance and raise important questions relating to the topic.

### 12.5.1 Will better reporting and greater transparency improve human rights?

As we have noted, various accounting practices in organisations can have implications on how human rights are considered both within the organisation's legal boundaries as well as in its supply chain. Still, they do not feature that prominently in discussions concerning accounting and human rights. Instead, much of both organisational practice as well as the recent legislation introduced in different contexts focuses on improving the reporting and disclosure on human rights.

The question that should be asked here then is how far does reporting for human rights ultimately take us? Does the preparation of reporting frameworks, such as the GRI, ESRS or the UN Guiding Principles Reporting Framework, indicate that organisations are now providing more and better quality information on human rights to their stakeholders? And even if they are, what are the implications? Do stakeholders act differently based on such disclosures? Consider for instance the examples we mentioned above, Marks & Spencer's modern slavery disclosures and Apple's conflict minerals report, prompted respectively by the UK Modern Slavery Act and the US Dodd-Frank Act. Which stakeholders are following such disclosures, and how is such information potentially influencing their decisions? Alternatively, we could ask whether the preparation of such public information on human rights, together with the fact that someone might be using it, has an impact on the organisation itself, i.e. do practices change as a result of such disclosures?

You may recall similar questions raised in the earlier chapters. Indeed, these are relevant considerations throughout sustainability accounting and accountability. Still, they might be more manifest in the realm of human rights than they are with carbon, water and biodiversity. One of the reasons for this relates to potential challenges in measuring and quantifying the human and social aspects of sustainability. It is easier to measure carbon emissions or water flows than it is to assess, quantify and potentially monetise how well human rights have been taken care of. At the same time, a substantial amount of research has over several decades highlighted the challenges related to corporate reporting. For instance, as long as companies have flexibility, some of this through operationalising the materiality concept, with regard to what, how much, and in which way they are reporting, it is unlikely that they offer open and comprehensive accounts of the challenges they may have encountered. Likewise, even if there is legislation stipulating certain disclosures as mandatory, it is unlikely that all organisations comply if such requirements are not actively enforced and monitored, including having public sanctions for any shortcomings.

**PAUSE AND REFLECT...**

In the early part of this chapter, we identified the important role of the citizen and consumer when it comes to human rights as they apply to organisations. It is perhaps a good time to take a moment to pause and reflect on this further through considering the question "How, if at all, are your own consumption habits influenced by the issue of human rights?"

You could draw on many areas to highlight this point: the food you eat, the hospitality venues you might visit, for example. But let's take the two issues that we have drawn on throughout this chapter: the clothes you wear and the technology you purchase.

Fashion: Would you stop buying clothes from a particular company if you knew there were likely human rights abuses in the supply chain? Has the discussion in this chapter made you stop and consider the companies from which you purchase your clothes from?

Technology: How concerned are you about the potential use of conflict minerals in your technology products? Again, does it make you rethink your purchasing behaviour, perhaps buying less (for example upgrading less often) or purchasing more ethical options (e.g. a Fairphone)?

You might like to take a few moments to look online and see what your fashion label or technology company of choice says about human rights. Do they report on the negative or potential negative impacts of their practices on human rights? Or do they simply write a vague commitment statement? Do they provide information you require as a consumer to understand the issue and to make an informed purchasing choice?

As we have highlighted throughout this chapter, many of the practices relating to accounting for human rights seek to make these issues transparent and to outline how an organisation is responding. But, an important aspect is also what consumers do with that information.

### 12.5.2 Reporting boundaries and accountability

As we have emphasised throughout this chapter, for many organisations human rights issues take place beyond the organisation's own boundaries. We have noted this as particularly true for organisations with complex supply chains spanning multiple countries. Here, we are again facing the question of how far does an organisation's responsibility reach? Or, in other words, how far beyond the entity's boundary can an organisation be considered to be accountable?

Think about fast fashion, for example, a topic which Antonini and colleagues (2020) focus on in their research. The business model within fast fashion is such that it appears no major high street retailer or internet store produce any of the goods themselves. All the products are acquired from a network of suppliers, in many cases residing across the globe. Furthermore, the supply chain network consists of multiple tiers, with some companies acting as wholesalers, others producing the clothes, some making the fabrics and so forth. While all of these suppliers are independent in the sense that they can themselves technically decide how they treat their workers, the actions of a major buyer have substantial implications. A buyer can, for instance, require that all its suppliers follow certain human rights practices or use external certification to ensure particular policies. On the other hand, the buyer can also, as noted above, demand fast delivery with a low price, creating pressure for the supplier to cut corners where possible. As such, it should be clear that a major buyer often exercises at the very least informal control over its suppliers, and hence should be held accountable for what happens in the supply chain.

Now, the question then becomes how is this portrayed and discussed in an organisation's sustainability report. The due diligence expectations and reporting requirements, as presented by the UN Guiding Principles, OECD Guidelines, GRI and ESRS, underscore the significance of identifying and addressing adverse impacts occurring across the organisation's value chains. Despite this, it is worth asking whether a given organisation accepts responsibility of the supply chain in earnest, even if those suppliers are technically outside the formal organisational boundary, or does it actively seek to distance itself from those suppliers? An organisation can in its sustainability report highlight that it follows high ethical principles, but at the same time emphasise how it is unable to control its suppliers since they are outside the organisation's control. We are therefore facing the question, who should be held responsible for the potential human rights impacts in the supply chain?

### INSIGHTS FROM RESEARCH: THE (NON)ACCOUNTING FOR VARIOUS HUMAN RIGHTS

Accounting research helps us identify areas where it is important to consider how accounting and accounting practices intersect with human rights. There are various areas that we could have included in our discussion, however we have chosen to feature four research papers that discuss labour rights, human welfare, and the rights of indigenous people.

Cooper et al. (2011) focus on a specific human right related to the workplace – "the right to work in a safe environment". They analyse a case study of an industrial accident and outline how we might account for human rights differently. They outline how current accounting is not sufficient for accounting for health and safety and suggest alternative ways – including the provision of multiple accounts – that is, accounts from the corporation as well as a public account from the health and safety authority. This research demonstrates how in sustainability accounting, and when considering accountability relationships that exist between organisations and various stakeholder groups, it is useful not only to consider the accounts of corporations or business organisations but also the accounts of other organisational forms and individuals.

Also interested in the context of the workplace, Yang and colleagues (2021) take on the topic of wage theft. Drawing on a case study from Australia, they illustrate how the issue of wage theft affects "industrialized as well as developing economies". The story in their paper is an interesting one – a university student who unknowingly started a resistance movement and a national debate on the topic of wage theft, in particular amongst precarious workers. These authors highlight the role that accounting plays both in concealing exploitation as well as helping workers enforce their rights. Linking again with discussions of counter accounting from Chapter 8, they also highlight important human rights issues relating to exploitation in the workplace.

Prem Sikka (2011), a prominent accounting author and public commentator who writes on many aspects of human rights, asks among other things whether traditional accounting principles such as going concern, accruals, consistency, prudence, entity, historical cost and other reporting methods are capable of responding to concerns for human welfare. While he recognises that sustainability reporting is one way in which corporations have responded and may facilitate more discussion of human rights, he does question whether or not reporting is a useful practice to enable citizens to confirm corporate claims. Again, this takes us back to some of the concerns we have highlighted with regard to the nature of sustainability reporting here in this chapter as well as earlier in the book. Sikka calls for a reconsideration and critical scrutiny of many accounting principles and practices which are often taken for granted and considered to be neutral and objective in societies.

McDonald-Kerr and Boyce (2020) provide an overview of how accounting has both historically and in contemporary settings been intertwined with colonialism, and how it has had and continues to have impacts on indigenous peoples in various contexts. They highlight how accounting practices have served in governing and controlling indigenous people, and also in creating and strengthening particular ways of thinking about different groups. One prominent example of this is how accounting relates to the ideas of possession and ownership, and subsequently how accounting practices have played a role in the colonisation of indigenous peoples and their lands, with further implications on indigenous cultures through marginalisation and disempowerment. While some may consider colonialism as a phenomenon of the past, McDonald-Kerr and Boyce (2020) highlight how accounting, as well as ideas associated with it, continues to feature in the at times problematic relationships between governments, businesses and indigenous peoples in contexts such as Canada, Australia and Alaska.

**Cooper, C., Coulson, A. and Taylor, P. (2011). Accounting for Human Rights: Doxic Health and Safety Practices – The Accounting Lesson from ICL. *Critical Perspectives on Accounting, 22*, 738–758.**

**McDonald-Kerr, L. and Boyce, G. (2020). Colonialism and Indigenous Peoples. In Edwards, J. R. and Walker, S. P. (eds), *The Routledge Companion to Accounting History*, pp. 553–577. Routledge.**

**Sikka, P. (2011). Accounting for Human Rights: The Challenge of Globalization and Foreign Investment Agreements. *Critical Perspectives on Accounting, 22*(8), 811–827.**

**Yang, D., Dumay, J. and Tweedie, D. (2021). Accounting's Role in Resisting Wage Theft: A Labour Process Theory Analysis. *Accounting, Auditing and Accountability Journal, 34(1)*, 85–110.**

### 12.5.3 Summary of questions concerning accounting for human rights

Along with a consideration of the limits of reporting, and in particular the reporting boundaries, the research discussed here involves considering the role that accounting and accountability research can play in "giving visibility to the plight of the marginalised people and showing the social cost of corporate profits" (Sikka, 2011, p. 824). This would seem important, given that much of the concern relating to accounting and accountability for human rights relates to the power that corporations and other large organisations have and how this can mean that human rights abuses or concerns remain "hidden".

Research we have considered above highlights the current limits of accounting for human rights in the workplace and calls for different forms of accounting. Engaging with such questions helps us to understand the links between human rights accounting and accountability. Some of this discussion also relates to considering who should provide the account, as an organisational account does not necessarily suffice in this context. For example, an account could be provided by the employees, health and safety authorities, indigenous communities or NGOs. There are interesting connections here to what was discussed in Chapter 8 where we considered the practice of counter accounting. It is hence perhaps a useful time to reflect on what we consider to be accounting, who we identify as the account provider, and how these could potentially be changed, or extended, in ways to improve accounting for human rights.

## 12.6 Conclusion

As we have noted, you cannot get a more important social issue than human rights. It goes to the very heart of what it means to be human as well as the values of freedom and justice. Human rights issues are broad and cross-cutting, but also complex and multifaceted. We hope that this chapter has enabled you to consider the role of sustainability accounting and accountability in the issue of human rights. This includes both understanding why the issue is of relevance to organisations and accounting, as well as critically reflecting on the current practices, and perhaps the lack of practices, in the area.

We also hope that this discussion has highlighted the relevance of academic research in this area by pointing to the relationship between practice and research. While we have indicated how some research, such as that related to human rights disclosures, has analysed current practices, and in many ways can be argued to trail behind what is occurring in trailblazing organisations, other research enables us to see how the conversations occurring in research can expose areas where further knowledge and practice are needed. We conclude this chapter by recognising that despite the longstanding awareness and commitment to human rights and human rights abuses there is still a lot to be done. We suggest that this topic of sustainability accounting and accountability will, given its importance, continue to be discussed and developed in the future.

## References

Anti-slavery (2025). What Is Modern Slavery? www.antislavery.org/slavery-today/modern-slavery/ (accessed 14 January 2025).

Antonini, C., Beck, C. and Larrinaga, C. (2020). Subpolitics and Sustainability Reporting Boundaries: The Case of Working Conditions in Global Supply Chains. *Accounting, Auditing and Accountability Journal*, *33*(7), 1535–1567.

Apple (2024). Conflict Minerals Report. https://www.supplychainreports.apple/home/default.aspx (accessed 15 January 2025).

Christ, K., Rao, K. and Burritt, R. (2019). Accounting for Modern Slavery: An Analysis of Australian Listed Company Disclosures. *Accounting, Auditing and Accountability Journal*, *32*(3), 836–865.

Cooper, C., Coulson, A. and Taylor, P. (2011). Accounting for Human Rights: Doxic Health and Safety Practices – The Accounting Lesson from ICL. *Critical Perspectives on Accounting*, *22*, 738–758.

ICAEW (2022). What Makes a Good Modern Slavery Statement? https://www.icaew.com/insights/viewpoints-on-the-news/2022/jul-2022/what-makes-a-good-modern-slavery-statement (accessed 15 January 2025).

International Labour Organisation (ILO) (2022). Global Estimates of Modern Slavery: Forced Labour and Forced Marriage. https://www.ilo.org/publications/major-publications/global-estimates-modern-slavery-forced-labour-and-forced-marriage (accessed 14 January 2025).

International Labour Organisation (ILO) (2023). The Rana Plaza Disaster Ten Years On: What Has Changed? https://webapps.ilo.org/infostories/en-GB/Stories/Country-Focus/rana-plaza#bangladeshi-garment-sector (accessed 27 February 2025).

International Labour Organisation (ILO) (2025). ILO Declaration on Fundamental Principles and Rights at Work. https://www.ilo.org/about-ilo/mission-and-impact-ilo/ilo-declaration-fundamental-principles-and-rights-work (accessed 10 May 2025).

Marks & Spencer (2024) Modern Slavery Statement. https://assets.digitalcontent.marksandspencer.app/image/upload/v1718891693/1252_20062024_Adhoc_Modern_Slavery_Statement_2024.pdf (accessed 15 January 2025).

McDonald-Kerr, L. and Boyce, G. (2020). Colonialism and Indigenous Peoples. In Edwards, J. R. and Walker, S. P. (eds), *The Routledge Companion to Accounting History*, pp. 553–577. Routledge.

McPhail, K. and Ferguson, J. (2016). The Past, the Present and the Future of Accounting for Human Rights. *Accounting, Auditing and Accountability Journal, 29(4)*, 526–541.

McVey, M., Ferguson, J. and Puyou, J.-R. (2023). "Traduttore, Traditore?" Translating Human Rights into the Corporate Context. *Journal of Business Ethics, 182*, 573–596.

OECD (2018). *OECD Due Diligence Guidance for Responsible Business Conduct.* https://mneguidelines.oecd.org/mneguidelines/ (accessed 14 January 2025).

OECD (2023). *OECD Guidelines for Multinational Enterprises on Responsible Business Conduct.* https://mneguidelines.oecd.org/mneguidelines/ (accessed 15 January 2025).

Ruiz-Ramírez, C., Castillo-Rojas-Marcos, J. and Molinero-Gerbeau, Y. (2024). Essential But Invisible and Exploited: A Literature Review of Migrant Workers' Experiences in European Agriculture. https://policy-practice.oxfam.org/resources/essential-but-invisible-and-exploited-a-literature-review-of-migrant-workers-ex-621604/ (accessed 15 January 2025).

Shift/Mazars (2015). The UN Guiding Principles Reporting Framework. www.ungpreporting.org (accessed 14 January 2025).

Sikka, P. (2011). Accounting for Human Rights: The Challenge of Globalization and Foreign Investment Agreements. *Critical Perspectives on Accounting, 22(8)*, 811–827.

UN (1948). Declaration on Human Rights (UDHR). www.un.org/en/universal-declaration-human-rights/ (accessed on 15 January 2025).

UN (2011). Guiding Principles on Business and Human Rights: Implementing the United Nations "Protect, Respect and Remedy" Framework. www.ohchr.org/Documents/Publications/GuidingPrinciplesBusinessHR_EN.pdf (accessed on 14 January 2025).

Yang, D., Dumay, J. and Tweedie, D. (2021). Accounting's Role in Resisting Wage Theft: A Labour Process Theory Analysis. *Accounting, Auditing and Accountability Journal, 34*(1), 85–110.

## Additional reading and resources

Agyemang, G., Dhanani, A., Ejiogu, A. and Perkiss, S. (2014). Researching Race, Accounting and Accountability: Past, Present and Future. Accounting, Auditing and Accountability Journal, 37(7/8), 1637–1664.

Denedo, M., Thomson, I. and Yonekura, A. (2019). Ecological Damage, Human Rights and Oil: Local Advocacy NGOs Dialogic Action and Alternative Accounting Practices. *Accounting Forum, 43(1)*, 85–112.

ICAEW (2024). Modern Slavery Signs That Accountants Are Well Placed to Spot. Available at https://www.icaew.com/insights/viewpoints-on-the-news/2024/jul-2024/modern-slavery-signs-that-accountants-are-well-placed-to-spot (accessed 2 March 2025).

Islam, M. and van Staden, C. (2018). Social Movement NGOs and the Comprehensiveness of Conflict Mineral Disclosures: Evidence from Global Companies. *Accounting, Organizations and Society, 65*, 1–19.

Kreander, N. and McPhail, K. (2019). State Investments and Human Rights? The Case of the Norwegian Government Pension Fund Global. *Accounting, Auditing and Accountability Journal, 32(6)*, 1742–1770.

Scobie, M., Finau, G. and Hallenback, J. (2024). Land, Land Banks and Land Back: Accounting, Social Reproduction and Indigenous Resurgence. *Economy and Space*, 56(1), 235–252.

Siddiqui, J. and Uddin, S. (2016). Human Rights Disasters, Corporate Accountability and the State: Lessons Learned from Rana Plaza. *Accounting, Auditing and Accountability Journal, 29(4)*, 679–704.

CHAPTER

13

# Accounting for economic inequality

Inequality comes in many forms. Gender, disability, race and ethnicity equality are likely to be familiar forms to many of you. While all forms of inequality are of importance to sustainability accounting and accountability, here, in this chapter, we look specifically at economic inequality. Economic inequality is a term used to describe the difference between individuals or groups in the distribution of assets, wealth, or income. Economic inequality can occur both across countries and also within countries. As we demonstrate below, economic inequality is a particularly important form of inequality for accounting and organisational accountability. Due to rising levels of economic inequality around the globe, it is gaining increasing attention as a sustainability issue. Economic inequality in societies has implications for the health and well-being of individuals, the prosperity and flourishing of communities, as well as the degradation and protection of the natural environment.

In investigating the issue of economic inequality, we structure this chapter as follows. First, we discuss the concept of economic inequality. Specifically, we distinguish economic inequality from poverty, outline the common ways it is measured and discuss why economic equality is an important issue for sustainability more broadly. We then consider why economic inequality is an issue for organisations and accounting before outlining key institutions and organisations that are relevant for the topic. Current accounting and accountability practices are then discussed. We conclude with some comments on the potential role of accounting and accountability mechanisms in addressing this issue of critical importance.

By the end of this chapter, you should:

- Understand what economic inequality is, its causes and its consequences.
- Understand why economic inequality is a sustainability issue that is relevant to organisations and accounting.
- Be aware of global, national and organisational level institutions and organisations in relation to economic inequality.

DOI: 10.4324/9781003533207-16

- Be aware of current accounting knowledge and practice in relation to economic inequality.
- Have considered the limits of current understandings and practices in relation to accounting for economic inequality.

## 13.1 What is economic inequality and why is it a sustainability issue?

### 13.1.1 What is economic inequality?

Economic inequality is a term used to describe the difference between individuals or groups in the distribution of assets, wealth or income. Economic inequality can take two forms. First, economic inequality can relate to disparities *within* a society, that is how equal or unequal people within a particular country are. Second, economic inequality can relate to disparities *between* societies, that is between two different countries.

Images that often come to mind when one thinks of economic inequality are those representing poverty; in particular, images of people living in poverty. This is understandable given the popular representations of the issue of economic inequality, including those you might see in the media. Economic inequality and poverty are indeed related. However, it is useful to recognise the difference between these two concepts (see the below "Pause and reflect").

**PAUSE AND REFLECT...**

Let's take a moment to consider the difference between economic inequality and poverty and why it is useful to make the distinction between these two related concepts.
Some key differences are:

- Poverty is focused on outcomes while inequality is focused on structures and systems. Poverty therefore results from inequality.
- Poverty is a condition of an individual or group whilst inequality is about the relationships between individuals and groups in society.

Thinking about these differences at a country level, for example, highlights that a nation can be both poor and unequal, poor and relatively equal, rich and unequal, and rich and fairly equal.

Furthermore, a consideration of the differences between the two concepts can assist us in reflecting on the response to addressing these issues. While much development work has been focused on tackling poverty through, for example, development aid, this is not necessarily effective in changing the systems and structures that can lead to poverty. While addressing poverty is clearly essential and urgent, the need to address the structures and systems associated with economic inequality which can lead to poverty is also evident.

Essentially, economic inequality can be seen as the system, while poverty is an outcome of that system. The SDGs list the two issues as different, albeit related, goals. Specifically, SDG1 No Poverty emphasises the need to end poverty in all forms everywhere, while SDG10 Reduced Inequalities is concerned with a number of inequality dimensions including economic inequality.

While poverty is clearly an important issue and one that requires attention, here in this chapter we focus on inequality as our aim is to discuss the structures and systems that ultimately need changing if we are to address economic inequality and poverty. Furthermore, we predominantly consider economic inequalities within a society. While we recognise that inequalities between countries are an important sustainability issue with implications for various organisations, we will demonstrate below how economic inequalities within a society have key organisational and accounting implications for *all* organisations.

### 13.1.2 Measuring economic inequality

Before considering some of the causes and consequences of economic inequality it is first useful to look at a few of the more common ways in which economic inequality is measured. This helps by giving context to some of the knowledge and understanding of the concept as well as enables the possible responses to addressing economic inequality, discussed below.

There are several ways in which economic inequality can be measured when seeking to understand inequality within a society. One of the most common ways is to look at the difference between the highest and the lowest incomes in a country. For example, Wilkinson and Pickett (2009) in their book *The Spirit Level*, a key text which we draw on in this chapter, measure economic inequality by considering income inequality between the top 20% and lowest 20% in each country analysed. This measure illustrates the income difference or income gap.

Another common measure is the Gini coefficient. The Gini coefficient measures inequality across the whole society rather than comparing the extremes as Wilkinson and Pickett do. The Gini coefficient can be used to measure income or wealth distribution and it scores each society on a scale of 0–1. Similarly to almost all widely used metrics, there is plenty of debate concerning the usefulness and nuances of the Gini coefficient. Still, the measure is amongst the most commonly referenced metrics of inequality (see Stiglitz and Rosengard, 2015). Let's therefore consider in simple terms how it works using income. Essentially, if all income within a society went to one person and everyone else got nothing (i.e. maximum inequality) then the Gini coefficient for that society would be 1. If everyone got exactly the same income within a society and there was perfect economic equality, the Gini would be 0. While some interpretation of the assumptions underlying the figures would be helpful and bring more nuance, in general terms, it is safe to say that the lower the Gini coefficient the more equal a society is.

**PAUSE AND REFLECT...**

We might not always pay much attention to the potential inequalities in the societies we live in or have visited. It is however a useful exercise to do at times, as it helps us be more attentive to how individuals and communities outside our usual daily lives, neighbourhoods and social bubbles live. While the Gini coefficient is not a perfect measure, it does offer a good starting point for discussions of inequality in societies as well as how societies differ from one another.

Gini coefficients for each country are available for instance in databases offered by the OECD and the World Bank. Have a look at the Gini coefficient of the country you currently live in. Next, consider it in comparison to that of some other countries, perhaps those you have visited, in which you may have relatives, or ones you consider yourself to be familiar with.

Are there any surprises in those numbers? Do the Gini coefficients you have found match with your experience or preconceptions of inequality in those countries?

You can continue further with this exploration by considering other key characteristics for those countries, such as GDP, life expectancy, access to education and infant mortality. Examples of good sources for this data are UN's annual Human Development Report (UNDP, 2024) as well as the Gapminder project, which allows you to compare and animate different metrics and see how they change over time (Gapminder, 2020; Rosling, 2018).

While wealth and assets can also be used to measure economic inequality, using income and in particular income disparity like the measures above is an arguably more useful measure as it has several advantages. First, income is much easier to measure than wealth and assets with income data being readily available in many countries. Importantly, income is a useful measure as it is an enabler of upward social mobility. Social mobility is a person's ability to move up in social groups, which has been noted to be a key aspect of reducing economic inequalities over time. The relationship between income inequality and social mobility is strong in high-income countries, with greater inequality reducing social mobility.

As you may have started to realise, organisations, in particular business organisations, are central to discussions of inequality. As key wage paying entities in societies their decisions and practices affect the distribution of income. We return to this below after first exploring some of the other relevant aspects of this issue.

### 13.1.3 Causes of economic inequality

There are many causes of economic inequality. One of the largest determinants is a person's starting position (e.g. the economic and social position of one's parents) as well as early life opportunities such as access to education and health care. That is, the long-term economic position of an individual is in many ways determined early on, and largely through circumstances that are not in an individual's control. However, several other causes of economic inequality include a number of global influences as well as tax and policy contexts relating to organisations and accounting. Let's look at some of these briefly as they help frame our discussion below.

Globalisation and the expansion of capital markets, which have made it easier for those with access to capital to invest across national boundaries, have had an influence on economic inequalities (see Piketty, 2014). Not being limited to a single economic market has created more opportunities for those with capital to increase their capital, often meaning that capital has been accumulated by a smaller number of people (i.e. high wealthy individuals). Similarly, the choices made within organisations, such as those relating to employee policies, can be significant. The types of contracts favoured (e.g. full-time, part-time, on demand) and how wages and wage structures are set affect people's income and the distribution of income in communities and societies. When it comes to increasing levels of economic inequality that we see occurring globally within countries, the swiftly rising high incomes and stagnant low incomes are a major cause. Finally, political decisions in each country also have an influence in terms of how inequalities develop over time. While decisions concerning social policy might appear somewhat distant to organisations and accounting, those focusing on employment legislation and corporate taxation are likely to have direct implications on them.

### 13.1.4 So why is economic inequality a sustainability problem?

Some people argue that some level of economic inequality is acceptable, or even desirable for our society. The argument here often goes that if everyone was equal people would have less incentive to work hard, save money and be entrepreneurial and creative. However, it is when we get high levels of inequality that it becomes a problem. And we are currently living in an age where in many countries the levels of economic inequality are not only high, but they are extreme. Oxfam International reports that at the same time as some 3.6 billion people live below the poverty line, the richest 1% of the world own 45% of all global wealth (see Oxfam International, 2025). So, while a small number of elite are ever increasing their share of wealth, and at alarmingly fast rates, many, indeed hundreds of millions, are living in extreme poverty without access to clean water and without enough food to lead a healthy life. Economic inequality, both between and within countries, is an issue of critical contemporary importance and while it is for many primarily a moral problem, it is also a problem that has various social, environmental and economic implications.

Some of these implications are explored in the book *The Spirit Level* by epidemiologists Wilkinson and Pickett. They outline the harmful effects of inequality on societies by drawing on their finding that for 11 health and social problems – physical health, mental health, drug abuse, education, imprisonment, obesity, social mobility, trust and community life, violence, teenage pregnancies and child well-being – outcomes are significantly worse in more unequal rich countries. Plotting health and social problems against income inequality in various OECD countries they show that more unequal societies tend to perform worse on each. Further, levels of trust within a society reduce as income inequality grows. Likewise, homicides are more common in more unequal countries. At this point, it is important to remember that this is not about the differences between high-income and low-income countries, but rather focused on the differences *within* a country. In short, economic inequality is an issue for *all* societies – not only low-income societies. The United States for example, while considered a high-income country, has high levels of inequality and therefore their performance is much worse across these aspects compared to those countries with more equality (see Collison et al., 2010). Another illustration here would be the "Glasgow Effect", which highlights the substantive effects stark inequalities can have on individuals' health and well-being: in the late 2000s men living in deprived areas of Glasgow had a life expectancy of 54 years, whereas the life expectancy of men in the affluent areas nearby was 82 years (Reid, 2011).

The basic argument put forth in *The Spirit Level* is that equal societies will almost always do better, that "everyone is better off when societies are more equal". Now, at this point, it is worth noting that questions of economic inequality, including its determinants and consequences, are politically highly contentious. As such, the arguments presented in The Spirit Level were and continue to be received differently across the political spectrum. While we can argue about how strong conclusions one should be making based on the statistics, in general terms the argument put forth by Wilkinson and Pickett seems to hold: lower inequality brings benefits to many, while higher inequality tends to favour the few.

We should also note that economic inequality is not just a social issue. It is also an environmental and economic one, meaning that the implications of economic inequality span the commonly identified three dimensions of sustainability.

While connections between economic inequality and the environment may not appear obvious to begin with, there are several key connections. Again, Wilkinson and Pickett (2009) outline some of these. They note the evidence that suggests that more equal societies consume less, and that the higher the income inequality in a country the worse the environmental indicators, such as waste production, meat and water consumption, biodiversity loss and overall ecological footprint, appear to be. Furthermore, and of significance to addressing other sustainability issues, more equal countries appear to be more effective in mobilising against the challenges of, for example, environmental degradation and climate change. This is likely due to the social context, such as greater levels of trust and an ability to foster collective responsibility. Furthermore, the relationship *between* high-income and low-income countries is affected by inequality *within* countries, which has significant effects on our ability to address sustainability issues at a global level. An example here is the ability to address climate change which, as we have noted, requires a global approach and thus cooperation.

Economic inequality is also an economic issue. For example, the range of social consequences noted inhibit economic growth and development. Moreover, in contexts with a high level of economic inequality, economic growth and development, which are generally seen as good for poverty reduction, are further problematised by the potential for "privileged elites" to benefit more from the positive effects of growth and development than those "at the bottom". In short, economic growth in contexts with a high level of inequality can often lead to more inequality as all do not share in the benefits. Furthermore, when speaking of economic growth, we should also recall the discussion presented in Chapter 2 concerning the fundamental dependence of human economy on the underlying ecosystems. In the context of economic inequality, this implies that attempts to solve inequality by spurring faster economic growth may not only worsen inequality, but inevitably also escalate other sustainability concerns (see Jackson, 2017; Raworth, 2017).

**PAUSE AND REFLECT…**

We have throughout this book discussed how alongside governments and organisations it is important to consider the role individuals' choices, desires and practices have in the global sustainability challenges. You may recall that in Chapter 2, we noted how the World Overshoot Day is getting earlier each year as a result of the increased consumption of resources. We have also referred to different types of calculations, such as ecological and carbon footprint, which you can use to estimate the environmental consequences of your personal consumption choices as well as to see how your practices compare with the average footprints of fellow citizens. Likewise, in Chapter 12, we highlighted how many of the choices we make in our personal lives may have human rights consequences, although those might not be immediately visible.

At this point, it is perhaps useful to take a moment to think about your own consumption. What drives your consumption and desire for products and services?

Inequality heightens competitive consumption. We often compare ourselves to those around us. The more the rich spend the more inferior those around them can feel which can drive us to desire more products and services. Wilkinson and Pickett (2009, p. 228) claim that "people in more unequal countries do the equivalent of two or three months' extra work a year. A loss of the equivalent of an extra eight or twelve weeks' holiday". This increase in work is considered to be the effect of a drive to have more money to consume.

Does this make you consider, perhaps even rethink, your own consumption habits?

## 13.2 What has economic inequality got to do with organisations and accounting?

As the causes of inequality discussed above reveal, economic inequality is very much an issue for organisations and accounting. In discussing many of the other sustainability issues in previous chapters, such as climate and water, we have used the distinction between impacts and dependencies. That is, how an organisation impacts the sustainability issue under consideration, and how the organisation is dependent on the same thing. While it makes less sense to consider how organisations are dependent on economic inequality (although, problematically there might be ways that they are), we can to an extent consider organisations' potential dependency of having less inequality in their operating context. Moreover, and to continue drawing on the idea of impacts and dependencies, we can consider the relationship economic inequality has with organisations and accounting from two perspectives: first, how economic inequality potentially affects organisations and accounting, and second, how organisational practices and accounting potentially affect economic inequality.

### 13.2.1 How economic inequality affects organisations

Organisations of all forms are connected to society and therefore are impacted upon, either positively or negatively, by levels of economic inequality within that society. Just as Wilkinson and Pickett discussed above identify that high levels of economic inequality are not good for all in society, the same can be said for organisations. That is, economic inequality can have negative effects on organisational performance.

Bapuji (2015, see also Bapuji et al., 2020) discusses the relationship between organisations and economic inequality and suggests two ways that economic inequality affects organisational performance. Indirectly via human development within the society, and directly via its effects on individual employees and their interactions in the workplace. This relates to our discussion above as there would seem to be advantages to organisations operating in a more economically equal society. For example, it is more likely that productivity levels of the workplace are higher when the workforce is in a healthier society with fewer social problems. More trust and co-operation would also have positive benefits for the workplace.

The second way in which economic inequality affects organisational performance is via the institutions within which organisations are embedded. This relates to the social, political and legal systems, as well as to the institutions governing those societies. There is, for instance, plenty of research discussing the linkages between corruption and economic inequality. While the exact causal relationship might vary, it appears evident that corruption features more prominently in societies with high economic inequality, which again has implications for organisations operating in those societies.

### 13.2.2 How organisations and accounting can affect economic inequality

The other element we need to consider here is how organisational and accounting practices affect economic inequality in a given context. Given that most economic activity in societies takes place through various types of organisations, it is probably not surprising that their actions have varying consequences. Likewise, given the power of accounting within organisations, used for instance in the allocation of resources and assessing success and performance of both individuals and organisations, accounting practices can have a range of implications for economic inequality.

Three areas where organisational practices and accounting are linked with economic inequality are introduced here and then focused on below when we discuss specific practices. First, accounting influences how economic activity is organised. Organisational structures, such as the gig economy, and the role of accounting within them affect economic inequality through for instance the relationship between organisations and the workforce. Second, wages and compensation schemes are an important way in which organisational and accounting practices are linked to economic inequality. Here, it is relevant to consider both how many people in societies receive their income from organisations and how organisational practices and accounting logics play a role in setting the level of wage payments. Likewise, we can also think of the consequences of accounting practices, such as how the payments to labour are treated as "costs". Third, organisations are significant taxpayers in many societies and have roles as intermediaries, such as in value added tax. Accounting, accountancy firms and the accounting profession are highly involved in tax, including being in the spotlight in discussions surrounding tax avoidance and tax evasion practices. These practices have clear links to the distribution of income in societies as we discuss further below.

### 13.2.3 Summary of how accounting, organisations and economic inequality are connected

In outlining the above, we are not claiming that these are the only areas where accounting, accountability and reporting are interconnected with economic inequality. There are definitely others, but a comprehensive discussion of all possible connections is beyond this chapter. Instead, we encourage you to consider these areas as illustrations of how broad-ranging and potentially powerful the implications of various accounting and accountability practices can be in societies. Moreover, we would at this point like to underscore that when considering the interaction between economic inequality, organisations and accounting we should not only see accounting as a contributor to the causes of economic inequality but also consider its potential role in countering inequality. Before discussing these accounting practices in more detail we will first provide a brief overview of the various institutions and organisations that relate to economic inequality as they provide important context.

## 13.3 Economic inequality: Relevant institutions and organisations

As with all other sustainability issues discussed, there are various institutions and organisations that affect economic inequality. Some of these overlap with other chapters in the book, especially the previous chapter on human rights. Again, this highlights the interconnected nature of sustainability issues.

### 13.3.1 International organisations

At the international level, there are a myriad of organisations, including many NGOs, that operate to address economic inequality and/or issues relating to economic inequality. Three key ones are introduced here.

#### 13.3.1.1 The United Nations Development Programme

The United Nations Development Programme (UNDP) is an international organisation under the structure of the UN that works with countries across the world to help "to eradicate poverty, reduce inequalities and exclusion, and build resilience so countries can sustain progress" (UNDP, 2025). The UNDP plays a key role in working towards the achievement of the SDGs which provide a key platform for their activities. While the UNDP has a focus on less developed country contexts, its work in 170 countries identifies their global reach as well as the international nature of the issues that they address.

#### 13.3.1.2 The International Labour Organization

The International Labour Organization (ILO) introduced in the previous chapter brings together governments, employers and workers to set labour standards, develop policies and devise programmes promoting decent work. The main aims of the ILO are to promote rights at work, encourage decent employment opportunities, enhance social protection and strengthen dialogue on work-related issues. It is through these activities that they have a role in both promoting and educating about issues of economic inequality and the role of organisations.

#### 13.3.1.3 Oxfam International

Oxfam is an international non-government organisation which aims to tackle inequalities that "make and keep people poor". Founded in 1995, it has a long history of working on issues of social justice and equality – including how our current economies enable a privileged few to accumulate wealth and power while many are left in poverty. Given the relationship between poverty and inequality, Oxfam aims to tackle the social structures of inequality which keep people in poverty. They have been successful in bringing attention to various policies and practices including tax justice and the under-taxing of corporations and what they refer to as the "race to the bottom on personal income". In recent years, Oxfam has annually published a new report on global inequality during the World Economic Forum's prestigious and widely followed Annual Meeting in Davos, thereby seeking to engage in a debate on social and economic development.

### 13.3.2 International social movements

In addition to the international institutions and organisations that operate to promote, educate and/or address the issue of economic inequality, there are a number of international social movements which have been successful in this space. While these social movements are international, it is important to recognise that they are often made up of a collection of national and/or local groups. Indeed, there is a vast infrastructure of national and community groups that operate in the context of economic inequalities. We will discuss just two here, but we encourage you to consider others that operate both globally and in your local area.

#### 13.3.2.1 The Occupy Movement

The Occupy Movement arose in the aftermath of the global financial crisis of 2008 and the public outrage expressed over the disparities between the high rates of pay for some (including bankers) and the hardship being experienced by those in precarious, part-time and low-paid work. Defined by the slogan "we are the 99%", representing the contrast between those very few (the 1%) that received excessive salaries compared to the majority, the Occupy Movement highlighted the issue of economic inequality on a global scale. While the Occupy Movement has been largely inactive since the mid-2010s, it is worth recognising that the movement played a key role in raising the issue of accountability for low, and particularly high, wages and salaries, into public discussion in numerous countries.

#### 13.3.2.2 Living wage campaign groups

Also operating across the globe are a number of what can be referred to collectively as "living wage" campaign groups. These movements have emerged as the result of low minimum wages in many contexts and the argument that these low wages result in a category of workers sometimes referred to as the working poor or, in the UK, the "jams" (just about managing). These terms refer to workers that, despite having jobs and being in paid work, are not earning enough to provide for them and their families. Living wage campaigners seek to eradicate this "in work poverty" through calling for the payment of a living wage. A living wage is an hourly wage rate that is calculated on what is needed within a particular context/location in order for someone to pay for the necessities of life and participate as a citizen. In many countries, the calculated living wage is higher than the national minimum wage.

Living wage movements seek to address the issue of economic inequality through actions directed at the payment of wages by businesses (in particular large corporations) rather than taxes. Indeed, central to some of the arguments used by these campaign groups is the recognition that when businesses and other wage paying organisations do not pay a worker enough to "live off" then the state often has to supplement their income through state payments in the form of benefits. Such campaign groups often note that the payment of a living wage would lead to benefits for all, including the businesses themselves – given the range of social, environmental and economic outcomes that result from more equality, as we raised above.

### 13.3.3 National tax, income and workplace policies

Policy which relates to both taxes and tax spending, that is the redistribution of income and wealth, as well as those relating to income and the payment of wages (for example, minimum wage rates and other aspects of employment benefits), are key ways in which rising levels of economic inequality are constrained. Such things are guided by government regulations and actions. Some examples include imposing new taxes or increasing current levels of existing taxes (e.g. wealth tax), controlling tax avoidance, and capping compensation levels (e.g. disclosure on CEO pay relative to median pay).

While all good measures, their effectiveness can depend on the willingness of individuals and organisations to comply with the regulation (consider here the use of tax havens) as well as on effective monitoring. There are also areas where governance and oversight are lacking, or at least lag behind current practices. A good example here is the gig economy and the use of various employment contracts such as zero-hour contracts. These things are discussed further below.

## 13.4 Accounting and accountability for economic inequality

When it comes to looking at accounting practices related to economic inequality it is useful to consider two aspects. The first relates to practices that are being undertaken to address economic inequality. That is, what some organisations, and the accounting that supports them, are doing in order to address, or respond to, calls to be accountable for economic inequality. Many of these practices are linked to an organisation's sustainability or corporate social responsibility strategy and are often supported by or discussed in research. The second area relates to those practices which draw attention, and for which organisations, and again the accounting that supports them, are being asked to be accountable. We consider both below as we seek to identify some areas of relevance for this topic.

### 13.4.1 The organising of economic activity

In considering how accounting and organising of economic activity relate to economic inequality, it is useful to begin from the bigger picture. That is, what is the role of accounting and accountability in societies, and how does this role affect the way economic and social activity gets organised? A grand theme, yes, but still something that needs discussing.

Accounting is involved in a range of organisational activities. Internally, management accounting and control is used to assess processes, evaluate alternatives and set targets. Externally, financial accounting frameworks and structures are drawn upon when producing accounts and eventually financial statements, which describe how an organisation has performed in the past financial year and provide an overview of its financial status. And so forth. Accounting information is then used for various purposes, such as allocating resources and setting priorities. All these practices, mechanisms and institutions have an impact on how organisations, individuals and societies value different things.

Take financial markets for instance, and companies listed on stock exchanges. In simple terms, the logic of the financial markets is based on the idea that share prices somehow reflect the future earnings of the companies. It is assumed that investors expect to receive returns for the capital they invest, and hence companies are expected to deliver a solid financial performance. If the profit, general profitability, or expected future profits are not in line with what the markets (i.e. investors) are looking for, organisational decision-makers are usually expected to engage in measures to improve financial performance. Of the range of measures available, cost-cutting is one of the more common. Within this is cutting labour costs. In order to ensure that those investing capital receive returns, an organisation can reduce the number of employees receiving income, or reduce the income of those employed.

Such cost-cutting mechanisms are an inherent feature of organising economic activity in a range of organisational forms. However, it is particularly so in listed companies, where the goal in most settings is considered to be increasing shareholder value. Accounting is closely involved, as it is the institution through which we define which companies, business units, investments and products are successful (i.e. sufficiently profitable), and which ones are less so. While the legal form of a limited liability company has had substantial influence in developing the modern society through for instance how it has incentivised entrepreneurs to innovate and made it possible to collect capital for risky projects, it has simultaneously created a structure which, amongst other things, encourages activities which can increase inequality.

The rise of the gig economy illustrates both the challenges related to the friction between investors and workers, as well as the debate on whether such friction is beneficial or detrimental for societies. The gig economy highlights how innovative organisational structures and forms of contracts can be used to create services which employ a great number of workers in what are usually low-paid and uncertain jobs. In more conventional organisational structures, the worker is employed by the organisation, meaning that the organisation pays the salary (and in many cases benefits such as sick leave and holiday pay) even in situations where there might temporarily be less work to do. However, the gig economy is based on the idea that employees only work when there is demand. In essence, the risk gets shifted from the organisation to the individual. This relates closely to legal disputes taking place in various countries concerning whether gig workers should be considered employees or entrepreneurs, with the latter interpretation again passing many risks onto the individual. Now, while it is clear that such arrangements based on forced entrepreneurship and/or on demand workforce are beneficial for the organisation using them, there is substantial disagreement concerning whether this is a good or a bad thing for societies and the individuals involved. Depending on the perspective, it can be claimed that such gigs offer opportunities for entrepreneurial minds and those who might otherwise not be able to find employment, or alternatively that such arrangements increase the share of precarious jobs in societies and hence cause increased uncertainty and inequality (Fleming, 2019).

### 13.4.2 Income and wages

The second aspect in relation to how accounting and organisations intersect with economic inequality that we consider is the payment of wages and compensation to employees. Here, we again note that organisations operate within social structures, which include different types of institutional arrangements and legal structures. These set the general boundaries on organisational activities, and as such, it is relevant to consider governments and the public sector more broadly as these institutions are the ones setting up the employment legislation, including regulation concerning income and wages. However, the private sector as wage paying organisations is also highly relevant. Business organisations, which both create and distribute "value", can both cause and help address income inequality. And given the role of accounting in facilitating wage decisions and in reporting, to varying degrees, wage payments, it is useful to consider accounting's role in inequalities and accountability for increasing levels of income inequality in many contexts.

When it comes to wages and income accountability, the differences in pay between top management and low paid workers in some private sectors has been in the spotlight for some time. The seemingly ever-increasing salaries for high-paid chief executives (sometimes referred to as fat cat wages), while wages for those at the bottom remain stagnant, have been the focus of the media and increasingly of the general public as well. For instance, and perhaps the example receiving the most attention was the employee wage raises announced by Amazon in 2018 were contrasted with the net worth and income of its CEO Jeff Bezos putting such increases into context. In addition to such high-profile cases, the phenomenon seems to be occurring also more broadly across companies: the Washington-based think tank Economic Policy Institute has followed the development of CEO compensations over time and noted that in the largest US public firms the ratio of CEO-to-typical-worker compensation has risen from 45-to-1 in 1989 to 290-to-1 in 2023 (Bivens et al., 2024).

Despite the high wages and lucrative compensation schemes many CEOs and other corporate executive receive, it is nonetheless unclear whether higher executive pay leads to better company performance. This has added to excessively high wages being in the spotlight as they have been identified as likely to be a reflection of the dominant bargaining position of executives rather than having much to do with how they perform at the position. In addition to society more broadly, these questions are also interesting for the financial markets, illustrated by how the US Securities and Exchange Council (SEC) set in 2022 new rules on how public companies need to report on the relationship between their executive's compensation and the company's financial performance. As these examples illustrate, organisations are increasingly being held accountable for their salary structures and decisions as well as for their role in perpetuating economic inequalities.

In similar terms, when discussing economic inequality it is also worth considering those organisations which have active strategies seeking to drive down wages. We identified above the drive to increase financial performance and how this can lead to a consideration of labour costs. This can manifest in multiple ways. An organisation can, for example, seek to set up its activities in a location which allows it to pay low wages. In addition to the organisation's own activities, such cost-cutting measures can concern its supply chain. In seeking to reduce costs some organisations are known to be aggressive in trying to find suppliers in countries with lower wage levels, or alternatively have suppliers compete against one another. As we discussed in our previous chapter on human rights, such situations can have negative social consequences, including greater economic inequality. Alternatively, the organisation can structure the work it needs so that it avoids any long-term employment commitments and relies instead on zero hours contracts or gig economy arrangements as we discussed above.

On the other hand, compensation strategies are perhaps also the direct ways in which organisations can reduce economic inequality in a society. Some employers have actively taken a stand and committed to paying employees a living wage, as such decisions have been noted to bring benefits to both the employees and the organisation. These firms are however only a small minority, as World Benchmarking Alliance (2024) reports that only 4% of the world's 2000 most influential companies pay their direct employees a living wage, noting also that only 3% support this in their supply chain. Other organisations engage with various types of employee ownership or payment structures, giving employees more voice in decisions regarding resource allocation and the use of potential profit. While potentially reducing the financial bottom line in the first instance, such decisions can be helpful for the organisation through enhancing work satisfaction and commitment, and subsequently to the society more broadly through reducing income inequalities. Finally, some organisations have also committed to pay structures that limit the difference between the top earners and those at the bottom, which means that any pay rise at the top has to be accompanied by a pay rise at the bottom.

Accounting is clearly relevant here, as it is the system that informs decisions on employee remuneration as well as records and measures workers through, for example, wage and labour costs. Indeed, some practices that are taken for granted within conventional accounting are perhaps problematic when viewed from a position which looks to address increasing inequalities. A key aspect here is the accounting treatment of labour and wages classifying them as costs. This is something accounting students learn early in their studies. What you may have also been taught is the accounting logic of costs as things to be reduced. Just think of the effect of this on how, in accounting, we treat labour and wages. We return to this discussion in Section 13.5 below.

Compensation strategies are a direct and key way in which organisations can address economic inequality. However, they are not the only way. In addition to paying wages to managers and employees, organisations also distribute income through other means of distributing profit. Common examples here include paying dividends to shareholders, engaging in corporate philanthropy (e.g. supporting charities and other community groups) and also, the payment of taxes. The latter, given its relevance to accounting, and its consideration in accounting research, is discussed next.

### 13.4.3 Taxes, tax avoidance and economic inequality

Taxation has a number of roles in society, including the redistribution of wealth and allowing targeted spending on things such as health and education. Essentially taxes and benefits are used to redistribute (often very) unequal incomes. While tax policies and the decisions concerning the use of collected taxes are the responsibility of governments, such practices rely on the payment of taxes. Accounting's role in the area of tax and the calculation of tax obligations for both individuals and businesses is one obvious way in which economic inequality is an accounting issue. While we could discuss many forms of taxes in the context of sustainability accounting and accountability (e.g. income, value added or environmental taxes), we focus here on corporate taxation. The reason for this is that it relates closely to accounting and accountants. It has also been subject to much public discussion.

Accounting offers a range of opportunities for tax planning purposes, such as developing a firm's capital structure and establishing several subsidiaries primarily for tax purposes (essentially seeking ways to reduce tax costs). The precise means vary according to each jurisdiction, as they are specific to the employed tax laws and policies. We should keep in mind here that tax planning is not illegal in itself. However, there are limits to it, and at some point aggressive tax planning can turn into tax avoidance or tax evasion. While the exact definitions of these concepts vary, it is useful to position them along a continuum, with tax planning sitting on the legal side, tax evasion being illegal, and tax avoidance hovering somewhere in the middle grey area between legal and illegal. The challenge with taxation sometimes is that it is not always very clear where exactly the boundary between legal and illegal is set. Hence, it is relatively commonplace to read a press release from a major corporation saying that the authorities are investigating their tax reporting and accounts, with potential future implications described to be in the tens or hundreds of millions of dollars. However, corporate tax payments clearly have an impact on equality, as less tax paid leads to less tax money to redistribute.

In recent years, we have seen media reports of a number of high-profile corporate cases in which the organisation has been using innovative schemes to minimise their tax payments. One frequently employed method has been setting up subsidiaries in low-tax jurisdictions, such as Ireland, the Netherlands or Switzerland, with the aim to take advantage of a lower or non-existent corporate tax rate. The founding of such subsidiaries doesn't always mean that an organisation would set up any meaningful economic activity in the state however, as a subsidiary can be operated almost entirely from abroad. Again, these arrangements can be perfectly legal, outright illegal, or somewhere in between. One such high-profile case has been the dispute between Apple and the European Commission concerning whether Apple's use of its Irish subsidiary was in effect an illegal structure used to avoid payment of taxes within the EU. After eight years of legal back-and-forth in various courts, European Court of Justice ruled in 2024 that Ireland had granted Apple unlawful aid, and ordered to company to pay Ireland 13 billion euros in unpaid taxes. This case also shows how the roles of different players in such disputes can vary, as here the state of Ireland essentially sided with Apple throughout by highlighting that the advantageous tax position the company held in Ireland was within the usual Irish tax rules and hence did not include any special treatment.

Sometimes such subsidiaries are founded in tax havens, or secrecy jurisdictions, such as Bermuda, Panama or the Cayman Islands, which in addition to low tax rates also offer organisations the benefit of low visibility. In other words, while in many countries organisations have a duty to file their financial statements into public registers, from which anyone interested can acquire them, secrecy jurisdictions do not require such filings and hence allow an organisation operating there to keep their records away from the public eye. From a societal point of view, such tax evasion practices imply that an organisation is not discharging its accountability, and also that it is not contributing to society via taxes. Many social movements, NGOs and other institutions, such as the Tax Justice Network, Oxfam International and the EU Tax Observatory, have been actively campaigning to make tax avoidance and the use of tax havens more visible in societies by providing facts and evidence about the extent of the problem. Such campaigns have also been successful in shifting public opinion on the legitimacy of tax avoidance and thereby making corporate taxation, tax avoidance and tax havens a question of public debate.

The challenge posed by the various advanced tax avoidance practices to societies and public funding has also been acknowledged relatively broadly by international institutions. Within the OECD, for instance, the BEPS programme (Base Erosion and Profit Shifting) aims at tackling tax avoidance strategies commonly used by corporations exploiting mismatches in tax laws applied in different countries. In simple terms, base erosion and profit shifting refer to various strategies through which organisations shift their profits to jurisdictions where corporate taxation is either very low or non-existent. There is sometimes nothing illegal in the use of these strategies, which have included, for instance, the use of multiple subsidiaries, high-interest loans and royalties, with some having been so commonplace that they have nicknames such as Dutch Sandwich, Double Irish, Single Malt, or Double Irish with a Dutch Sandwich. Nonetheless, the BEPS collaboration and associated framework is based on the understanding that the widespread use of such practices is detrimental to societies in general, and lower-income countries in particular, as those states are often more dependent on corporate income tax. As such, reducing aggressive tax avoidance, both legal and illegal, would be helpful for reducing global inequalities.

OECD was also a key player in facilitating what is known as the Global Minimum Tax agreement, which was signed by some 140 countries and became applicable from the year 2024 onwards. The core ideas of the deal include seeking to make multinational companies pay more tax to the jurisdictions in which they actually do business, known as pillar one, and ensuring that multinational companies pay a global minimum tax rate, which is an effective rate of 15% on corporate profits, as set out in pillar two of the agreement. With this structure, the goal is also to reduce the race to the bottom by making it less attractive for nations to serve as tax havens for multinational companies. Several jurisdictions previously known for low tax rates have indeed adjusted their legislation concerning major companies according to pillar two, including Ireland, the Netherlands and Switzerland. While the Global Minimum Tax agreement is seen as a considerable step forward, it is unlikely to mean the end of tax competition between jurisdictions, as there are also other means, such as subsidies and credit schemes, which are regularly employed to attract businesses. Moreover, some concerns have been raised after the incoming Trump administration in 2025 immediately announced that the US would pull out of the agreement, with potential broader ramifications on pillar one in particular. Still, while the exact implications of the Global Tax Agreement on global tax distribution remain to be seen, the agreement is nonetheless considered to change the landscape substantially.

### 13.4.4 Economic inequality disclosure practices

In addition to legislative and regulatory contexts discussed above that govern organisational behaviour related to tax and income distribution, again, as we have seen in other chapters, much of the governance regimes that exist at the organisational level relate to reporting and disclosure. Here, we once again see the link between transparency and accountability in relation to the role of accounting. We will next outline how economic inequality features in the reporting frameworks, and follow this with a discussion of current reporting practices. While taxation is the most prominent element in this area, other aspects of inequality also feature at times.

#### 13.4.4.1 The Global Reporting Initiative

As with the other topics discussed in this book, the Global Reporting Initiative (GRI) has a series of standards that relate to both tax and income distribution-related disclosures. GRI Disclosures on tax and payments to governments were published in December 2019. The aim of these standards is to help promote greater transparency in a reporting organisation's approach to taxes. This revision was perhaps the result of the continued attention, and concern with, aggressive tax avoidance and evasion practices around the globe. It is worth noting here that while the disclosure items listed under management approach disclosures focus mainly on organisational policies, employed mechanisms and approaches as well as governance structures concerning taxation, Disclosure 207-4 sets out some fairly detailed expectations concerning an organisation's tax calculations, payments and tax rates in the jurisdictions it operates in. If provided, such country-by-country (CbC) information has the potential to provide stakeholders considerable detail regarding an organisation's practices. Upon publication, the GRI called it the first global sustainability standard for public CbC reporting on tax. Since then, public CbC reporting requirements have emerged in several jurisdictions, such as Australia and the EU, with the OECD's BEPS programme discussed above serving as an influential catalyst (see "Focus on practice" below). It is noteworthy here that the public reporting requirements set in Australia in late 2024 position GRI Standard 207 as the source of primary guidance, illustrating the important role GRI continues to play in the global sustainability reporting landscape.

**Focus on practice: Tax transparency through country-by-country reporting**

Public country-by-country (CbC) reporting has long been promoted as a potential tool to reduce harmful tax avoidance. The underlying logic is transparency. Much of tax avoidance takes place in the shadows, for instance through complex networks of subsidiaries and with the helpful assistance of tax havens and secrecy jurisdictions. Likewise, tax and accountancy professionals have over the years developed intricate mechanisms, through which companies have been able to shift profits to low-tax jurisdictions, effectively eroding the tax base of others (hence OECD's Base Erosion and Profit Shifting programme). Public CbC reporting is essentially an accounting practice, which will make corporate activities in each jurisdiction more transparent, thereby allowing those outside the entity to see whether the company has engaged for instance in profit shifting from one country to another, possibly tax havens. In principle, such reporting requires firms to disaggregate their economic activities, profits and losses for each country, thereby making it harder for firms to hide their tax avoidance practices behind global aggregate figures.

While OECD adopted a private CbC reporting scheme as part of the BEPS process in 2015, the GRI 207–4 Disclosure published in 2019 was the first widely recognised reporting standard for public CbC reporting. In addition to Australia mentioned above, EU has also set requirements for public CbC reporting that applies to major companies which either domicile in the EU or have significant activities there, although it is relevant to acknowledge that the EU requirements are less ambitious than those set by Australia or GRI, as they for instance only require disclosing CbC information on EU member states and some other selected jurisdictions.

In addition to the tax-related disclosures, there are other disclosure indicators as part of the GRI that are relevant here. Under economic performance, disclosure 201-1 "Direct economic value generated and distributed" requests the organisation to provide information on how the economic value it has created gets shared between different stakeholder groups, including employees. While the disclosure does not provide any direct information concerning employee compensation or wage levels, it does provide an indication on which groups are benefitting the most, as well as offer an opportunity for comparisons with other similar organisations. Likewise, if the information is provided separately at country, regional or market level, as the GRI recommends doing when relevant, it helps understand whether the value generation differs across the contexts an organisation operates in.

Another relevant disclosure item is included as part of GRI Standard 202 Market Presence, where disclosure 202-1 is entitled "Ratios of standard entry level wage by gender compared to local minimum wage". This disclosure focuses directly on a theme relevant for economic inequality, as the distribution of wages between different groups, such as women and men, or local and migrant workers, as well as the level of those wages, has direct consequences on how economic inequality in a given context develops.

#### 13.4.4.2 Economic inequality in other reporting frameworks and practices

In addition to the GRI, some other reporting frameworks also include guidance which could, depending on how they are interpreted by the reporting organisation, relate to economic inequality. For example, disclosures relevant to economic inequality could be guided by the EU's ESRS Standard. Within the ESRS, there are disclosure items concerning remuneration metrics, focusing in particular on the potential gender pay gap in organisations. Moreover, the standards also include disclosures regarding potential impacts on affected communities, under which aggressive tax minimisation strategies are mentioned as one example, especially in the context of corporate value chains and Global South. In contrast, economic inequality or taxation do not feature in the IFRS S1 and S2 requirements.

Another accounting practice worth mentioning here is the production of value added statements, which we briefly mentioned above. Value added statements are statements which report on how the organisation both creates and distributes value (Haller et al., 2018). It is a broader statement than the conventional profit and loss statement, and includes information on how much of the value created by the organisation is distributed among various stakeholders and how much has been retained by the organisation itself. By providing further insights on, for example, how value is distributed to both employees and other stakeholders, value-added accounting practices and statements are relevant when considering accounting and economic inequality. The use of value added statements goes back to the 1970s when they enjoyed some popularity for instance in the UK. In the present day, value added statements feature in the GRI Standards through Disclosure 201-1 Direct economic value generated and distributed, which is intended to provide an indication on how the organisation has been creating wealth for its different stakeholders.

Other disclosures too could be considered through an economic inequality lens. Fees paid to directors disclosed as part of governance reporting, as well as the disclosure of high earning employees, can help in understanding various aspects of compensation. However, to what extent they are useful, and whether simply the reporting of these things is sufficient, is discussed in the next section.

## 13.5 Economic inequality: What is still left to resolve?

With inequality increasing across the world it is not surprising that attention being paid to the topic is on the rise. There is also an increased focus on how such inequalities may be reduced and, in relation to the focus of this book, the role of accounting and accountability. While practices related to accounting and accountability for economic inequality are emerging, there are many aspects that require further consideration. We discuss some of these as they relate to the practices discussed in Section 13.4 above.

### 13.5.1 Improving accounting for equality in various organisational forms

Given our discussion regarding various organisational forms and inequality (e.g. limited liability companies and those operating in the so-called gig economy), it is worth considering whether alternative forms of organising might be helpful in reducing economic inequality (see Chapter 2).

While a limited liability company is a common organisational form, there are other options such as co-operatives, social enterprises and benefit corporations. These alternative organisational forms, in principle, offer space for reducing inequalities in society. Various types of collectives and co-operatives, for example, are based on wide ownership, including employees, with the inherent idea of being more democratic in terms of decision-making (i.e. one cannot invest more capital to receive more influence). Different types of benefit corporations, both of a particular legal form and certified organisations, have broader goals than those typically pursued by a traditional limited liability company. In practice, benefit corporations and B-corps explicitly aim at particular social and environmental outcomes alongside financial performance. A consideration of how accounting could support these alternative organisational forms which foster equality is needed.

Now, we need to underscore that the organisational form does not dictate in itself whether an organisation causes more inequality or helps reduce it. And we should not dismiss the idea that accounting and accountability practices could, for example, be changed to help limited liability or gig economy organisations to be more equitable. However, organisational structures do have an impact on things such as organisational goals that are considered natural and worth pursuing. Indeed, alongside a consideration of accounting in alternative organisational forms, how accounting could assist in the promotion of equality in existing organisational forms such as limited liability companies is needed.

### 13.5.2 Changing accounting logic in relation to labour

We discussed above the accounting treatment of labour and wages. Essentially we highlighted how accounting classifies labour and wages as a cost and as such, something which accounting logic tells us should be reduced. This can affect economic inequality through a drive to reduce the distribution of wealth and income.

Sikka (2015) has considered the possible effect of changing this logic, for example, what would it mean if we thought of labour as an investment rather than as a cost. Our "Insights from research" section below discusses this further and we would suggest it is something useful to consider. For many of the topics we have discussed in this book, we have encouraged a consideration of how accounting might be done differently to support the transition to a more sustainable society. This example demonstrates that some of these accounting basics are likely to need reconsidering.

#### INSIGHTS FROM RESEARCH: FROM COSTS TO INVESTMENTS?

In his paper published in 2015, well-known critical accounting scholar Prem Sikka clearly exposes the links between accounting and economic inequality. He calls for the scrutiny of accounting concepts and categories which "help businesses to control costs, promote competition, profits and efficiency, but also facilitate inequitable distribution of income and wealth" (p. 47). Sikka focuses on accounting calculations, practices, and discourses in relation to the determination of wages and taxes to illustrate his point.

He argues that the labelling of wages and taxes as costs and burdens dictate that they are to be considered "always and only as a necessary evil to be reduced". As such, the payment of wages is not "seen as legitimate rewards for employment of social and human resources, but as barriers to expansion of capital" and that accounting practices "celebrate the gains to capital, but do not give visibility to the human consequences of the drive to reduce wages and tax payments" (p. 58).

He argues that the negative portrayal of wage and tax payments supports discourses that erode the workers' share of national income and wealth, and thus fuels the economic crisis.

Let us take up Sikka's (2015) call for more scrutiny of accounting concepts, categories and practices which facilitate the inequitable distribution of income and wealth. In addition to the labelling of wages and taxes as costs and burdens, what other accounting concepts, categories and practices that facilitate inequitable distribution of income and wealth can you think of?

**Sikka, P. (2015). The Hand of Accounting and Accountancy Firms in Deepening Income and Wealth Inequalities and the Economic Crisis: Some Evidence. *Critical Perspectives on Accounting, 30*, 46–62.**

### 13.5.3 Accounting's role in tax

We have discussed how tax, and corporate tax in particular, has a role to play in economic inequalities. Like cost allocation and budgets, tax planning appears to be a taken-for-granted element included in the training and education of an accountant. In accountancy textbooks and degree programmes, students go through tax laws and discuss how a firm could optimise its taxation. In essence, it appears that tax planning is generally considered to be a natural part of an accountant's professional skillset. As such, it is worth considering further the role of the accounting profession and major accountancy firms, in particular the Big4, in how corporate taxation and tax planning take place and are discussed in societies.

Many of the corporate tax avoidance strategies affecting the amount of tax funds available for redistribution in societies involve the use of some fairly complicated accounting. Someone needs to design those structures for the companies, as well as innovate new types of tax avoidance practices as some of those more frequently used in the past are made illegal by the states. Major accountancy firms play a role here, as tax planning and tax consultancy are amongst the services they actively offer to clients.

It remains contested whether the active engagement of major accountancy firms in the area of tax planning eventually benefits societies and works for the public good. Addison and Mueller (2015), for example, highlight this tension by discussing how the activities of the Big4 in this area can be framed either as illustrating the dark side of the profession or alternatively as a legitimate and innovative service in an increasingly complex field demanding substantial professional expertise. Sikka (2015) is more adamant with his position as he notes that the sale of tax avoidance schemes by accountancy firms and the erosion of tax revenues negatively affects the state's ability to redistribute wealth. In recent times these issues have received substantial attention through concerns about tax avoidance by some large technology companies. You might remember seeing some of this in the media. However, the level to which accounting firms engage in such behaviour, as well as how accounting practice (and the accounting profession), could be improved to help address this issue is in need of further consideration and change. The recent initiatives on tax transparency and Global Minimum Tax might hint at potential ruptures in the practices and discourses that have dominated the interplay of accounting and taxation, although it remains to be seen whether the new era of geopolitical tensions and increasing de-globalisation turn the tide on such initiatives requiring international collaboration.

There is also an increasing phenomenon related to transparency and accountability. While accountancy firms and the profession more broadly are keen to highlight how they are actively involved in developing new types of sustainability metrics, assurance services and initiatives of social responsibility, they are substantially less overt about their involvement and competency in taxation. You might not easily find any Big4 company advertising their services with slogans such as "last year we helped a major client save 100 million euros in taxation", even though this is very much at the heart of what their tax advisory and consultancy services are about. In similar terms, while many organisations highlight various achievements in their annual reports and websites, you might not come across a CEO praising her tax department for doing a tremendous job with optimising (again, reducing) taxes. Instead, the occasions when tax planning and avoidance are discussed in the public sphere tend to relate to some major controversies. Disputes regarding the tax practices of a household multinational company, like Apple, Starbucks or Meta, or big media leaks bringing vast amounts of previously hidden financial information from secrecy jurisdictions to public knowledge, as was the case with *Panama Papers*, *Swiss Leaks* and *LuxLeaks*, are some examples here. Oftentimes, these cases show that accountancy firms have been heavily involved in the processes. It is perhaps not a coincidence that in the public eye, tax planning is often associated with something clandestine.

### 13.5.4 Limits in current reporting practices

While we see some developments in relation to reporting on issues related to economic inequality, there is clearly much scope for development. While some disclosure practices seem to be on the rise due to the increased legislation in many jurisdictions (e.g. disclosures in relation to gender inequality and reducing the gender pay gap), disclosures of economic inequality beyond that required by regulation are more limited.

Taxation has emerged as somewhat of an exception though, as in recent years there has been an uptick in how corporations have published some tax information in different forms. One such example would be tax footprint reports, typically including a list of all types of taxes and payments to governments during the financial year. These are often described as being a transparent way to highlight how an organisation is taking care of its tax duties and hence providing a fair contribution to society. It needs to be noted however that these disclosures tend to focus on taxes where organisations have relatively little leeway, such as value added tax and employers' social security contributions. Less attention then has been given to areas where an organisation can actively seek to engage in tax planning and avoidance, such as corporate taxation. Materiality considerations are also a relevant factor here, as for some organisations taxation may be perceived to feature in the lower left quadrant of a materiality matrix, and has therefore been left unreported as a less significant matter.

Moreover, it is worth considering whether an organisation is providing the information in an aggregate form – that is, across all jurisdictions it operates in – or whether information includes details broken down on a CbC level. As you may recall from our discussion above, this is the kind of information that regulatory requirements set recently in Australia and the EU seek to get into the public domain. It is worth keeping an eye on how the evolving corporate practice will eventually match the expectations set for such reporting. Moreover, it also remains to be seen how much public disclosure there will be available on potential other elements states might use to attract firms, such as various subsidies or credit schemes. From a user's perspective, increased transparency and additional details can potentially offer an opportunity to consider for instance how aggressive an organisation is with regard to tax planning, avoidance and potential use of low-tax jurisdictions, as well as how actively it seeks to compete states against one another when for example considering major investment projects.

The role of accounting in income inequality emphasises the need for increased transparency and disclosure. Transparency and disclosure enable understanding and scrutiny of organisational practices, so without disclosure, or when disclosure is not sufficient, organisations may be able to operate without scrutiny. This leads many, including a number of accounting researchers, to argue that more disclosures relating to economic inequality are needed. For example, accounting researchers Ravenscroft and Denison (2014) argue for further corporate disclosure on transactions that contribute to current income inequality in three areas: compensation, taxation and non-business expenses. Other researchers highlight the role of value added disclosures discussed above and how they could help improve sustainability reporting (e.g. Haller et al., 2018).

However, just like with many of the topics covered in this book, the limits of disclosure and reporting require highlighting once more. In order for disclosure to work it needs to enter into decision making. For example, a company could disclose high manager salaries and bonuses and low wages for the majority of workers, but disclosing won't resolve the issue in itself – there also needs to be a willingness to act.

## 13.6 Conclusion

We have discussed accounting and accountability for economic inequality in this chapter. In many ways inequality brings the issues discussed in the book together – and hence considering economic inequality is perhaps a useful way to conclude our discussion of sustainability issues related to accounting and accountability. For example, we have highlighted how economic inequality is interconnected with various other sustainability issues – social, environmental and economic. How these sustainability issues need to be considered and addressed together – not in isolation – can be seen starkly here. While we need to address poverty, and to do so urgently, we must alongside this address economic inequality as a major driver of poverty. Furthermore, and as outlined above, economic inequality has serious implications for the ability for us to address climate change and other key sustainability issues. This chapter has also highlighted how our current accounting and accountability practices, some of which we take for granted, are problematic when addressing sustainability. Indeed, as highlighted throughout this book, accounting and accountability practices still have a long way to go if they are to be "fit for purpose" in a sustainable world.

## References


Addison, S. and Mueller, F. (2015). The Dark Side of Professions: The Big Four and Tax Avoidance. *Accounting, Auditing and Accountability Journal, 28(8)*, 1263–1290.

Bapuji, H. (2015). Individuals, Interactions and Institutions: How Economic Inequality Affects Organizations. *Human Relations, 68(7)*, 1059–1083.

Bapuji, H., Ertug, G. and Shaw, J. D. (2020). Organizations and Societal Economic Inequality: A Review and Way Forward. *Academy of Management Annals, 14(1)*, 60–91.

Bivens, J., Gould, E. and Kandra, J. (2024). *CEO Pay Declined in 2023 - But It Has Soared 1,085% since 1978 Compared with a 24% Rise in Typical Workers' Pay*. Economic Policy Institute. https://www.epi.org/publication/ceo-pay-in-2023/ (accessed 31 January 2025).

Collison, D., Dey, C., Hannah, G. and Stevenson, L. (2010). Anglo-American Capitalism: The Role and Potential of Social Accounting. *Accounting, Auditing and Accountability Journal, 23(8)*, 956–981.

Fleming, P. (2019). *Sugar Daddy Capitalism: The Dark Side of the New Economy*. Polity Press.

Gapminder (2020). *Worldview Upgrader*. www.gapminder.org (accessed 31 January 2025).

Haller, A., van Staden, C. J. and Landis, C. (2018). Value Added as Part of Sustainability Reporting: Reporting on Distributional Fairness or Obfuscation? *Journal of Business Ethics, 153*, 763–781.

Jackson, T. (2017). *Prosperity without Growth: Foundations for the Economy of Tomorrow* (2nd edn). Routledge.

Oxfam International (2025). Takers Not Makers: The Unjust Poverty and Unearned Wealth of Colonialism. https://www.oxfam.org/en/research/takers-not-makers-unjust-poverty-and-unearned-wealth-colonialism (accessed 31 January 2025).

Piketty, T. (2014). *Capital in the Twenty-First Century*. Harvard University Press.

Ravenscroft, S. and Denison, C. (2014). Social and Environmental Implications of Increasing Income Inequality: Accountability Concerns. In Mintz, S. (ed.), *Accounting for the Public Interest: Perspectives on Accountability, Professionalism and Role in Society*. Advances in Business Ethics Research, vol 4, pp. 91–113. Springer, Dordrecht. https://doi.org/10.1007/978-94-007-7082-9_5

Raworth, K. (2017). *Doughnut Economics: Seven Ways to Think Like a 21st-Century Economist*. Random House.

Reid, M. (2011). Behind the "Glasgow Effect". *Bulletin of the World Health Organisation, 89*, 706–707.

Rosling, H. (2018). *Factfulness: Ten Reasons We're Wrong about the World – And Why Things Are Better Than You Think*. Sceptre.

Sikka, P. (2015). The Hand of Accounting and Accountancy Firms in Deepening Income and Wealth Inequalities and the Economic Crisis: Some Evidence. *Critical Perspectives on Accounting, 30*, 46–62.

Stiglitz, J. E. and Rosengard, J. K. (2015). *Economics of the Public Sector*. W. W. Norton & Company.

UNDP (United Nations Development Programme) (2024). *Human Development Report 2023–24: Breaking the Gridlock: Reimagining Cooperation in a Polarized World*. https://hdr.undp.org (accessed 31 January 2025).

UNDP (United Nations Development Programme) (2025). About Us. https://www.undp.org (accessed 31 January 2025).

Wilkinson, R. and Pickett, K. (2009). *The Spirit Level: Why Equality Is Better for Everyone*. Penguin.

World Benchmarking Alliance (2024). 2024 Social Benchmark. https://www.worldbenchmarkingalliance.org/publication/social/ (accessed 31 January 2025).

## Additional reading and resources

Closs-Davies, S., Bartels, K. and Merkl-Davies, D. (2024). How Tax Administration Influences Social Justice: The Relational Power of Accounting Technologies. *Critical Perspectives on Accounting, 100*, 102758.

Finer, L. and Ylönen, M. (2017). Tax-Driven Wealth Chains: A Multiple Case Study of Tax Avoidance in the Finnish Mining Sector. *Critical Perspectives on Accounting, 48*, 53–81.

Laguecir, A. and Hudson, B. (2024). Too Poor to Get Social Housing: Accounting and Structural Stigmatisation of the Poor. *Critical Perspectives on Accounting, 100*, 102757.

Tweedie, D. and Hazelton, J. (2015). Social Accounting for Inequality: Applying Picketty's Capital in the Twenty-First Century. *Social and Environmental Accountability Journal, 35(2)*, 113–122.

Tweedie, D. and Hazelton, J. (2019). Economic Inequality: Problems and Perspectives for Interdisciplinary Accounting Research. *Accounting, Auditing and Accountability Journal, 32*(7), 1982–2003.

Wilkinson, R. and Pickett, K. (2018). *The Inner Level: How More Equal Societies Reduce Stress, Restore Sanity and Improve Everyone's Well-being*. Penguin.

PART

# IV

# Conclusion

CHAPTER

14

# Closing remarks

Let us congratulate you on making it to this, the final chapter of the book. We have traversed a large amount of content. We have highlighted areas where accounting and accountability practices are developed yet still evolving and emerging and also encouraged you to reflect on areas where more is required or where those practices are insufficient. We hope that you have found the content we have covered both informative and challenging. We also hope that it has not only provided you with a basis to understand accounting and accountability and its role in the transition towards a more sustainable society but also encouraged you to engage with the challenge of sustainable development, through discussing these topics with classmates, friends and family, changing your own practices and behaviours, and hopefully even considering how you might engage with the contents of this book and the challenges it poses in your current and future work roles.

There are a large number of things we could cover in this closing chapter. As we have demonstrated, the connections between accounting and sustainability are many, and they are also complex. It is not possible to summarise all the contents of this book and its key points in a single short chapter. Nor is this perhaps appropriate, given the content of each chapter largely speaks for itself. As such, what we aim to do in this short chapter is to outline a few of the most important implications – and leave you with a consideration of what all this means for the future of accounting and accountability.

## 14.1 Hope and/or despair?

One of the central threads running throughout this book has been a consideration of the potential role of accounting in the transition towards sustainability. We have considered how accounting and accountability concepts and practices demonstrate how accounting and accountability can be, indeed need to be, a positive force in the transition towards sustainability. However, we have also contrasted this with the stark reality that our current systems and structures, and the responses from

DOI: 10.4324/9781003533207-18

organisations and accounting, are yet insufficient to enable the transition needed – and definitely not at the pace required. So, what does this leave us with – hope or despair?

Sustainability considerations are everywhere. You have probably noticed this more as you have engaged with this book. Take food, where the vast interest in plant-based meat substitutes is spurring companies to work on research and technological development at a swift pace, potentially allowing substantial reductions in the production and consumption of meat- and milk-based products with a major ecological footprint. Or transportation, where the variety and availability of electric cars consumers and businesses can choose from has rapidly expanded with potential for the reduction of fossil fuel consumption in traffic and personal mobility. Or electricity, where the share of renewables in the global power production keeps taking major strides forward. There is therefore a lot of promise and plenty to be hopeful about.

At the same time, however, the signs of ecological collapse, including the breaching of planetary boundaries, keep getting stronger and the alarm bells louder. Indeed, as we were updating this book we found many areas where the situation had gotten worse and few where it had got better. Wildlife species populations continue to collapse, with, for example, the loss of wild bees and other pollinators due to pesticides, climate change and loss of habitat causing serious threat to global food security. In 2023 and 2024, we saw the manifestations of the climate emergency, we witnessed extreme temperatures across the globe, especially in the Arctic, and experienced massive and devastating wildfires in the United States and devastating floods in Spain and Germany. And we could go on. There are also events at the state level, including the rise of the far right that contain within them anti-environmental and social sentiments.

There are therefore reasons for hope, and there are reasons for despair. There is vast momentum in different areas of society, ranging from urban infrastructure to financial markets, as sustainability appears to have become a core agenda item in many spheres. And, as we have highlighted, the same activities can be perceived in different ways. While some find the regulatory changes within the sustainability reporting sphere to be a move forward, others fear they are a move in the opposite direction given the prioritisation of financial considerations. Whatever our position, we must remind ourselves that having sustainability on the agenda or having various targets does not suffice in itself. Targets can serve as aspirational goals and spur governments, organisations and societies to innovate, but given the seriousness of the sustainability crisis, there is an urgency to get the changes to materialise. There are numerous examples, such as the Aichi Biodiversity targets agreed upon internationally, where goals have been set with much fanfare, but the social and organisational changes needed to accomplish those goals never fully materialised. There are declarations of a climate emergency, but without the actions resembling an emergency response.

We also need to acknowledge that sometimes goals may contradict each other. Take the UN Sustainable Development Goals (SDGs) which we have highlighted throughout this book. There is every reason to strive to achieve the targets included in the SDGs, such as reducing poverty, ensuring education and revitalising ecosystems. Still, the SDGs are neither perfect nor without contradictions. Can we simultaneously achieve sustained economic growth and live in harmony with nature, both of which are called for by the SDGs? And, as the above illustrates, just because we have a set of goals and commitments to achieve them does not mean the job is done. Will the SDGs become another set of goals that appear to hold much promise, but by 2030 remain unachieved? It would appear that way at present.

These situations bring us to the uncomfortable reality of inherent trade-offs, which prevent us from having everything. Despite ongoing innovation and sustainability trends, individuals, organisations and societies have still plenty to do in seeking to achieve social models, which avoid both ecological overshoot and social collapse, as Kate Raworth clearly and usefully depicts in doughnut economics. In this context, sustainability accounting and accountability have a very important role to play.

## 14.2 Accounting and accountability in the transition to sustainability

As we demonstrated in this book, there are significant sustainability accounting and accountability considerations across the entire spectrum of accounting functions. Inside organisations, we need assessments, measurements, comparisons and foresight, which take into account social, environmental and economic considerations, thereby enabling managers to make decisions that will not only benefit the organisation, but provide value to stakeholders and steer organisations to less unsustainable practices. We need sustainability reporting, which allows stakeholders to hold organisations accountable and helps evaluate whether their past performance, current activities and future plans show signs of transitions towards sustainable and low-carbon operations. In the financial markets, investors need financial and non-financial information, which incorporates externalities and thereby provides investors a basis for decisions, which would unleash the power of the markets to facilitate societies' aspired sustainability transformation. Furthermore, we need vigorous social groups and civil society to produce innovative counter accounts, which continue to challenge laggards and push leading organisations further in all sectors (e.g. private, public or third sector).

It is evident that sustainability accounting and accountability is highly important, and its relevance will only continue to grow. As we have discussed in Part III, accounting practices and knowledge focusing on specific areas of sustainability, such as climate, water, biodiversity, human rights and economic inequality, have taken major steps forward. These areas are likely to remain important, and we need more and better information that allows us to assess, evaluate and report on these complex and intertwined sustainability questions. Moreover, there are many other topics that we could (perhaps even should) have covered here, and novel topics will emerge as science progresses and organisational practices evolve.

While activities and developments since leave no doubt that the accounting community (academic researchers, practitioners, the profession) have increased their focus on sustainability, the need for accounting and accountants to respond to these questions more still remains. Steps have been taken, but much more is needed. Furthermore, this is a collective effort. There is little space for complacency even for those leading the pack: everyone needs to raise the bar and up their game. Accounting can be a powerful force for sustainability only through continuous innovation and critical work. Accounting, accountants and accountancy need to step forward and rise to the sustainability challenge, and show what it means for accountancy to serve the public interest. There is a need to reflect on past and current actions and activities, as well as develop and advance new ones. We hope that this book has reached a number of readers interested in developing accounting in a way that responds to the sustainability challenge. It is time for action!

# Index

Note: **Bold** page numbers refer to tables; *italic* page numbers refer to figures and page numbers followed by "n" denote endnotes.